'One of the few people made seriously famous by television ... An engaging read from a celebrated and unashamed champagne-Bentley-and-woman enthusiast, the more so for Whicker's scornful attacks on present-day smiley blondes who usually pronounce the week's destination to be "a land of contrasts". He has a point.'

Independent

'Alan Whicker is a giant of broadcasting, a pioneer who set TV standards with the legendary magazine programme *Tonight* and the unforgettable *Whicker's World* TV series ... In a fascinating book he launches a trenchant attack on falling standards of television.'

Daily Mail

'Alan Whicker, unlike so many familiar small-screen faces, is so utterly indistinguishable from his television persona it initially takes you by surprise. The carefully brushed hair, the trademark glasses, the neat moustache, the well-cut suit and plump silk tie, the distinctive voice – here's an instantly recognizable figure from all our yesterdays and tomorrows ... Now here's another book, *Whicker's World – Take 2!* Mopping up the best bits from the last decade and more.'

Woman's Weekly

'The extraordinary life of one of the everlasting Greats of television ...'

Michael Parkinson, BBC Radio 2

'Highly entertaining'

Hello magazine

Other books by the author

Within Whicker's World
(Autobiography)

Whicker's New World
(Living with Uncle Sam)

Whicker's World Down Under
(Living with Waltzing Matilda)

Whicker's World - Take 2!

Alan Whicker

Photographs by Valerie Kleeman

André Deutsch

For Valerie
who saw it all happening . . .

First published in 2000 by André Deutsch Ltd

This paperback edition published in 2002 by
André Deutsch
an imprint of the Carlton Publishing Group
20 Mortimer Street
London W1T 3JW

Reprinted in 2009

A catalogue record for this book is available
from the British Library

ISBN 978 0 233 05019 5

Typeset by Derek Doyle & Associates, Liverpool
Printed and bound in the UK by
CPI Mackays, Chatham ME5 8TD

Contents

I remember you in black-and-white . . . vii

Everyone he meets sells out, in a way . . . 1
Commercial break . . . 32
I tell you, it was awesome . . . 49
The television we deserve . . .? 70
A pinch of aggro to bring the box alive . . . 94
Whatever you do east of Suez doesn't count . . . 119
Bang – I shot him right between the eyes . . . 136
Never thought of an airliner as home before . . . 153
The baritone put a bomb on board . . . 201
Luciano, you *have* to sing tonight . . . 213
Last assignment . . . 241
The other side of the one-way mirror . . . 248
A land of wild and preposterous death . . . 267
People who do *that* can finish up dead . . . 281
The public execution drew an appreciative crowd . . . 296
My anxiety tube was a poor investment . . . 306
A hot mother on the dark edge of magic . . . 312
Why should I travel when I'm already *here* . . .? 319
The wantability factor . . . 327

Acknowledgements 336
Index 337

I remember you in
black-and-white . . .

Only when friendly viewers sidle up and murmur 'I remember you in black-and-white' does my lengthy television life click back into focus. It seems there are not too many TV men still at the coalface after forty-five years hard, still watching progress from both sides of our mesmerizing window on the world . . . who have seen it through, man and boy, all the way from Shepherd's Bush to satellite, then on to Internet and into cyberspace. Since we're counting, it's also hard to think of anyone who's been as lucky, both personally and professionally, and as blessed. If I had a gold ring it would long ago have been cast into the sea to placate the gods.

When I arrived at Lime Grove W12 from Fleet Street in the late 1950s, colour was still eight years ahead. The tiny tentative audience watched occasional documentary and news programmes that copied cinema newsreels of the time by transmitting silent film voiced by unseen commentators. Then BBC's *Tonight* and *Panorama* introduced visible reporters who involved viewers directly, who were responsible for what they said, and blamed or encouraged for their attitudes. The seductive television set had become personal, and viewers began to spend more time with presenters than with their friends.

I was fortunate to be one of the first to come from behind the screen and appear nightly before an exploratory but ever-growing audience which was also only just getting to know a magical medium that seemed full of delight. One early viewer wrote to ask what I thought of her new living room curtains.

This new television life as *Tonight*'s man-around-the-world was not unlike my previous years of anonymous wanderings around the globe as a news agency Foreign Correspondent. I was still landing in Singapore at dawn to interview the Chief Minister and talk to the Triad boss, still considering the Dream Deaths in Hawaii and wondering what Hong Kong *tai-tais* discussed when they met for tea at the Gloucester each day . . . still reporting from everywhere about everything. Yet suddenly I was being stopped in the street by amiable strangers with a conspiratorial 'It *is*, isn't it?', told to shake hands and 'Sign this!'. Television, which was making us better-known than the neighbours, had also converted us into familiar public property.

Today, after a few million miles and almost as many *Whicker's Worlds*, I find myself still on television, cable and radio, but now also Travel Ambassador for AOL Online. Such transmissions seem a long way from my vox pop mark on Shepherd's Bush Green, where I clutched a stick-mike and talked to passers-by before the double camera the BBC had just created. That Neolithic monster required two men to lift it on to a massive tripod, and was an early shot at miniaturization. Now the Travel Channel of the largest online community in the world uses equipment light as a butter-fly. Going with the millennium flow may not be promotion but surely puts me in line for a long-service medal . . .

At a recent BAFTA awards dinner I was sitting next to a top executive from one of the networking companies who was giving me a hard time for undertaking some television project she considered unsuitable. Her reaction was noticeably straightfor-ward. 'You,' she said indignantly, 'You – you're a fuckin' icon.'

I thought *Wow* – the title of my next book! We all funked it, in the end.

Since I got on my happy treadmill, TV has become the nation's muzak: always *on*, everywhere – yet despite the Niagara of chan-nels bringing changing standards and techniques and a diffusion of viewer-response, it remains an exciting and agreeable place to be. Its relationship with those who watch is excellent. The wonder may be fading, the technical miracles become commonplace, but my years on-screen have never once provoked an unhappy expe-rience, off-screen – which says a lot for viewers' tolerance.

Around the world and down the years my unseen travelling companions, should they ever descend upon me in reality in street or aircraft, have always been generous and encouraging: windswept archaeologist on Easter Island, fraught businessman on Tokyo's Ginza, Maharajas in Rajasthan, mafiosi in Las Vegas, British homesteaders in Alaska or Palm Beach have all accepted a detached and professional eye on the world, and seemed happy to share my experiences.

I must have made familiarity easy, even for those original black-and-white viewers, by rarely changing my style down the decades, my delight at who and what I come across, my attitude – or my wardrobe. I had not noticed this last unenterprising facet until the other day, when asked to appear as myself in a feature film set in the cool era of 1977. The young wardrobe mistress intent upon transporting us back in time with the help of her hangers of swinging gear with kipper ties under wide collars, was worried about what I might have been wearing, back in those distant days.

This was no problem: 'You're looking at it.'

I confessed it could well have been the blazer that was present and correct as we spoke, and admitted that even older suits were still operational and on-camera. They checked this unlikely story with programmes shot a quarter of a century ago and were disappointed to find that even in my wilder days I had never gone for flares or frilly shirts, platforms or Cavalier hair.

Call me unimaginative – lazy, even – but I was comfortable with the unobtrusive rig that had carried me through the Korean war, the Egyptian revolution and various Royal tours, to name but a few dressy occasions. At a push, a blazer can be worn in the Outback and at the President's reception that evening. A conservative style, I always tell myself, never goes out of fashion. My tailor, Doug Hayward, is not amused.

The film's make-up department was equally anxious. They were aware that on-camera my best side was the back of my head, but like Wardrobe were hoping to create some evocative 1970s figure. They had colourful visions of punks, Rolling Stones, Starsky and Hutch . . .

After studying old production stills they reluctantly decided I could get away with an inch on the sideboards and a touch of darkening pencil on hair and moustache. Since I have so far never had time for a facelift, it seemed a fair trade for years of action on all fronts. I was relieved and duly thankful.

Fortunately the people I met in *Whicker's World* through the years were *far* more colourful and adventurous . . .

Everyone he meets sells out,
in a way . . .

As soon as I heard that the Sultan of Brunei would be happy to appear in *Whicker's World* – that he was actually ready to join me on television and talk to us all, just like a real person – I knew we had some self-imposed problems. Two worlds were about to meet; although he'd seen my programmes he had of course never been interviewed on television before. Unthinkable.

An Absolute Monarch and twenty-ninth direct descendant in one of the oldest royal dynasties, he was also Brunei's Prime Minister and supreme religious leader. He alone among all the world leaders represented unimaginable Wealth combined with total Power and the sure authority of Belief. Constitutionally Brunei seemed in the early Tudor period, somewhere between Henry VII and Henry VIII. The fact that the Sultan was also one of the richest men in the world was an anticlimax.

As with other potentates, the line between the Sultan's private and public purse is blurred. It is impossible for outsiders to separate his wealth from the nation's income and its phenomenal earnings from oil and gas, which are state secrets. Any closer examination would be seen in Brunei as disrespectful.

As that Texan Senator said, 'A billion here, a billion there, pretty soon it adds up to real money.' However you add it up, the Sultan, with his privately owned country, is worth real money and, in simple available cash terms, must be the richest man who's ever walked this earth.

I had first moved into the Richest Men league back in 1963, with

J. Paul Getty and *The Solitary Billionaire* – a television breakthrough that an American network showed twice in one week – and my professional eye had been on the Sultan for some years. I was also up to speed on Absolute Rulers, following programmes with General Alfredo Stroessner of Paraguay, President Ferdinand Marcos of the Philippines and Dr François Duvalier of Haiti.

Our remarkable Brunei saga came about quite casually – and mainly because in London we usually stayed at one of his properties: the Dorchester. Before its reopening after an eighteen-month rebuild I was invited to a celebratory lunch at which the Duke of Edinburgh unveiled a plaque and said a few royal words to a small group of loyal regulars. Since Prince Philip's stag night had been celebrated there and he lived just down the road, he was seen as one of us.

After lunch the Sultan's man in London, his former ADC and friend, Major Christopher Hanbury, came up to talk about the commemorative piece I had written for their hotel magazine. A jolly Irish Hussar, enthusiastic polo player and all-round good egg, Hanbury asked what was happening in *Whicker's World*. Thinking aloud, I wondered whether, as the Sultan was about to celebrate the Silver Jubilee of his accession and pay a State Visit to London, it might be a good time to consider a Brunei programme.

A few weeks later Christopher and I were sitting in an ante-room in one of the Sultan's great mansions in Millionaires' Row, Kensington Palace Gardens, ready to launch that unlikely project. We had passed through heavy security, layer after layer, and were surrounded by an anxious bevy of supplicants who, it appeared, had been waiting for hours, or days, in the hope of an audience.

Such a guarded ante-room world was then a new scene for me – especially one at Notting Hill Gate. I suspected it could be a mere taste of what awaited in Brunei, should we go to watch the Sultan ruling his Kingdom.

However, in W8 protocol was relatively relaxed. The Sultan, smiling and welcoming, said he'd watched *Whicker's World* and though he had no experience of television, seemed prepared to undertake a programme. His only concern was that his English might not be good enough.

His anglophile father Sultan Omar, who hero-worshipped Churchill and drove around his dilapidated capital in a black London taxi, had owned several homes in England; as Crown Prince, the Sultan had left the calm of 27 Redington Road, Hampstead NW3 to tackle two years within the brusque military world of Sandhurst. He now lived among English speakers, his second wife was a quarter British, yet despite all this his command of the language was limited and constrained by natural shyness.

More important, this bashful billionaire was not experienced at answering questions: 'I *never* give interviews.' Certainly none of his courtiers or his people would ever dare ask him anything.

Handsome, laughing easily, disarmingly shy, he seemed to have no hidden depths. Indeed I found it surprising that an Absolute Monarch could remain so balanced and sensible and – you could say – ordinary. 'HM', as they called him, was small, muscular and boyish, with greying hair – indeed one of our points of contact was that we shared a barber. More significant, we were both Bentley enthusiasts who always chose two-door models. A good solid basis, you may think, for a relationship. Unfortunately our similarities diverged quite noticeably when we began marching to a different income . . . The annual expenditure of the Sultan, his three brothers and their families had been estimated at well over £1bn.

One of the occupational hazards of being such a monarch, I reflected as we considered opening his closed world to the ultimate intrusion of television, was that he must suffer the inevitable disturbance of reality that comes from having too much money, and too little to spend it on. If he can think of it, he can have it; but how many palaces, cars, ponies, diamonds, airliners . . . could he cope with?

With expenditure limited only by imagination, he can do or buy or control anything he wants and, with that sort of power, surely never hears the word 'No'. What's more, how can he tell who his real friends are? A rich man's jokes are always funny so he's surrounded by a lot of hearty laughter. Everyone an Absolute Monarch meets sells out, in a way.

At that first meeting we had one of those amiable conversations which drift along pleasantly – but afterwards you're not quite sure what has been achieved, if anything. However we had broken the ice and been invited into his Kingdom. That was a giant stride for mankind. It would be his first and, he added with fervent conviction, his *last* venture into television. It seemed as though he felt it was something he ought to do, just once, to get it over with and on the record; *noblesse oblige*.

In due course we set off for Negara Brunei Darussalam – a 24-hour three-flight journey from my home in Jersey. I did not then know that I should have to fly backwards and forwards across the world three times to complete our documentary on this ordinary man in an extraordinary position.

Out of Singapore on the last leg of the journey we were enveloped by the soft leather seats of a Royal Brunei Airlines 757. Its loo was vast, like a brilliantly lit throne room with golden fittings. I couldn't find the jacuzzi. Once upon a time it must have been part of the Royal Squadron – a private fleet larger than the national airline.

I assumed life was going to be golden from then on, in the lavish tax-free land at the end of the Sultan's rainbow, but when we checked into the most modern hotel in his workaday languid little capital, Bandar Seri Begawan, it was brown and basic – though between 'Postage' and 'Pressing' in the guest facilities brochure: 'Prayer Mats'.

In that unmemorable huddle of Chinese shops and riverside stilt houses, the Sheraton Utama was a sort of international ante-room of the Palace. When the Sultan was at home, it was full of arms dealers, jewellers and deal-makers of every description, all eager to sell him a Van Gogh to go with his £50m Renoir. Or possibly a warship, a customized 747, a few clusters of emeralds too big not to be real. Some of them waited months in that rather limited hotel in the hope of a rare Royal summons.

Its commonplace lounge was the Mecca for salesmen from all the right places, from Cartier and Asprey and Van Cleef, from Rolls-Royce and Boeing and British Aerospace . . . right down through the sales spectrum of eager flatterers to the chancers and con men who beat a path to Brunei to sit and wait, to scheme and dream about separating the Sultan from some of his easily earned cash.

Though we were expected and awaited, we still had to join the struggle up through the Palace bureaucracy before getting in to the Royal presence. Afterwards, back at the Sheraton, all the anxious supplicants wanted to touch me in the hope that some of my luck might rub off. It was glory, slightly removed – like dancing with the man who danced with the girl who danced with the Prince of Wales.

As at some watering hole on the Silk Road to Samarkand the traders gathered, smiling sincere smiles and eager to be charming. We mingled in the Utama coffee shop and, like them, I came to rely upon Brunei noodles as the just-acceptable Dish of every Day.

We had to adjust quite quickly to the fact that in Brunei – the size of Norfolk, but richer than Australia – the Sultan was no longer just a dashing youngish chap behind the smoked glass of a souped-up white Mini-Cooper vrooming happily round and round Hyde Park Corner. No longer just the slight, elusive figure slipping through the Dorchester lobby about whom its Assistant Manager told me reflectively, 'The Sultan? Oh, he's a nice little fellow – no trouble at all . . .'

At home HM was so Royal, so elevated, so protected by court protocol that it became like trying to reach God for a chat. A rather charming deity, I must say, who despite his power was almost diffident – though his subjects, from hereditary noblemen to rainforest tribesmen, fell silent and abashed in his presence.

He has spent more than half his life as King, a role both ceremonial and functional; as Prime Minister he presides over a Cabinet of eleven, which included two brothers – until Prince Jefri's downfall. Spiritually, he is Protector of the Faith. Financially, he signs the cheques.

Once we'd moved up through the barriers of guards, flunkeys, officials, ministers . . . and finally reached the Godhead, the Sultan was always open and friendly, shy but rather jolly. He brandished a copy of my autobiography and noted a picture of a heterosexual group getting closely acquainted in the jacuzzi at Plato's sex club in Beverly Hills. 'Which one is Mr Whicker?' he asked Christopher, conspiratorially.

Though detached from reality, he was more Action Man than Intellectual – and certainly not one of your effete royalty. He flew his Airbus and his choppers, played furious polo, drove his Bentleys flat out with escort struggling to keep up . . . and looked back wistfully on his days in 1966 as an officer-cadet at Sandhurst.

He had just organized a reunion for his class of sixteen from the Royal Military Academy, summoning cadets who had served with him to a dinner at the Dorchester and a night on the town. Most of them, now senior officers or grey executives, flew in from around the world to help the Sultan relive his carefree days. 'It was great fun,' he told me. 'They are always the same.' He, of course, was not.

Today he rules alone, the Last Emperor – though a long way from those African sergeants who make themselves presidents after each *coup d'état*. Around the world most surviving royal families have been on their thrones for a century or two, if that. The Sultan's family has ruled for some six hundred years, so he is perhaps the most royal of all the Royals.

A visitor sees a pleasant, smiling man – then notices with surprise how both haughty and obsequious prostrate themselves to kiss his hand. This made me recall Papa Doc, in Haiti – a most unkind comparison. President Duvalier, a small, hesitant Creole, was exceedingly polite and welcoming to me and grew to enjoy being interviewed. Standing among Tontons Macoutes in his dark suit and dark glasses he seemed merely an insignificant little doctor who wrote poetry – until one noticed that upon his arrival everyone was transfixed with terror. They knew him better than I did.

Remembering how we've come to view our Royalty, these days, it was hard to adjust to the almost mystical awe surrounding the Sultan in his deferential little Kingdom. Such national reverence, rooted in religious and cultural history, contrasted with the relentless triviality of his treatment by the international press, which concentrated upon his wealth, his wives – and the confrontations his rakish younger brother Prince Jefri had with American bimbos and Armenian property men.

In those days there was also the Sultan's $10m contribution to Oliver Stone and the Contras, and whether he *had* given Mohamed al Fayed the money to buy Harrods . . . That story ran and ran. Because so little reliable information came down from his lonely privileged pinnacle, reports of his lifestyle were always extreme.

A speck on the island of Borneo, Brunei is rather smaller than the ranch in Australia's Northern Territory bought to provide its meat. It lies between the South China and Java Seas next to the Malaysian states of Sarawak and Sabah, and must cope with the problems of being very small and very rich.

Because its wealth comes from oil and gas, most foreigners believe Brunei must be somewhere in the Middle East, though the 280,000 Bruneians have only oil and religion in common with Arabs.

No one could accuse their capital Bandar of being stimulating – or indeed much fun. There are few duller places in the world. Though only two or three flying hours from the thrust of Singapore or the excitement of Bangkok, it feels like an indolent colonial outpost without Parliament or political parties, book-shops or concert halls, discos or bars . . .

However, it does boast two remarkable features: the enormous Omar Ali Saifuddin mosque, with a prayer hall almost a hundred yards long and three million 24-carat golden tiles glowing on its dome. Then, below that religious radiance, the Kampong Ayer on the Brunei River – the world's largest water-village where the Sultan's father was born and lived, and his own modest birthplace is now a place of pilgrimage.

Traditional wooden stilt houses cover several square miles of river. They impressed the first European explorers in 1521 when Brunei was the main imperial power in the region, and fascinate their few visitors today. Though their lives are little changed since the sixteenth century and they still know no plumbing, the 30,000 residents are fiercely loyal to the waterborne life of their ancestors and extinguish destructive fires lit by disapproving city authorities who had hoped they were not looking.

Brunei is only 300 miles north of the Equator and mainly jungle, so its climate is humid and stifling and the rainy season lasts six months. In this steamheat, court etiquette demands that Westerners going into Royal orbit wear suits, collars and ties.

For a guest of the Sultan this debilitating situation is amelio-rated by a constant supply of black air-conditioned limos, bought by the hundred and taken over by Bruneian drivers not always familiar with new roads built by an administration anxious to find ways of spending money. One of my drivers set off, flat out, along the wrong side of a dual carriageway. Despite language difficulties I managed to draw this to his attention, just in time.

After near invisibility during the early years of his reign the Sultan, now more confident, often leaves his palaces – so we followed him around, filming endless polo games, various audiences and visitations, and went wandering and wondering through his vast homes. Until the 1950s and the arrival of oil, the old Palace was on stilts in the harbour. Now his main home is the Istana Nurul Iman, the world's largest private residence, bigger than the Vatican, several times grander than Buckingham Palace; a monumental slab on the scale of Grand Central Station or a 747 hangar. This sultan-size palace has 1,778 rooms – but then, it is his office as well. At its heart, sixteen acres of marble amid a total floor space of more than fifty acres. Cosy it is not.

Red carpet runs more than a hundred and fifty yards from the entrance across gleaming marble amid pools and fountains, past waterfalls and guards snapping to attention, and ends at two commonplace shopping-mall escalators. It is not easy to gild an escalator. The Sultan likes all his desires to be fulfilled without delay, so it was designed in two weeks by a Filipino architect, Leandro Locsin, who had never seen the site – which is perhaps why it does look rather better from the sky. Should its monumental atmosphere become too oppressive, the Sultan has twenty-five other palaces to fall back on, and at least a score of large guesthouses.

On my first exploratory visit to that Palace the Sultan was again totally charming. Christopher told me he had said, 'I've seen *Whicker's World.* He doesn't just want a programme about me, he wants to look at the country and the people.' This was partially true.

He agreed we could film as he piloted his Airbus – when travelling abroad his workaday Boeing 727s just brought back the shopping. We were already using an army helicopter for aerial shots, but had to keep above 3,000 feet over his Palace. I said an ideal height would be 500 feet, and he agreed – though was sensitive about the size of his home. 'Everybody says it's the biggest palace in the world – that sort of thing. I don't want too much of *that,*' he said. He didn't seem to appreciate that it was a hard place to miniaturize.

He did not want his wives filmed, nor his huge and almost unused Royal yacht, but offered instead: 'Tomorrow we're going to the mosque. You can film that.'

Yes, but filming any conversation with him anywhere always proved far more complicated than seemed probable. Each one became an escapade unlike any confrontation I've known during over forty years in television. For a start, the Sultan is always reluctant to make up his mind about anything until the very last moment. This must be the prerogative of Absolute Rulers. He had not even decided definitely about his three-day State Visit to Britain, which required a certain amount of organization on both sides. Our planned meetings had to be some way down that Royal 'To Do' list.

He had invited us to join him when he went to pray, but traditionally would not reveal which mosque he was attending until just before leaving his Palace. On Friday mornings this kept every place of worship in Brunei in a state of extreme agitation.

Sometimes, we were told, he would suddenly decide to pilot his helicopter to an up-country mosque, leaving his road-bound entourage in desperate pursuit below. It was a 'Follow that chopper!' scramble of dignitaries and senior officers, and reminded me of some Ealing comedy with Peter Sellers. As we prepared to film, informed opinion was that today he would drive. That was a relief. We were given two fast cars, so we could slip into the motorcade behind his 150 mph Bentley.

As we waited in the fierce heat for the Royal mind to be made up, we were joined by his *chef du cabinet* who had been at college in Wolverhampton, but still did not know which prayers were going to be blessed that day. A chopper flew low overhead: HM, coming in from the Palace where he had spent the night.

After half an hour word came that His Majesty was about to leave. Everyone quivered to attention, ready for the chase, engines running. Then we learn by telephone that he has decided to go to a mosque in the Kampong Ayer – by *boat*.

This throws everyone. 'Unfortunately not even this car will go on water,' says the *chef du cabinet* from the Midlands, helpfully. We drive down to the jetty, anyway. The wide river is thick and dark grey. The Sultan arrives, says hello, gives a grin and a wave, jumps into a noisy launch and heads off in a cloud of spray.

After a few minutes of confusion and fury, a sort of rowing boat with an outboard passes and is commandeered for us. It is already overloaded with retinue. My cameraman, recordist and director leap in. As I follow, the shaky boat jumps away with a roar, abandoning the *chef du cabinet*. Everyone is drenched – including four of the Sultan's party, exquisite in their turbans and national costumes of turquoise silks. They smile wearily.

We go bounding and splashing up river. Facing the stern, I cannot see what's happening or where we are going because if I turn, the fragile craft could capsize. My shirt, sodden from perspiration, is now soaked with smelly river water. My crew are damp and disorganized. The Royal launch has disappeared. I have been happier.

After a mile or so we are met by a police boat which had apparently received a message to rescue us. In a wobbly operation midriver we transfer to the more secure craft and renew the chase, feeling more Keystone Kops than ever.

The problem now is to find where HM has gone to worship. The Kampong, home to 30,000 Bruneians, has six mosques. By the time we discover which one I suspect its service will be ending . . .

We approach the landing stage, fretting – and there is the Royal boat coming towards us bearing a smiling Sultan, amused to see us damp and bedraggled. He had made a block or two around the village while waiting for us to catch up, which was thoughtful. Ashore, we follow him through respectful crowds into a huge mosque where hundreds wait, and film him at prayer.

When he leaves, his people go wild. Suddenly he's not at all remote. Normally undemonstrative and timid, the democracy of worship now permits them to surge around, for many still believe his touch can heal – or, at least, bring luck. Others, more practical, thrust petitions at him. All want to kiss his hand. Pushing through this crowd of thousands we follow him back towards his boat, filming.

The Sultan clearly enjoys such public adoration. Spotting me amid the swirl, he gives a nod and, as he gets into his launch, suddenly says, 'Come with me.' I do not need to be asked twice. So there I am, finally sitting with my target in the Royal boat, alone together amid a demonstrative crowd. Perfect location, great pictures – except that my film crew are somewhere on shore, and out of sight.

In desperation I say, 'Look, we *must* film this.' He considers. 'All right, get the camera.' Our police launch arrives – but no sign of my crew. I realize that they must now be in some car, racing back to the Palace to film our return. The Sultan is unconcerned. 'They'll be here in a minute,' he says cheerfully. I very much doubt it, but do not wish to depress his happy innocence.

Never underestimate the power of an Absolute Ruler. Within three minutes they turn up in another boat.

The Sultan's man bars their way on board. 'One person, only one person.' I go over his head: 'Must have my recordist.' The Sultan says, 'All right, two.' They jump in and we go bouncing down the river towards the Palace, triumphantly struggling with mikes and leads and cameras amid the spray and heat.

We prepare to record a conversation but the outboard is so noisy we cannot hear each other. By Royal command the boat slows, and we start filming. At last – this is why we came! Everything's going to be all right. The conversation is just getting going when we reach the Palace jetty and the Sultan announces cheerfully, 'We're here. I think that's that.' And it was.

He goes ashore, gives a last wave and leaves in a cloud of Bentley dust. Still at least we have filmed our first conversation, sort of. I had also taken the opportunity of reminding him of various other situations in which I wanted to film him, and he had replied agreeably, 'Yes, we'll see.'

Later Christopher explains that, at court, 'We'll see' is the polite way of saying 'No.'

Bond Street's gentleman jeweller, John Asprey, knows how to keep his A-list clients amused. He had flown out an English polo team to play Royal Brunei for his Asprey Cup at Jerudong Park, the Sultan's multimillion-pound polo complex housing several hundred of the world's finest ponies. The high-goal home team would be led by Christopher Hanbury, strongly supported by HM and Prince Jefri; a pair of Royals is an unbeatable hand. Preparing for their first stick-&-ball at the Polo Club, the Bond Street boys receive news that their afternoon knock-up is to be the actual Cup match – an unsettling play ploy.

The Sultan arrives in the Bentley Continental he had just bought off the stand at the Geneva Motor Show, with second wife Princess Mariam, daughter and baby. Catching sight of me as he leaves the clubhouse he comes up and says, unexpectedly, 'You're looking very young.'

This was one of the more disarming observations I have had to face from an Absolute Ruler, and I had little to offer except: 'Nicest thing that's been said to me all day.' At which he got on his pony – the only one permitted scarlet bandages – and galloped away. He doubtless believed that was another interview – but at least my morale was much improved and the muddy water forgiven.

During the afternoon while he was playing I chatted with his daughter, who was wearing gold trainers. Brunei children tend to have more designer clothes and more Mercedes than most children. I wondered who was going to win. She did not need to consider form: 'My Daddy *always* wins,' she said, with simple conviction. Princess Fadzilah was six at the time.

The Royal children were well attended, and by all the best people: Kevin Keegan and Jack Nicklaus were flown in to give football and golf lessons, Ray Reardon and Steve Davis to make sure the Crown Prince, Prince Al-Muhtadee Billah, got the right cues, despite his diabetes and poor eyesight. Champion tennis players, disco dancers, aerobics teachers arrived to attend, if and when required. Rod Stewart was brought in for a children's party, Michael Jackson and Elton John for the grown-ups.

HM was always well mounted on the best ponies money could buy, and played well – if not quite up to the almost professional standard of Jefri. A tough polo game must have been almost therapeutic for the Sultan; at last this shy restrained man could shout at people.

After six chukkas, HM demanded another two. The final score was, I believe, Royal Brunei 24, Asprey 4 – or about par for that course, since the home team was beefed up by a ten-handicap hotshot Argentinian on contract and liable to pick up a $100,000 bonus. Fortunately Asprey had prizes for everyone, already gift-wrapped in purple and green back in Bond Street.

Once in a later game against the Sultan's team it looked for a worrying moment as though Asprey's might win. Fortunately, with extra effort from both sides, that danger soon passed.

When players gathered in the pavilion for drinks and small eats after each match I was always hoping Prince Jefri or even HM might look in for shrimps and chicken legs, ginger beer and 7-Up. They never appeared nor, I discovered, were they expected. It was explained that if any Royal had entered the room all Bruneians would leave, believing themselves unfit to be in such company. Royal isolation was total.

The camaraderie of the car broke down some barriers, and the Sultan escorted me around one of his garages to admire his fleet of Bentley Continentals – one in every colour. Unfortunately he would not let us film that gleaming motorshow scene; I suspect he was afraid of appearing a tad ostentatious.

Fortune magazine reported he had 153 cars, but a craftsman from the Rolls-Royce team flown out to reupholster the Phantom VI he was using at his coming Jubilee celebrations told me it was 200. In such a league it was just: Think of a Number. Even so he was exasperated by a press report that if his cars were placed nose to tail they would stretch from London to Turkey. I was suitably shocked by such blatant exaggeration and suggested that in reality they would stretch only as far as Switzerland. I'm relieved to say he laughed.

Driving around Brunei I had been pleasantly surprised to find that we were expected. Signs along most roads announced 'AWAS' – which of course as everyone knows is the acronym for the Alan Whicker Appreciation Society.

It seemed very decent of them to make such a fuss about our arrival. We all agreed they need not have gone to so much trouble, but took some pictures to send to the Society's Chairman, John Ferdinando, who was busy evangelizing and spreading the good word back in Sussex.

Later we learned they were road signs, warning traffic to slow down.

However disguised, such nationwide encouragement seemed an auspicious omen as we joined the Sultan on a tour of his jungle kingdom, watching him hand out keys for new subsidized houses, inspect soldiers, receive petitions, listen to speeches – the usual royal rigmarole among a people who had come far, and fast.

Children of Brunei parents who still cannot read or write are now doctors and lawyers. The brighter students at the underused university fly away to study in Cairo or London, and – unhappily for their country – are often reluctant to return. It's hard to keep them down on the farm . . .

So today most of the country's professionals are expatriates, usually eager to become citizens of this multiracial society and so benefit from one of the world's highest living standards. To get that passport they need to have been resident for twenty-five years and to speak Malay – which limits the queue.

The distribution of free benefits remains somewhat uneven. In the 550-bed hospital at Bandar all its superb state-of-the-art equipment is duplicated. One set reserved for the Royal Family, the other for the 280,000 people of Brunei.

On tour upcountry the Sultan was at his most relaxed, as he always was when doing something practical, something technical in which he could lose himself – like flying his Black Hawk helicopter: 'That's right, I like to be in control and not need to depend upon anyone – when you're flying you're too busy to worry about anything else. I like to be responsible for myself.'

His inspections were most thorough. He entered every classroom, talked to the children, examined recorders in the language class. Each time he caught sight of me he broke into the smile that lights up his face: 'Hello, how are you? Everything all right? Enjoy yourself!' He always seemed most concerned.

However, it began to dawn on me that in his mind each of those passing salutations – a few of which we filmed – was an interview. Indeed later, when I am pressing for more access, he tells Christopher, 'We've done interviews all over the place.'

The jovial hail-fellow-well-met was endearing, but unfortunately in television's eyes didn't amount to a hill of Brunei beans.

The Sultanate was powerful back in the fifteenth and sixteenth centuries, and its enduring relationship with Britain began a hundred and fifty years ago when there were pirates to suppress. Brunei was probably saved from extinction by our Treaty of 'Friendship and Commerce'; it was never a colony but a 'protected state', and its survival through the centuries has been a happy fluke.

The real splendour began in 1929, when oil flowed from the tiny backward land dozing amid equatorial jungle, and soon in an emerging state the sons of fishermen, farmers and hawkers became ministers. Today oil gushes from fields that will not run dry for another twenty-five years. The Sultanate has formidable financial clout; its purchases are not only from Harrods and Cartier. The Royal Brunei Navy, for instance, had just spent £200m on Clydeside for three patrol ships; settled, no doubt, out of petty cash.

Back in 1962, before oil revenues escalated, the Sultan's late father embarked upon Brunei's first and only flirtation with democracy: he permitted an election. The newly-created People's Party won a landslide victory, but when it was not allowed to take over the Legislative Council there was an armed rebellion.

The Sultan's call for help was answered by 2,000 British troops from Singapore, mainly Gurkhas, who put down the tentative uprising within a week. Since then Brunei has lived in a perpetual but relaxed State of Emergency, renewed every two years. Its only noticeable effect: the banning of fireworks.

The Sultan's unthreatened government collects in taxes and royalties eighty-five per cent of Brunei Shell Petroleum's massive oil earnings from production now held back to 170,000 barrels a day. Gas was discovered in 1963; from 1973 Japan took the total output – and Brunei was rich rich rich. These revenues pour into the National Exchequer far faster than they can ever be spent – though some members of the Royal Family do their best. Now even this Niagara of wealth has been overtaken by the ever-growing earnings of international investments. All Brunei's financial figures are stratospheric and beyond normal comprehension; we're talking the mileage to Mars here.

There is no trade deficit, no national debt in this unique fiscal dreamtime. Unlike other oil-rich but overpopulated lands, there are only 280,000 Bruneians lining up for their share. Mere residents don't count; only citizens need apply. No tax, of course, and in this Shellfare State everyone gets free education, health care, scholarships, interest-free loans, pensions, you name it – and each family runs about four cars. With Royalty, of course, that's several hundred cars.

The Sultan, a Sunni Muslim, had married his cousin Princess

15

Saleha when he was nineteen and she sixteen. Though Islam allows four wives, he has taken only one more and, by religious precept must treat them equally – so the youngest of six children by the Raja Isteri was born two years after his second marriage to an air hostess flying with Royal Brunei Airlines.

Mariam Bell's father, Jimmy Bell, was a head clerk for the Brunei Customs Department, with a Japanese mother and a British-Brunei father. Her mother was Bruneian, but of course she had no royal blood, so the Sultan's autocratic father and all noble traditionalists strongly disapproved of a marriage they believed would demean the monarchy. Turning his back on the family tradition of intermarriage, the Sultan went ahead anyway and wed his quarter-British Princess in 1981, a marriage finally made public a year later. They now have four children.

Each wife has her own palace, and both are popular. They take State Visits in turn: the Princess goes to India and Pakistan, the Raja Isteri to London.

In the streets I found the Sultan was greeted by a sort of reverential delirium – and these days not too many of the world's rulers can wander safely through their own capitals. Shielded from public view by the elaborate court system, by ancient codes of hierarchy, protocol and rank, HM is obsessive about his privacy – as well he might be in a world eager to get in on his immense wealth.

The first time I followed the red carpet stretching through the Palace into infinity was when Prince Edward was paying his official call upon the Sultan, who stood to greet him in one of his audience rooms wearing traditional Malay costume of yellow silk – the colour reserved for royalty – with brilliant diamond buttons. Unused to being kept waiting, even for seconds, he grew uncomfortable and restive. We watched silently from the sidelines, unable to contribute or attempt to put him at ease. Then Prince Edward arrived with his aide, a flustered Major-General, and the High Commissioner, Adrian Sindall.

In such an audience small talk is by numbers, and safely anodyne; neither Sultan nor Prince is a great conversationalist at the best of times. Having struggled with a sort of Royal interview that morning it was a relief for me to stand aside and let others take the strain: 'Er, how was the flight?' 'Um, are you tired?' 'How is your Mother?' 'You must come and stay in our home in London – the weather is sometimes good in November . . .'

Later, recalling that uneasy audience, the High Commissioner – soon to be Ambassador to Syria – topped it with memories of a dinner party he gave at the Residence, a small elegant Beverly Hills-style villa on a hillside facing the sea, when on an official visit in 1985 Mrs Thatcher wished to return Royal hospitality. The dinner was attended only by the Sultan with two of his senior ministers – both clever Oxford-educated barristers who of course spoke perfect English.

The Commissioner and Mrs Thatcher were taken aback when these two sophisticated men sat for the entire meal with eyes downcast, never uttering a word.

The unease was accentuated by the fact that the Sultan himself was in turn somewhat in awe of the Prime Minister, so her dutiful questions about Brunei received monosyllabic replies. The desperate Commissioner, who had to defer to two Leaders, risked an anecdote which tailed off after a few minutes, ice unbroken. The chemistry was just not right. Mrs Thatcher struggled on manfully with further questions to a diffident and uncomprehending Sultan. His two silent ministers just sat.

Afterwards the High Commissioner held a more successful reception for Prince Edward, before he left to inspect the rainforest. We were there filming jolly Brunei Brits enjoying his diplomatic alcohol in that newly dry land when invitations arrived summoning us for dinner within the hour with Prince Sufri, the Sultan's youngest brother, who was almost a recluse compared with the hyperactive Jefri; the number plate of his modest Lexus was BLISS. He suffered from an unfortunate skin complaint, side effect of drugs taken for serious throat trouble. He had married a Malaysian pop singer, and was shy but popular.

Spurred by the fact that a Royal actually *wanted* to see us, we made our excuses to the Commissioner and slipped out of his party, much to the relief of Prince Edward who, after our brief conversation about Prince Charles's television technique, had been eyeing my camera warily – as though The Really Useful Company was getting its own back. He was so uneasy and unhelpful it was hard to see him as a coming television front man.

We raced down to the vast secluded Istana Edinburgh, built for

Prince Philip on his last visit to Brunei. He stayed one night, after which it became just another guest palace-in-waiting. Followed by the camera car, my black saloon swept up to the imposing entrance hall where Prince Sufri and various ministers were lined up to receive us. This was a mistake. They had assumed our cars contained their Royal guest of honour, Prince Edward, who was still at the Residence smiling dutifully at local Brits.

At the Sultan's Palace such harmless confusion and loss of face would have been a major disgrace for all concerned, and heads would have rolled; but this, I realized with relief, was a casual evening. There were smiles and tolerant murmurings of 'Oh, *Whicker's World . . . Whicker's World . . .*'

My next surprise, after so many dressy 'Decorations-will-be-worn' days, was that our host was wearing an open silk shirt and scruffy, shapeless trousers – though doubtless Armani. All the ministers were in the Brunei version of rat catcher. The dress code was obviously 'not quite smart casual'. We, fresh from the High Commissioner's cocktails, perspired in our dark blue double-breasteds. For the first time in more than forty years of television filming I realized that my camera crew were the best-dressed people in the room.

Christopher Hanbury, slightly embarrassed at being out of step, murmured, 'Perhaps we'd better take our jackets off?'

This presented a far more serious problem. I was 'miked up' – wearing a radio mike with wires and leads, battery in hip pocket, dangling aerial, microphone on tie. This rig meant I could go into an instant interview without the intrusive mike in shot, and was standard time-saving practice. However, in a guarded gathering heavy with protocol and suspicion, within a closed and uncertain community, such exposure would doubtless have revealed me to the ever-watchful security men as a British spy or suicide bomber. I would then be hustled out by armed guards and shot.

I hastily suggested shirtsleeve order might not be a good idea as Prince Edward was about to arrive in his regulation dark suit. 'Ah yes,' said Christopher. 'Perhaps we'd better not.'

It was a relief to get into dinner. There were thirty of us at five tables in a room large as a tennis court, brilliantly lit by five enormous chandeliers hanging from a bright blue ceiling. Next to me sat Brunei's Head of Protocol. As face was all important he must have been an extremely busy official, making nice judgements all day and deciding whether the third wife of the Sultan of Sarawak took precedence over Sabah's Minister of Information . . .

'I like *Whicker's World* very much,' he announced to my great surprise, awarding himself instant precedence in my eyes at least. It transpired he had spent six years at Exeter University.

During the only delicious meal I ate in Brunei, this discerning man surprised me again by springing into outraged action: my enterprising director, David Green, had suddenly appeared with the camera crew and started filming. This meant they were standing taller than the seated princes, so were beyond the protocol pale. What was worse, they tended to chat to people in a friendly fashion as they moved about. This was another major gaffe – almost as bad as blowing your nose in HM's presence. I passed the urgent message that they must bow low while taking pictures. The cameraman was not well pleased.

In Brunei, there's more to filming than getting the exposure right.

Our programme transmission had to coincide with the Sultan's state visit to Britain which, following his procrastination, was due within weeks, so I was writing commentary at every available moment – usually at 3 am while recovering from a change of time zone. By the end of the shoot I had done seventeen drafts, and recorded guide tracks in my room. Since we so far had little interview material each script took thirty-five minutes to read.

The need for a long commentary was growing more obvious by the day, for we were coming up to Ramadan when everything closed down, especially the Sultan. We prepared for another twenty-four hours travel, going home.

At a goodbye dinner with Francis and Simone Medlicott, old Brunei hands who had brought up a family during sixteen years in the Sultanate, I was disconsolate about our lack of progress. He reassured me: 'Don't feel unhappy about getting less than you want. Half is marvellous – that's the most you ever get in Brunei. Most people don't get anything.'

We returned in August, this time without Christopher, who had broken his leg in three places playing polo. Once again we had to go through the ritual of getting into the Palace and attending upon the Sultan, who was now even more nervous about being filmed and required further reassurance. This time I was escorted by a nobleman with whom I had become friendly, the Sultan's representative in London, Pengiran Dato Setia Yusof Sepiuddin, a courtier who learned to stand and wait during a year working in the dining room at Blakes Hotel, SW7.

He now lives near Marble Arch but is losing enthusiasm for London as his wife has recently been mugged at knifepoint. She handed over her handbag with money and cards so was not hurt, but the experience made boring equatorial Bandar seem even more secure and reassuring. Despite this, he says, he plans to retire to Cheshire, or maybe Eastbourne.

The Sultan sends his Private Secretary to show us where in the Palace we can interview him: along the red carpet, of course, and in his Audience Chamber, where we must not move furniture because the Royal chair has a precise position.

We approach this location through an ante-room crammed with brilliance and esoteric artefacts, most of them gifts rained down upon the Sultan in the hope of generosities to come. A shotgun, its stock made of lapis and mother-of-pearl, its barrel gold with diamond-encrusted trigger. Two golden pyramids surrounded by gold palm trees with ruby coconuts and in between, a golden tank. A jade and onyx watering can has diamonds around its rose. A golden helicopter with blades of diamonds protecting a golden pen.

Lots of gleaming jewelled flower bowls and vases; a rock crystal centrepiece with coral poppies and lapis cornflowers, jade leaves and sheaves of corn made from pearls and diamonds. Occasionally there's a flower centre that is empty – carefully removed, perhaps, by some crafty cleaner who then retired for life?

The most insignificant item: a small rock-crystal flask trimmed around the middle with gold, rubies and emeralds – evidently some afterthought gift from which no one had even bothered to remove the price sticker: £49,500.

The Audience Chamber is no anticlimax. It is by *Arabian Nights* out of *The King And I* and has a curious dazzling quality as soft brilliant light falls upon scintillating jewellery scattered among gold-silk furniture. The carpet is extraordinary: pink and glowing with – it would appear – flecks of real gold. It's like disco lighting, but more expensive.

Everything seems solid gold – even the tissue box. The ornaments on each table are encrusted with diamonds and rubies. I notice several jewelled flower arrangements from last year's Asprey catalogue. An amethyst fruit bowl eighteen inches wide decorated with cherry blossom branches of rose quartz and jade, with diamond centres and gold stamens. Large pink, blue and green tourmalines on *pavé* diamond stalks. Two huge blue urns decorated with enamelled pansies, with diamond centres and stalks. A golden model of the house in Kensington where I met the Sultan, its roof picked out in diamonds with lines of rubies and diamonds at its base, set upon a malachite stand. Embossed gold-silk cushions, all with zips at the back – a relief to see something commonplace.

Where else in the world can there be two such rooms? Stunned, feeling inadequate and out of place, we move on to view the empty Throne Room, impressive in a different way: big as a football field with a gilt mosaic five or six storeys high at one end, and 3,000 red plush chairs under a dozen chandeliers, each weighing a ton. Throughout the Palace there are 564 chandeliers and 51,490 light bulbs.

Amid this scintillation our cameraman gets out his exposure meter: how does the room look with *all* the lights on? Click. It's blazing – but one vast chandelier fuses under the strain. I hear the pop but amid the brilliance am loath to point it out because we are already being blamed for most things. When I brace myself to tell them everyone is greatly perturbed. They now have to change about 800 bulbs; at the going rate that should take several weeks.

As we leave after our dazzling tour I thank the Sultan's gentle and amusing Secretary for his guidance and concern. 'That's all right,' he says. 'I'll bill you.'

Most wealthy Bruneians are compulsive shoppers; Christopher Hanbury's wife Bridget – an efficient Colonel's Lady if ever there was one – is kept busy at long range by the Royal Family, particularly the two Queens. She sends the glossy fashion magazines out to Brunei each month, and the family mark up everything they want – which is normally quite a lot. Louis Féraud is favourite. Then, three days a week, the cool Bridget hits Knightsbridge to spend, spend, spend. Best of all, it's Other People's Money.

The wife of another official told me that when she asked the Queen if she had done much shopping during her last flying visit she replied in surprise, 'What's the point of going to London if you don't shop?'

This went some way towards explaining the compulsive buying of those with bottomless purses. The acquisition of some new object is what triggers the orgasm, not the pride of possession. Once bought, packages are often unopened, for new targets have appeared.

This may be why Prince Jefri had six hundred cars – though surely by now any new car must offer only a momentary tingle. I suspect Mr Hertz and Mr Avis get more satisfaction from their parking lots.

Although Brunei is governed in almost total secrecy it could not contain the palace upheaval that followed the enforced collapse of Prince Jefri's Amedeo Development Corporation under debts some estimated at £10bn. His spokesman dismissed them as only £500m and 'quite normal for a business of that size'. Nevertheless its demise gravely damaged the economy and may have signalled the end of Brunei's playboy era.

A former Finance Minister, Jefri had already been replaced as Chairman of the Brunei Investment Agency which controlled a £35bn nest egg against the days when the oil might run out. These savings had apparently dropped to £12bn. A worldwide hunt started for the missing billions. There has been no report of any sightings.

The extravagances of this international playboy with four wives and a lot of form were first exposed at a time when Brunei had begun to feel the effects of Asia's 1997–8 economic crises. Following that financial upheaval, annual revenues from oil and gas, which usually fluctuated around £1–1.5bn fell back towards £900m.

The Sultan's fortune was halved from a high of £25.6bn, due mainly to the Asian depression, the price of oil and, somewhere along the line, a measure of old-fashioned graft. Prince Jefri did his bit too; his outgoings were significant. Amedeo had bought some of the world's leading hotels, including the Palace in New York, the Bel Air in Beverly Hills and the Plaza Athénée in Paris.

With little sense of what money is worth, Prince Jefri had also picked up Asprey in Bond Street for £243m – before discovering that he had been its biggest customer. It was his corner shop. Nevertheless he carried on buying and the following year spent another £70m – a third of its turnover – and lent it a further £277m.

Aston Martin sued him for £4m; he had dropped by its showroom one day and, it would seem, did not like to leave without buying *something* – so ordered twenty-five Astons. They were not cheaper by the dozen.

Prince Jefri has several homes in Hampstead, including a £20m conversion of two houses in Bishops Avenue; also what was once the massive Playboy Club and casino in Park Lane, next-door neighbour to his brother's Dorchester. Risking even greater exposure to the sin of gambling at its very heartland, he built the largest private residence in Las Vegas. Among his thirty homes around the world was the new £500m 600-room Jerudong Park in Brunei, with eight swimming pools and nine restaurants. It had originally been planned as his country's first deluxe hotel, but was later seen as just another residence for the Prince.

He faced lurid lawsuits in California and London, none of which proved him guilty though all tarnished his name and that of his family. Allegations of his brother's sexploits seriously embarrassed the Sultan, as did his vast yacht called *Tits*, with tenders *Nipple 1* and *Nipple 2*. Reports that forty prostitutes had been installed in the Dorchester were used by Fundamentalists in Brunei to underline his threat to Islamic purity.

This palace intrigue and his various dismissals from office were brought about by his estranged older brother Prince Mohamed, soft-spoken and far less extrovert. This devout Foreign Minister was supported by shadowy religious advisers, including a group of forty 'teachers' from Iran. The Royal confrontation had Shakespearean echoes of some medieval Venetian or Florentine court, as brother plotted against brother.

Prince Jefri wrote to *Le Monde* explaining why he believed he had been attacked by Islamic Fundamentalists: 'This is a power struggle between those supporting an open modern and pro-western policy, which I represent, and others wanting a conservative religious regime.'

Certainly during the months of our visits Fundamentalist influence had grown perceptibly firmer, and the powerful religious conservatives seemed to find it easy to make up laws as they went along. 'Every week, some new restriction,' one resigned expatriate told me.

Rotary and Lions Clubs were denounced by the state Mufti as part of 'a Zionist conspiracy' and banned. Later they were permitted to re-form, but Freemasonry was still suppressed. Pig farming stopped, and the Mufti outlawed alcohol – making Brunei the only 'dry' country in South-East Asia. Chinese restaurants around town echoed Prohibition by serving beer in teapots, to be drunk out of mugs. Then even that 'special tea' was banned.

Women of the Royal Household, TV announcers and schoolgirls appeared with heads covered, and a dress code was even imposed in the town's amusement park. Islamic authorities ordered the withdrawal of three hundred Japanese tyres imported for Mitsubishi jeeps when the treads were seen to resemble a verse from the Koran.

When Buddhist temples were closed and some priests and nuns asked to leave the country, there was concern that Brunei was changing from a relaxed Muslim nation into a theocratic Islamic state – especially when, during the Sultan's absence abroad, Christmas was cancelled as 'a foreign intrusion into a Muslim land'. Trees and decorations were removed from public places, and Rudolf the red-nosed reindeer went into exile.

Soon afterwards there was a problem with the Chinese New Year. As elsewhere in South-East Asia, the Brunei-Malaysians have more conflict with the 46,000 pushy Chinese who run their country's commerce than with the 6,000 expat Brits who merely administer and help to keep the system going, yet in the end the Chinese celebrations were allowed to continue.

The world's only museum commemorating our wartime leader Winston Churchill was in Brunei, and his was the country's only statue – gesturing defiantly. Like Queen Victoria in Bombay, he was demoted, and disappeared. The museum now shows a collection of royal regalia.

The language of Brunei's courts is still English, as is its

Common Law, but mild censorship is pervasive. Kissing scenes are removed from films on Brunei television – twenty-two minutes from one *Miami Vice.* The local *Borneo Bulletin* controlled by Prince Mohamed is of course in tune but published under religious and political censorship which also applies to publications arriving from the outside world. Foreign newspapers are sold with pages full of holes where offending stories and pictures have been neatly removed. My *Herald Tribune,* printed in Singapore, sometimes looked as though a cabaret artist had been cutting it up for some trick – though missing stories, if interesting enough, arrived soon after by fax. A *Time* cover story on breast cancer in America had its illustrations laboriously blacked out.

Bland and even sympathetic articles are often cut, for obscure reasons; the mood and intention of any censor anywhere is usually hard to decipher. Before a classical concert a foreign quintet was sternly questioned: 'Are you playing Communist music?'

Should the British Council bring out a Shakespeare play or a mime artist, the performance must first be 'scrutinized'. BADS, the British Amateur Dramatic Society, planned to stage one of those brittle Noël Coward comedies of the 1930s. It submitted the required thirteen copies of the script to the 'Language and Literature Bureau'. After *seven months*' consideration the script was returned, with twenty cuts. The Master would have been enchanted.

In their jungle longhouses Brunei's Iban people are traditional and picturesque, though now 'not a positive image'. Officials prefer to show the world pictures of modern but commonplace housing estates. They were reluctant to let us film the old Brunei of the rainforests, but I insisted. We had to have some local colour.

It took a long time to organize two boats to carry us up river. Then we had to wait for a third, to carry our drivers – which suggested they had some security role and were really there to keep a languid eye on us; certainly their driving abilities were limited, and they never offered to help carry the camera gear.

Finally we set off, launches riding on top of the water and banging about. We roared through mangrove swamps for an hour, then drove a long way in Jeeps before reaching the jungle longhouse they proposed we should film.

It housed seventeen families – about a hundred and thirty people – and had just been built. Amid the picturesque traditional longhouses, this showplace looked like a new school in the home counties, put up by Wates.

What's more, it had left the traditions of the Iban jungle people so far behind that after looking round I was asked to sign a visitors' book.

As our set piece conversation with the Sultan finally approached, my recordist went into the royal chambers to put on his radio mike, a delicate operation that required actually touching the Godhead. He was quite relaxed, even if his guards were not.

While I waited for HM to emerge I pondered the problems of interviewing an Absolute Monarch on his own territory. Such small television skills as I have are usually used to uncover attitude, flavour and information. Here the problem was just to keep him *going*. He could not be asked thoughtful questions for if he did not understand or the question was problematic he would laugh nervously, and dry up.

A written interview would of course have been simple – just link a few disjointed phrases into an unbroken considered quote; but television was watching what we both said. He was showing courtesy by talking to me in a language with which he was not comfortable, and deserved every consideration – but a good question might equal silence and discomfort for everyone, including the viewer. He had to understand, at least. Yet should I coax or encourage too much I could already see the *Guardian*, *Observer* and *Evening Standard* critics complaining that I had not given the smiling billionaire King a damn good going-over.

However, I was confident once we got through our first hesitant interview his assurance would grow and subsequent meetings would be more revealing.

So finally it's 'Turn over – *Action!*' We set off along the red carpet, filming. We're silhouetted against the light for some of the walk. He's laughing nervously, as expected. Those damn fountains are too noisy. That guard got into shot and stared. Never mind, keep turning.

To the cameraman's surprise the Sultan diverts me into his golden Cabinet Room, never before photographed. This will later throw the Household into a fret; another precedent set, after five hundred years.

Then into the even more golden Audience Chamber, for our relaxed chat. As expected, he was tense and anxious, but since this was only our first filmed conversation, it was not too crucial. I could afford to jolly him along while he warmed up and played himself in, painlessly.

In contrast I found myself cooling down, because when you're being casual and informal it is off-putting to find his entourage approaching on their knees, keeping below his level. It was also disconcerting to know that, as we filmed, four ashen aides were crawling around anxiously behind my settee. It was not easy to comprehend their task, nor what they were achieving.

The Sultan explains he is reconciled to his role as an Absolute Monarch: 'God wished me to be King, God gives me happiness – I have no complaints.'

I wondered whether one day he might have to follow Malaysia, Thailand and Japan and accept a constitutional role within a democracy? 'We already have a constitutional role, we have a Cabinet,' he said. 'It's up to future generations – but there might be some adjustment.'

Money may not go out of fashion these days, but conspicuous spending does, so he was determined to deny that he was the world's richest man. 'I don't understand how it comes out like that. It surprises me. How do they know? I have three hundred watches, but I can only wear one,' he adds, sounding reasonable – though little else was, in his improbable Kingdom.

Could there be anything in the world that he wanted? 'Well, even the richest man needs something. However rich you are, there is still something you miss.'

This at *last* promised a revelation: 'What is it then, in your case?'

'That's my secret.' OK, thanks.

However, he did tell me, amid many chuckles, that he had never owned Harrods: 'I wish I did.' I suspect that, as with everything else in the material world, if he hasn't got it, he doesn't want it.

We talk for sixteen minutes. Afterwards, pushing it along, I ask what time we shall be seeing him on Monday? 'Oh, you want to do it *again?*'

'Of course we do.'

'Well all right, but perhaps more informal next time.' At last, he's singing my song.

My director and I decide that the conversation just filmed will be useful, though merely as mute under my build-up commentary; tomorrow's meeting will be the main interview.

I was happy – and, as I walked him back to his chambers, so it seemed was the Sultan. We considered filming him playing on the private golf course he had carved out of the jungle, flying his Airbus, playing badminton; the ice has been broken and nothing now seems impossible. Do we have lift-off?

No, we do not. That evening he injures his leg playing polo and is laid up. So we pack and fly home again. It felt like commuting.

We returned for the third visit in October to film his Silver Jubilee celebrations. After years of planning, everything went smoothly this time. At Brunei's previous Independence celebrations in 1984 the King of Tonga had stayed in one of the palaces built for visiting royalty. A special bed was constructed to accommodate his enormous bulk, and a huge loo. Unfortunately this king-sized convenience had a standard Brunei-sized door which the King could not get through – not even sideways. This time there was no such pressure on guests.

Prince Edward represented the Queen and sat in the Throne Room looking young – as HM might have said – among the King and Sultans of Malaysia, the Crown Prince of Thailand, the Presidents of Singapore and the Philippines. Each Royal guest and Head of State was provided with a new Rolls-Royce flown from England for the occasion; the hundreds of less-exalted guests were all allocated new Mercedes.

As the Sultan's guests, we were well seated for the ceremony. After a delay of almost three hours, the Royal procession along the red carpet was well worth waiting for, brilliantly bejewelled and suitably spectacular. The Sultan's wives wear identical costumes and equally splendid jewellery. They process behind him, regally, to sit on either side of the throne. 'Do you think those rocks are real?' whispers an unworldly American wife.

The brilliance in this wide room far exceeds any Coronation or Durbar I have ever seen around the world. We grow almost weary of magnificence.

After the religious ceremony the Sultan leaves, to be pulled by soldiers through the streets of his humid little capital in a golden Cleopatra chariot, before most of the population. Their reception was cordial yet strangely impassive, a respectful people seeming too awed to cheer and wave and let themselves go.

Celebrations around town were predictably extravagant, though muted – but then they were organized by Brunei's Department of Religious Affairs and included a Postal Exhibition, some top-spinning and a Cookery Fair showing how to steam glutinous rice. None of this stimulated the wild carnival spirit; there was not much abandoned dancing in the streets.

However the climax of the celebrations that night was a state banquet for five thousand bejewelled guests at the Royal Palace, when a splendour of Rolls-Royces disgorged glitterati into the sultry night.

It was here I revealed, to camera, the gift we had brought the Sultan, the man who really does have everything. The great and the good and the rich had arrived bearing piles of magnificent presents, and we knew he had enough watches. With some trepidation I had risked asking him what he wanted. Fortunately he did not request another Bentley; with much giggling it was decided he would leave it to us.

So we contrived a highly personalized spectacle case for his glovebox, which Valerie had skilfully embroidered with our Best Wishes on one side, the Bentley emblem on the other. This required much work, but the end-product was elegant, unique – and affordable. In it we put a pair of very stylish dark glasses with frames containing flashing lights. The Sultan, as I said at the time, would be beside himself.

We hoped it was well received and, if not left in the glovebox of one of the Continentals, might even find its place among the important bejewelled gifts in the Royal museum. We never discovered what happened to it. They don't do thank you letters.

Though apparently relaxed among his massed guests, the

Sultan remained diffident about further filmed conversations. With so many crowned heads and political leaders to entertain, with Heads of State discussions and the whole Royal minuet, we were not high priority and became wearily aware that our warm-up chat was all we were liable to get. He had done all those interviews ('How are you?' 'Everything all right?') and now had significant political work to do. We were becoming an afterthought – like that £49,500 vase. The circus was moving on.

This was our third visit, and it was getting more and more difficult to retain our eager enthusiasm. We could not keep flying a television crew backwards and forwards to the Far East, not even for an Absolute Monarch. We had almost achieved our profile-in-depth. It required only a few more hours of the Sultan's time, and Brunei's archives would have gained a permanent record of life as this unique land entered the twenty-first century – a bequest future generations would see as far more interesting than the memory of yet another wooden Royal meeting or polo match . . .

So we set off home again, for ever. We left a gentle land and its handsome people, a Royal Family divided between traditionalists and self-indulgent playboys, a nation trying to adjust to an informal Islamic lifestyle while striving to find a future somewhere between the muscular traditional and the easygoing modern. Above all, it was learning to cope with the predicament of being very rich in a poor world in which dynastic rule is always vulnerable, and learning that it cannot spend its way out of every problem.

With all our filming we already had a good programme in the can, which on eventual transmission achieved an enormous audience – 55 per cent of all viewers – but of course, it could have been so much better . . .

It was shown around the world. The Sultan enjoyed it, I was told, and at a time of international discord it helped to keep HM happily on the Commonwealth team, buying British warships; in an emergency, Brunei could always rescue sterling.

Having finally made up his mind about dates, the Sultan arrived on his State Visit. He was met at Victoria by the Queen and Prince Philip and – as Prince Edward had suggested – stayed at their home for a few days. He also lunched at Number 10 with Prime Minister John Major and was entertained by the Lord Mayor and City of London at the Guildhall, before completing his holiday at The Aviary, his mansion among forty-seven acres of Southall.

His magnificent banquet honouring our Royal Family was held at the Dorchester amid banks of orchids said to have cost £250,000, which mesmerized the Queen. Our *Whicker's World* had just been transmitted and the Queen was gracious enough to thank me, as did some ministers. I was most appreciative – particularly since one or two critics had, predictably, attacked me for being too polite to the Sultan. There's a surprise.

HM had come to Britain bearing ceremonial gifts, of course, and certainly the quixotic generosity of Bruneians can be startling. There are endless stories of the Royal Family's elaborate and exotic presents emerging from their golden Aladdin's Cave. The Sultan is said to have given his daughter an Airbus 340 in her favourite colours on her eighteenth birthday. Prince Jefri once ordered half-a-dozen BMWs to be airfreighted into Brunei and left outside friends' homes, gift-wrapped with bows and ribbons – and gold ignition keys from Cartier. He also paid £3.2m for ten watches set with jewels showing a couple copulating every hour, on the hour.

As we were leaving Brunei for ever after filming, a dignified messenger arrived from the Palace to deliver a bulky gift from His Majesty. We held our breaths. Oh really, you shouldn't have ... Within a massive velour box lined with Royal yellow satin was a small yellow plate showing the Sultan's portrait.

At least it was Spode.

Commercial break . . .

In the early years of ITV it was not considered proper for serious actors or documentary people to make commercials: those profitable sidelines were generally left to the lower echelons of showbiz. Then Laurence Olivier went on American television, rather quietly, selling Polaroid cameras. This encouraged other names to drift overseas and film, bashfully, in Japan – where it was considered unlikely the rising *Sun* would break their cover.

Smart advertising agencies then started to enlist familiar on-screen personalities. I was asked to support cars, hotels, beer, shoes, wine . . . but I refused all approaches, however financially appealing. I could not see myself flogging soap powder or coffee; not being snooty, you understand, but my heart would not have been in it.

Then along came British European Airways. Their agency, J. Walter Thompson, suggested that as television's first Travelling Man I should front their new campaign for flights and holidays. That caught my attention. I used BEA constantly and usually found them excellent – so I would not be expected to enthuse over something I did not believe to be true. What's more, I would be supporting what was then the taxpayers' airline.

Once I was enlisted and on the team, the advertising fandango began; this was new to me and all rather agreeable. I attended lots of script meetings and lunches. When an agency is spending a fortune on eighty words dropped carefully into forty seconds of airtime, each syllable is priceless and must be endlessly considered.

After weeks of rewrites and argument I went on location one sunny morning to film my first commercial. It was at good old

London Airport, where a large camera crew, BEA airliners and smart uniforms were lined up for our dramatic opening shot.

I had learned the script. It was only a hundred words or so – a trifle compared with the long pieces I daily struggled to memorize for *Tonight*. In a departure concourse the director asked me to walk alongside picture windows looking down at well-orchestrated BEA activity on the apron below while chatting our much discussed script to a tracking camera. This I did.

They cut, and a long baffled silence followed. Director and crew looked at each other in some confusion. I wondered where I had gone wrong.

It appeared I had shocked them all by doing the entire script in one take. This was to be the work of several intensive days. All they had expected from me was the first phrase. I was suitably shamefaced by my brash excess of fluency, and spent the next three days obediently repeating each phrase in a different setting, backed by scores of extras. There is nothing so simple that cannot be complicated if exposed to enough creative thought.

The intensity of impact of commercials – and much of their phenomenal expense – is created by the endless changes of location, shot, casting, angle, background, inflection, atmosphere, considered necessary to hold an audience credited with an attention-span of three seconds. This is now standard practice, as you will observe from ever more frantic commercials.

Later we flew down to Sorrento to shoot two more which, when edited and presented, delighted BEA. J. Walter Thompson, well content, booked hundreds of slots in all TV areas and prepared to launch its blockbuster campaign. We workers celebrated at Annabel's.

The day before the first transmissions, the Independent Broadcasting Authority cancelled the whole campaign – because of me. Their sudden veto was 'expressing the view that Whicker is a central feature of serious journalism, and an important objective view on ITV'.

BEA had spent hundreds of thousands of pounds; JWT had signed scores of contracts; schedules covering transmissions during future weeks had been booked; but now JWT and BEA executives lost jobs, went to Siberia or out of business, all because the IBA had decided that for me to support our national airline would be against the code of ITV – which owed its very existence to advertising!

Our harmless and jolly forty seconds was hardly a *Hitlerbefehl* or Papal *diktat*; not even a parliamentary ruling or court order. It was just me, musing about reliability and cabin service and hotels with lovely views.

After this bizarre and disruptive decision heads rolled; a major airline and advertising agency were furious and financially damaged – and poor JWT had to settle my contract anyway since it was they who had omitted to send the scripts to some ITV committee. At the end of the fracas I preserved my advertising virginity, but had been involuntarily at the epicentre of a PR disaster.

IBA's draconian concern for my probity may have been flattering – but it seemed I was being flattered rather more than anyone else in television. Little discouragement was offered to actors or mimics who were then impersonating me in various commercials. The admirable Ronnie Barker was able to extol the virtues of Japanese watches in Whickeric upon the mandatory desert island, after his agency had asked permission for me to do the pitch but been refused. Robert Morley went on to record my banned airline commercials, rather differently. My old *Tonight* colleague Cliff Michelmore spoke for London Docklands instead of me, and a disc jockey called Jimmy Savile stepped in to make his name on the 'Clunk–Click' safety-belt campaign, which I had to refuse.

When I protested at being singled out by this curious determination to ensure that I should not be deflowered, the Director-General of ITA/IBA, Sir Brian Young, explained that I was not on a black list but indeed proudly included on a white list. Whatever the colour of his list, it emasculated my earning capacity for years, as though I were ITV's only true voice from abroad. To recoup I had to go to distant lands beyond the control of the IBA and speak for Air New Zealand, who had smartly picked up BEA's idea.

After ten more years under their implacable embargo, the cogs finally moved within that curious hierarchy and Sir Brian wrote to tell me that finally and inexplicably I was unchained and a free man: 'You are losing your divinity,' he wrote, sadly. I replied, 'Emancipation, even late in life, comes as a great relief – though I suspect that you have defended my virginity so fiercely and for so long that after many expensive courtships word has gone round that I am unattainable. Impregnable, even.' At least I could now imitate Ronnie Barker.

Though liberated and finally as free as everyone else, I continued to refuse commercials, since nothing that was offered seemed suitable or interesting. That blanket ban under which I was clutched, protesting, to the IBA's protective bosom had prevented my doing what I would in almost every case have rejected anyway. Before agreeing to appear in a commercial there was always a great deal to be considered – including your entire future. An ill-chosen project could explode in the face of an over-eager huckster.

Bernard Braden had just ended his BBC career by advertising Campbell's soups at a time when he was fronting a consumer programme, so Saatchi & Saatchi flew an ingratiating account executive to Jersey to convince me it might be interesting and profitable to replace him. On reflection I felt it unwise to upset my television life by getting in the soup, however generous their offer and however appealing the prospect of free cream of chicken for the rest of my life.

Actors of course can go anywhere they are invited, and even some of us who appear in documentaries and current affairs programmes may move into commercials painlessly if a suitable product or service is involved; if it is not right, a hard sell can cause a jolt of public disbelief each time it appears.

Back in the 1980s my successor as winner of BAFTA's Richard Dimbleby Award was the botanist Dr David Bellamy, he of the fierce enthusiasms and tortured speech. Along with all those impersonators, I enjoyed seeing him deep in foliage explaining in that distinctive voice 'That's *arctostaphylos uvae-ursi* – it's very good for PMT . . .' But then to hear him urging me with equal enthusiasm to use a certain lavatory cleaner – no, no, that just drove me round the bend.

I was also taken aback to find myself advertising Rank Xerox printers along with John Major, the Prime Minister, and Trevor McDonald, the newsreader. Without asking permission, our images had been kidnapped. It was a strange sensation to be splashed across the important public prints supporting a product of which one had never heard.

Twelve-inch double-column advertisements in all the serious broadsheets showed Trevor McDonald bringing information from the network and John Major adding glorious colour, while I was well connected. The implied endorsement with its big colour pictures passed us off as supporters of that product. This was financially damaging to me, as other advertisers saw I was contracted to that major company. Trevor McDonald was even more displeased since his agreement with ITN had a 'no endorsements' clause. 'Bit shocking,' he said, 'to find Rank Xerox maintaining that because they'd bought the rights to my photo from some library for a few pounds, they could use it without permission.' The Prime Minister was also unamused.

The *Guardian* ran an article under the headline 'Barefaced Robbery', and I grew uncomfortably aware that should some other advertiser decide to be as unethical, I could find myself selling sex aids, cigarettes, suspect airlines, miracle cures or nuclear-waste disposal, in colour, anywhere.

We complained to the Advertising Standards Authority, but that professional body did not uphold our objection. Anyone, it seemed, could be used to advertise anything, whether they liked it or not. An unhappy state of affairs. At least Dr Bellamy was being paid for enthusing about loo disinfectant.

Later the more responsible Council of that Authority did an about-turn, overruled their own recommendation and upheld our complaint. It concluded that 'because the advertisements implied endorsement, advertisers should have obtained the complainant's permission'. The Authority told Rank Xerox to withdraw the offending displays.

That curious company then declined to pay our costs, and we were too busy and too weary of expensive soliciting to go to court; but at least we had discouraged their dubious practice, and perhaps other innocents will in future be spared such blatant theft.

In the United States they handle things rather better. A Canadian software company used pictures of the beautiful Hedy Lamarr in her 1949 film *Samson and Delilah* on their graphics packages, without her knowledge or consent – doubtless believing she had gone to that great studio in the sky. Happily she had not. Then eighty-four, the actress immediately sued them for millions. Later, out of court, she granted them a five-year licence to use her image – for an enormous sum.

After the unhappy experiences of Rank's cheeky imposition and the abortive BEA project, no advertising I could support wholeheartedly came up for several years, so I made no use of my new freedom. Then a major campaign was suggested for a service that fitted my lifestyle precisely. All I had to do was keep doing what I was doing anyway, while pausing now and then in some exotic location to recall that Barclaycard had qualities 'unlike some charge cards I could mention . . .'

It was the intention of their enterprising agency, Collett Dickenson and Pearce, to spread the word that credit cards could be used internationally for all sorts of purchases in all sorts of jet-set locations, not just at the neighbourhood supermarket and garage.

At a time when its competitor Access/Mastercard was producing commercials with talking cartoon lobsters, Barclaycard had made an equally slapstick approach to television with the comic actors Peter Sellers and Dudley Moore. The intention now was to move away from film stars and show a real person doing real things, so they asked a known traveller to flash his card around in California and Kenya, Portofino and Ephesus, Tucson and Seville – where I might well have been working and using my card anyway.

Amid a television lifetime filming *Whicker's World*s for BBC and ITV, my only additional chore would now be to peel off for a couple of weeks each year to record two or three Barclaycards. These would be produced in the same sort of places on my flightpath with the same sort of people – sometimes, after CDP's entertaining copy had been slightly Whickerized, even with the same sort of script!

The agency, starting off as it intended to go on, set the first commercials in the photogenic Alps and on the Côte d'Azur. No pain, there – or so it seemed at first. After a last-minute rush from Munich to Hochgurgl I was hurriedly kitted out in the hotel shop and found myself seven thousand feet up a mountain in ski boots so small I could hardly stand, let alone ski. However, they were the right scarlet colour, which was all that concerned the art director. On that chill mountainside, I felt like a Japanese bride with cute little feet. It made somersaulting on skis quite an ordeal . . .

Portofino was far happier, as we went cruising around that enchanting harbour while a tenor in a nearby boat sang 'Just One Cornetto' and I chased the throwaway inflection for 'Isn't he in the wrong commercial?' We had broken the taboo against referring to another product, and rather enjoyed it.

Then there was that Turkish bath with a lot of noisy slapping and twisting, and the wonder that is Ephesus. The ten-hour drive back to Istanbul competing along narrow roads with Turkish juggernauts made even the local airline seem secure. On Mykonos I achieved a lifetime ambition – to smash a lot of plates in a seaside taverna. We never got around to throwing glasses into the fireplace.

By chance, or because of commitments or schedules or availability, wherever we went to film the climate was always at its most scorching, so behind the camera they worked stripped. In front of the camera, in Seville in June, my suit, shirt and tie were soggy within minutes. Occasionally the director would add to the furnace by topping up available light with enormously hot brutes. Flushed with the success of the Joan Collins/Leonard Rossiter Cinzano commercials – also made by CDP – he decided it might help the script if in one shot wine was thrown all over me.

I had only three gaberdine suits to ruin, but he was confident he would get the shot in three takes. This seemed unlikely, since he had been averaging about ten. Fortunately the price of my Doug Haywards got through to the producer just in time to spare me a refreshing flagon of Spanish red straight at each gent's single-breasted button-one 9 oz tropical-weight.

In Beverly Hills we introduced to the underprivileged viewing world those stretch limos that are so long – and now so commonplace. As an extra, ours had a small jacuzzi full of blonde bimbos on the back, which has yet to be spotted on the M25.

My favourite of all was the dolphin at Long Beach. The script called for me to be talking to camera by a waterside and as I made an emphatic gesture while holding my Barclaycard, an invisible sea monster would leap out of the waves and bite it from my hand. Well, yes, great, but wait a minute, steady on . . .

As a man with little understanding of big-game fish I was slightly unnerved that this enormous shark-like creature, which could easily have been a killer whale, was planning to rear up behind my back while I stood innocently chatting away in the Californian sunshine, and grab at me. This was going to happen while I was looking the other way, and seemed so unfair.

I know dolphins are meant to be wonderfully well disposed towards us, but I had seen those teeth – and what if he didn't like foreigners in his territory? I had visions of losing my right hand, or at least a few fingers. It was crunch time. They would never transmit that, surely? Perhaps I might get off lightly, with just a gash?

Not wishing to appear chicken to a fish, I located the unit first-aid kit, a fixed grin, and went ahead with my spiel. Right on cue the dolphin leapt ten feet out of the water – and gently removed the Barclaycard from my hand. I didn't even feel it go. There was a small splash, and silence. No blood at all. It was a new enchantment.

Needless to say the cameraman, my old colleague Brian Tuffano, wanted another take, then another and another. I fluffed a couple of times. Then the sound man wasn't happy. The dolphin was perfect, every take.

I assumed his trainer had worked on this new trick for weeks, but when I asked how long it had taken the fish to get the hang of it he said, 'About two minutes.' Made me feel quite redundant, and rather slow.

After the wrap we hung around to play with him for a while, but even as we were leaving Marineland our star carried on mugging the camera – even though he could see it was now off the tripod. He kept flipping his ball out of the pool for us to throw back. His professionalism and spirit of fun were so admirable and endearing that I have never since felt the same way about Japanese cars.

We flew on to Tucson, to face a more worrying challenge. This time the Barclaycard had to be *shot* out of my hand. I had more confidence in the dolphin – he was a real pro.

After a few cowboys were flung out of bar windows between me and the camera, my stagecoach was attacked by Indians. Covered in arrows, I had to discourage a mother who was about to board with her family: 'Don't put your daughter on the stage, Mrs Worthington.'

The whole campaign was proving wonderfully successful: the commercials were entertaining, good to look at and usually amusing. We enjoyed making them, and research told the agency that viewers enjoyed watching them.

Of one achievement there could be no doubt: the impact of commercials is quite extraordinary. During the last forty years I have done many hundred *Whicker's Worlds*, usually well received; but the public reaction to that catalogue of hour-long documentaries sometimes seemed overshadowed by a score of happy but piffling 40-second ads.

At the airport check-in or the supermarket checkout, on a bus or in a bar people still grin and ask, 'Barclaycard, I suppose?' My last credit-card commercial was more than ten years ago! Advertisers sometimes do get their money's-worth.

One of our constant production problems was that each series had to carry a bigger jolt than the last, and needed to be more visually exciting, funnier, further-flung. At the agency in Euston Road they decided our next location would be Kenya. The producer explained: 'We want more drama, more excitement, more – well, more sort of everything. We've found a paradise beach, an unspoiled wildlife reserve and we'll be having six days under canvas in the shadow of Kilimanjaro.'

The project seemed exotic enough. The scripts featured wild animals, dhows, balloons, jungles, helicopters, Masai warriors and the snows of Kilimanjaro – hard to top, and a natural winner. It was also the last Barclaycard we ever made.

After months of planning, writing and rewriting, we followed the crew out to Nairobi, well injected and Paludrined. From Nairobi, another couple of hours in a small plane to Kiwaiyu, a honeymooners' hideaway near the border with Somalia, accessible only by air or sea. It was the perfect backdrop for any Robinson Crusoe dream: coral reef and wide white beach, banana-leaf huts by the water, each with a gigantic white bed surrounded by fluffy mosquito nets; all very pretty, with excellent food and no communication with the outside world. Behind our thatched hut a shower with rattan screens was pure South Pacific – chilly, unless you washed that man right out of your hair some time after midday, when the sun had warmed the water.

That night we dutifully lit our anti-mosquito coils and settled down behind nets to repel hungry anything, while listening to the exotic and agitated sounds of the African night.

Half an hour later, just dropping off, I felt something moving across my chest. Panicky struggle for the torch. It was a large and unsquashable sort of cockroach and/or venomous thing. Out of bed, recovering from the shock, I remembered to up-end my slippers, cautiously. Something large and repulsive emerged, like a hairy snake. On closer examination by torchlight it turned out to be a long-haired and obviously poisonous centipede which would doubtless have torn off my toes. This was not friendly territory.

Shaken, we settled back insecurely beneath the net. Later, in the darkness, Valerie reached out a comforting arm and gently touched my shoulder. I hit the thatch. At three o'clock, still shaking, we gave in and took sleeping pills, to keep everything at bay.

At dawn the monkeys arrived – but at least we knew what and where they were. A horrified shout came from the next hut: 'There's an animal in my shower.' Monkeys steal everything loose, so we scrambled our suitcase locks and hoped the combination would fool them.

Our first sequence was shot on board a dhow which, under its great white triangular sail, had been dressed to look super-exotic with rugs, cushions, palm fronds, trays of giant crayfish, golden coffee sets and photogenic boatmen. By the time our camera crew and all the extras got on board we were low in the water and looking more like a boatload of Vietnamese refugees.

Our chopper flew overhead to film us sailing away – and knocking the young son of the resort manager off his surfboard. We ploughed on, unaware. The child survived, but the mother was hysteric, the manager apoplectic. On the other side of the reef, in a high swell, the dhow's engine conked out and our treasure ship was stranded. It was the first sign of gathering clouds.

Next day we flew south to Mombasa and put to sea in a powerful big-game fishing launch, which was quite another speed. I spent several hours strapped in the seat at the back wrestling with a fishing line pulled taut by the strength of some enormous shark. It was in fact a heavy oil drum, which bent the rod satisfactorily and was equally exhausting to reel in.

Later we looked at the monolithic Fort Jesus, and a local resident took us for tea at the old Mombasa Club – ancient, deserted and unloved. I had last been there during the 1950s while covering the Royal tour of East Africa, when it was very elegant and white Raj. It remained gloriously traditional, with lovely tropical gardens, white rattan chairs on its long empty terrace – and the usual snarling Club servants: 'It's 5.15 – no more tea!'

We crossed by ferry and drove into the jungle, to Shimba Lodge, built with timber walkways through trees around a flood-lit elephants' watering-hole. We were there for several days, but caught a glimpse of only one elephant. It was just the way it is all round the world: 'You should have been here yesterday, we had twenty-two elephants.' I decided it must be another BYO place – bring your own.

However, it was all so beautiful and well designed that we settled for the deafening chorus of bullfrogs and remote possibility that animals might arrive tomorrow. There was also considerable promise in the next day's call sheet: 'Artists Required: Alan Whicker and one cheetah.'

I expected some cuddly furry bundle, but when I went to check him out in his cage on the back of a truck, he was long and lithe and gorgeous, almost full grown and called Chaos. Enormous golden eyes, a ruff of baby fur still around his neck and huge paws like some giant Labrador puppy. He was quite stunning and never stopped purring, though undid this amiability by refusing to look you straight in the eye.

He belonged to David Hopcraft, an impressive third-generation Kenyan whose other cheetah was a full-grown eight-year-old. I never discovered what his bumper-sticker said. Though not overfriendly, the two cheetahs used to go hunting together in the bush and then glide home to his farm outside Nairobi. Since they could run at 60 mph with 20-foot strides, it was not surprising he was untroubled by poachers.

Released from his cage Chaos lay around our set observing everything languidly, but keeping a sharp watch-out for elephants. If annoyed he stopped purring, gave a high-pitched squeak and – sometimes – a half-hearted nip. For this Barclaycard he had been contracted to stroll nonchalantly through shot on a jungly walkway as I talked to camera. He brushed by me quite well the first few times but then, not unreasonably, lost interest and was reluctant to take further direction. He had done that.

Chaos doubtless sensed that we had an insecure director who required the shock absorber of many takes and who, from behind the camera, had begun treating him just like another bloody-minded extra. This was discomforting, as I was the one standing next to him and liable to be the first to know if he got cross.

'Get him to do it again,' the director kept saying – to me, of all people. Chaos looked around thoughtfully through those wonderful golden eyes and clearly did not care about the director, nor me, nor his Equity card. It is not much fun, working with a rather cross cheetah – especially one who always stares over your shoulder.

In our tiny chartered plane we flew, wondering and daunted, around the summit of the great equatorial iced cake of Kilimanjaro – which was to star in the next commercial. We landed in Amboseli National Park braced for all the drama and excitement that had been plotted back in the Euston Road. Instead we found ourselves in a desert: just dust and scrub. It looked like the end of the world – a harsh and gritty Dali landscape complete with animal skulls; only the melting watch was missing.

In an old Land Rover with a Jack-the-lad driver from Nairobi, we headed for our safari camp. We were looking forward to one of those stylish set-ups as seen in the brochures, where Ava Gardner met Clark Gable and Ernest Hemingway considered the short happy life of Francis Macomber.

CDP had flown out a team of fifty-six, which was joined by another 110 locals who set up a camp in the middle of the reserve: forty olive-green tents pitched in a semicircle on ground inches deep in dust and the droppings of wildebeest, zebra and elephant. Our tent had two narrow iron beds, two wire hangers, a washing-up bowl, a pitcher of water, a mirror strapped to the tent pole, a lavatorial bucket and two jumbo tins of insect spray. I had never seen so many flies in one place, not even on an Australian sheep farm. It looked like the kind of camp where you assembled Kalashnikovs. There was no sign of Ava Gardner.

We went to recce the first location, an elegant pavilion built by our chippies on top of an observation hill overlooking a brown river and the whole of Africa. The Kenyan crew had gone to the forest, selected and felled trees, milled the wood and created a splendid gazebo which, after a couple of days filming, would have to be pulled down. There we sat watching a glorious sunset: hippos wallowed in muddy pools, baby elephants hid beneath their mothers, zebras took fright and stampeded across a lunar landscape. Suddenly all was serene and worthwhile.

Our advertising account executives were becoming captivated by the magic of Africa. They had kitted themselves out with safari hats and suits and desert boots, and the most dashing sunglasses south of the Groucho. Transmogrified into Euston Road white hunters, they were all doing Robert Redford.

We decided to leave the Kalashnikov camp to them, and drove to the Amboseli Lodge, in the heart of the park. Halfway there in the African night we were stopped by two evil-looking poachers with ancient rifles. Our city-slicker driver was very frightened. After some confusion, they turned out to be game wardens – the good guys. Although we did not look like ivory hunters, no movement through the Reserve was permitted after dark. They were placated by cigarettes and a lift to the cheerful bar at the Lodge – leaving any poachers to get on with it.

Our room at that threadbare establishment appeared not to have been cleaned since it had been built, around 1952, but despite worn carpets and soiled blankets, after the camp it seemed like the Dorchester. We were virtual prisoners, forbidden to walk out of the garden unescorted; a group of American tourists had just been murdered nearby. A high-voltage electric fence surrounded the place, supposedly to keep elephants out – though it must be hard to shock an elephant. I assumed the marauding gangs of poachers were more threatening.

In this depressing confinement we could not even turn to comfort food, since everything available was horrible – yet we felt guilty when leaving anything on a plate because the poverty of the staff was all too evident: sad and depressed, they shuffled from table to table, the 'wine waiter' usually tipsy and lurching about. They knew their usual tourists on one-night safaris were unlikely to tip.

They lived behind the Lodge in huts grouped around a small mosquito-breeding swamp. The Indian owner had refused to drain it, but instead placed duckboards over its pools of stagnant water. The Kenyan government had just reneged on a promise to supply the local Masai with running water if only they would leave the wildlife in peace – so they poisoned seven lions. It seemed to me the Indian manager had to read the omens if he hoped to avoid the strychnine sandwich that was coming to him.

Late one afternoon Valerie sat outside on the veranda of our dilapidated bungalow, doing her sewing. There was a soft breeze, a smell of cut grass, and zebras grazing behind the fence. She could have been a faded photograph, she said, in someone's attic.

After bonding at singsongs around the campfire each night our pale advertising folk were now deeply smitten by the great outdoors and their safari gear, so moved their tents away from the lines to experience the real feel of the bush. During their first night alone, Africa came to them with soft, ponderous steps: in the early hours, attracted by the scents of the camp kitchen, a herd of elephant arrived – and reached their tents first.

Masai warriors engaged as extras were camped near by; they knew all about that kind of behaviour, so attempted to shoo them away. Our boys joined in this splendid new game, chanting 'Bugger off! Bugger off!' Finally the elephants swung round to face them, heads lowered. The advertising men buggered off, in turn. Later they repitched their tents within the reassuring confines of the camp.

The scenario for our 40-second commercial was so magnificent and orchestrated it felt like attempting another *Gone with the Wind*. A horde of red-daubed Masai warriors with spears had to tramp in line abreast up a hillside above the empty plains, climbing into the frame just as the sun rose over distant hills. The cameraman, crouching in a well-positioned trench, would widen his shot to reveal me in the basket of a balloon – talking about Barclaycard, of course. The balloon would slowly ascend into the sky as the camera pulled out further to reveal majestic Kilimanjaro and its snowy peak. Wow. That was just for openers. An award-winner, at least.

The only snag, as locals kept telling us, was that Kilimanjaro's peak, up there at 19,330 feet, was always covered in cloud in August. Our white hunters had convinced themselves that if the production was sufficiently lavish and enough money spent and everyone wished hard enough, all things, including mountaintops, would be revealed.

So each day, ever optimistic, I got up at 3.45 am and bumped along tracks for an hour or so to the location, to catch the sunrise. By the time the sun was scheduled to appear the camera operators in their trench were tense and ready, the Masai lined up in position, and I was freezing quietly in my balloon – though poised to float up up and away, chatting to camera.

Each day Kilimanjaro remained hidden. Sometimes not even the sun appeared. So it went, dawn after dawn, until it was too late to accept advice and move to the Masai Mara.

Far more worrying, the proud Masai warriors were unhappy because our construction crew had cut that camera trench into their sacred hill. This damaged its magical powers and boded ill for all concerned.

Soon, as they had predicted, bad things began to happen. A member of the camera crew fell into that sacrilegious pit and injured his leg. One of our carpenters almost severed his thumb with a panga. A tent boy who had been looking after some of the lines died of meningitis, casualty of an unpublicized Nairobi epidemic which was then killing some fifty a week. A couple of safari flights bringing tourists into the reserve crashed on the airstrip, killing almost everybody. In our camp a driver reversed his truck and ran over a foot – which turned out to belong to the unit nurse, who was badly needed.

By day four the curse was still operating, and we had only about ten cut seconds in the can. The weather stayed overcast and grey and no blushing African dawn emerged under those vast skies. Kilimanjaro never appeared.

On our last night some divine compensation brought a little much needed magic. The Masai arrived on set looking as usual effortlessly elegant and aloof. Tall and slender, graceful posture, ochre-coloured beads and *shukas*, braids of ringlets Brylcreemed-down by muddy ochre, they were dramatic and peacock-proud.

Our make-up girl wanted to embellish their intricate face painting with some ideas of her own, so they got kittenish and flirtatious with much giggling and hiding behind their *shukas*. They were fascinated by her technique, sensing she might know something they did not.

One particularly beautiful youth whipped out a small mirror and studied himself with solemn intensity as he was made up, more critical than any catwalk model. All these aristocratic dandies had a fine and well-deserved conceit.

Then bonfires were lit against a pitch-black sky and the Masai danced, unconcerned by cameras and our small and silly dramas. They seemed to have forgiven that desecrating trench.

Liaison with them was handled by Carolyn Roumeguere, whose French parents had moved to Kenya when she as an infant. Her anthropologist Mother later married a Masai chieftain and went to live in his camp. Brought up among the women and children, Carolyn was trilingual; her home is still a hut in the Masai Mara, where she designs jewellery.

When she arrived to meet our massed Barclaycard tribesmen they made some extremely personal remarks about her among themselves. She took this in silence until the excitement had died down – and then gave them a Masai mouthful. The group stood stunned in horror and disbelief before this stylish Frenchwoman who spoke Masai better than they did.

After the confusion had subsided they came up humbly and apologized: 'Sorry – we thought you were white.'

Next day we prepared to leave Amboseli, without any regrets at all. Our jolly crew bounded with relief up the steps of the aircraft, looked back scornfully at the white hunters and offered a final judgement on the director: 'He's two sandwiches short of a picnic.' Chaos knew it all the time.

Back home again, it was found that the Amboseli filming was so thin and unsatisfactory that even forty seconds had to be supported by library footage. We could have stayed in Euston Road and used back-projection.

To complete the disastrous scenario, the slow editing meant that the four commercials failed to meet transmission dates. Barclaycard was already losing patience with CDP, and this was the final embarrassment. At their Northampton headquarters, the new executives who had been replacing tolerant old friends were no longer prepared to put up with arrogant treatment that was becoming inefficient. They decided to let other advertising agencies bid for their coveted £25m account.

Sir Tim Bell later told me he had not even bothered to present because, as he warned a friend from another agency who did plan to pitch, 'It's been such a successful series and supplies exactly what Barclaycard needs, so it's not even worth trying to displace them.' She knew more than he did about the new marketing people and their reaction to CDP: 'They hate them,' she said. She was right.

Nine months later I was on a train cruise around Scotland and, arriving at Dunrobin Castle for drinks with the Duke, found an urgent call awaiting in the dungeon that was his office: Barclaycard's new marketing manager told me the new agency which had been chosen planned to deliver a different message; they were going back to comedians, again. So that was that. I went upstairs for a dram.

After six years as the public face of Barclaycard, the end of the affair was curiously cold and charmless; but nobody ever said credit-card banking was stylish. Except me, I suppose.

Until the Amboseli experience all our expeditions had been happy and much enjoyed, and a lot of Barclaycard's success in the marketplace came from CDP's flair. This had lifted a struggling and characterless credit-card company to a financial peak which, unlike Kilimanjaro, was not shrouded at all. They got no thanks, either.

Barclaycard then had thirty-three per cent of the UK credit-card market. During the following five years their share dropped to twenty-eight per cent, and 1,100 staff were dismissed. Pure coincidence, of course.

Yet this decline was not for want of advertising funds. The producer of their new commercials, John Lloyd, previously had a budget of £250,000 for his entire *Blackadder* series on BBC1. Now he spent that much – the total budget of a major weekly light entertainment show – on each 40-second Barclaycard commercial. Still its market fell.

After many years documentary-making on a tight budget it had been an experience for me to observe how lavish filming for an advertising agency could be. Leaving Hong Kong after making eight hours of *Whicker's World*s with a BBC crew of six, I had flown to make those fateful hundred African seconds with a crew of 156 – not counting Masai warriors but including a skilled group of balloon captains and helicopter pilots, six chippies, lots of painters, gaffers and a unit nurse – until the Masai curse got her.

During those six years I had been brushed lightly by Hollywood production style within a rarefied cocoon in which people hurried to open my limo door, get me a chair, bring me lunch and laugh at my jokes. I never once needed to carry the tripod . . .

I *told* them not to dig that trench.

I tell you, it was awesome . . .

Television has left the world few secrets. Buckingham Palace, Kremlin, White House, Vatican, Presidium, Cabinet, Pentagon, MI5 . . . all doors have opened. Kings and Presidents, Princes and Potentates, Papa Doc and the Sultan of Brunei have welcomed the enquiring eye and told all – or at least, some.

One final international mystery remained protected and hidden for almost half a century: 'How *do* they elect Miss World?' That fateful jury room preserved its virginity, you might say – until *Whicker's World* boldly went through the chaperone cordon.

There we filmed the whole exotic operation, right up to the breathless moment when the final judgement was handed down. Deliberations behind locked doors, layers of security, guarded examinations, secret interviews . . . while around us, eighty-three international beauties postured and sought to enthral. I tell you, it was awesome.

It was all happening down there in darkest Africa in 1993, where my infiltration of an endangered species was supported by a glitter of international gypsies: Joan Collins, Ivana Trump, Kim Alexis, Sidney Sheldon, Gary Player and five other judges, all bowed by sudden responsibility. At the end, one nineteen-year-old accepted a sizeable fortune and a year of queenly obligations, while the others returned to their homelands and obscurity.

Since the first Miss World was created to promote the Festival of Britain in 1951, a judge has always held an unusual role. After appointment, this usually imposed the tolerable burden of a few days in some exotic location amid a mass of what were once called 'bathing beauties' who had flown in from around the

49

world with national costumes and dazzling smiles, eager to please.

They were all thrilled to be on parade for, win or lose, they had already achieved quite a lot on their home grounds; each had been through many heats and contests before selection as a national winner. Now they were preening before twenty million.

For a judge suddenly surrounded by smiles, it was a sunny environment where every judicial joke was acknowledged by one and all to be tremendously funny. So, was everybody happy?

No.

In the late 1980s strident feminists pushed on stage and brusquely swept poor Miss World aside. Physically, that competition was unequal. Though vocal, the antis were, more often than not, deeply unattractive. Their hostility towards younger and more favoured girls was easy to understand, as were their public displays of contempt, derision and, doubtless, envy. 'Cattle market' was the accepted pejorative, along with 'meat rack'. Poor old Bob Hope was flour-bombed at the Albert Hall, while in India a woman indicated even stronger disapproval by setting herself on fire.

The sisterhood insisted that the international beauties – who were all having a lovely time – ought to be too proud to let themselves be admired. This campaign had some effect. The first and most telling feminist victory was to get Miss World banned from British television, after forty years of top ratings. So in 1989 she went off to Hong Kong and Bombay and Atlanta, and carried on parading, though the whole carnival seemed effeminated.

Curiously the women who so resented the admiration won by their more comely sisters seemed unconcerned when women took up boxing professionally and began to punch each other to the ground before cheering crowds. Evidently there was little to be jealous about in such an androgynous spectacle, so they concentrated upon the 'exploitation' of contented catwalk beauties.

By November 1998, after ten years in the middle distance, Miss World returned to terrestrial television from the Seychelles – though in the UK paraded only before Channel 5. Even so she earned that marginal channel what was then its best rating ever for an original programme: 2.6 million viewers. The contest had planned without much success to avoid those 'demeaning' swimsuits and white stilettos – but the beauties had forty-seven years of inbred tradition to sidestep, so they often crept into view.

That Miss World was Miss Israel, and she won £62,500 in cash, holidays, jewellery – and an electric car. As though creating a Miss World was not demeaning enough, Israel had also just won the Eurovision Song Contest ... It was an upsetting year for them.

By December 1999 most feminists had run out of steam, and venom – or perhaps just felt less threatened – so Miss World's catwalk wound its way right back to London, where it all began. The ninety-four international beauties could be watched live from Olympia, no less, by viewers who had Channel 5. On the night it was a clear win for Miss India – and for her Den Mother Julia Morley, who recalled their 1989 expulsion from TV: 'A bunch of left-wing ladies influenced television men with weak minds, who were not up to their jobs.'

Channel 5 had topped Sky's £850,000 bid for the event, and recruited the heavyweight world champion Lennox Lewis, racing driver Eddie Irvine and TV's Superman Dean Cain to help choose the winner. She was Yukta Mookhey, a twenty-year-old zoology graduate from Bombay.

Outside Olympia a score of small shaven screamers reverted to flour-power and some of the audience arrived in white clouds, very cross. The new Miss World had little time for those snarling protesters who, she believed, 'would not object to watching an obscene movie on television'.

The Miss World pageant, with Michael Aspel asking bemused contestants for their views on world inflation, was not a programme I ever watched, but it was always enormously popular internationally. The axe had finally fallen following pressure by a Thames Television executive – and his wife – who at the same time dismissed the clever but saucy comedian Benny Hill. After decades of worldwide popularity, his regular televised humiliations by busty women were suddenly seen as chauvinistic.

Salacious obscenity and dirty talk on television was then acceptable, but lewd innuendo and silly slapstick set to music was not, despite persistent worldwide popularity. The late Benny now has a new website complete with high-speed video feeds, and his seaside postcard humour remains a cult in America.

Though I had never given much thought to Miss World, I must declare an interest: in a 1965 *Whicker's World* series we took a look at the formative years, devoting a programme to beauty contestants. We opened with shy abashed girls at church fêtes being urged by their jolly vicar to compete for the prize of a kiss from the town clerk. Then we followed the more professional stilettos of eager Miss This and ambitious Miss That along provincial catwalks, through factory Saturday galas and up the seaside slopes towards the very peak – Miss World, in London.

After transmission the Controller of BBC Television, Huw Wheldon, wrote to my director Jack Gold to say he had found our film 'delightful, and *most* touching' – adjectives rarely applied to any head that bears the rhinestone crown.

Despite that pleasant exploration, I found it hard to work up enthusiasm or hostility towards an innocent pageant that gave eager participants, families and friends much harmless pleasure, so Miss World escaped my eye for some thirty years, during which she carried on parading. Then one day while filming a *Whicker's World* in Bophuthatswana around a remarkable but little-known tycoon, my troubles began: I found myself judging Miss World in a casino in South Africa. As I said anxiously at the time – at least I wasn't wearing a fur coat, and smoking. Even so, it was going to be a field day for jeering politically correct Trots.

In a curious way, Southern Africa's return to the community of nations after forty years in exile was signalled by the arrival and celebration of the Miss World gala, as apartheid and sanctions fell away. Well, you've got to start somewhere.

Financial support for the international contest had been provided by the subject of my programme: Sol Kerzner, then considered one of the most powerful men in that stricken land, though little known outside it. He was a cataclysm waiting to hit the world.

A college boxing champion whose family had escaped to Africa from the Ukraine, he was small, muscular, sharp and tough – his temper tantrums rocked the chandeliers. A Damon Runyan character in a land at the end of the line with few personalities, where dressed-up ladies still wore white gloves, Sol was strong medicine indeed.

On closer acquaintance he revealed a disarming giggle and

surprising sensitivity within that formidable redneck exterior. This foul-mouthed perfectionist had a soft side somewhere, for some of his nervous staff had stayed with him longer than his wives. I was not quite sure what that proved, but suspected that the secret of his commercial triumph was a perpetual turbulence which was doubtless easier to take in the office than at home.

Twice divorced, once widowed by suicide, working eighteen hours and smoking sixty cigarettes each day, he survived the megamillionaire's mandatory heart attack, so gave up smoking and took to handling his stress by click-clicking away at a set of worry beads. He gave these such a hard time that *they* collapsed. He had to carry a spare set.

Born in 1935, Sol worked in his parents' Johannesburg café: 'The neighbourhood I grew up in, there was no time for charm. If you wanted to be OK, you'd punch your way through.' By the time we met, skilful punching had brought him thirty-two hotels and casinos in Africa, Mauritius and the Comoros and three casinos in France. Just ahead lay a gambling empire in the Bahamas and a £200m resort in Connecticut to be developed and managed for the Mohegan Indian tribe.

His empire constantly expanded: turn your head, and he had sold Southern Africa's biggest hotel group plus his French casinos, and bought most of Paradise Island in Nassau and the oldest casino on the Atlantic City boardwalk.

To examine his latest creation we flew in to Nassau after dark and high-rolled up to Sol's new gambling resort on Paradise (formerly Hog) Island in one of its mandatory stretched limos. As we drove across the bridge a firework display was exploding behind the vast moonlit monolith that was not there the other day but now contained a couple of thousand bedrooms and thirty-eight restaurants. It looked like a title sequence from Disneyland.

In the daylight it was stylish and far more real, and you could see where £500m had gone. Atlantis, the biggest theme resort in the world, was another of Sol's pink cities – though this one was slightly submerged. Amid a fourteen-acre waterscape of pools (eight million gallons of fresh and salt water, if you must know) the ruins of Atlantis had been re-created in a maze of underground passageways surrounded by 100,000 floodlit fish. Seven species of shark cruised around menacingly, stingrays fluttered about the aquarium floors, six-foot green moray eels glared from rockpiles and 300lb groupers just looked fat and cross. In that cobalt waterworld there were of course dazzling rainbows of tropical fish.

I also observed that a small bar amid the underground caverns was serving Bloody Marys – and being watched intently by four hundred piranhas.

The staggering display of marine life was tended by its own staff of sixty, including a fish curator, aquarists – and cooks preparing gourmet meals in what had to be the world's only kitchen *for* fish. A favourite dish with the regulars in this fish restaurant was a tasty combination of shrimp, squid, sardines and minnows, all fresh and locally caught.

That varied and generous menu must have been why the residents did not seem interested in eating each other, as I had been expecting. I have never seen such placid fish, all being extremely polite.

Yet there was also an ominous Predator Lagoon full of giant sharks, the Stingray Lagoon, the shoals of furious barracuda . . . This is why guests going for an early dip in one of the resort's eleven swimming areas, or a look-see in the seven-acre Snorkelling Lagoon, were advised to inspect their surroundings carefully before jumping in. Sharks are rarely at their best first thing in the morning.

Behind glass were tunnels for five hundred lobsters, transparent clouds of iridescent jellyfish, Australian wobbegong sharks, swordfish . . . an improbable scintillation swimming over, under and around visitors who were reduced to silent wonder, or gasps. Audio-animatronic animals will never survive this outburst of reality.

We sat in the Fathoms restaurant before a wall of glass fronting a deep soft-lit aquarium where shoals of fish were so dense that when stationary they looked like bushy-topped trees. Sharks circled, watching thoughtfully as I ate my mahi-mahi while trying to look casual, and vegan.

Resort activities for humans were also available. The gaming floors, which paid for it all, had a thousand slots and eighty tables. The casino broke with tradition by having windows which allowed in natural light, so you could see the dawn arrive. They'll be letting clocks in next.

The Bridge Suite in the Royal Towers is reserved for the highest-rollers of them all, for even Sol found it hard to put a price on its ten tall rooms stuffed with the gold chandeliers, mandatory grand piano, ten-foot-high four-posters and his-and-hers everything which was launched by tiny Michael Jackson – who must have felt rather lost.

Sol was convinced the resort's £10m marina for forty large boats would become another Monte Carlo, and already one liner-like private yacht was tied up, gleaming quietly. For the land-locked there were five waterslides at the Mayan Temple, where the Leap of Faith started with an almost vertical sixty-foot drop before sending riders down an acrylic tunnel submerged in a shark-filled lagoon. You get the picture.

Sol was a mite weary after that massive building feat, aided by his evocative design team: Wimberley, Allison, Tong & Goo. He was cheered by the sale of his French casinos, where he told me local Mafia and trade unions had caused more upset and strife than the rest of his empire put together.

He had the panache of a tycoon from another era, when financial pioneers thought big and did not hoard their cash in secret. He brandished his, flinging it across the countryside and defying critics. In South Africa, accused of paying a bribe of half a million pounds to the then leader of the Transkei Homeland to secure sole casino rights, he claimed the money had changed hands because of extortion. The case never came to court.

The agreement with President Lucas Mangope which led to Sun City was also not easy to win; Bophuthatswana was then one of the four tribal homelands given a certain independence in the dying days of apartheid.

Sol told me: 'Every man and his dog was trying to get this gambling concession. We knew there were going to be offers made, and all sorts of stuff. The President took me inside his office, a very modest place, and said some people were offering a deal that was better in terms of percentages than what we were offering.' Along with that agreement, the President told him, went a big suitcase: 'and it wasn't full of clothes'.

That was the first consignment of £50,000, in notes. 'The

President said, "I want you to know that we asked those people to leave. I'll tell you this, Sol – you'd better not let me down." '

So Sol built his gaming resort in the Daliesque landscape of a volcanic crater – a smiling colour-blind place safe from the angry streets of Johannesburg, seething just beyond the rim. That original Sun City was conventional Nevada drear – white plaster, twinkling pink neon, massed fruit machines. Its four hotels and 1,200 rooms could have been on the tired rim of Vegas. So Sol decided to go after a better class of gambler – the punters who were blissfully ignorant that they were supporting Miss World.

Sol dreamed the impossible theme, and built an African fantasy, a brand-new ancient caravanserai overlooking his commonplace complex. Two million cubic metres of earth and rock were moved to create the Lost Palace, which was vast and bizarre beyond belief, looming like a crazy mirage above a non-descript landscape.

In the bare bushveld, as in the Bahamas, Sol had magicked a sort of Disneyland-south – though there was nothing Mickey Mouse about the budgets. In Africa it took £200m to turn a fanci-ful folk memory into false reality, where Flintstones and Indiana Jones met Mozart and chandeliers.

With the help of design studios in Dallas and Las Vegas he built a vast hotel complex in red local stone which was both brilliant and outrageous. Through twenty-five-foot bronze doors too heavy to close – fibreglass, of course – the lobby seemed as big as St Peter's. Its circular ceiling high above arriving guests had been repainted three times because Sol did not like the animals' attitude.

Mosaic floors with semi-precious stones laid by Italian crafts-men, balustrades of crystal from Poland and a rampant replica of Shawu, the Kruger Park elephant with the largest tusks . . . This was no ordinary hotel; it was Jaipur's Rambagh Palace crossed with the set of an MGM musical and quite beyond taste, a phan-tasmagoria defying cynicism.

Africa has no palaces to copy, so everything in the Lost City was unreal, right from the 'legend' behind its creation. Amid 5,000 well-designed acres, eight-foot waves created in man-made lagoons crashed on to silver sand. ('Are the waves high enough for you, Sol?') Rivers thundered down concrete canyons – and were then pumped right back up the mountain. Acres of languid lakes and tinkling waterfalls cooled the searing heat – everywhere, the sound of water. Amid smoke and a thunderous soundtrack, well-controlled earthquakes shook a bridge built on an air cushion which was, like Sol, just waiting to explode. Grass on the tees of two golf courses was painted green.

It was unnerving, and quite a relief to find that, at the heart of it all, Sol's casino would accept *real* money.

'We have five slides here,' said Sol. 'We call it the Temple of Courage. It's the height of a six-storey building, and takes you two minutes to come down through the dark. You reach thirty mph. I wanted it to be very natural, so we blew the mountain away, put in the slides, and then put back the mountain.'

The day the recycled waters were turned on after two years' work and did not disappear or overflow . . . was the first night in twenty years, Sol told me, that he had slept a full eight hours.

The Temple of Doom was surrounded by a designer jungle – 750,000 trees, some three hundred years old, had arrived from everywhere. There was a rainforest and a dry forest; both looked centuries old, but were not there last week.

Rocks seen to be the wrong colour for his scheme of things were replaced by boulders of painted cement that looked far more natural. Such landscaping skills came in useful later when Sol bought a seahouse at Eze-bord-de-Mer, near Cap Ferrat in the South of France, and wanted to enlarge his rockpool. The Côte d'Azur authorities are noticeably reluctant to permit anyone to change anything along the water's edge, but Sol convinced them their coastline would be safe in his hands.

When we lunched in that lovely setting I sat wondering what rocks were natural, which had been improved – and which had come straight from his workshops . . .

At the Lost Palace, visitors bought a ticket into a fantasy. Our suite was vast, with everything to scale in jungle baroque. Big paintings, big curtains, big tables with antelope-head legs too heavy to move, chairs like twisted branches upholstered in imitation zebra skin. The four-poster's tree trunks were bound with wooden ribbon, the wonderful carpet woven with leopards and plants – all designed by a clever American decorator and made locally.

Our terrace could cope with a hundred guests, who would certainly have a problem living up to the décor – and this was not one of the important apartments. The four presidential suites with grand pianos, all too splendid to sell, went to high-rollers, compliments of an optimistic casino.

I stood on the top terrace of one of the towers as the chopper carrying my cameraman approached over the rim of the crater and flew straight at the Lost Palace, zooming-in on me at the end of the track; ideal title shot.

The chopper surprised me by repeatedly coming and going. Without radio communication, I had to keep dashing outside to do my duty on the terrace, smiling and looking dominant. I did this many times.

Later we discovered it was not our chopper but one hired by *Time* magazine. Their photographer must have been bemused by the constant appearance in frame of some madman leaping on and off the terrace, gesturing expansively and grinning at him. Our helicopter arrived later, by which time my smile was fading.

In the depths of apartheid South Africa had become a pariah state. Sol planned the development of gambling resorts in Atlantic City and Queensland, but each time news of these projects was published there was uproar in local legislatures and he was forced to withdraw.

It was also a problem finding entertainers who would defy the sanctions and risk becoming Untouchables. 'Don't play Sun City,' sang Cat Stevens. He knew nothing of the local situation, so Sol thought this 'a cheap shot'. However after checking Sun City's total disregard of colour, Frank Sinatra arrived and enthused. At his first rehearsal he stopped the orchestra and said, 'I don't believe where I am – in the middle of Africa and in the best room in the world!'

In this citadel of crafty kitsch, black and white got along splendidly without a cross word. It was the way Southern Africa hoped to be. The local tribe of Tswanas supplied all the staff. Soft-spoken, they had great sweetness and were controlled by the Chief Operations Officer, a pale New Yorker in a heavy Armani suit who had been running boutique hotels in Manhattan.

Gerry Inzarillo arrived with an Oriental cover-girl wife, and suffered severe culture shock. He had left bare Philippe Starck bathrooms and stylish resting actresses working as butlers, to control more than five thousand Tswana tribesmen. Hotel school had not prepared him for this.

The charming illiterate Tswanas, never before employed and unfamiliar with knives and forks, suddenly had to cope with cool international diners who thought what you ordered was what you *were*, with five-star silver service and state-of-the-art cash machines. Such problems had not faced Gerry at Club 54 – though his African staff were certainly far more agreeable.

As his anxious eyes darted watchfully around the bar, Gerry told me: 'Our first headache was to persuade them to keep their shoes on. Then to get them off the escalators – they just wanted to ride up and down all day. If someone asks for a Scotch and water, a good employee will reply, "What brand, sir?" Here they don't know what scotch *is* . . . We're starting from a much more modest base. Still,' he sighed, 'we're training waiters – not building a nuclear power plant.'

He believed in hard sell and management by aphorism, and had a rich store of smart inspirational phrases – the effect of which may have eluded his massed Tswanas. He called 3,500 of them into Sun City's Superbowl for a motivation lecture, anyway, and got them chanting positive slogans – which must have been fun, if confusing. Keeping smiles on was easy; keeping shoes on remained a problem.

'There's no worry about adrenalin here,' he said. 'It's rock 'n' roll, big time.'

Because Lost City was as widespread as Sol's imagination, a room-service waiter serving twenty breakfasts had to walk four miles, which took time. On the stepping stones across an artificial pond outside our suite a nervous maid had just dropped the Managing Director's only suit as she was returning it, freshly-pressed, for a conference. Too frightened to tell anyone, she hid the sodden suit – and went home. The Managing Director went to bed.

Training employees may have been a problem, but training guests was far more difficult. Even South Africans admit their countrymen, brought up to be pampered by many staff in their homes, are demanding; their clothes lie where they drop.

They can also be light-fingered. At the opening of the hotel the week before our arrival local guests, carefully chosen, had methodically stripped most rooms of movable objects and ornaments – even the shower heads.

I discussed South African attitudes with that acute social observer Nigel Dempster and recalled that in his native Australia 'Sydney society' had been a contradiction in terms; how then did he see Johannesburg society? He recalled an Englishman who made a fortune in South Africa, and then moved home again: 'At a London dinner party it was said of him, "Too big for South Africa, too small for Sunningdale." '

Sol, however, was rather too big for London, let alone Sunningdale. The promoter Harvey Goldsmith reflected, 'Ninety-nine people out of a hundred in Europe have never heard of him – but you come out here and he's moving mountains.'

I flew in Sol's overworked Challenger jet the 800 miles down to his estate at Hout Bay, on the Atlantic coast outside Cape Town, and we talked about how it all happened. A depressive wife committed suicide and a daughter became a junkie, but he survived to marry and divorce a Miss World, and build other homes in the South of France, Johannesburg, Cadogan Square, Ibstone near High Wycombe, and a massive international business empire. He was then engaged yet again, but confessed, 'I guess I'm just not good marriage material.' The engagement was duly broken off.

To open his Lost Palace in the empty bush he invited not only the Miss World jamboree but a scintillation of judges offering varying degrees of skill and expertise: Joan Collins was judging Miss World for the third time and had played a beauty queen in her first movie *Lady Godiva Rides Again*; Ivana Trump was experienced at divorce, plastic surgery and parties. Sidney Sheldon was a silver-haired Bestseller. Gary Player, champion golfer who designed Sun City's courses, was amusing but perhaps a little naïve: I heard him earnestly asking Ivana whether she would ever *consider* having cosmetic surgery? She said, yes, if she ever needed it.

Sol also invited one or two African stars to be judges and – getting his own back on an interrogator – me. It was my first time, I admitted. 'All right,' said Joan. 'I'll deflower you.'

We were joined for the spectacular show by Billy Dee Williams who was in *Batman*, another fantasy; Jerry Hall, without a Rolling Stone; the galactic Brigitte Nielsen, an enormous gladiatorial Dane who had dropped her far tinier husband Sylvester Stallone; and Kim Alexis, American supermodel from 400 glossy covers. Jean-Michel Jarre brought his *Light Show* with thirty-three tons of equipment and wife Charlotte Rampling; Richard Branson brought his pullovers and plans for Virgin flights to Africa; eighty-three international beauties brought chaperones and guards. It was a considerable party.

The contestants had flown in from their homelands around the world. They ranged from Miss United States, a self-confident Florida blonde from a tougher world where you can not come second, who wore jewels won on some catwalk . . . to wondering East European and African beauties who carried their possessions in paper bags. Miss US was strikingly dressed by Fredericks of Hollywood; a Caribbean beauty wore her mother's cut-down wedding dress.

In that year, 1992, South Africa's own beauty queen was, for the first time, non-white. A self-possessed and articulate teacher, Amy Kleinhans disproved the claim of a former Miss South Africa who said that no black girl would ever win the title because 'they're all pregnant by the time they're fourteen'. Even during apartheid, people noticed that was not PC.

They were guarded and chaperoned so strictly that a few of the more sophisticated grew restive, and there were even whispers of mutiny. That could have been unwise. Though most men are scared of beauty queens, some it appears are not scared *enough*, so they and their companions were watched and escorted through hordes of swivelling eyes. It reminded me of a crocodile of giggling schoolgirls walking up the Via Roma in Naples.

'We have girls of seventeen here,' said Julia Morley, their Den Mother. 'There are eighty-three nationalities and they speak twenty-two different languages – it's like a mini Olympic Games. For most girls it's the biggest event of their lives. Some have never flown before. Last year the girl from the Cook Islands was seen off by practically everyone on the island – they'd all sent to New Zealand to buy material for her dresses. We *have* to look after girls in our care.'

For their first morning at Sun City the contestants assembled, as was right and proper, on a sandy beach to play with beach balls, lie gracefully on rocks and pose for photographers. I felt I'd never left Morecambe.

Falsies and artificial aids were of course taboo, and surely unnecessary among such firm young flesh – though I did discover that one much-photographed model posing there among transplanted palm trees actually had false teeth. She was an enormous and well-behaved elephant with damaged tusks. Gleaming and splendidly-curved plastic falsies were placed over her unphotogenic stumps before each photocall, to sparkle beguilingly in the sunshine.

Next morning we all went on safari, bumping through the dawn around the Pilanesberg National Game Park in the back of an open three-ton truck. It was 104°, so some beauties dressed down for the occasion. Others, fearing photographers, were more dignified: pretty Miss Ireland wore a cartwheel hat and a white piqué garden-party outfit.

Because of recent rain everything was greener and more attractive than game parks in Kenya; my instant suspicion was that Sol had transported the foliage, and had it spray-painted. Unfair – even the animals were real, and not the least bit tame. This was a relief.

We saw groups of rhinos, lots of zebra, herds of antelope and springbok. There were hippos in the lakes and big black snakes on the road. Giraffes lolloped about, doe-eyed and statuesque. At every sighting the beauties oohed and aahed and screamed appreciatively. They were good company.

Because so many wild animals were watching, and no doubt hungry, our escorting game warden insisted we remain in the truck, but after a morning's filming I badly needed some establishing shots of our rumble in the jungle. So we stopped and unloaded my hesitant cameraman. He walked warily away into the bush to set-up and film us passing and, doubtless, waving. The reflex action of every beauty queen is to wave at every camera, anywhere.

The girls were in a jolly mood; they had spent days knee deep in paparazzi, so instantly plotted to give at least this pesky cameraman a proper scare. As he stood there alone in the long grass and prepared to film, they all suddenly screamed and screamed, terrified, pointing at something behind him in the bush.

He leapt a foot in the air, white and shocked. It was heart-attack time. Casting around wildly, he looked desperately for the threatening animal, wondering whether to climb a tree or race back to the truck.

Total victory, this time, for the beauty queens.

We stopped at a kraal for breakfast. Behind the stockade they sat together in the scorching heat eating their scrambled eggs, protected from stalking paparazzi outside, who were always after unkind shots. I was hoping that some of the animals might stroll up and take a look through the bars at these denizens from another game park who were also endlessly stared at, spied upon and guarded.

The most endearing and surprising thing about them all, I discovered, was how friendly and uncompetitive they were among themselves; I had seen more jealous spite among the wannabes at church fêtes. Affectionate and happy, they shared their clothes and make-up with less-privileged contestants, clung together for support, and always sounded like a joyful aviary.

So they were looked after in luxury for the week and entertained royally. In return their workload required them to spend a day answering questions from judges, to attend press conferences and photocalls, to parade in their national costumes, and join international celebrities in a theatrical spectacular televised around the world. At its climax, one fortunate 35–24–35 would find herself wearing a crown, holding £40,000 in cash, accepting another £40,000-worth of clothes, jewellery and perks, and a contract for a year's lucrative modelling when representing her country at charitable events.

It was hard to see them as victims, or hate figures.

Easier, I suppose, to dislike the judges. Joan Collins, delightfully natural in every way, changed her hotel only once – but then Ivana Trump did have a bigger suite. She was pathologically unpunctual, so behind that niceness lay a touch of the Joan Crawfords, an echo of *Dynasty*'s Alexis maintaining precedence on set by making everyone wait.

Ivana, keeping up the tradition, refused to join us as we prepared to film a chat with her in the enormous hotel lounge under a chandelier fifteen-foot wide, until everybody was poised and waiting. It was the kind of thing the *Rich and Famous* man Robin Leach told me Americans do all the time. Joan Collins and Barbara Walters, he said, refused to go into an interview room because they both insisted that the *other* must be in place and waiting before she entered.

Ivana was surrounded by a resistible retinue, without which she evidently would not get out of bed. She had brought with her from New York, sixteen flying hours away, a daughter, a fiancé, assorted bodyguards and staff, a constantly attentive hairdresser and two particularly unlovable female minders described as PA and President of Ivana Inc. Like snapping barracuda these New Yorkers were there to smooth Ivana's path and obstruct everyone else's.

As my crew prepared to film us taking tea they were told she would not like that table, she must have this one, she had to sit here, the humidity from that door might affect her hair, we should move to another restaurant . . . an endless and charmless exhibition of job-justification.

She finally arrived and stood smiling and pink through all this snarling nonsense: perfect Bardot hair over reconstructed face, perfect smile, perfect legs, smoky eyes which calculated every move. Her champagne glass was instantly hidden: 'When you have too many pictures holding a glass, they make you an alcoholic.'

I wondered who she would prefer to do without, at a push – her hairdresser or her bodyguard? 'I could do without both,' she said, bravely. A sensible woman in many ways, she was totally self-promoting and self-absorbed.

I filmed another happy chat with Richard Branson, who was considering Virgin's service to Johannesburg. He was agreeable and smiling, and we were both pleased with the interview. Afterwards as we stood to say see-you-later, he suddenly got apoplectic. 'That *can't* be used – we have to do it again!'

He pointed to my pen, which could have been in shot. It was marked British Airways. After much ridicule he finally backed down, but grabbed a knife and scratched off the lettering. 'Send you a Virgin pen,' he said. He never did.

Sidney Sheldon and his handsome wife, fearing attack by

terrorists or feminists, had demanded protection as the price of his appearance, so unarmed guards sat, day and night, outside their suite. Not a high-profile politician or a high-rolling gambler – or indeed recognizable – he did not seem an obvious target for attack by assassins. Perhaps he was afraid someone might steal his last chapter?

He and Ivana earnestly considered what to do in the event of attack by some radical group. Ivana said she would drop to the floor, but didn't want to discuss kidnapping – it made her uneasy. The bodyguards on whom they relied said they would run to the telephone. This was not reassuring – I suspected they would probably get a wrong number, anyway. Only Brigitte Nielsen was unconcerned, but with her bulk and muscles that was understandable.

I had thought being a judge in Miss World's time warp might offer an enviable Noël Coward-pasha lifestyle; in fact it demanded considerable concentration during several days. On my schedule for the first judging day, every moment from 8 am until 8 pm was occupied.

A vast Sun City ballroom with guarded doors had been set aside for our first official meeting with contestants. Inside eleven tables, well separated, each with three chairs. These were for judge, contestant and, if necessary, interpreter.

On that interview day we had to assess which girl had the mental capacity and authority to reign as Miss World for a year; a daunting prospect – I didn't even *know* eighty-three different beauty-queen questions. To make life worse, Eric Morley's marking system was desperately complicated, evidently devised over decades by a group of mad accountants. Despite our confusion, the system was sacrosanct.

To take the task seriously – as I observed all judges did – much effort and application was required in encouraging more than a smile out of nervous girls, while giving each one fair consideration and forming an opinion of her capabilities.

The beauties slipped through in groups of eleven and settled down for the revealing conversation. Some of their costumes were out of pantomime. After three minutes a school bell rang, and they moved to the next table. This minuet went on for seven hours, beauty after beauty. A few were bright and confident, some shy and monosyllabic, others knowing and challenging. Those three minutes could seem quite a long time, or vanish in a puff of happy chat.

We bent to our task, murmuring questions and putting at ease while marking for intelligence, charm, character. I heard Ivana, in a pink silk trouser suit with huge hair, asking one tongue-tied African girl, 'What is your five-year goal?' Confronted by this apparition most contestants were speechless, mesmerized by pinkness, floored by materialism. Ivana explained their overawed reaction: 'Nobody home,' she said.

Sidney Sheldon, a humorous man, said one of Ivana's encouraging questions was: 'You call yourself *pretty*?'

Joan was less daunting, and more practical. 'It's like engaging an au pair,' she told me. 'It's the hardest work I've ever done for not getting paid.'

In the late afternoon we returned – I confess with some relief – to the old routine: they paraded before us on stage and in ritual bathing costumes, turning once, twice, as requested. It was like an identity parade, and quite took me back to those 1965 catwalks.

Like viewers criticizing anyone who appears on television, we judges felt remote and licensed among ourselves to make extremely personal remarks. 'For young girls they've got the worst arses I've ever seen,' said Joan, in an indelible whisper. 'That's why you have to see them from the back as well.'

I had not noticed that earlier: 'Perhaps their bottoms sag in the afternoons?' We went on in that shameless way, as cruel as any viewer. 'I'd rather die than do anything like this,' Joan admitted.

After a lifetime promoting and protecting beauty queens, Eric 'now in reverse order' Morley is still their best salesman, ever defensive and on guard to resist constant criticism. His bright and capable wife Julia, with dimples of steel, remained the power behind the parades and spent the year escorting the winner around the world, making appearances and opening things.

Eric had faced more problems than triumphs during nearly fifty years of contests: political storms in national teacups, contestants who ran off with ski instructors, winners with hidden husbands, jealous boyfriends, unmarried mothers and an all-American girl, Marjorie Wallace, who celebrated victory by announcing she intended to make love to as many men as possible. She did her best, before resigning her crown after 104 fun-filled days. It was not an easy world to control.

'They're an entirely different lot of girls today,' he said, recalling our first meeting thirty-five years earlier. 'Most of them are students taking a sabbatical and using Miss World to let them visit places like Miami or London. They're girls who usually go on to be computer engineers, doctors, lawyers – except, by the way, those from the UK. We happen to have a good one this year, but normally the British always stick to models. Other nations see us as a way to get an education, because Miss World has to be able to talk to ambassadors and people like Alan Whicker. One has even *become* an ambassador.'

As a judge-elect I said it might be hard to be totally objective, and recalled that when one of my early *Whicker's World* subjects, Eric Gairy the Prime Minister of Grenada, had been a judge, Miss Grenada had instantly become Miss World . . .

'Well, yes,' said Eric. 'That was unfortunate.' He admitted he never found women judges very good: 'That's why we always have a predominance of men.' But the judging, he said, could not be fixed; certainly his tortuous marking system *had* to be uncrackable.

Julia Morley said her den had already discussed the problems of winning and losing, and realized some girl had to come first, and that on another day a different group of judges would probably choose another girl. It seemed a wise thought to implant.

Eric had been watching all our filming with growing concern; the regulation disciplines of his lifetime were being overturned. Finally he could no longer contain his outrage at my camera's intrusion behind traditionally closed doors. 'In nearly half a century no one has *ever* filmed our judging,' he kept saying, indignantly. 'You're incredibly privileged.'

We could reveal secrets, it seemed, as closely guarded as the formula for Coca-Cola or Madonna's telephone number. We might even influence the odds: people bet thousands on the outcome of Miss World. The town clerk's kiss was only a memory.

With all the respect due to an eighty-year-old, I told him we were in that African comic-strip version of Monte Carlo dancing around and trying to breathe life into his tired old pageant. This did not appease his sense of invasion and damaged protocol. We called in Sol Kerzner as umpire. He had bought the contest for hard cash and was not a man to be overawed by machinations behind a beauty parade, however rooted in tradition; so it proved.

At the dress rehearsal Sidney Sheldon asked to see his introduction on the autocue. After reading a string of accolades he pointed out, 'I also have an Emmy.' Joan Collins then wanted to see hers too, while blaming me, and started to read: 'International superstar Alan Whicker . . .'

'Seems reasonable,' I said, impervious to ridicule. 'But why do they call you a starlet?' She has a great giggle.

On the night, the spectacular show ran for more than three hours before an audience of 6,000 in the auditorium, and went well. It was televised to fifty countries and claimed 600m viewers.

The South African television director defended our frivolous evening: 'It's pointless to say that because people are starving in Somalia we can't have a beauty pageant. The amount of money we're going to raise is not going to solve the world's problems, but we *are* beginning to achieve something more than just watching a bunch of pretty girls walk up and down to no end at all. There's nothing wrong with froth and nonsense if it helps people less privileged.

'We're already being knocked in the South African press because there aren't enough black girls in the contest, but that's inverted racism. Tokenism is not what it's about either. Every girl's here because of merit. End of story.'

The MC was Billy Dee Williams, amiable *Batman* actor who seemed incapable of reading his autocue, which in that vast auditorium had letters eighteen inches high. During rehearsals his fluffed lines had been cut down and down until, after a Sol outburst, they were taken from him and shared between Deborah Shelton, JR's *Dallas* girlfriend and former Miss America, and Jerry Hall. All he now had to do was announce the event – but still he got the date wrong and welcomed us to Miss World 1999, seven years ahead. Oh, well.

Jerry Hall had spent much of the rehearsals asking everyone for jokes to pep-up her introductions. In the end she even telephoned London to get advice from Eric Idle, ex-*Monty Python*. He came up with: 'Alan Whicker has spent the last six months finishing a book. He's not a fast writer; he's a very slow reader.' Even a Python is entitled to an off day.

Now time has healed wounds and no government will be brought down, perhaps I can reveal the nations in my short list were the Misses Denmark, Finland, Hungary, India, Romania, Spain, United Kingdom, Uruguay and Venezuela. A worldly cross-section, you might think; but tastes vary, and other judges thought otherwise. India, Spain and Uruguay, all ravishing, did not even appear in the final ten.

After the declaration people asked, 'Was it a fix?' Certainly it was not – though there was unspoken acknowledgement that should the noticeably gorgeous Miss Venezuela follow compatriots who had won the last two contests on to the dais, it might be too much of a good South American thing. Otherwise no one tried to influence my decisions in any way. I detected no hint of the tiniest bribe, or offer.

Instead, I tried to nudge fellow judges towards a would-be television presenter called Claire Smith who was fresh, natural and bright. The fact that she was Miss UK and came from Chester was totally coincidental, I swear. I believe my little group at the table – Joan Collins, Gary Player and a South African actress – all voted for her; but I gathered the sulky son of French actor Alain Delon and a few African judges were not smitten.

In the event and in reverse order the deserving Miss Venezuela was third. Claire came second, one point behind Miss Russia, Julia Kurotchinka, a six-foot Moscow teenager with a lot of hair and very long legs who had not been in my Top Ten. She then rode her chariot with aplomb, suddenly significant and briefly rich, heading towards her year of charity chores.

Some Miss Worlds become film stars or diplomats and appear on postage stamps. Most are instantly forgotten, for beauty is a glorious but trivial thing.

I was sorry about Claire's narrow defeat, and after the ceremony was filming a post-mortem with her when her mother came up, in tears. I consoled our rueful runner-up as best I could and sent her off to face her chosen career, in television.

What a fate.

The television we deserve . . .?

Revealing future plans, the BBC announced, 'We are trying to find another Alan Whicker.' This was a surprise; nobody had warned me I was about to be cloned. I was not sure whether to feel flattered – or abandoned. It was gratifying to be a role model, but seemed alarmingly like an early obit.

I checked my diary and found I was still on parade every day. I had just flown out to film on Grand Cayman for the BBC, introduced *Whicker's Week* on BBC Choice, which featured my programmes every night – and fifty *Whicker's World*s on the Travel Channel. I had accepted the Travel Writers' award, written and introduced *Around Whicker's World* for BBC Radio, completed a second *Whicker's New World* series and prepared *Whicker's World Down Under*, planned a TV project called *Journey of a Lifetime*, been selected as one of the first names in the Royal Television Society's Hall of Fame and in that self-denigrating BBC programme-title jargon, become one of *Auntie's All-time Greats*. As though that wasn't quite enough thank you, I'd been appointed cyberspace travel Ambassador for AOL on the Internet, and so on – and on.

Well, all right, all right; but you'll understand I did get the feeling that the world was adequately Whickered – even, you could say, *over*-Whickered.

Still I have to admit 22,000 travel agency clients elected me the person with whom they would most like to travel. In their next poll I was among the people with whom they would *least* like to travel. What a difference a year makes . . .

Another poll decided – and we're talking *serious* accolades here – that I was the ideal dinner party guest. When they discovered I was going to Hong Kong and could not attend their presentation dinner, the party left town. I was instantly *un*ideal. Forget it, they said, turning to ideal guests with spare time.

The BBC later revealed that a new 'me' had finally been discovered. The tension was unbearable. He turned out not to be one of the newer fellahs from Current Affairs, nor a battle-scarred News veteran, not one of those Monty Pythons, nor a suitably moustached and well-spoken member of the Alan Whicker Appreciation Society . . . but a small chirpy and popular pianist who once fronted a funky Newcastle music show with Paula Yates.

Quite a challenge, no doubt, but in that curious quest for a replica he still did not seem to strike exactly the right note; different performance, different theme. A considerable distance, indeed, from all those documentaries, all those air miles as foreign correspondent and war correspondent, from the books and the features produced while landing on virgin beaches and pushing on through primeval jungles protected only by background music. Then during long years of television legwork, interviewing everyone in sight from the Easingwold goat with milk that made women pregnant, to the Sultan of Brunei, who made them rich, and Papa Doc, who made them dead.

The BBC's choice seemed somehow . . . out of synch. Yet on reflection, could that be the way television is going, these days? Are Absolute Ravers replacing Absolute Monarchs? Is thought giving way to hype? Are reality and television separating?

Well, yes.

The *Sunday Times*' incisive TV critic AA Gill reviewed my clone's first report: 'The programme was a spectacular of mediocrity and tired travel film clichés . . . a nadir in the television cult of lazy, self-regarding, charmless youth amateurism. Although Holland must be well into his forties, his voice is still truculently twelve.' I just hated myself for enjoying that.

Come to think of it, how often do we turn on TV these days with that old curtain-up anticipation of pleasure to come, with the expectation that what we're about to see will make us truly conversational tomorrow?

The family radiogram had been replaced after the war by a box in the corner which was welcomed as a source of wonder and illumination. Every night its window offered a surprise, a new view of something or someone, an unexpected experience to be shared across the land. It was becoming the nation's meeting point.

Now it has lost that concentrated authority and pushes out all those game shows we have to dodge. Often several hours of snooker or darts. Endless posturing music videos. Unavoidable cooking – ninety-six food and drink shows each week on the main four terrestrial channels, for appetizers, and not one of them a patch on the *Cook's Tour* Mireille Johnston made in 1992. As viewers tire of looking at food, selected desert island castaways come splashing in from all sides.

The outpouring from a couple of hundred digital channels looms, and the urge to zap grows ever stronger. To see you is not *always* nice, for programme makers are now as short of ideas as they are of money. Any rare success is ravenously copied in the scramble for the brief attention of a fragmented and diminishing audience as ratings are chased downmarket towards the desperation of trash television.

What that box reflects is a world of its own creation, promoting tension and irritation. We watch what we are offered, so mass-audience programmes promise something for nothing: Lottery results, or the chance of winning £1m by naming the capital of France.

Television has decided that audiences grow more stupid by the day, and the subsequent dumbing-down is justified as chasing younger viewers with shorter attention spans who cannot absorb a simple message unless delivered by two or three grinning heads shouting in turn. Even the warmed-up applause of well-drilled studio audiences must be reinforced by 'encouraged' laughter tracks, in an attempt to convince viewers that they are having an equally hysterical time watching kiddie programmes before 9 pm, and occasional filth afterwards. On Channel 4 parents giggle conspiratorially as their sons discuss mum and dad's sexual preferences, in detail. Hard to view without cringing.

Apart from some shafts of sumptuous costume-drama brilliance, even the reliable old BBC has fallen upon uncertain days. Peter Salmon, Controller of BBC1, scornfully cancelled the long-running comedy *One Foot in the Grave*: 'I am the net-curtain comedy killer,' he announced proudly, 'the man who took out a contract on suburban sofas and knitted pullovers, and will *do* for

the dreary 1950 scenarios that have affected too many comedies.'
Tough talk, indeed.

He then had to eat humble custard-pie. In what was a promising situation for a sitcom, he hurriedly went into reverse and
brought that suburban series back from the dead in a desperate
attempt to overcome the BBC's dearth of good light entertainment.

After other disastrous decisions – like the £3m BBC1 wasted
luring the ill-fated *Vanessa* confessionals away from ITV – the
nation's premier channel seemed to shrug and give up, for the
first time since its recovery from the initial commercial onslaught
in 1955.

Its magnificent catalogue of sports events was surrendered –
right up to the FA Cup Final and Test matches. England's winter
cricket tour went to the home of mindless call-ins, then called
Talk Radio. Premier league, rugby internationals, Formula One,
Ryder Cup golf, FA Cup matches were all too expensive for the
BBC – though £50m a year could be found for the almost
unwatched News 24, and £28m for management consultants –
£4m to McKinsey. They could even afford to advertise a new post
called 'Head of Diversity' who would be responsible for 'driving
and developing the BBC's new diversity strategy'. There's money
well spent. Pity about the programmes. The Corporate Policy
Unit had 300 staff, and impoverished producers observed flocks
of unproductive planners at their earnest seminars and country
hotel awaydays, draining money and talent from core
programmes.

'BBC1 is a mess, a shambles,' said Alasdair Milne, former
Director-General. 'Comedy is non-existent and there is no
contemporary drama worth talking about. Most of its decent
programmes are repeats. Sadly, the creativity has gone out of the
BBC.'

Consoling itself that in the long run only quality mattered, the
BBC held up its hands and submitted – without admitting it, of
course. It withdrew and left ITV to walk away with the mass audience; a public defeat that could have been dramatized, peak
time.

This was a disaster, for as television fragments it becomes
impossible to overestimate the importance of the BBC. Our

national institution embodying common values is part of the social glue that holds us all together. Its main characteristics were quality and the assumption of a basic level of intelligence in viewers – both of which have recently been disregarded.

Finally in the summer of 1999 the BBC governors and the outgoing Director-General, Lord Birt, ordered a review of BBC1 in an attempt to lead that confused and unhappy channel back towards its old dominant role. This belated call for an overhaul criticized the 'lack of distinction' of daytime shows and the despatch of *Panorama, Question Time* and *Omnibus* into the night to make way for silly sitcoms like *Birds of a Feather.*

Executives were rebuked by the governors for the marginalization of serious current affairs and arts programmes. The output of the excellent *Omnibus* had been halved and that of *Arena* and *Bookmark* cut – so for twenty-four weeks each year the BBC had no arts review programmes at all. This was a misguided reaction to ITV's display, night after night, of mass audience game shows.

Peter Salmon later attempted to cover his channel's retreat by accusing ITV of 'abandoning journalism'. One of his stars, Noel Edmonds, then abandoned the BBC, complaining of 'salmonella poisoning'.

Spring 2000 is the time for Lord Birt's swansong and any legacy of quality television he may hope to leave. At the moment he seems most likely to be remembered for his ban on any BBC reference to the sexuality of his friend Peter Mandelson.

Reactions to his programme judgement have rarely been enthusiastic. His personal sortie into creative television was with LWT back in the 1980s, when he produced the most boring, static and heavy-going current affairs series ever broadcast. At least it did not patronize viewers, so despite its stultifying tedium *Weekend World* and his Mission to Explain manifesto with Peter Jay set him upon a path towards his wobbly television summit.

Yet even with such an overview it seemed that he and the governors had only just noticed the progressive degradation of BBC1. Somehow they had missed the market-led formula broadcasting, the emasculation of quality programmes, the frequency of patronizing trash. Where had they *been* all that time?

'The BBC makes a mistake if it merely apes a formula from the competition,' said the governors, urging the Corporation to 'dare to be different' once again. Ratings were not the be-all and end-all, and controllers must have the confidence to commission 'an unashamedly public service schedule' which did not merely copy its rivals.

The growing tackiness of BBC1 had long been obvious to every viewer except, it seemed, to the executives on the sixth floor of Television Centre – and the D-G and governors, of course.

To reinvent public service broadcasting Greg Dyke, supporter of Labour and Roland Rat – but at least a considerable TV professional – was appointed new Director-General, despite protests from all sides. Chairman of the Board of Governors and leader of the LWT cabal, the implacable Sir Christopher Bland, who railroaded Dyke's appointment, had earlier warned the world's Public Service broadcasters that they had the responsibility of protecting viewers from a tidal wave of cheap, low-quality television arriving to fill ever-expanding airwaves. He did not discuss the flood of bad news closer to home.

Lord Birt had been convinced that the BBC could only save the licence fee if it competed with the market. Certainly, in its uninspired and declining days, the Corporation could hardly remain aloof from the nation's social readjustment. Its main audience has always been that very middle class which forms the majority of the population. New material prosperity brought a cultural decline and the audience for even mildly intellectual diversion, has been eroded. The BBC has to cater for those it was created to serve – the viewers who pay £101 a year, or else, for services which were once a serious viewing alternative to a tacky ITV.

Yet no longer is the BBC seen to be the essential public service broadcaster it once was, nor is it all *that* popular. In 1998 its annual audience share fell below thirty per cent for the first time as the proliferation of new downmarket channels chipped away at viewing figures. In 1999 a professional analyst predicted it would be below twenty per cent within ten years. The BBC needs to be popular, just as it *should* be distinctive; but since funding follows audience, it anxiously chased the nation's sliding standards in case remaining viewers asked for their money back. In these days of speculation and spin, sizzle defeats substance. As current affairs and news morph into entertainment, we watch the old structures of television's authority breaking down; even politics becomes showbusiness for ugly people.

British and American networks fragmented after the 1980s, opening the air to cable and satellite shows that experimented with low-budget studio talk formats and tabloid news. Alarmed US programmers replied by increasing the airtime for news, though not improving its quality. Interpretation almost disappeared, and famous anchors followed the trend towards *Oprah* and worse. Their considered newscasts were replaced by lightweight opinionated chat. With so much time to fill on new and less restrained channels, authoritative and thoughtful newscasters were elbowed off-screen by a noisier, scruffier bunch. In five years, the networks lost their significance – and a fifth of their audience.

In this trend, as usual, we follow the US, where weighty evening news programmes were for generations the model for all television journalism, and were imitated around the world. Today those mighty news divisions mindlessly cut away from live coverage of the first threatened Presidential impeachment for 130 years – to get back to football.

Worldwide news reporting that exposes and illuminates is expensive, but talk is cheap, so television's new role model is the chat show – television conversations offering incoherence and triviality. The line between broadcaster and entertainer has almost evaporated; the smooth presenter ascends – and *News at Ten*, humbled, is sent into the night, along with *Panorama* and *Question Time*.

Documentary series that were television events are banished to the 11pm ghetto, at best, and the excellent *Pull of the City* series concludes around midnight. TV now speaks with the shrill persistent voice of Entertainment, offering a raucous babble wrapped in frills and tinsel. When everything is Entertainment, everything shrinks to predigested visual pap.

The *Brideshead* repeats reminded us what drama could do when directing, acting and resources were running strong. Travel programmes once stimulated yearning and daydreams; now mandatory blonde presenters wander the world to discover they're in 'a land of contrasts', taste some strange and exotic foreign dish like spaghetti, gasp, 'Mmmm, luvly' – and run squealing into the waves. It is apparent such travellers can't tell their Aran from their Elba.

Certainly the documentary pendulum has swung. When I started in television viewers were driven to the 'off' switch by earnest nanny-knows-best programmes about Safety at Sea and Britain's second-longest river. That sorry status changed after a few years, and I still have a couple of Jictar Top Ten ratings from the 1970s showing *Whicker's World* at number one, followed by some aspiring programme called *Coronation Street* . . . Wonder whatever happened to that?

On ITV, most documentaries are now screened for night-owls – unless about sex and sleaze, or fronted by some momentarily hot comic who can cope with autocue. Controllers have taken us back to the 1950s' belief that viewers are incapable of absorbing reality without some frivolous decoration to take the taste away.

Film was once expensive, so treated with consideration; every shot had to earn its place, and we would debate whether we could shoot another roll of mute. Now reusable tape means that directors attempting fly-on-the-wall revelations, docusoaps or survivalism can let their camcorders run, gulping up hours of desultory chat like a whale absorbing plankton – and about as stimulating.

The more thoughtful programmes have reverted to well-written commentary behind compilations of old library footage: *The Nazis, 50 Years War, Channel Tunnel, Cold War, War of the Century* . . . All lucid and absorbing, few as creative as the remarkable *Escape from Colditz.*

Shamed by the standards of BBC1 which had fallen so much that even the D-G and governors noticed, the Director of Television Alan Yentob promised to rescue *Question Time, Omnibus* and *Everyman* from the graveyard slots to which they had been banished by the Controller of the Corporation's shop window, Peter Salmon. They would be transmitted 'no later than 10.40 pm', he promised. Coming in from their cold night, it seemed almost peak hour.

Only one television category consistently improves: those enchanting wildlife and natural history programmes on all five channels. Armand and Michaela Dennis, Hans and Lotte Haas would be staggered to see that we can now fly alongside the condor, mingle with prides of lion and swim with elephants. They would marvel at the patience, ability and man-hours behind each astonishing shot, at the apparently invisible cameras of daring film-makers. Even the birth of Attenborough's polar bear cubs in a Belgian zoo rather than the Arctic seemed totally acceptable.

On his way to becoming BBC's Director-General, the courageous but abrasive Alasdair Milne one day told me that he had spent the afternoon junking a selection of old filmed programmes, most of them mine. Later, in 1987, he became the first D-G to be fired – though not as a direct result of such vandalism. It was a falling out with the Thatcher government that cost him his career and his knighthood.

The culling may have sounded Luddite, but BBC archives were overflowing with great cans of deteriorating film, and it had been decreed that the pressure must be reduced to make room for the outpouring of current programmes. A reasonable decision, and I was not too concerned. Only afterwards did I realize how much irreplaceable record, how much living history had been casually destroyed.

The BBC also miscalculated when, in 1988, it sold its valuable photographic library to a cable TV entrepreneur for £1.5m. He promptly sold it on for £10m to investors who resold it again for £30m to the grandson of J. Paul Getty. Bidding against Mark Getty was the richest man in the world, Bill Gates – so the next sale had to be considerably higher. Having sold off part of its heritage at a closing-down price, the BBC instantly spent £70,000 hiring some of it back for just one drama series.

A feeling for the past was once essential in journalism and television. Today we live emphatically in the present and ape the US, where they lack any real sense of history – as the standard of their occasional historical documentaries can indicate. In American cities the Present is so powerful that the Past is lost; what little survives around the country becomes themed, fibreglassed, Disneyfied.

We all look with delight at old photographs of, say, Piccadilly – the clothes, the carriages, the empty street . . . Library footage of any fifty-year-old scene glimpsed in a documentary is even more fascinating, for it shows us the way things were just the other day. If such passing pictures can intrigue and enlighten after a few decades, how much more significant will surviving footage seem in the centuries to come?

Viewers in the twenty-fourth century, say, will be able to see and hear and evaluate the thoughts and concerns of their distant ancestors and learn how we lived and died, what we celebrated and worried about. Once only the rich and powerful could buy immortality with their portraits, their paintings of homes and horses. Future television archives will feature the neglected men and women in the street who were merely tiny background figures for Canaletto, Gainsborough, Seurat . . .

Imagine if we could now listen to a conversation with Albert Einstein, Marlowe or Leonardo da Vinci, see London as it was before the Great Fire, hear a vox pop among Shakespeare's audience at The Globe . . . That's how our current output will be viewed in centuries to come.

A few attempts are now made to replace the wastage of such records when thought to be socially and historically significant. Sometimes interviewers are despatched to try and capture the memories of vanishing groups, like the 370,000 survivors of the dying British textile industry who worked the gloomy woollen mills. They will reminisce before a tape recorder for a couple of hours about the way their families lived. Such captured recollection goes into sound archives and its illumination will one day be as invaluable as surviving documentaries.

Yet – the pity of it – to save a little space in a suburban warehouse the BBC once casually destroyed some of its unique store of local and national happenings, its panorama of the country's small conflicts, triumphs and disasters. Future viewers will never know the concerns of those Ramsgate landladies, who starred in my first programme in March 1957, explaining how their seasonal livelihood was in jeopardy. It was an occasion – and Mrs Evelyn Stone's poodle Candy wore a new red and blue jacket.

As it happened I went on to do more television, but those anxious landladies did not; that conversation in front of the bombsites along Nelson Crescent was both initiation and swansong. Then, Candy and all, they hit the cutting-room floor; goodnight and goodbye for ever. Sob.

From the late 1950s and early 1960s the *Tonight* programme was recording the nation's major and minor concerns, but also changing viewing habits and setting the agenda for conversations next morning. This was the dawn of a shared national experience, and television's impact. We were writing the grammar across a blank screen, and learning as we worked. It was an early self-help version of that channel which, forty-two years later, Lord Bragg urged should be set up to train media studies graduates at a cost, he estimated, of around £50m a year. Our way was cheaper.

Television's manning pendulum has always swung wildly. When I started *Whicker's World* around 1957 the union, the Association of Cinematograph Television and Allied Technicians, was still not recognized by the BBC, so I could set off around the world with only a cameraman and a recordist. The three of us produced many hours of programmes. By the time Yorkshire Television started in the late 1960s the ACTT had been allowed in to the BBC and its control over ITV was total and destructive. Crews of thirteen had to be sent to attempt what we three had achieved without strain; the only difference being that the equipment had become lighter and easier to handle.

Since we often filmed in places that were dangerous or uncomfortable, the Union granted a dispensation, as crews were not always eager to go to Algeria, Paraguay, Haiti ... It decreed smaller crews could be used in 'Whickers and war zones'. Even so I seldom escaped with fewer than five – often it was seven, including an assistant sound recordist whose main contribution was to pin on my neck-mike occasionally, and grumble away idle hours.

The negative and restrictive grasp of the Union has been loosened today, and in some production companies the crewing pendulum has swung to the other and equally unsatisfactory extreme: multi-skilling, or the one-man crew. Some wretched learner desperate to get into the business is expected to research his own programme, then film and record the material himself while shouting questions from behind his shaky camcorder.

Spared Union headaches, *Tonight* could be endlessly enterprising. For seven years it produced a pioneering fast-paced magazine which overflowed with adventurous items covering the world from Shepherd's Bush to Alice Springs every night and casting a wry eye on presidents and prostitutes. Its pioneering programme decisions were tracked by competitors and Fleet

Street. Its editorial crystal ball was ever-alert to trends – yet could be clouded . . .

In 1963 one provincial pop group had begun to impress and charm listeners. They were unknown to me, but such was the improbable impact of those four adolescents that in February 1964 it was suggested that I should travel with them to film behind the scenes on their first cautious American tour. They were pleasant chatty lads, welcoming and evidently pleased with the idea; *Tonight* was a prestigious programme and its vast audience would provide telling exposure.

I began my research. Then at the last moment . . . *Tonight* cancelled the project. Our schedules were crammed, I was about to film in Alaska – and producer Donald Baverstock had decided that the group had peaked. By the time their two-week tour was over and my reports on American reactions had been edited for transmission, the public would have wearied of such overcoverage. They would be growing old hat and ready to fade back into the provinces and obscurity, like any other passing craze.

His judgement was supported by newspapers; the *New York Times* believed they would last a year, at most. After a disastrous Paris performance, *France Soir* derided them as *vedettes démodées*. It seemed these lads were going from Unknowns to Has-beens, with only a Royal Command Performance in between.

So I never got to film the Beatles, at the very start of Beatlemania. Let it be.

All of us on that pioneering, but not infallible, programme would watch transmission anxiously every night and grieve that we had not done better. On such a significant new scene, everything mattered very much indeed. There was usually a fraught post-mortem led by Baverstock, a little Welsh firework, and Alasdair Milne. Nationally admired interviewers, then poised to become government ministers, were sent reeling out into the night, white-faced and stunned by a torrential analysis of what had just gone wrong, and why. We learned quite quickly, that way.

Today there seems little internal criticism in television production. Presenters and directors are inevitably thrilled with their programmes, and green rooms echo to triumphant congratulation.

As a visiting interviewee, relaxing after appearing on some so-so show, I have often been baffled by the surrounding chorus of mutual delight in full cry. Those in front of the camera rarely have journalistic skills, but a confidence born on some showbiz periphery – so it's kiss-kiss, you were wonderful, darling. This is pleasant to go along with, but you don't learn much.

Such easily earned approval accompanies the Australianization of television, which was at first resisted, but is now taken for granted. As programmes chase the lowest common denominator, viewers learn to be satisfied with little thought and less effort, and clever Rory Bremner commands only a tiny audience; and all this before the coming Niagara of digital, cable and Internet.

As standards sink, it is not a smart career move for the presenters of trendy youth programmes to speak grammatically or use accepted pronunciation; they should laugh a lot and shout the going mantra. In many series they will be ahead of the game if they gutter-speak. So much for role models.

Some fifty universities today offer media studies, and eighty per cent of those students want to work in television – an outpouring of 30,000 eager apprentices each year. According to a departmental head at Coventry University – which has the high drop-out rate of twenty-four per cent, and where subjects considered worthy of course study include the Teletubbies, skateboarding and body mutilation – many of these would-be communicators cannot write a sentence.

Fortunately that University, desperate to fill empty places and qualify for funding, gives them all a let-out in the course handbook before they start: 'There is no single correct form of English. Rather, there are many different versions.' Tell that to Fowler.

It adds, helpfully: 'Try reading back your work to get a sense of where the gaps come, both in and between sentences. Short pauses often show a comma is needed. Longer ones where you breathe in can indicate the beginning of another sentence.' Such budding student scriptwriters, Listening with Mother and breathing heavily, would doubtless be employed by Melvyn Bragg's £50m channel.

Established television stars pulling in huge salaries can also run into difficulties when attempting to read the autocue. Not to write, mind you – to read. Pretty former bra model Kelly Brook, was nineteen when she became co-presenter on the *Big Breakfast*. Reported as accepting £200,000 a year for the task, she still had to be protected from herself. The programme's writers were told not to tax her capacity with long words; her intros and links must be as simple as possible. They were warned: 'Words that have recently caused her trouble include "intrepid" and "satirical".'

Jake Lloyd, the actor who played Anakin Skywalker in *The Phantom Menace* put his honest eleven-year-old finger on their embarrassment: she was also boring. 'I've been asked that a thousand times,' he told her, reasonably. 'Ask me something new.' The idea of creating a whole new question on the spot all by herself was a terminal problem which the producer later resolved by dropping poor Miss Brook.

All conversational television can be enlivened or ruined by the interviewer. Any guest – including childish skywalkers – can be diminished by bus-queue questions. Even Peter Ustinov or Billy Connolly could seem dull if poorly interviewed, while a sensitive interviewer can stimulate and animate the dullest person, the most obscure topic.

Everyone who gets to perform on the small screen now is a star and believes that, apart from the occasional artful word, television is easy – when patently it is not. After thousands of *Whicker's Worlds*, I have yet to be wholly pleased with any of them, and after each transmission must come to terms with my degree of dissatisfaction and decide what to try and improve next time.

Writing the television grammar at the start of it all, the disciplined *Tonight* programme agonized over every question posed within its fast forty-minute format. Our thesis was that since the interviewee should have at least nine-tenths of the airtime, the interviewer's one-tenth had to be as telling, had to contribute and guide. Interrogation has come a long way since then. In *Whicker's World* I always intend my questions to be short, as in normal conversation, and to offer viewers the sense of eavesdropping.

The other extreme is aired every morning on Radio 4's generally excellent *Today*, which unfortunately has come to rely upon the harassing interview, presumably developed because of the pressures of time to which they constantly refer – despite having the luxury of three solid hours to fill. The late Brian Redhead introduced the incursive technique now pursued by an often waspish John Humphrys, who attacks or scoffs, by the thoughtful James 'I must interrupt you' Naughtie, and sometimes even by sensitive Sue McGregor.

The enterprising programme usually has so many inserts and guests from all over, that few get an adequate hearing, unless politically important and approved, in that rush through relevance towards *Thought for the Day*, the weather or *Money Matters*.

After the usual lengthy opening question, interviewees are rarely permitted to finish their first reply before being talked down by the inevitable supplementary, or overridden by some opinion the interviewer is determined to put forward. This is the time when radio sets across the land get abused by the mildest listeners. Then it's, 'I have to stop you there'.

Thankfully the *Today* team is usually too professional to fall back upon the excrutiating 'How?' question, which lazy reporters on lesser programmes and the news inflict upon listeners and viewers: 'How does it feel to have lost your home and family?' 'How upset are you that your son is missing in the Sahara?' 'How surprised were you to be in that terrible train crash?' The traditional *Today* harangue can be accentuated by the fact that sometimes the interviewer's microphone is adapted to override those of guests, so any interruption however inconsequential drowns out the interviewee – who has been invited to give his opinion and is trying hard. Whatever the host wants to say takes precedence through volume alone, driving exasperated listeners over to Radio 5 Live, or their local station. Such domination techniques rarely survive on television where they are seen to be unacceptable – except when dealing with politicians . . .

Some producers do get away with a political line. A man interviewed on film for one long-running, but now defunct, current affairs programme told me he was asked various forms of the same question eighteen times while the director struggled to manoeuvre him towards the sound bite reply he required. In the end the crew gave up and wrapped, very cross, and his unwelcome answers hit the cutting-room floor.

Whicker's World never approached a programme with such a hidden agenda. I went to Rio or Devil's Island to find out how it was, not to massage the facts and confirm prejudice; not even to satisfy Lord Birt's Orwellian injunction to write the script before setting out to film – and then try to find evidence to support it. With that technique the message, however suspect, could never be outmanoeuvred by the facts.

Once we were in the assured hands of presenters we trusted: David Dimbleby, Attenborough, Wheeler, Day, Taylor, Philpott, Dando, Pettifer ... Now there is rarely a known documentary presence on screen to steer us through what is being shown – apart from those vapid holiday programmes, when they intrude. Often we must make do with muffled paparazzi questions shouted from behind the camcorder, which allow talking heads to present their own view of themselves, or offer meandering and evasive call-in chat.

The producer of a series of films I made around the world for British Telecom was an intelligent advertising executive and former speech writer for Margaret Thatcher. He fretted because interviewees were not answering my questions exactly as they had on the recce, so might not slot precisely into his script. I tried to dilute his preconceptions by explaining they were not actors, but real people speaking real thoughts, which were rarely repeated with precision. As a good copywriter, he was not convinced; in advertising they were used to total control. He later hurried us from Tokyo down to Kyoto, because Tokyo did not *look* like Japan.

Having once produced four *Whicker's World*s on the *QE2*, I watched the BBC's *Cruise* programmes to see how things had changed. I never found out. No one selected to talk during that series was even close to being informative or interesting – proving once again that unguided dull people remain unguidedly dull. I learned nothing about the ship, passengers or destinations, but instead spent ten minutes watching a casino employee trying to rollerblade. This was peak-hour viewing?

As a build-up cliffhanger for the final programme, we waited on tippy-toes to see whether an unknown singer performing in the ship's theatre would receive an ovation. This was suspense? The BBC later went on to make a programme about her wedding. *Please.*

It gets worse. At the National Television Awards ceremony in the winter of 1998 I was asked to present the trophy for the best documentary series of the year before 5,000 in the Albert Hall and millions watching ITV's two-hour transmission – the mass audience that had voted for those *TV Times* accolades. Among the four programmes on my shortlist was – you've guessed – *The Cruise*. These things happen. I got my mandatory grin fixed, and started to announce the four contenders.

Then I opened the envelope – and the winner was . . . Michael Palin's *Full Circle*, a follow-up to the series suggested for me which I had originally turned down. The clip Trevor McDonald had used to introduce us was from the 1962 *Whicker on Top of the World* series in which I stopped a massive train in Alaska's frozen wastes simply by waiting alongside the line and holding up my hand, as at any request stop. The *Full Circle* director copied that sequence twenty-five years later – and won an award. There's not much new in television, these days . . .

Some years ago Channel 4 showed a superb series about the construction against the clock of a New York skyscraper. Men ran urgently along massive girders in the sky above Manhattan, frantic to complete on time. *That* was suspense. As it grew from its foundations into the clouds the tower occupied a camera crew, on and off, for a year. Television can now rarely afford production time for such revelation – far cheaper to film some singer's honeymoon.

The excellent *Airport* spawned a succession of imitators, but lost it all with a self-indulgent second series when its real-life cast got showbizzy and started to perform. Now so-called documentaries stage scenes – even script interview replies. After *Hotel* we got bland docusoaps like *Driving School* with its petty recreated happenings. Maureen, the starring learner, woke in the middle of the night, started to ruminate about her test and – what luck – a film crew just happened to be in her bedroom too.

Each documentary generation appears watered-down and weaker, straining and suspect as fly-on-the-wall producers learn to cheat, and viewers face the fakery of Central's *The Connection* and Channel 4's *Rogue Males*.

Most people have learned not to believe everything they read in the newspapers, but since the start of television, seeing has always been believing. In the sure hands of the BBC and the ITV companies, that trust was sustained. Then the airwaves were

Interviewing the Sultan, an Absolute Monarch, was like trying to hold a conversation with an amiable deity. Our main points of contact were a barber and a Bentley …

His palaces exist in a haze of gold, their salons crammed with brilliant and exotic artefacts; even functional items are rather more jewel-encrusted and golden than your average tissue box …

Brunei saluted our arrival with road signs welcoming the Alan Whicker Appreciation Society. We all agreed it was decent of them to make such a fuss of AWAS, but they shouldn't have bothered …

The Barclaycard crew dug a trench into the Masai's sacred hill, but despite their warnings our make-up girl went ahead and topped-up the warrior's traditional red body-decoration ...

Our cheetah, the languid Chaos, walked through his first few takes just as contracted, but then lost interest in the director, me – and his Equity card ...

Our dolphin, however, was a real pro; never put a tooth wrong. He was perfect, every take. I didn't even feel the card going ...

One more smile from eighty-three international
beauties, all longing to wear Miss World's rhinestone
crown – and apprehension from a lone Judge …

Sol Kerzner at the Lost Palace in Sun City. He
brought this international carnival to
Bophuthatswana which, in a curious way, signalled
the end of apartheid …

As an impartial judge I can now risk revealing my distinct leaning towards
Clare Smith. The fact that she was Miss UK and came from Chester was totally
coincidental, I swear …

Judges preparing for weighty decisions watch a dress rehearsal: Ivana Trump, Sidney Sheldon, Joan Collins, briefed by Eric Morley, granddaddy of every Miss World since 1951 ...

One of the MCs, Jerry Hall, was so worried about her lame television introductions that she telephoned a Monty Python in London to ask for a new joke. It arrived – but was hardly worth the price of the call ...

Laying the hard word on a sister judge. Sidney Sheldon said Ivana Trump's first question was: 'You call yourself *pretty*?' Unfair; she really asked them an easier one: 'What's your five-year goal?' ...

The week's Best Buy in your friendly neighbourhood gun shop can be a Kalashnikov. Having a Nice Day in California is still possible; Having a Nice Night is something else …

Juliet Mills, film-star daughter of Sir John, and her then husband Michael Miklenda in the shooting range at their Beverly Hills home. Their experiences of survival in California were chilling …

Josephine on her last adventure, around the Wonders of the World in 37 days …

Harbourmistress from Wareham, Mrs Babs Elvins, whose luck became too much of a good thing …

We prepare our revenge on that Monty Python mob by revealing that the real problem of Whicker Island is that there are too many millionaires – and not enough Whickers to interview them …

By the time we reached Iguazu, tourists had become travellers. We shot the rapids below the Falls while smiling casually and not even getting our lifejackets wet …

At New Delhi our waiting transport showed the usual Indian indifference to road signs …

Facing another 37,000 miles in a private jet, I assume a natural position. (Isn't that one of those rare portable typewriters?) Constant travel during forty-three years has left me set in my airways …

In Spain, all senses are heightened as though by some elevating drug; the air is cleaner, sun brighter, people more gracious, more cruel, more grand – while the savage ritual of their corrida reveals unexpected instincts …

thrown open to as many would-be production companies as could make up a smart name and afford a telephone.

It is hardly surprising that among eager untrained wannabes, some prepared to work for nothing, sharp chancers emerge desperate to make money and their names – and along the way squander the trust built-up with viewers over forty-five years.

I was invited to a BBC governors' seminar when, as though to sustain that disturbing trend, 156 significant communicators spent a day considering 'Factual programmes; is seeing believing?' That theme – alarming enough – grew more worrying when a cross-section of the industry's senior producers and directors appeared to accept deception as a matter of course. The main problem was, how it should be presented.

Calm discussion centred on how staged scenes admitted as fake could be shown and justified. Were captions warning 'reconstruction' enough? Indications in the commentary? Known actors, with scripts? 'The beauty and danger of a drama-tized account is that you don't need to prove anything,' someone explained. Yet these were documentaries – which my belief and my dictionary hold to be 'pictures or interviews with people involved in real events to produce a factual record or report'.

The concern at our seminar was not whether it was right or wrong to squander integrity by deceiving the viewer, but whether such reconstructions in the middle of an otherwise honest programme might devalue sequences around it.

Today documentaries face the problems of success, rather than of disinterest. Appetite for the ordinary has overcome viewers' curiosity about the extraordinary. Even a dreadful series full of the trite and the obvious like *The Cruise* can achieve a large audi-ence. Better series like *Airport, Pleasure Beach* and *Hotel* create their own stars, who stop being ordinary folk and start to employ agents, make appearances and open fêtes. *Driving School*'s hope-less learner – but useful old actress – is garlanded for her perfor-mance by a *Radio Times* cover and *This Is Your Life*, just for being a bad driver.

General acceptance of the fact that some documentaries try to create actuality is deeply disturbing. *The Connection* won Carlton's Central Television eight awards. In it we watched a Colombian mule swallowing fingers of cocaine before flying to London, and the sinister No 3 of the Cali cartel, heavily disguised, discussing plans to run drugs into the UK. Gripping material, dramatically ill-lit – but all staged and acted. The drugs were sweets, the No 3 a retired bank manager. A gleeful press exposure followed, and another bond of trust with viewers was broken.

The Independent Television Commission later fined Carlton a hefty £2m for 'a wholesale breach of trust between programme makers and viewers', and warned against television's employment of 'key personnel with little or no prior TV experience'.

BBC's *Watchdog* cut old footage of a Greek hotel restaurant's unappetizing food display into a programme criticizing a hotel in the Caribbean – and was deeply sorry when somebody noticed. In Nottingham security cameras revealed that a television crew had imported young people to pose as homeless beggars. *Daddy's Girl* was pulled before transmission when viewers of its trail noticed it was not interesting incest but a recognizable couple of live-in lovers hoaxing a gullible producer. BBC's *Everyman* withdrew an episode when its professed sex addict was seen to be a *Sun* reporter; another £50,000 plus down the drain.

Channel 4 bought a documentary about young male prostitutes; the producer was called Devine and her company, Basement Productions. They filmed the activities of rent boys and their clients on the streets of Glasgow – but the men negotiating for sex were members or friends of the production team. Another fine for Channel 4: £150,000.

One documentary after another fell at the barriers of truth. Sometimes producers were duped, sometimes they were merely crafty and desperate to produce a BAFTA winner. Small independent companies, working hand-to-mouth and staffed by untrained ill-paid eager learners, are now expected to uphold the dignity of television.

Most planned programmes, by the time of their first presentation to the network, are oversold and underdeveloped. To complete the sale, each producer is desperate to deliver whatever might interest or intrigue the commissioning editor. Every docusoap, though supposedly reality, now requires upfront easily identifiable heroines/villains/comics to carry the series along, week by week, and remind viewers who's who; so the real people in its cast must often be moulded by plausible directors or clever editing to stay on the storyline.

In Germany a television producer faked a number of films: Nazi links with the KKK, whose pointed hoods and white gowns had been run up by his dear old mother; toads with secretions that gave a high when licked; drug runners crossing borders at night with sugar-filled bags of 'cocaine'. All entertaining – all totally bogus. He was sentenced to four years in jail, for fraud. Neither the BBC nor the ITC has the authority to seek such a cautionary deterrent.

In these tabloid ways reconstructions copy real happenings and, if done well, are hard to detect; yet deceptions endanger all our factual programmes. Television may be more strictly regulated than the newspapers it is quick to reproach, but unlike German viewers our basic protection still remains the conscience of the director and that still small voice warning: 'Don't do it – you might get found out.'

Amid the BBC governors, I sat wondering whether I should try to restore the balance by reminding their seminar that in more than forty years of filming documentaries for BBC and ITV neither I nor my directors and producers had ever for one second considered faking a single significant shot; the possibility of trickery was inconceivable.

I finally decided it would be thankless and pointless to attempt to discourage the pushers who were busy conning their way into the ratings and devaluing our currency; and, I suppose, feared appearing holier-than-thou among the few sharp operators who in that company seemed to be accepted – even justified.

The innocent days when viewers automatically relied upon television's professional honesty were dissolving before our very eyes as the memory of innocence and honesty grew fainter. So the wallpaper closes in, and I await the revelatory docuseries *Junkies Chatting at Bus Stop*. On autocue, of course. With actors. Someone might get away with it . . .

Haphazard television crusades can sometimes affect a foreign nation's delicate balance should we ever try to impose our present values and judgements. They recall those well-meaning missionaries who knew without doubt what was best for the natives, and can prove as unwise as judging the injustices of the Boer War or the Indian Mutiny by today's standards and outlook. Life and times have changed; infantrymen in the two World Wars were not at all surprised to find the enemy shooting at them, and contrived to survive that unpleasant experience without counselling.

One current affairs series always relished any story critical of British institutions: police, judiciary, right-wing politicians, diplomats, conglomerates, army . . . were favourite targets for attack. One of its secret camera programmes found a scandal in an Asian clothes factory which supplied a major British chainstore. In that isolated village, workers – some of them children – were paid the local rate which was of course low by western standards, but enabled their primitive equipment to compete in world markets. The TV producers, scandalized by such rapacity, attacked the factory management so successfully that the British company was forced to cancel its contracts and withdraw. The factory then closed and its workers went back on the streets, unemployed.

Such televised campaigns are rarely followed up, but this one was. It was found that most of the destitute children and women workers had been forced to turn to the only other local employment available to them: prostitution.

Having destroyed the income of the village, the crusading programme moved purposefully towards other revelations elsewhere, leaving its stunned but liberated victims to get on with what was left of their lives . . . They may have been half-starving, but at least they were no longer underpaid.

Equally misguided are those grotesque studio confessionals in which gloating presenters urge on the ravings of exhibitionists who are real enough – though their confessions may not be. Actors or anguished, they will be applauded and cheered if suitably shocking and contrite. Confession on television has become equated with pardon and usually, approval. It can be far more detailed and graphic than MPs manfully 'fessing up in the House of Commons, and is mainly controlled by the monstrous regiment of interchangeable chat show As: Trisha, Ulrika, Leeza,

Melinda, Mariella, Vanessa – all aping the shout-shows of Springa . . .

BBC1 poured millions into the little-watched 9.45 am *Vanessa*, milking the budgets of better programmes. As its audience fell to half that of ITV, *Vanessa* began to use entertainment agencies to supply made-to-measure TV guests who could provide its confessionals with instant emotional outpouring.

Despite a large budget and a production team of twenty-eight, the disappointing viewing figures only perked up a little when newspapers revealed that the battered suffering wife was in reality an unmarried actress, that feuding sisters were strippergram girls who had just met in the green room. *Vanessa* was cut from seventy to forty-five minutes and three production staff and a couple of researchers were sacked. A few weeks later it was put out of its misery and cancelled.

That was supposed to be victim television, the exploitation of misfortune for the purpose of entertainment, a splattering of emotions, postures and pain across our screens; but these days you cannot even believe what you hear from the confessional or the dock. *Kilroy*'s chastened paedophile, like his fantasizing potent hypnotist, was a hoaxer.

Such lurid talk shows feed the psychoses of attention-seekers desperate for their fifteen minutes, so every day we are offered deranged or grubby behaviour simplified and displayed as entertainment. Though usually tedious and pathetic, it is shaming to admit that sometimes the revelations of such assembly-line TV can be fascinating – even though you suspect many distressed victims have Equity cards.

The networks' only answer to such trickery seemed to be: chuck a few production staff off the sledge to distract the triumphantly pursuing press.

In the late 1960s when Yorkshire Television came on air I moved from the BBC to ITV and briefly shared an office in Leeds with Jess Yates, who played the organ lugubriously and presented the popular *Stars on Sunday*. Newspapers labelled him The Bishop, until he was destroyed by vicious Sunday tabloid treatment punishing him for not living up to the name they had given him. Today he would have gone on *Kilroy*, shed a tear to much applause – and increased his viewing figures.

He had been an effective producer who spread a small programme budget cleverly, paying Vera Lynn, Harry Secombe and any reigning Covent Garden diva once, but getting his good billings by using small slices of the original performance on Sunday after Sunday.

This technique was reinstated for the *Hollywood Women, Men, Pets* . . . vox pops, and subsequent nudge-nudge 'pretend documentaries' concerned only with ratings at the expense of insight. In such Sunset Boulevard compilations a small repertory of Hollywood exhibitionists eagerly revealed their shallowest thoughts. The series was put together with sliced-up snatches of to-camera statements – the outrageous sounds stronger when not qualified. The assumption was that if each volunteer said only a few words before the tape cut to another bubblehead, viewers' attention would not wander.

Advertising agencies with only forty expensive seconds at their disposal have always attempted to override viewers' hummingbird attention span by frenetic editing. That is acceptable in the commercial break, but when we settle down for an hour to watch a documentary, the frantic technique confuses and irritates. Such programmes do not move forward, do not take the viewer anywhere; they merely repeat versions of an opening phrase which carries us as far as we shall go during the next fifty-three minutes.

More serious programmes can be emasculated by the networks' lack of urgency, since all channels enjoy an inpouring of projects jostling for transmission time in schedules already full for the next year. My series of eight programmes on Hong Kong sat on a BBC shelf for seventeen months while Tiananmen Square happened and the handover approached. Before transmission I had to fly back to update. Unlike wine, documentaries do not improve with age.

ITV Network Centre, considering future *Whicker's World*s in its new cost-conscious free for all, asked for full details of anything I might shoot during the next year or two, as though commissioning drama. They required location, cast and content of all future topical programmes.

Exasperated by such lack of contact with the actuality of the big world outside, I was finally goaded into admitting that in the year

2002 I would be covering an earthquake in Nicaragua, a mass cult killing in California, a revolution in Indonesia – and next July we collide with Mars.

They made notes.

A pinch of aggro to bring
the box alive . . .

I have spent a lifetime interviewing people in front of cameras – though rarely where people are *supposed* to be interviewed: in a television studio. During the 1950s and 1960s I occasionally sat in with Cliff Michelmore, Geoffrey Johnson-Smith and Derek Hart, but as *Tonight*'s man-around-the-world was usually in Alaska or Tasmania or wherever, far from our cosy studio in Lime Grove, W12.

The *Tonight* on-camera team separated naturally into those who toiled Indoors, and those Outdoors. Indoors, they always seemed better combed and dressed, calmer and warmer: Cliff, everybody's cheery uncle; Geoffrey, blond and tennis-anybody; Derek, Mrs Dale's mellifluous nephew and tiny actor. Outdoors we could be windswept and struggling with real life in some far-flung setting; yet whether it was Fyfe Robertson or Trevor Philpott, Ken Allsop or Julian Pettifer, we always seemed to be having more fun and making more impact than the sedate studio trio who were jealous of our roving lives while, on occasion, we envied their comfort and regular hours.

Indoors, they worked on that night's interview during the afternoon, met the subject in the green room, and talked on camera for four minutes or so. The interviewees would have been delivered into the bewildering chaos of a studio where even today, when television's routines have become so commonplace, people are not always relaxed or assured. Made-up and dusted down, growing tense under powerful lights, those about to appear on the small screen would be propped precisely into chairs – hard and minimalist for serious programmes, soft and chintzy for happy chats – and told where to look. They were made aware that when the red light on their camera came on, ten million viewers would be studying them intently: their hair, posture, teeth, clothes, honesty, incoherence . . . would be examined as never before. They would then attempt to concentrate upon interviewer and questions, while in the background cameras slid around urgently, headphones whispered, sound men waved extending booms, floor managers soft-shoed about making wild hand signs suggesting fearful emergency but usually meaning *wind-him-up*!

Outdoors, I would take my camera crew and talk to interviewees on their home grounds, where they were most relaxed: in sitting room, workplace, local street, favourite restaurant. I have always believed this the most natural way of learning about people – to be an invited guest while they paused in the middle of their daily lives. The interview on the road also had the advantage of requiring travel, which I always relished, of getting to know people on their own territory and being part of their scene, whether it was palatial living in India or drug-running in Rio.

Whicker's World was still turning happily as I celebrated my first quarter-century in television, which resulted in retrospective series on both channels. ITV put out three hours of *Around Whicker's World in 25 Years*, and BBC1 followed with six 40-minuters they called *Whicker's World – The First Million Miles*. I seemed firmly set in my long-haul airways. Then to my surprise BBC Manchester invited me to come inside, at last, and do a talk show.

This required other disciplines, and turned out to be a greater change of emphasis than I had expected. Instead of a two-month shoot across Australia, say, and flying home to view one hundred hours of rushes which then had to be edited down to eight hour-long programmes, each with my commentary written precisely to film, a talk show required only a few days' organizational foreplay, telephoning and research for each programme, climaxed by an intense forty minutes in the studio, being casual. Instead of months of work, it meant that when the red light on my studio camera went out, that was that. Another one in the bag. Quick post-mortem, and off home.

From 1957 the *Tonight* studio set-up had been a couple of

chairs for guest and interviewer – a basic two-camera situation without the possibility of much development. Our international magazine programme was far more intense and businesslike than any talk show, though these became the popular and persistent format. Most programmes would follow the showbiz approach of NBC's pioneering late-night chat shows with Steve Allen, then Jack Paar and afterwards Johnny Carson. More than forty years of television talk based around a desk and a couch have brought little change of format, only of hosts.

Eamonn Andrews, too pleasant to be incisive, handed the torch down to the disastrous Simon Dee, who went on to drive a bus. Saturday-night talk was invigorated for years by the excellent Michael Parkinson, and reinforced midweek by an affable Michael Aspel. Terry Wogan moved in on the early evenings, and despite overexposure, could be surprisingly good. Russell Harty wrung his hands in anguish each week, and was different.

There were many sideshows, not all successful. Clive James wrote well but found it hard to interview. The barrister Clive Anderson adopted judicial condescension and felt the need to top every guest, so appeared tiresomely smart-arse. Clever Chris Evans had a brash breakthrough. Comfortable Des O'Connor just wanted people to singalong with him, and was adoring. Paxman was scornful.

Across the Atlantic Oprah Winfrey blazed her intelligent style among studio audiences, imitated all the way down to the dreadful Vanessa. Today it is often interchangeable blondes being bright and giggly and not quite understanding anything.

The BBC decided to call my talk shows *Whicker!* They were to be different from the accepted run in that they would have no audience, no musicians, no steps to walk down modestly, no warm-up, no off-camera cheerleaders, no claques or canned laughter. We should be looking for interesting talk in a calm setting with the kind of people the viewer might not normally come across but would be pleased to have for dinner.

The format of each programme was for three guests to meet in a comfortable study-like setting and consider one overall theme each week about which they were well informed – say terrorism or divorce, finance or power. I hoped to offer good after-dinner conversation and that sense of eavesdropping that often came across in *Whicker's World*. We planned to avoid 'celebrities' plugging shows and books, and go after little-known tangential experts with something to say on our subject.

There was a price to pay for such self-denying decisions, since chat-show familiars got that way by being confident, funny and famous. It was like saying: 'We've heard Peter Ustinov's stories and Billy Connolly's jokes, so instead we'll talk to the Bush Bishop of Kalgoorlie – nobody's heard of him.' After a few minutes' conversation it might become apparent *why* nobody had heard of him.

I would be inviting viewers to be interested in people who might be monosyllabic or embarrassingly shy, even in a relaxed and unstressed programme which was not chasing one-liners or expecting funny sound bites.

The series was to be transmitted by BBC2 in the rather dead 9.30 pm Friday-night slot. We had a good budget and production team, elegant set and first-rate technical back-up but, for many guests, Manchester proved one flight too many. We could be chasing someone to join us from California or Cornwall who might find travelling to London was an expedition. The prospect of a further flight made some feel there were just too many airports for a 40-minute conversation, however agreeable.

In our first programme we had one Name: Professor John Kenneth Galbraith of Harvard, distinguished economist, ex-Ambassador and adviser to four Presidents. Also the Chairman of an advertising agency, Peter Marsh, who gave the world the Age of the Train, the Listening Bank and other haunting jingles. Finally there was Jane Deknatel, a strikingly handsome woman with silver hair around a youthful face who was then Vice-President of Home Box Office and controlling a budget of £50m. She had been described to me as 'a powerhouse who wants the lot – and she's almost got it'.

These disparate folk had just met at my welcoming buffet: the LA-based daughter of an Oxford trade-union official, a fey but pushy huckster, a bleak disapproving American eagle. Well all right – I *said* we were attempting a new style . . .

On transmission Professor Galbraith, enormously tall and curmudgeonly, took against Peter Marsh, a small rotund figure who showed his elevator shoes to the camera and told the formidable academic to stop match-playing and let him finish.

The Professor retaliated by refusing to understand advertising jargon: 'My God, what is tunnel vision? You're an Englishman, why don't you speak English? With all your public bamboozling, you regard showing off as your ultimate achievement?'

'No, Professor, it's just part of one's character when you're as self-centred as any ambitious person must be.'

'Why does a person have to be self-centred?'

'Would you mind not interrupting.'

'It's impossible to listen to your nonsense and not interrupt.'

Marsh went on to talk about the significance of 'restaurant presence', which in his native Hull he had found that he lacked. The Professor knew nothing about this social knack, doubtless relying upon his great height to intimidate *maître d's*. His frown lines deepened. The studio chemistry was certainly working, though not quite as expected: viewers were watching hostility, not the usual chat-show lovefest of mutual admiration and stroking.

'*Whicker!* got the weekend off to a rousing ill-tempered start,' wrote Herbert Kretzmer in the *Daily Mail* next day, 'with the eminent economist growing increasingly irked and outraged by the utterances of a small garrulous advertising chief described as "Britain's most vulgar millionaire". Mr Whicker did not seek to calm things down. Our Alan has been in TV long enough to know there's nothing like a pinch of aggro to bring the box alive.'

Actually it was Jane Deknatel who brought it alive for me, as we considered the problems of successful executive women who, when leaving university, would be asked, 'Do you want to be a nurse, teacher or librarian?'

She denied being a dragon lady, but graphically outlined her social problems: 'My image as a successful and tough business-woman always seems to get in the way of any kind of personal relationship. I was in Paris the other day having dinner with a friend on a warm Saturday night. He was a very elegant, good-looking European who was in the process of getting divorced. About midnight after we'd drunk a bottle or two of rather good champagne, he said, "Jane, I'm having a fantasy about you."

'I thought, "Well, *this* might be interesting!" I asked what kind of fantasy, and he said, "Oh no, I can't tell you." "Why not?" "I'm too embarrassed – please forget it." By this time I had visions of swinging from chandeliers and God knows what else – it was very provocative. "Now you *have* to tell me." "No I can't – impossible."

'Finally after a lot of persuasion he mumbled, "Would you . . . could I . . . would you ever consider . . . going into business with me?".'

Among the thousands I've talked to on television down the years, the person who stimulated the most reaction from viewers was not Papa Doc or President Marcos, not Paul Getty, the King of Tonga or James Bond, but an unknown pneumatic blonde from the San Fernando Valley. Kathy Wagner was married to a Beverly Hills cosmetic surgeon who she had encouraged to operate on her, endlessly: 'He'll never have to divorce me, he can always change me.' Some viewers thought she was the shape of things to come, others that she needed a head transplant.

Ten years later, considering themes for *Whicker!* and noticing they were not making mirrors the way they used to, I took another look at Kathy's foible, which since her riveting 1973 confessions had become commonplace. Dr Howard Bellin, then Assistant Professor of Plastic Surgery at the New York Medical Center, flew over to bring us up to speed on the improving knife. He was quite happy to escape from Manhattan where he was being sued by a patient complaining that he had replaced her belly button 2½ inches off-centre.

We were joined by Italian-born author Gaia Servadio who had just had her eyes debagged, even though married to William Mostyn-Owen; he was in charge of old masters at Christie's so should have appreciated a few character lines.

Our third guest had undergone an emergency facelift and had his nose reshaped in a Paris clinic – an experience followed, he said, by the most excruciating agony of his life. He was the Great Train Robber Ronnie Biggs, safe in sunny Rio.

Because of technical confusions in Brazil I sat in the studio chatting with his rearranged face on the monitor for a full hour before our programme began; we talked ourselves out while no one was listening. Then after we went on air they pulled the plug in the middle of things, so we lost our line and our elusive Train Robber escaped once again. This technical shambles was thankfully not apparent to viewers.

Apart from surgery, the bald and smiling Dr Bellin had one

other enthusiasm: collecting Air Miles. He transferred our booking to PanAm, since it was theirs he needed. He told me he was
about to use his Frequent Flyer perks to take a girlfriend on a
romantic African holiday. For their exotic escape he had selected
Lagos, Nigeria, which he thought sounded right for an Ernest
Hemingway fantasy . . . I was able to warn him in time. When we
met in New York some months afterwards he entertained us at a
soul food restaurant in Harlem – also an acquired taste.

His most popular operation was, predictably, breast enlarge-
ment. 'It's generally thought men desire women with large
breasts,' he said, 'but it's actually a fixation of women. It really
changes a woman's personality – an amazing phenomenon. She
becomes sexier, livelier, pregnant, and every other thing . . .'

He was also proud of an operation that made people taller: 'It's
horrendous, actually. My son underwent it, because he had a
short leg. It involves cutting the bone, putting in a little device
that spreads the bone little by little, stretches the muscles, nerves
and tendons, and at the end of a month or two they take a bone
from the hip and transplant it into the gap that's been created.
You can do that for both legs, or both thighs, on young people
who are abnormally short – providing they're willing to undergo
a lot of torture. It's one of the few procedures in plastic surgery
that is very painful.' Increasing or decreasing the size of buttocks
seemed merely uncomfortable; after that operation the patient
could not sit down for three weeks.

Dr Bellin explained that the agony Ronnie Biggs had suffered
when seeking permanent disguise was quite pointless. 'You
cannot change the way someone looks. You can make them
better-looking, more beautiful, but you cannot make them unrec-
ognizable. You can add to cheekbones, jaws, chins, change the
nose – a lot of things – but the person will still be recognizable as
themselves.'

He had once operated on a rather suspect South American
who urgently required his appearance changed and had arrived
for his new look supported by CIA credentials, presumably
forged. 'I did a facelift, fixed his nose, did hair transplants,
changed the pitch of his voice. I did jaw implants, cheek
implants, a chin implant. Several months later I read in the paper
that he'd been arrested, anyway.'

Ronnie Biggs, cheery and confident, told us, 'The guy that escaped with me had an inch or two off his nose, but I had the nose job and the full facelift, which involved 144 stitches.' The operations cost them £40,000, though this package deal *did* include a couple of fake passports – an item not normally seen on surgeons' accounts.

'I went into the operation thinking it was going to be plain sailing, but when I came out of the anaesthetic I experienced pain like I've never known before in my life. I really did think about jumping out of the clinic window – but I couldn't get out of bed. For the amount of money I paid I was assured I'd get the finest surgeon in Europe, but I think it was somebody learning the business who'd come straight from a butcher's.'

Dr Bellin admitted having collagen injections to remove lines from his face and intending to have his eyelids done: 'People say you can tell every nose job. You can't. You can only tell every poor nose job. There's no way good cosmetic surgery can be detected.'

I reminded him that President Reagan's inaugural had looked like a masked ball, and that the taut Duchess of Windsor was said to have had five or six facelifts. Dr Bellin said the most any of his patients had undergone was three. 'The first should last five to ten years, the second ten to twenty years.'

Despite the initial pain, Ronnie Biggs seemed a good advertisement for the improving knife, at least. I reminded him that in Melbourne his ex-wife Charmian had told me how when his Paris operation healed he had put himself about like Jack the lad, very proud of his new look.

Ronnie had other memories. 'When I came out of the clinic the guy I stayed with said, "God, they're never going to dig you out with a face like that – you look like a bloody Chink." ' He said a number of Canadians were having their faces changed at the same time, to avoid arrest, which he could quite understand, 'but for anyone else contemplating surgery, my advice would be to steer clear. There's a lot of beauty in wrinkles.'

Dennis Potter arrived bristling for a fight. The obvious target for the afflicted, acidulous playwright was Manchester's massive bearded Chief Constable, James Anderton, the lay preacher who had armed his police during the city's riots. Separating them was

Daphne Rae, attractive wife of the Headmaster of Westminster School. She had experienced a Gothic childhood, and at first seemed like another Potter target. Then he discovered she was a volunteer worker in an Indian leper colony. 'Hope it's not catching?' he muttered, edging away.

Potter had suffered from psoriatic arthropathy for twenty-seven years, which had shrivelled his hands and his life. He called it 'biblical leprosy' and certainly did not need the real thing. She tried to allay his apprehension: 'Ninety per cent of us are immune, and only ten per cent of leprosy is infectious – so you can work that one out.'

In the studio, with leprosy on hold, Potter's crippled hands coped with his chain-smoking as he faced up to a potential opponent, a do-gooding neutral – and I don't think he was too thrilled about me, either, although in an earlier career as television critic of the *Daily Herald* he had written approvingly of *Whicker's World.* Vehemently articulate, he was forever lashing out at the world, and once wrote, 'The only meaningful sacrament left for human beings is for them to gather in the streets in order to be sick together, splashing vomit on the paving stones as a final blow to an apparently deaf, dumb and blind God.' There was little that was gentle in his writings.

He had been furious when Alasdair Milne, then Director-General of the BBC, banned his play *Brimstone and Treacle* in which a couple's brain-damaged daughter is raped by a satanic man. A sense of despair and disgust, hatred and loathing emanated from Potter plays: religion parodied, young woman dying of cancer, boy mentally retarded, another burnt to death, heroine's illegitimate son returning to seduce her . . .

When I recalled that during a remission from his crippling disease he had written the brilliant and relatively upbeat *Pennies from Heaven*, he was quick to deny any gentle instincts: 'I don't know whether it was much happier because it ended with the man on the gallows and the girl becoming a prostitute . . . It was about the use of cheap music as a direct line of descent from the psalms and from all the religious yearnings of human beings who say, "Life isn't *really* like this, is it?"

'There are only two kinds of plays. Tragedies assume the world exists in an ordered sequence and that there's an inevitability about people's actions which leads to disaster. Comedies assume that the world is not so organized – it's the gap between the organized and structured, and the chaotic, which creates the comedy.'

I wondered whether, despite his almost permanent state of aggression, his determination to retaliate first, he found people reluctant to defend themselves against him because of his affliction? I recalled being interviewed on Radio 4 by a man who was waspish and unpleasant – but also blind. This neutralized my defensive reaction, as he coped bravely with misfortune.

'I don't deal with it bravely,' Potter said, 'I deal with it because it's there – I don't have any choice. I think people are far more heroic than they ever know, since few get the chance to find out what they're made of. Not that I look at the world with loathing and detestation – far from it. I actually do have, for want of a better word, a religious sense of the world, of its gleam, of its shine, of its possibilities, of its humour, of its eternal and perpetual yearning that things should be better than they are. That bitterness is expressed in the most unexpected places and in the most unexpected ways. It's expressed in what's called the dregs. It's expressed among the people whom Mr Anderton's police arrest.'

'Perhaps,' I interjected, 'also among the police?'

'Of course it's expressed among the police. Of course it is.'

Chief Constable Anderton was in charge of a force of 7,000. He was also the President of the British Association of Accordionists – a position from which he must have squeezed a lot of pleasure. He was concerned that all violence on television – even the clip we showed of my San Francisco Police patrols – every bloody scene pushed back the threshold to a point where viewers no longer regarded it as unusual. 'Young offenders seek to copy the violence they see. What worries me most of all is that somehow the whole community may begin to feel the problem of violence is so great, so overwhelming, that they are not in a position to do much about it – so they become less caring. I wouldn't censor the news, but I think a lot of our local problems – like football hooliganism – is the direct result of too much publicity.'

'That might be true, to a degree,' said Potter. 'Young men will react with aggression, and the media beats it up, obviously. But at the same time it's the automatic condemnation of a young man's energetic violence that I find odd.'

'Energetic violence,' I protested, 'left that poor old man we saw in the San Francisco tenderloin hotel with a cracked skull. Are you condoning that?'

'No, I'm not condoning violence of any kind, but violence is eddying and surging around them and needs to be anaesthetized in ads which are full of summer and couples running together through buttercup meadows, selling them a version of life which is other than the reality around them. That was the history of the penny dreadful, that's why pubs existed in Victorian England. People can only take so much apparent reality, just as a cheap song is a reduction of the yearning in a psalm.

'Society is in itself crippled and damaged, tempting you to say that nothing very much matters. The way we run ourselves at the moment is so out of kilter with what we really want as a people that you're going to get stresses and groans and upheavals. The more you articulate your dismay, the more you're going to be seen as apparently giving comfort to people who break the law.'

I suggested to Chief Constable Anderton that in Manchester he was a law unto himself. Nobody could gainsay him, apart from the distant Home Secretary. The local Police Committee, which was extremely left-wing and had often complained of his actions, could only advise, suggest or exhort. It was fortunate that he was a reasonable man . . . 'Every unreasonable man hopes he's reasonable,' Potter muttered, bleakly.

Daphne Rae sat calm and pretty between these reasonable men, protected to a degree by her unusual brain condition which meant that she could retain no memory of anything. After talking to you she would turn away – and by the time she looked back, you would have become a stranger again. She had worked with Mother Teresa in Calcutta, but had no time for her. 'Mother is a megalomaniac.'

In her autobiography she recalled how the wife of a house-master at a leading public school had attended to the sex educa-tion of her husband's sixteen-year-olds, pleasuring around a hundred or so each term, and getting very few refusals.

Mrs Rae had run away from her school, as had her husband, a present headmaster; three of their six children also decamped from schools. I wondered whether all this said something about our education system – or her family.

'It might well be our family. There was so much going on at home that they wanted to get back to see what was happening. I had a marvellous childhood.'

Not everyone would have thought so. She was abandoned by her mother at the age of five. Her guardian, Uncle Bob, was a doctor who attempted to rape her. He regularly enjoyed his patients on the consulting-room couch, under which she would hide, and he amputated his dead wife's finger so he could give her ring to his mistress. Her early life, I suggested, sounded rather like a Dennis Potter play – except that she had a happier ending.

Chief Constable Anderton said he thought the message of the Dennis Potter plays was that life did not change at all and never had, down the ages. 'Also, that life is good. Evil and sorrow and joy live together all the time, and this is the human condition. It's certainly true in the whole context of policing. There is nothing surprising to us in 1984 – it's just the same as it was in 1884, I suspect.'

Dennis Potter's prickly hostility was undermined by such sweet reason, so I ended the programme with his exasperated tribute to the burly religious policeman: 'You are a truly subversive dangerous man!'

Once upon a time I would occasionally meet a quiet schoolboy when he slipped away from Eton to the sanctuary of his aunt's Belgravia home. I assumed he was still spending his pocket money in the tuckshop until I heard he had won an Oscar for his first feature film, *Chariots of Fire.* He then spent £30m of Warner Brothers' pocket money directing *Greystoke,* a visually stunning Tarzan film. This led me to invite Hugh Hudson, still slim and tousled, to join one of Hitchcock's leading ladies from *The Birds,* and a white-bearded explorer from darkest Africa, for a more modest production in our Manchester studio.

We discussed wild animals, for Tarzan and Jane and all those apes were about to swing through the jungle for the umpteenth time since the original 1918 movie, though the haunting cry that now rang out from the treetops had a different accent: Hugh's

Tarzan was a Frenchman with soulful eyes and a slight squint.

Tippi Hedren, one of those cool blondes Hitchcock preferred, lived with her daughter Melanie Griffiths some forty miles north of Los Angeles in close proximity to ninety-seven lions and tigers, which wandered at will through their home. Gregory was a problem, she complained. 'Can't keep that tiger out of my kitchen. Keeps coming through the window – once when it was shut. I've had to put up bars to stop him hurting himself. Natasha, one of our tigers, always settles on the living room sofa. She's very fond of television – especially action scenes like ice skating or dancing girls.'

All the animals were totally adorable, she assured us – though every now and then they did put her entire family into hospital. Fortunately their doctor was a plastic surgeon.

While making her film *Roar*, Tippi was bitten on the head by a lion, her leg was crushed by an elephant and she suffered black gangrene. Her husband, bitten on hand and thigh, was left with eight scars and a limp. A daughter needed plastic surgery after a lioness clawed her face. One son was bitten, another had fifty-six stiches after a clawing and a third lost several teeth when an owl, of all things, went berserk – which may have been the revenge of *The Birds*.

This catalogue of casualties made it hard to see the appeal of wild animals in a home where communication was spasmodic. 'We didn't take against the animals – the only thing we ever did say was, "I'm not working with that cat again". That's what I said after Charisse bit my head – and the elephant didn't intend to hurt me, because if he did I wouldn't be here.'

Tippi kept her lion and tiger population down by putting them on the pill, and seemed to value her animals more than her family. During the making of the film no animal got hurt, though most of the cast did.

Some observers believed things went wrong because her husband Noel Marshall had directed *The Exorcist*, so they were 'using the Devil's money'. That argument was later supported by the fact that among Tippi's deeper scars was her broken marriage with that successful director.

Our third guest was a Fellow in Zoology who after thirty years in Kenya had also been bitten by most things. Dr Malcolm Coe of

St Peter's College, Oxford, had published papers on wildlife, from the necking habits of giraffe to the decomposition of elephant dung. Since he and Hugh Hudson had studied chimpanzee communication, they whooped away in ape.

Hugh had needed to brush up his chimping while on location in the Republic of Cameroon, where on each set real apes intermingled with fifty small actors – below 5' 4" – in carefully created monkey suits. To get their postures right they had all studied monkey business for six months, from treetop athletics to mating, and wore different masks for different moods: threat, joy, fear, affection . . . All the animal costumes were controlled by a 'primate wardrobe supervisor' who after the film went to work for Leonard, the Mayfair hairdresser.

Unlike Tippi's casualty list, there were no walking wounded during the Tarzan shoot, though West African life was so tough the benevolent film company occasionally flew in to their jungle location a group of young ladies from the nearest big town, to help restore the crew's spirits. They arrived with the unit's fresh food and, apart from jolly company, unfortunately also contributed what became known as 'jet-fresh clap'.

Not a word to Jane about that.

As we go about our lives these days none of us is quite as safe as we believe. In *Whicker!* we considered the sixty terrorist groups around the world that range from small cells to state-supported mini-armies. Those who should know had told me there were thirty-one terrorist organizations in Britain alone, which was hard to believe.

At that time Americans were preparing for the Los Angeles Olympic Games, and fearing that the Palestinians who had killed eleven Israeli athletes at Munich might attempt an encore. Such madness is still with us today, as Islamic Fundamentalists destroy American embassies in Africa and Aid workers are kidnapped in Eastern Europe, Bosnia, Africa . . .

To join us, to speak the unspeakable, I invited a man I had long admired: Sir Geoffrey Jackson, small and resolute, who as British Ambassador to Uruguay was kidnapped by the Tupamaros and kept in an underground cage for more than eight months while up above thirty thousand police and troops searched for him.

During those 244 days he showed such grace under pressure that his captors were finally casting around for some face-saving excuse to release him.

We brought in another quiet expert, Stephen Sloan, from his university in Oklahoma. As a Professor of Political Science he spent his days simulating the seizure of oil refineries and the hijacking of aircraft, while teaching corporate officials how not to be kidnapped. He brought us some bloodthirsty film clips to undermine any remaining sense of security.

Dr Richard Clutterbuck, alert and perky, a former Major-General then lecturing in politics at Exeter University, was an international authority on a bloody trend which could still produce biological or chemical horror, or even extortion by nuclear bomb. Despite the availability of Russia's crumbling nuclear arsenal, this scenario has so far reached only thrillers, but any day could explode into the headlines.

'Such extortion would be very easy,' he said. 'A crate containing a nuclear bomb could be substituted for a crate of motorcar parts coming from Rotterdam into a British port, with radio-monitoring to follow it and radio-control to fire it. When it reached Britain the message would be sent: "Unless you release our prisoners by ten o'clock tomorrow, it will be detonated."

'That has been possible for years but, touch wood, they haven't done it yet. The reason they haven't is because it's complicated, so there's far more likelihood of their being caught. Terrorists are not frightened of the death penalty but they *are* frightened of being caught – that's as far ahead as they look.

'If their threat was challenged and they exploded the bomb, the political price would be so high that their political movement would be finished. It's perfectly feasible for a nut or anarchist who doesn't mind blowing up the world, but it's very unlikely that one nut could manage it alone – so it's far easier for him just to point a gun at somebody.'

Professor Sloan was less sanguine: 'I'm concerned about rogue states – Libya, Iraq. One always wonders if combinations of zealots who've already indicated they'd be willing to die for their cause might be able to acquire low-grade nuclear weapons, and not care about world opinion.'

Sir Geoffrey said, 'You'd only get that kind of action from

raving maniacs. My own belief is that no terrorist is normal anyway, but these would have to be real nutters – and the less nutty nutters would be on their tails. I would say the professional terrorist would be the first person to kill that kind of terrorism.'

Dr Clutterbuck recalled that before martial law in the Philippines a politician required an army of 300 to protect him as he moved around the country, with groups travelling ahead and behind to prevent ambush. Sir Geoffrey, who had good cause to know, said, 'The old theory that the bomber always gets through also tends to apply to the terrorist. My kidnappers told me that even my primitive precautions in that age of innocence caused them to cancel their operation eight times. In the final attempt they were ready to wipe out my armed protection, and possibly my wife.'

I recalled that when I interviewed Run Me Shaw in Singapore, the Chinese tycoon who was a Triad kidnap target showed me how he defended his Rolls: at the touch of a switch by his seat the Phantom III became live and would electrocute anyone touching it. It also seemed a useful way of coping with traffic wardens.

Sir Geoffrey said his experience as a potential target in the Middle East and South America convinced him that local protection should be left to the host nation. 'If you bring your men out from England the population will say, "Why are these gringos killing our boys?" Foreigners are always in the wrong, even if "our boys" are Tupamaros.'

I was pleased to find his technique for maintaining dignity and establishing some personal contact with kidnappers supported the style I had found useful when dealing with Tontons Macoutes in Haiti, gangs in Brazil and terrorists in Egypt. I have always believed that if you smile – or better still, even manage to make the man with the gun smile – that whatever his original intention he is not going to hit you with his rifle butt. Once you've looked him in the eye as amiably as you can manage, a glimmer of contact has been established which can save your life, or your jawbone.

A Tupamaro doctor called in to inject Sir Geoffrey saw he was doodling their five-pointed star emblem and observed it was a seditious pastime for an Ambassador. 'I asked him to tell me whether I was in purgatory, or was I still alive? When he said

"Alive" I asked for a certificate to that effect, so I could pin it up in my cage. He said "Certainly – but in the circumstances you'll understand if I don't sign it." I thought: a sense of humour! I'm home and dry. No further trouble.'

'The Sardinians who kidnapped the Schildt family were straightforward bandits in it for gain,' said Dr Clutterbuck. 'The politically motivated terrorist is a far more dangerous and vicious animal. The Dutch industrialist kidnapped in Ireland was held for six weeks by two IRA people; one was a professional bank robber who was quite a human being, and they got on some sort of terms – they argued, had a dialogue. The other was a girl of twenty with a lifetime of IRA indoctrination, and for six weeks that girl never said one word, never acknowledged even by the flicker of an eyelash that he existed. She was completely dehumanized. She was the political animal which is so different from the criminal animal.

'In the kidnapping of the OPEC oil ministers in Vienna, a policeman had his gun on a girl about five foot nought with a machine-pistol in her hand. He grabbed her gun, but of course she had a handgun as well – and shot him dead. If she'd been a man he would have shot her first. Because she was a girl, he died.'

We considered the conditioning needed to allow a human to kill another. 'By experience and studies, it takes about seven years. None of the Red Army faction or the Baader–Meinhoff group killed anyone until they were twenty-five. The people who seem able to sink fastest to this condition are those with higher education. I can't think why this is.'

Sir Geoffrey believed the Red Brigades attracted the mad, but could also madden the sane. 'One of the best of my gaolers had his gun behind my ear and said, most regretfully, "You do appreciate that in certain circumstances I'm going to have to pull this trigger. I shall hate doing it, but I certainly *will* do it." I could tell he had not yet killed, for there was still a human being in there. By the time he had killed a couple of times he would have been the sort of animal Richard is describing.

'Living with terrorists is like living with a jug of nitro-glycerine in your lap. I've always maintained that psychopaths can be totally logical, but they can never be reasonable. You have to locate the point beyond which it's not safe to push them. Even a word can do it. I've seen a young man go over the edge because the name of the President of his country was spoken – it was enough to trigger him.'

'The Chinese have a proverb,' said Dr Clutterbuck, 'Kill one, frighten 10,000. But they have to kill someone who might be you. Killing a soldier doesn't do that, nor does killing a policeman. Killing somebody on his doorstep in front of his family does. Terrorism is theatre. It's aimed at the audience rather than the victim – and at the media.'

I recalled that as a war correspondent in Korea I had gone into the invasion of Inchon, an extremely hazardous landing behind North Korean lines. The three American news agencies – AP, UP and INS – were fiercely competitive, and as we prepared to get into landing craft and head for the beaches in that surprise amphibious attack, we heard that one of them had released news of the invasion and its location – and this had been broadcast! For an agency scoop he had jeopardized the lives of thousands of his countrymen – not to mention mine. In our boat war correspondents were not popular.

Afterwards the correspondent of one of the agencies that had not broken the embargo was reprimanded by his New York office: 'Are you working for the Marines, or INS?' Professor Sloan understood that murderous irresponsibility: 'Ratings are the game, and I don't care what the guidelines are – we don't have D-notices. I don't see any way you can control that, in an open society.'

'You can defeat terrorists, but only if you have a controlled press and a totally closed society,' said Dr Clutterbuck. 'Today their weapons are very small and very lethal. You can get a machine-pistol about a foot long and shove it in a briefcase. It'll fire twenty-five rounds a second – or 100 rounds a second with a four-barrel version. Its laser sight projects through a hole in the case, so the terrorist stands there in the airport lounge until its orange disk is on the heart of his target, jiggles the handle – and *Brrrrr*, twenty-five rounds every second go through that little orange disk. Nobody knows who the hell has fired because the thing is silenced. Then he walks away.'

That was in 1984. We know how terrorism has changed and machine-pistols 'improved' since then. Today the late Dr

Clutterbuck would be appalled to learn that every year around the world there are at least 12,500 kidnappings.

Large international companies flourish by selling corporate security among multinationals, banks, law firms and any group that sends employees into peril. One has annual sales of more than £120m, another helped secure the release of hostages in 840 kidnappings – in most of which a ransom was paid. The kidnapping and ransom-insurance market – or K&R – has an estimated annual premium income of about £76m. Such cruelty is big business indeed.

Sir Geoffrey Jackson, the kidnapped Ambassador, then believed that four or five hundred terrorists could bring down any state that had not got its eyes open. He put his faith in some sort of Neighbourhood Watch: 'The greatest safeguard against takeover by terrorists are nosy old ladies and inquisitive little boys and gossipy people telling each other what's going on around the place.'

It was rather comforting to hear that experts who could consider mass death so calmly believed our first line of defence against silent machine-pistols and nuclear holocaust was a gossipy old lady.

As soon as we get out of bed and dress, we start to signal something about ourselves. So if we are what we wear, do we become what we buy? Fashion has always created its own dictators, and I was joined in our studio by three dedicated followers.

Lady Rendlesham, formerly of *Vogue* and then ruling Yves St Laurent's British empire, was tiny, taut and formidable, and one of the few Englishwomen capable of intimidating the directrice of a French couture house. Those who had cause to flinch called her Lady Rattlesnake. She had been known to deny eager customers permission to buy some garment she considered unbecoming. At the other end of the style scale, Molly Parkin, former Fashion Editor of the *Sunday Times* but then writing soft porn, or even not-so-soft porn, with undemanding titles like *Cock-a-Hoop* and *Up And Coming*. Between them sat Malcolm McLaren who, with Vivienne Westwood, had designed Confrontation clothes projecting a sense of menace and sold in a Kings Road boutique called, predictably, Sex. He had an instinct for trends and the seamier side of pop and created – and was abandoned by – Adam Ant, Boy George and the Sex Pistols.

The clothes such gurus wore were revealing. Lady Rendlesham chose a classic St Laurent pale-pink cableknit cashmere cardigan with pink chiffon scarf and wide trousers. Molly Parkin, plumper, wore a long black medieval dress topped by a hat like a black jewelled ice-cream cornet sprouting feathers, and a beaded snood. She dressed with the kind of enthusiasm men reserve for cars or footballers. Despite our hot studio lights Malcolm McLaren refused to remove a dark-grey off-the-shoulder overcoat several sizes too large which looked like a great blanket but was doubtless most expensive.

'Clothes make you feel important,' he said. 'If they don't, they're a waste of time. I don't sell clothes, I sell the act of rebellion, I sell the ability to climb up the drainpipe and get to the girl's bedroom window, rather than going in gently through the front door.'

He was proud of the Sex Pistols – 'They made cash from chaos' – and untroubled by his turbulent managerial career: 'I've had a lot of battles but it's better to be hated than loved, because you get more done. People love rogues – they forget heroes very quickly. Everybody remembers Dick Turpin.'

Molly Parkin scolded him for excessive prices in his boutique. 'I don't like spending a lot of money on clothes, it's immoral. These old socks came from Oxfam, this hair hanging down cost seventy-five pence in the Brixton market, though the snood cost a bit more – but I do know how to put things together. Malcolm borders on the obscenely ridiculous, the way I do.

'I knew how I wanted to look when I was seven: dramatic. Now I'm evidently also ridiculous and when I walk into a place people laugh – not to say, snigger. I don't mind because I've come to the time of my life when I'd like to be a comedienne.'

For our sideways glance at politics I was joined by two of my oldest television friends from the early *Tonight* days of 1957: Sir Geoffrey Johnson-Smith, Under-Secretary of State for Defence and one of the first television knights, and (soon to be Sir) Antony Jay, co-author of all the delightful *Yes Minister*s.

With them, a former resident of No 11 Downing Street, the

biographer Edna Healey, who told us about the trials of being a political wife. 'If you know anything about the Treasury you will know that it's a man's world if ever there was one. I was the wife of the Chancellor and we were there for five years, but in all that time I had three meals in the official dining room. I'd be watching television upstairs and see people on the screen going through the door at No 11 and say, "Oh gosh, that's where he is tonight – turn off the oven."

'You're a great deal alone – though I don't expect you to get your hankie out and weep for the Westminster wives. In the nineteenth century you had a baby every year, so there was a very good reason why you would be invisible. It's probably still true today that if a wife gets two lines in her husband's biography, she's lucky.'

With the publication of my own autobiography and all the pleasures and pains of a publicity tour only just fading, I could understand Tony's delight that his *Yes Prime Minister* scripts were being published in an omnibus edition, when he would have something solid on his bookshelf. 'It goes out on the air and people laugh or not, as the case may be, and it's gone. But some of the things you'd like to think are recorded somewhere are in a book, which is more satisfying if you belong to the print generation, as we do. You can't pull a video out of your briefcase on a bus . . .'

In the fertile field of backbiting politicians, I reflected, he was surely not short of material, for he must have been knee deep in calculated indiscretions from Members who wanted to get their retaliation into his shows first. 'They think you've already got the other side's story,' he explained, 'so they want to be absolutely sure you've got theirs as well.'

Had Sir Geoffrey been one of Tony's Deep Throats? 'I did suggest a story to him, that's perfectly true, yes, and I knew it would be treated with the greatest discretion. I put an official in touch with him, just to check the authenticity of the background.'

After we had watched a clip of the machiavellian Sir Humphrey manipulating his baffled Premier, I wondered whether Ministers could ever dominate their crafty senior civil servants? 'Some do, in some respects,' said Tony. 'One of the factors is the intellectual capacity of the Minister, because he's dealing with very intellectual people. If he's not up to it, everything he suggests will be treated as though by a headmaster marking the essay of a rather backward pupil. You need great force of character – but above all, you need to be there for a while. One of the reasons Denis Healey was successful in the Department of Defence was that he was there for six years. The average tenure of a Minister in office is about eleven months, then he's moved to something else or the government falls or there's a reshuffle.'

Dominance could be achieved in many ways: he had been drawn to some research into the status structure of a colony of monkeys, who all recognized the top monkey by the colour of his scrotum: the darker the scrotum, the higher in the hierarchy. 'One poor little monkey was left out of it all because he was the palest Cambridge blue, as opposed to the deep magenta of the number one, so the scientists painted his scrotum an even darker blue than all the rest – and immediately the other monkeys sat back and let him eat first and all the females flocked around him. The poor chap didn't know what had hit him!'

I wondered about politicians' fascination with showbiz: Mrs Thatcher had appeared with Sir Humphrey, Sir Harold Wilson was interviewed by Mike Yarwood, Neil Kinnock did a double act with Tracey Ullman; lately Tony Blair and William Hague sat on Des O'Connor's sofa. 'We've grown out of the nineteenth-century innocence pre-1867, when an MP knew all his constituents,' said Tony. 'Now Sir Geoffrey has about seventy thousand and can't possibly know them all – and the only way they can find out anything about *him* is by watching television.'

I recalled my bafflement in the *Tonight* days when, after a hard session in the studio, Geoffrey would hurry out into the winter's night to go door-knocking around St Pancras for hours, wearily chasing votes. As a popular television man, well paid, loved by millions and able to get home to his wife every night, why did he do it?

'I felt at the time that fascinating though it was being in television, meeting interesting people, interviewing politicians, I was still on the outside looking in. I wanted to be on the pitch, close to the people making the big decisions. I like to be close to power and I like to exercise power myself. I won a case for my local hospital recently; they were going to close Obstetrics, but I was able to see the matter was properly argued in front of the Minister, fairly and squarely and democratically. We won – and that's a tremendous thing to be able to do. I also like to think I'm doing something for the country and helping people who without me would find life drabber and nastier.'

As we closed the programme I observed that when taken out of a studio and transferred to Westminster, even a television idol began talking like a politician. I could tell Sir Geoffrey was *very* deep blue, where it mattered.

We considered a growth industry: divorce. In America every other marriage breaks up, though in Britain, merely one in three. This means that if your two best friends are happily married, it's your turn next.

My first guest was Fiona, Baroness Thyssen, top model who married a multimillionaire and was immortalized, you could say, in a 1963 *Whicker's World.* She and Heini were living a blissful fairy tale in St Moritz, but as soon as my back was turned after the programme, they divorced.

To join her we flew over from Beverly Hills America's best-known divorce lawyer Marvin Mitchelson, who by then had separated more than two thousand couples, expensively. The long list of Hollywood husbands who regretted their wives had ever met him included Marlon Brando, Mick Jagger, Rod Steiger, Eddie Fisher, Tony Curtis, David Bowie, Adnan Khashoggi, James Mason, Bob Dylan and many others, today wiser and poorer. They were doubtless not displeased when he was later convicted of theft, and gaoled.

Marvin first 'hit really deep pockets', as American lawyers say, back in 1946 and, though apparently a soft and smiling man, had once reduced a defendant to death. The poor man suffered a heart attack during cross-examination. 'I'm not proud of that, but he was lying. I did mouth-to-mouth resuscitation in court, and thought of giving up law for the rest of the evening.'

My third guest was the delightful Mel Calman, who drew pocket cartoons of anxious married couples for *The Times,* evoking the strife of marriage and the melancholy of the single: his little man in bed reflecting, 'I even miss her cold feet.' Another sighing, 'For a moment I thought I was happy – but it passed.' His drawings evoked rueful smiles, and had been well researched: he had been divorced twice, and was not keen on lawyers.

Mel died tragically of a heart attack in a Leicester Square cinema, sitting beside the long-term live-out lady he had not married. He was a funny man who looked gloomy, whereas Marvin Mitchelson was a happy man who created gloom. After the much publicized Lee Marvin case which gave the world the dreaded word 'palimony', his client Michelle Marvin became 'the Joan of Arc of live-in ladies', he told us proudly, glossing over the fact that the court awarded her only $104,000.

Lee Marvin had enjoyed a sort of reverie, after the case: 'I thought I'd catch Mitchelson in his Rolls in the parking lot and I'd take out one of my guns and blow his leg off. He'd be lying there screaming and I'd bend down and say, "It's OK, I've called an ambulance." He's sighing with relief – then I blow his other leg off.'

I suggested to Mitchelson that one of these days such daydreaming could come true; he was going to open his front door, and two shots would ring out. 'I try not to think about that,' he said. 'I did represent a lady married to someone in the Mafia who sent me a gun as a present. Some time later a man who had been threatening me came to my office, so I got the gun out of the safe, but didn't put any bullets in. When I practised aiming I blew off the top of my desk! He'd left one up the spout. It was his idea of a present.

'I won a case against a doctor who was on crutches, and as I was walking out of the courtroom a crutch hit me on the back of the neck and sent me sprawling. The judge wanted to put him in gaol, but he'd just given me a good award of attorney's fees so I didn't feel like prosecuting.'

His highest award for temporary support was $75,000 a month to the wife of Sheikh Mohammed al-Fassi. This turned into a final award of $82m. Will she ever see the money? 'Well, she'll see some of it.' His critics said all he won in such cases was publicity.

I told him it was hard to take Californian divorce cases seriously when the wife of actor George Segal could ask a judge for $600,000 damages because as an ex-wife she would suffer the social indignity of no longer getting the best tables in restaurants.

To ease her inner torment she needed regular applications of her husband's money.

Once such a divorce hearing could be as emotional as a murder trial, he said, 'but now we have no-fault divorce, and no more adultery or fault-finding, most cases are rather dull. It's just a matter of the real-estate appraiser and the business manager coming in and saying what they're worth.'

Mel Calman explained that all his cartoon husbands were very vulnerable, which could have been autobiographical. 'Psychologically I had a bossy Jewish mother, so I'm attracted to intelligent, interesting – and therefore difficult – women. They can chop a man down to size very quickly by saying, "Darling, you've told that story before." Still, one husband did reply, "Darling, I can't change my stories but I can change my wife." '

Fiona recalled her upheaval following our 1963 programme *Model Millionairess*: 'As we know, it's largely due to you that I'm divorced! After all, if you hadn't asked me all those lethal questions I probably could have floated through life happily married for another fifteen years, without thinking too much about my situation. I don't reproach you for it, though, because I do think – for me at any rate – it was the better solution.' Her divorce from Heini Thyssen was 'totally good-natured' but she regretted that 'my daughter never heard the dominant voice of a male in the home'.

I told Fiona that after a second programme we did, a viewer from Park Crescent in Brighton wrote to say, 'If you don't ask that lady to marry you, you're mad.' Unfortunately she always seemed to prefer other chaps merely because they were handsome and charming and rich . . . 'Absolutely untrue. You were much too busy. I like somebody who's available, not trotting around the world.'

It was the best argument yet for running a static talk show in Manchester and becoming an Indoors man.

Whatever you do east of Suez doesn't count . . .

There are few friendships like those of foreign correspondents, which are deep – though spasmodic. Once side by side you have faced snipers across the Sweet Water Canal or watched North Korean hordes advancing implacably up the hill towards you – even endured the stultifying rigours of a royal tour in Africa – you meet with delight in the street after twenty years and instantly pick up the conversation.

This is particularly true of war correspondents, whose task requires that they constantly insinuate themselves into dangerous situations, so bond intensely for reassurance and company. Wars almost always break out in unpleasant places, so a press camp is as close and self-protective as a mining village, and even richer in shared experience and conflict with authority.

The first war reporter, William Howard Russell, sent hand-written despatches from the Crimea to *The Times* a century and a half ago, stories of the Charge of the Light Brigade, the Army's ammunition shortage, the way British soldiers lived and died. Some of these upset the War Office, but were the start of the multi-million-pound media industry which now springs up around every modern battlefield.

Following occasional reportage during the Boer and Great Wars – mainly from GHQ, as the only source of information – correspondents emerged as an organized and regulated body in World War II. They wore battle or service dress with 'C' badges in green and gold, and were non-combatants with the honorary rank of Captain – in the US forces, Colonel. Fed and quartered in press camps near the frontline, correspondents were escorted wherever they sensed a story by Conducting Officers who had often arrived at that posting after being wounded.

The War Office had not forgotten William Howard Russell, so their reports were censored before despatch. They chafed against such control, naturally, but were grateful for the facilities provided, for protection and welfare – and company. It was a friendly, almost comfortable way to cover a war – at least when we were winning.

North Korea invaded the South in 1950 after five years of uneasy world peace, and President Truman reacted with what he called a UN 'police action' – so there could be no war correspondents. I arrived in Tokyo within three days – the time it took to fly there.

Neither accredited nor supported, we were itinerant uninvited civilians with notebooks, wandering the warfront. We wore whatever seemed suitable, slept and ate with any hospitable unit that might welcome us. Most did. At the dawn of this media age, all units in the field were delighted at the prospect of being written about, or having their pictures taken for the local paper back home.

The American army vainly attempting to stem the North Korean invasion was mainly a disorderly collection of young GIs from the Occupation forces in Japan, with little training and less discipline. They had believed the war was over. Those 'Ginza cowboys' were then supported by one British brigade which I had watched sailing into Pusan from Hong Kong. It seemed likely that together we should be pushed back into the sea.

A few dozen newspapermen and photographers covered the rout. There was little television. The solitary BBC crew arrived late: a cameraman and a reporter, Rene Cutforth, whose main concern was radio. The Korean War – eventually stabilized – was one of the under-reported conflicts of the century, yet casualties following the Chinese intervention across the Yalu were enormous. The US sent a massive army to that theatre; more than 30,000 were killed in action, and another 20,000 in various accidents. Before the armed truce the South Korean army lost 46,000 men, the Chinese enemy an estimated 400,000.

Yet during those three desperate years home newspapers showed little interest in that distant war and the plight of UN

Forces rushed in to stem the invasion. Each day as we struggled to report the battle we were aware that our stories would probably be spiked, or cut to insignificance.

We may have been welcome visitors when we reached soldiers then facing only danger, discomfort and defeat, but from our viewpoint it was not a well-conducted war; our first problem was how to reach them. With no transport we had to bum rides and cover the warfront by thumb. This was not difficult, but also not comfortable. Moving around on a tank was even worse than in a truck – except for one lone three-tonner with a cheery driver which stopped to pick me up. I clambered into the back and as we set off, found it full of bodies.

Since we were not accredited, there was at least no censorship. The main problem was how to get our stories back for transmission from the cablehead in Japan. US Army Signals in the field had other messages on their minds.

Korea, the first of the modern local wars, saw the start of front-line competition by wire services and newspapers, all frantic to be first to report each victory and defeat, every advance or retreat, to reveal exclusively any plan High Command might wish to keep secret. Amid the desperate life-and-death military action, we civilians also fought a ruthless media war of old-fashioned hold-the-front-page scoops. There was none of that traditionally gallant 'Gentlemen of the French Guards, file your story first . . .'

Chinese and North Koreans showed little respect for the Geneva Convention and did not distinguish between heavily armed GIs and unarmed Gentlemen of the Press. At that time correspondents suffered the army's highest casualty rate, due mainly to air crashes as we flew backwards and forwards to Japan in overloaded supply planes with uncertain crews who had been dragged from desks and orderly rooms and press-ganged into emergency duty. In one C119 I passed a fraught flight pushing shells out of the back as we skimmed the waves and braced to ditch in the Yellow Sea.

By the time of Vietnam, from 1965, the power of the media had expanded; correspondents were not only accredited, but courted and lionized. Television had grown so significant on the home front that President Johnson could wail, 'If I've lost Walter Cronkite, I've lost the war.' Reporters seen on the screen every night were no longer out of their depths and humble amid military brass, but would browbeat PR officers with demands. Helicopters, aircraft, jeeps and boats were at our disposal.

In this rush to freedom, to report a war Sixties-style, TV networks repaid an eager and acquiescent Pentagon by going for instantly dramatic stories, by showing napalmed children, burning villages, weeping women, forests stark and arid from agent orange. Even worse for viewers' morale were the nightly vox pops when bewildered GIs recounted real nightmares to camera, wondering why they were fighting, knowing only that they might at any moment be killed or wounded or, even worse, captured. It was one-note coverage – or, if you will, it was showing things as they were.

The sense of possible defeat grew. No need for the Viet Cong propaganda machine to attempt to demonize their American enemy; they were doing a masterly job on themselves – which ultimately proved fatal.

Television is a short-term high-impact medium in which new images constantly obliterate the old – so before the army noticed the war was lost behind their backs, on distant screens unused to bloody reality. When I later interviewed the commanding General William Westmoreland at his home in Charleston he told me that if Washington could have resisted public opinion for one more month, the Viet Cong would have been beaten . . . It was not to be; viewers had had enough. As far as they were concerned it was over, over there.

By the time of the Falklands and the Gulf, the War Office and Pentagon knew only too well that although they were fighting for freedom of speech, a nightly display of bodybags and despairing servicemen would destroy any nation's spirits, so no longer did we have free run of the action. Correspondents were carefully corralled, and fed controlled information. There were few photo opportunities to reveal reality and upset delicate sensitivities watching aghast in their sitting rooms at home.

In the Yugoslavian fighting, NATO took the same line. A few correspondents remained in a Belgrade hotel, to be suffered and controlled by Serbians, and travel only with escorts. Others prowled the borders of neighbouring States, recording what they could.

Such warfront free-for-all had first started back in Korea, when Tommy Thompson of the *Daily Telegraph* and Steve Barber, *News Chronicle*, shared the Jeep I liberated from North Koreans – who had captured it from Americans. It was not in showroom condition but, as it lurched and groaned towards Pyongyang, was better than clinging to a tank.

We three went through discomfort and anguish, laughter and fear for many hideous months but were as merry as you could be in an Asian war. They were my brothers. Then the war waned, left the front pages, and we dispersed to other assignments around the world. We never met again, ever.

Less stressfully, correspondents who covered the royal tour of East Africa and Mauritius travelled in a DC3, bumping around behind the royal aircraft. This ponderous and unstylish transport much irked Kenneth Ames of the *Daily Mail*, who had been a wartime Spitfire pilot. Nineteen years later, while filming in Vienna's Kärntnerstrasse, I was accosted by a blond and joyful figure: Ken was then bureau chief for a group of American financial magazines, with an office near Sacher. That night we hit the inns and the new wine of Grinzing with his wife, the novelist Sarah Gainham, who had just written another best-seller and with her royalties, bought him an aircraft faster and more stylish than our Dakota. Back on a jolly professional impersonal level, we reminisced the night away and could not have been in better spirits; such a relief to be a long way from Dar-es-Salaam.

Next day Ken sent round to my hotel some Austrian political background he thought might help my commentary, with a note: 'Let's not leave it for another nineteen years'. The following day some family situation became intolerable; he cut his wrists and drowned himself in his office bath.

Another friend also had women trouble: Arthur Cook of the *Daily Express* was between wives when he came to stay in my Richmond flat for 'a couple of nights', later extended to a year or so. We had worked together in the Middle East. In Iran he got a scoop on the suicide of Premier Mossadegh, which I missed. The *Express* splashed his story across the front page. It was graphic and arresting, but unfortunately untrue. While we attempted to confirm or deny, his unhappy foreign editor sent a telling service message: 'Either Mossadegh dead, or you are'.

Arthur moved cheerfully on to the *Daily Mail* and was covering south-east Asia from Singapore when next we met at the Oriental Hotel in Bangkok – a crumbling wooden riverside structure when I first drank there with Randolph Churchill on our way home, with great relief, from Korea in 1950. At the crossroads of the Far East, it had slowly grown into one of the best hotels in the world.

Its General Manager since 1967, Kurt Wachtveitl, controlled the impeccable place with precision and earned total loyalty from regulars. One American stayed many times a year at this luxurious and expensive hotel, so when his visits reached 200 Kurt organized a small party for him in the Authors' Wing. In the middle of the celebrations the businessman spotted a hotel photographer arriving to record the event, and leapt nervously behind one of the white peacock chairs.

He was the organizer of a large American charity and alert to the fact that if potential donors saw him living in a state of perpetual luxury, their generous donations to the Asian poor might evaporate.

Kurt himself received a gift from Mohamed al Fayed: one of Harrod's clip-on ties which, like made-up bow ties, tuck in under the shirt collar. These lifeless things are often worn by police, doormen, bodyguards or anyone liable to be grabbed aggressively, when the tie would come away and leave its wearer at a safe distance.

Out of politeness to his guest, Kurt wore the awful tie next evening at a dignified banquet. Al Fayed, knowing something other diners did not, strode up to him in the middle of dinner and with his usual unerring charm, grabbed the tie and tore it off.

Though he was an enterprising manager, not every one of Kurt's ideas seemed constructive. On my last visit I ran into former toastmaster Ivor Spencer who runs a school for English would-be butlers hoping to get rich serving oil men in Texas or thereabouts. He had been invited to instruct Kurt's army of Thai butlers. It was hard to believe that any of those silent smiling room attendants needed to be taught how to arrange orchids on breakfast trays and night-time pillows, or carve fruit.

One day as I was returning from filming the Governor of Tarlac in the Philippines, the former war correspondent Ninoy

Aquino, I ran into Arthur Cook hobbling around the Oriental lobby. During the Emergency in Malaya he had joined an army jungle patrol and fallen from an improvised bridge into a river, damaging a leg.

Years later, after he had retired to the peace of a picturesque old house at Haut-de-Cagnes in Provence, an internal growth detached itself one night and he was carried down to the Cagnes clinic in agony. To save his life, they cut off his leg.

The clinic was competent and caring, but the artificial limb they later provided was from Long John Silver, and the ghost pains were excruciating. With the help of Kenneth Allsop of the *Mail* – who had also lost a leg during the war – and the RAF Association, we managed to get him into Roehampton. His sympathetic surgeon told him, 'By the time patients reach me I usually have several fat files about them. In your file there's only a letter from Mr Allsop and a letter from Mr Whicker.'

Arthur was later returned to the South of France with the latest high-tech leg, a life-enhancing light-hearted cripple.

I was discussing such spirited fellowship with Sir David English, editor-in-chief of the *Mail*, during the Hong Kong handover. We were in the lobby of the Mandarin awaiting the arrival of Lady Thatcher. I had just lunched at the Peninsula with Simon Winchester and Jan Morris who, as James, had climbed Everest, almost, establishing a *Times* base camp at 22,000 feet from which he scooped the world on Hillary's conquest. He then went on to cover the troubles in the Canal Zone, where I was established at Moascar outside Ismailia with David Walker of the *Daily Mirror*. Non-competitive, we three shared a hut most harmoniously for several months.

After the Egyptian revolution King Farouk went into exile and James went into Morocco for a trail-blazing operation, emerging as Jan.

I was stunned by that surreptitious snip. I have no gay or trans-sexual hangups, yet from then on was always apprehensive about my first post-operation meeting with James/Jan, who I liked enor-mously and greatly admired; we had seen a lot of action together. So, should I shake his hand? Kiss her cheek? Buy him a beer? Offer her cucumber sandwiches?

After some forty years of postcards and occasional phone calls,

Jan and I collided naturally and with glad cries in the crowd outside the Hong Kong Club. 'You haven't changed a bit,' she said, smiling. 'Can't say the same for you,' I said, observing the twinset and pearls.

She was belatedly appointed a CBE in the 1999 Birthday Honours List, so I wrote to offer a throwaway line for use with downcast eyes in any acceptance speech: 'Of course, it's nothing like a Dame . . .'

When I mentioned this nostalgic reunion to David English he instantly set about organizing another foreign correspondents' get-together from among the scribes and old China hands gathered in Hong Kong to watch the Union Jack lowered for the last time. With the consistently excellent Ann Leslie of the *Mail*, Sir Nicholas Lloyd, ex-editor of the *Express*, his wife Eve Pollard, ex-editor of the *Sunday Express*, we sat in the Excelsior restaurant high over the harbour and relived old Fleet Street days until 3 am.

Mourning the disappearance of such camaraderie, we agreed it was of course due to the restructuring of Fleet Street, the transmission speed of television – but above all because most journalists no longer drink. 'They have a sandwich and a mineral in front of their screens,' said David. 'Not much fun and fellowship in *that*.'

Nostalgia and alcoholic intake restored, I returned to London – and walked innocently into the kind of journalism that shames our craft. I had been asked to take *Whicker's World* across to BBC radio. Though a visual series, it worked surprisingly well, thanks to our interviews, and two further series were commissioned. When Jim Moir, Controller of Radio 2, revealed his new schedules I was invited to his press conference, along with Terry Wogan, George Melly and various radio heavies.

As I had also just won a travel writer's award for what with typical understatement they called 'a lifetime of extraordinary achievement in documentary television' the *Mail* requested a longer interview; I set aside time to discuss our series with their reporter. The paper was an old friend, so I was certainly not braced for what used to be called 'a demolition job'.

It was an unusual experience – and one I suppose that must happen to many unsuspecting subjects in these tabloid days. A substitute reporter of a certain age arrived with her own sharp agenda and an air of weary defeat. I was not aware that she had an angle, though I did notice she disliked the pleasant BBC official who had arranged our meeting almost as much as she instantly disapproved of me; Miss Publicity was pretty and – even worse – young, while I was still professionally active.

It soon appeared that this grim reaper had come, not to write about my forty years of television but to put down men, particularly me, and to establish that I was older than she was. Even if true this did not seem of much national import; hard, indeed, to think of anything less interesting. However, when she mentioned she had left her former job reporting for ITN upon reaching her on-camera sell-by date, all became clear.

Since I spend so much of my life interviewing people I always feel obliged to do the best I can for those who, in turn, are assigned to interview me. I talked to her slowly for two hours while she struggled to fill her exercise book with laborious long-hand while keeping up the conversation. It was apparent that only a very rough approximation of what was being said would emerge, if anything. To fill her page she would need to rely upon old cuttings. So it proved.

Her silly piece, heavy with ancient inaccuracies, told us a lot about this sad lady, very little about me, and nothing at all about television. It was hard to fathom how the stumbling individual she patronized in print had actually survived a lifetime in our demanding craft. Just as television can trivialize the world, so we in turn are trivialized.

The one tiresome consequence of her baleful piece was that it would for ever lurk in cuttings' libraries to await resuscitation by any equally pedestrian interviewer without shorthand but with malice; or, even more unfortunate, by well-intentioned writers merely seeking information they assume will be correct. Serial inaccuracies can be preserved indefinitely by culling the cuttings. Indeed a *Mail* columnist who had interviewed me thirty years before as she arrived in Fleet Street – and whose daughter I subsequently tried to help journalistically – instantly used this amateurish piece as a peg on which to resurrect some silly dolly-bird fantasy of the 1960s. With unhappy ladies, no good turn will go unpunished.

I felt like protesting, 'It's only a radio series, Ingrid.' I was not seeking Cabinet office. For the first time I could understand why Dame Diana Rigg refused to be interviewed by the female reporters she called 'grubettes'. She found them dissatisfied, or jealous: 'They are so mean, and abuse you so cynically in print.'

Upon my return home following that sour demolition job I was surprised to find a courteous fax waiting from the *Mail* features department. It asked me to write a thousand words about the current state of television: 'You would recall your early days at the cutting edge of the new TV phenomenon . . . pick your favourite programmes, personalities, television ideas and techniques of previous years compared with the turkeys of today. Many of our readers are increasingly frustrated by the plummeting standards of what used to be the best broadcasting service in the world.'

Well yes, thoughtful points which stimulated many interesting reactions – but wasn't that exactly what their elderly interrogator was supposed to be interviewing me about, for free? That's what I was there for. The piece they commissioned was well paid, but not printed; I assumed it was conscience money.

To retain balance: two sour experiences out of a lifetime of interviews can be shrugged off – though it is always the silly spleen you remember, and the sorrow at being briefly ashamed of our craft.

I was particularly unhappy that it was the *Daily Mail*, since I have for years worked alongside and admired many of their writers. As a youth I travelled with Alex Clifford, their noted war correspondent, and his wife Jenny Nicolson. Ralph Izzard drove me in his open Packard through hostile villages in the Nile delta on our way to cover the Cairo revolution. Don Iddon, who first offered us the brash flavour of New York. Vere, Lord Rothermere – who wished he had been a correspondent and not the boss. The gentle Lachie Macdonald, injured in Korea, who I ran into back in his native New Zealand. G. Ward Price, the Grand Old Man of Fleet Street, at his last battlefront. Noël Monks, from whom Ernest Hemingway stole a wife. Arthur Cook with his terrible Iranian suits and high spirits. Walter Farr in the desert, Vincent Mulchrone in the floods, Jack Starr in Paris, the sprightly David English, who combined power and boyish enthusiasm. Great friends, great men, great memories – and surely not to be corroded by one defeated lady soon to quit journalism and be instantly forgotten.

Even so, it *did* feel rather like being savaged by the old family spaniel.

I first met Richard Hughes, Rabelaisian Australian newspaper-man, when he was Hon Sec of the Tokyo Press Club, harbour of R&R for Korean war correspondents. He was also Chairman of the Far Eastern chapter of the Baker Street Irregulars, and solemnly flew to London with a plaque to place on the Criterion wall in Piccadilly Circus to commemorate the first meeting of Sherlock Holmes and Dr Watson. It was instantly stolen.

Dick was large and Pickwickian – though financially closer to Micawber. Even today when I think of that endearing man, I smile. He had been immortalized as old Craw by John Le Carré in *The Honourable Schoolboy*, as Dikko Henderson by Ian Fleming in James Bond's *You Only Live Twice*, and as Yer Grace by his admiring friends.

He appointed me to the ranks of Hatmen, a foreign corre-spondents' group whose loyalty to each other was such that should news arrive that one of us was in trouble, every member's first reaction would be 'Gimme me hat'. We met when possible in a room at Jimmy's in Hong Kong Central, a regular booking under the club's title: Alcoholics Synonymous.

In true Hatman tradition, Dick dropped everything and flew to London to say kind things on my *This Is Your Life* programme, recalling the time when I was reported – with some exaggeration – shot down in flames in a spotter aircraft on the Korean front. It was Dick I first saw when I entered the Radio Tokyo Press centre, to learn that I was a ghost. 'My God,' he whispered, 'you're *dead*!' This is a conversation-stopper.

To prove it, he showed me the story he had filed detailing the whole grisly incident, supported by the tapes and a (rather short) piece on the front page of the *Daily Mail* which reported the death in action of yet another correspondent. That seemed to settle the matter. I was a statistic – and so young.

In fact the Royal Artillery had that morning put up two Piper Cubs as aerial observation posts over the frontline. I was flying and spotting targets in the one that was *not* shot down. I cabled

ExTel's London office: UNKILLED UNINJURED ONPRESSING. Transmission then cost 1/1½d a word so it seemed, to me at least, that a well-spent forty old pence covered the situation economically.

When the war ended most Far Eastern bureaux moved from Tokyo down to Hong Kong, where it was cheaper to live. The Press Club was in a fine villa on Mid-Levels. It had been the setting for the William Holden film *A Many Splendoured Thing*, written by Han Suyin about her love affair with *The Times* man Ian Morrison, an early fatality in Korea. Dick also worked for *The Times* and *The Economist*, and wrote for the *Far Eastern Economic Review* – or rather, rewrote for them. Its editor, Derek Davies, complained ruefully that although an entertaining and creative columnist Dick had, as he neared retirement, developed a tendency to recreate the same piece.

He was larger than life, funny and jolly right up until his death, which left a void that for me clouds every return to the Far East. At his memorial service at St Bride's, Fleet Street, I sat with Denis Hamilton, then running the *Sunday Times*. After a lifetime of bylines and journalistic significance, Dick had faced retirement still strapped for cash, so Denis arranged a substantial ex gratia payment. Dick instantly gave this to his son, who was playing a piano in the Sydney Press Club. 'Typical,' I said, 'the last generous man.'

'Yes, *but*,' said Denis with exasperation, 'this just meant he and Anne were still hard up, and we were still feeling obligated.'

On that sorrowful day I decided to surrender to a mixture of nostalgia and self-indulgence and devote one of my *Whicker!* talk shows to the campfire conversation of a congenial group of foreign correspondents, before it was too late.

We gathered at my studio in exotic farflung Manchester: Jack Le Vien who, after service with US Army PR in North Africa and Italy, had returned to Pathé in New York as news editor. From the late 1950s, when TV put that cinema newsreel out of business, he produced a series of remarkable television features based on Winston Churchill's memoirs, *The Valiant Years*, followed by *A King's Story* with the Duke and Duchess of Windsor. *The Black Fox*, his account of the rise and fall of Hitler narrated by Marlene Dietrich, won an Academy Award in 1963.

Jean Rook starred in the *Daily Express* in its glory days as 'The First Lady of Fleet Street', though self-styled as 'The Bitch of Fleet Street' and parodied in *Private Eye* as Glenda Slagg. Starting on the *Sheffield Telegraph*, she had married her deputy news editor: 'I never met anyone else – I was on the two-till-ten shift.'

Then there was my good friend Noël Barber, the quintessential foreign correspondent and compulsive writer: 'I did a thousand profitable words this morning, before coming here'. He had reached the South Pole before Hillary and got into Budapest during the revolution of 1956, where he filed his story with two Russian bullets in his head.

He managed to get to a Freedom Fighters' hospital for fifty-two stitches – unfortunately just *after* their anaesthetic had run out. The surgeon had to clamp his wrists to the operating table to stop him jerking about. He fled from that hospital in his pyjamas and finished up in the London Clinic, where his first visitors were the Duke of Windsor and Lord Rothermere.

Noël, half Dane half Yorkshire, had married Titina, a volatile Italian who told him, 'I'm not so sure I really *like* journalists – but I'll marry you because you've got such beautiful blond hair.'

'Two years later,' said Noël, 'it was all shot off in Hungary. She came to terms with it. She didn't much like my travelling, my going away for six months a year, so we did a deal. She said, "If you sleep with any of my friends I'll kill you – but whatever you do east of Suez doesn't count".' He settled for that.

Safely eastern, Noël reported from the Hunza Valley on a man of 118 he met at a christening, where the eighty-nine-year-old father stood around chuckling and looking forty. The rules for longevity, he discovered, included drinking glacial water and the liquid in which the food had been cooked – and of course, eating all that yoghurt. Disease seemed unknown in the serene valley which had never seen cancer, heart attacks or tuberculosis. Children never caught measles or mumps and could not play cops and robbers because they had no idea what cops and robbers *were*. In Lhasa he had to sit, anxious but fascinated, while the Dalai Lama took his wristwatch to pieces . . . and meticulously reassembled it, in a way. It was a leisurely interview.

Noël wrote thirty factual books about his adventures, which all sold modestly. Then he wrote *Tanamera*, a romantic fictional doorstopper around his family home in Singapore. This sold hundreds of thousands. From then on he fictionalized his factual books and pursued a new career as best-selling novelist. On his seventieth birthday I organized a *This Is Your Life* around him, and reintroduced his Budapest surgeon.

In our elegant yet cosy set in Manchester, Noël recalled an intensely personal experience in Antarctica. The communal lavatory at the McMurdo Sound base camp was a long row of open seats like a pew, and unheated – though it was minus 40°F. Sitting there one morning he leaned forward – and was stunned by a searing pain. His penis had frozen to the steel pan.

His alarmed neighbour on the next seat cried, 'Don't move!' and rushed off for hot water, which he poured on the icy mass. Noël was finally released, weeping frozen tears through closed eyes.

We had proof of this improbable story and were able to show viewers a photograph of the warning sign put up afterwards, which would have saved him much personal pain. It read: 'Caution. Use toilet paper to avoid sticking penis to steel part of commode during sub-zero temperature. If this occurs do not attempt to pull away until someone can bring you a can of warm water to pour on it.'

However, like any enterprising correspondent, Noël made constructive use of his near-vasectomy, for the obliging man on the next seat had been the Admiral, the Post Commander – a useful contact who invited him for a medicinal whisky and reassurance, 'Don't worry – you won't be needing it for months, anyway.'

That was cold comfort, but the Admiral then added, 'You think you're in a bad way, but we've got a chap at the South Pole who's in real trouble. He can't eat – he's broken his dental plate and he's losing weight. We've got a team of eighteen there with a doctor, but no dentist – so I have to fly one up tomorrow.' Noël said, 'I'm still in pain – but can I thumb a lift?'

'I got there on Friday 13 November 1957, before Hillary,' Noël continued. 'Then the Antarctic winter arrived, the temperature went to minus 60°F or 70°F. We were supposed to fly back that same day, 826 miles, but the DC3 was a mass of twisted metal within a few hours and we couldn't get out. On one terrible day it was minus 84°F. We were on two solid miles of ice. I was stuck up there for three months.

'Hillary came overland. He'd done a huge double, conquering Everest, then the South Pole. He had already run into Ralph Izzard and James Morris up Everest, so when he arrived on 4 January I went out to greet him and his first words at the Pole were: "Not the fucking *Daily Mail* again!" I was the first Englishman there since Scott, though admittedly I'd taken a different route.'

Jean Rook had just returned from Washington after interviewing President Reagan: 'He was sweet and adorable, but she was absolutely icy, with this amazing redone face and bulletproof hair.'

On the way home her Concorde lost an engine. 'There was a loud crash and all the surrounding businessmen started gulping their whiskies. I really thought we were about to explode – that I was dead. They say your life passes before you, and I did see my son in his school uniform – in colour. I thought, I wish I'd been nicer to my husband. My next thought – and it's dreadful to admit – was, Will my memorial service be in St Paul's or St Bride's? Then I thought: I haven't done my expenses.

'Later the pilot came back and said, "Sorry about that rather sporting vibration. We shall be a quarter of an hour late at Heathrow." I was so pleased I was with the British – I would have hated to die on a French Concorde.'

Jean could understand why even the remaining swashbuckling foreign correspondents were, in the public mind, grouped with other journalists and almost as disliked as MPs and estate agents: 'There's so much digging and spite and abuse today. When I'm working on my column about things that've happened during the week, there's one Sunday newspaper I won't touch. I won't comment on anything in it because I know half of it's phoney – made up. All Fleet Street's going that way.' I was soon to learn how right she was.

Jack Le Vien was a table-hopping socializing and most likeable New Yorker. 'When Pathé News folded,' he said, 'I had just read Churchill's six volumes of war memoirs and thought they'd make a great television series. I went to the three networks and the big production companies in New York but they all said Churchill would never grant an American the television rights, so I set out to prove them wrong. After a year or so of negotiation we finally signed the contract on Onassis's yacht *Christina* in Monte Carlo – marvellous! While he was signing Winston Leonard Spencer Churchill in three places I kept thinking, Why does he give these rights to me? Finally I came out with it. You know what he said? "No one else ever asked me." '

I recalled meeting Churchill when covering the Congress of Europe at The Hague and afterwards the Council of Europe at Strasbourg; as a correspondent I had not found him an easy man to get alongside.

'Maybe he was more mellow as he got older,' said Jack. 'Very sentimental man – certainly had a sense of humour. I took my daughter to Chartwell and at lunch she was sitting between him and Beaverbrook. She was fourteen or fifteen at the time and very pretty. Beaverbrook asked what she was studying at school and, thinking it might please Sir Winston, she said "Political Science". Churchill poked her in the ribs and said, "Why don't you study cooking?" '

On that happy basis Jack went on to corner the market in televised Churchilliana. He made the twenty-six-part series *The Valiant Years*, a film about Churchill's life called *The Finest Hours* and a dramatized version of the first volume with Richard Burton playing Churchill. Then *Churchill and the Generals*, with Timothy West in the role.

On the strength of that record the Duke of Windsor agreed that Jack could film his memoirs. 'He was an enchanting man. She was not *quite* as enchanting, but she was dynamic and devoted all her life and energies to making him feel he was still a king. Like Churchill, he also had a sense of humour and whenever he called he'd say, "Hello, Jack, this is de Dook." Took me a while to realize he was imitating my accent.'

I recalled that the boyish Prince of Wales had charisma at a time when other Royals seemed cardboard cut-outs; he liked ladies and lived an apparently dashing life full of human weakness. Noël Barber agreed. 'During the eight years when I was editing the *Continental Daily Mail* I found him absolutely charming. Very often when she was out we'd have lunch together, then he'd go off and play golf. However, I did find him – for want of a better word – just a little bit *dim*. I think he was led – she was a very aggressive person.'

In the making of *A King's Story*, Jack created an extraordinary situation on film, using the former King to re-enact his Abdication speech which Jack then intercut with the actual recording, so on that *Whicker!* we and the viewers watched a clip of the Duke giving up his Kingdom and Empire in 150 stricken seconds. It was most affecting.

'One of the most emotional moments in my life,' said Jack. 'To have the former King Edward repeating his Abdication speech – the most precious and one of the most poignant speeches of our times – thirty years after the original. We used the actual microphone and the original desk, and shot it in his mill house outside Paris. We cleared most of the technicians out of the room, so there was just the cameraman, the sound man, the Duchess and myself.

'The cameraman was wiping his eyes behind the viewfinder, the Duchess was in tears, the sound man was lifting his earphones to wipe his eyes. The only one who wasn't emotionally shook up seemed to be de Dook.

'When in the editing I listened to the speech we had filmed, it didn't sound much different from the one he had made on the radio thirty years before – the same little fluffs, and so on.

'Both the Duke and Duchess were always very professional about filming. If I said Please be on set tomorrow at nine o'clock, they were there promptly. Very few retakes, believe it or not – though he did have to repeat the Abdication speech eight or nine times. Working with them was like walking in history.'

Our forty television minutes of campfire reminiscence passed like a short happy session in some Press Club bar. Not long afterwards the indestructible Noël Barber died, and so did the sturdy Jean Rook. My friend Jack Le Vien, that golden-tongued charmer, had a fearful stroke which left him in a wheelchair, and speechless. Our last get-together had been only just in time.

Bang – I shot him right between the eyes . . .

I have always been haunted by the bumper-sticker I saw while filming a *Whicker's World* about staying alive in California. Like many of those mobile messages it seemed to offer an unsettling truth: 'If guns are outlawed . . . only outlaws will have guns'.

That chill forecast grew more telling after the mad scattergun massacres in Hungerford, Dunblane, Atlanta, Tasmania, and the anti-Semitic shooting frenzy in Los Angeles. Then, at the Wedgwood Baptist Church in Fort Worth in September 1999, seven youngsters were shot dead and four critically wounded when a man in black, smoking and swearing and reloading two automatic pistols three times, spread gunfire around a prayer service before shooting himself. It was America's twelfth mass bloodletting in nine months. Each time the impact grew less.

Since 1997 the US had seen twenty-one schoolyard killings, with twenty-nine dead and seventy-six injured. Then one morning in the Denver suburb of Littleton, the Columbine High School massacre: another fifteen dead and sixteen wounded. Perhaps the worst aspect was that in all this classroom slaughter, children shot children.

After Dunblane suffered the execution of seventeen pupils and a teacher by a homicidal maniac, handguns were outlawed in Britain and Australia; yet despite universal shock and distress many Americans still saw them as vital personal protection – and that was not just their obsessive gun lobby, the 3.5m members of the National Rifle Association under their President Charlton Heston. Giving people the right to carry concealed weapons, the Hollywood star believes, 'creates a climate of uncertainty for criminals. In a world where the wolves cannot tell the lions from the sheep, the entire flock is safe.' Another of these unhappy but telling maxims.

Lethal weapons were a major ingredient at the Boston Tea Party, and members of the NRA have always upheld that free men bear arms, slaves do not. They seem to forget that the Second Amendment to the Constitution governing the right 'to keep and bear arms' was answering the need for a well regulated militia to defend a newborn nation with muskets – not licensing disturbed children two centuries later to wield machine pistols. A heavily armed anti-government rabble of youthful mass killers, ghetto gangsters or manic survivalists was *not* what the Founding Fathers had in mind.

Also unforeseen: suburban screenagers turning their passing dissatisfactions into lethal performance-art, rich kids prepared to scatter hatred and alienation – and answer any imagined affront with semi-automatic fire from mail order guns.

Yet after studying crime statistics a Chicago law professor, John Lott, discovered that there is an argument for Mr Heston's disturbing mantra: 'More guns means less crime.' In the forty-three States with laws permitting concealed handguns, the murder rate has dropped by eight per cent. Violent crimes against women, normally the easiest victims, fell even more. It seemed that criminals in those States had taken on board the possibility that their victims could be armed and might even, at a push, shoot back. The flock was indeed safer.

So far gun legislation has been minimal, and even that almost ignored. The National Rifle Association want to see the imposition of punitive federal law for firearms offences – and the remaining States joining those permitting concealed weapons. This policy is supported by many experts who believe it would lower crime and help the economy. Sterling Burnett, of the National Centre for Policy Analysis, calculates that the deterrent effect of 'defensive gun use' would confer an annual net benefit on the nation of between $1bn and $39bn, while Professor Lott calculates that if every State permitted citizens to carry a gun, fifteen hundred lives would be saved each year.

These are unpalatable thoughts one does not wish to face, and seem quite mad: you *save* lives by distributing even more lethal weapons around a country already saturated with small-arms and ravaged by violent death?

It has been estimated that there are some 225 million firearms at large in that land. Deduct children and the aged, and every citizen is armed. Fearful householders see the house-gun, the glovebox pistol as some protection against the national epidemic of casual violence – the muggings and drug killings, the aimless drive-by shootings, the gang warfare that inflames cities where an uncertain legal system repeatedly puts dangerous felons back on the streets.

A handgun in the home changes capabilities and attitude; it is the last-ditch defence against the mad prowlers haunting our urban nightmares. 'You almost never need a gun,' a Californian friend told me, 'but when you do, you need it *bad* . . .'

The first wave of gun proliferation in the US started with the arrival of crack cocaine in the 1980s, adding to the irreversible national saturation by lethal weapons. Such an arsenal can never be decommissioned, and leaves many frightened people wondering whether safety may now lie in an alarming extreme: arm *everyone*.

Some argue that individual dignity depends upon a willingness to fight back against crime, to join in the hard-fought police campaign. In an anarchic world of gun law, owning a gun and mastering its use could become a duty of citizenship, and an armed society a safer one.

The belief that God made men but Sam Colt made them equal, the impossibility of banishing the Colts and Lugers and Berettas, the Walthers, Smith & Wessons, Mac-10s and the whole deadly catalogue of Equalizers, has imposed upon America a fearful price. Four assassinated Presidents, for a start.

The millions of handguns in America's bedside tables and gloveboxes make killing – deliberate or accidental – instantly available. Last year 34,040 citizens were killed by firearms, and another 100,000 wounded – indeed more Americans are slaughtered by guns in a week than in the whole of western Europe in a year. So much for their defiant Constitutional Right to bear arms, and the NRA's homely image of the faithful gun.

A sidearm is sold somewhere in the US every few seconds. For many it will offer a sense of escape from despairing, humbling impotence; for others, only fear. Each year a quarter of a million Americans face a threatening weapon; for many thousands of them it is the last moment of their lives.

A change in gun law might delight lawmakers, might even make possession illegal, but it would be much like passing a law to ban the Mafia: legislators could feel a sense of achievement, outlaws would hardly notice.

Though crime has been decreasing in much of America, apprehensive citizens are not convinced that the taut blue line of police can protect them against a fatal future. Having a Nice Day may still be possible but as sirens scream through the dark, Having a Nice Night is something else . . .

So across the United States we see the birth of Enclave Man living within gated and walled communities. These have grown up wherever people feel themselves threatened, mainly by the arrival and concentration of Latino immigrants in southern States like California and Texas, Arizona and Florida.

The get-out-of-town drift began back in the 1970s when many Americans, exhausted by the violence and disintegration of their cities, retreated to the suburbs, usually into the sanctuary of small protected communities created by enterprising builders. In such anxious areas, a third of all new houses are built behind the high walls of guarded estates. Across the land some 30,000 suburban fortresses protect eight million people.

Within them daily life can be regulated and restricted – it is like joining a rather strict club: you must be quiet after 10pm, you must not own a dog weighing more than 20lbs . . . The rules may be irritating but, on the other hand, you and your family do get to keep your possessions, and live.

Such secure developments with private police patrols were once restricted to the rich and famous in the original million- aires' ghettos. In today's drug culture they house the newly threatened middle classes. Within them children's playgrounds are carefree and parents experience the unfamiliar sense of secu- rity and community that comes from living behind twelve-foot iron fences and floodlit bulletproof guardhouses.

A new housing estate selling well in Nevada has at the top of its amenity list, not the usual golf courses, tennis courts and swimming pools – but rifle ranges. A development in the desert sixty miles south-west of Las Vegas is a sort of Disneyland for gun enthusiasts. Ignatius Piazza is spending $25m to build a variation around the familiar golf resort theme. His 'First Sight' across 550 acres of desert will be the world's largest non-military firing range, with its own airstrip and, instead of fairways, '360-degree live fire simulators'. Firearm training on twelve ranges will exceed any police course.

Four months before opening Mr Piazza had already enrolled 3,000 students for his first $2,000 course. They hope to become 'combat masters' with handguns, shotguns, rifles and machine guns. For the less aggressive, he offered a $900 four-day 'defensive handgun' course. Such developers zero-in on Nevada because it is the only State permitting residents to own 'Class 3 weapons' – automatic machine guns.

Another attack weapon becoming available in every State can be made at home and penetrate all residential defences: pipe bombs, like those scattered by student murderers around the anguished Denver schoolyard. They only require such innocent hardware-store items as soap, petrol and propane, and the recipe is on the Internet. Hundreds of books and manuals explain how to mix the ingredients for bombs that are easy to hide and devastatingly powerful: a metal pipe bomb less than a foot long will kill at a range of 400ft, and a stash can be made in an afternoon.

So today's alienated youth-culture can become pariah-culture, with a video-game mentality that deadens all feelings except blame and rage, backed by an Internet which supports murderous fantasies. One website sponsored a national 'Bring-your-gun-to-school' Day, with instructions for making pipe bombs and napalm.

These fatal recipes for home-made death cannot be restricted because of America's First Amendment, which guarantees Freedom of Speech. You are quite free to say and read anything you like, as you die.

Americans now spend $80bn a year on security and $9bn on guns and ammunition. The gardens and gates of the rich bristle with warnings against a threatening world: 'Attack Dogs On Duty', says one. 'Any Unauthorized Person Entering Will Be SHOT'. Whatever happened, I wonder, to those old Welcome mats?

*

In Britain we have always been reassured by the comforting belief that however bad things become here, crime is *far* worse over there among all those gangsters. It is unsettling, then, to face statistics showing that America has cut crime dramatically and now has proportionately less than we do. After seven years of decline, their crime rate is the lowest for twenty-five years. You are more likely to be mugged or robbed in Britain than in the US.

London street robberies reached an all-time high in January 2000, with 4,138 muggings – 1,300 more than the previous year. Some 140 people were being attacked each day. The capital had fewer police than any comparable western city. Fighting cancer of the jaw, elderly John Aspinall also had to fight muggers on his doorstep in Belgravia. For a £500 watch and some jewellery, they smashed him and his wife to the ground. It was just another standard West End mugging, and made the gentle gorillas in his Kentish zoo seem civilized.

The unwise report by Sir William Macpherson on the murder of Stephen Lawrence had handcuffed the Metropolitan Police, who he branded as 'institutionally racist'. His recommendations were one of the consequences of agitation by lawyers who have made careers out of confrontation with the police. The findings clung to one constant: that the police were bound to be in the wrong.

The report offered open-season to professional muggers who instantly took advantage of the inevitable police reaction: a dispirited reluctance to stop and search suspects for fear of being branded racist – and then not being supported by their senior officers. This left the police subdued and defensive, and encouraged the creation of no-go areas in cities and the withdrawal of county forces into urban barracks. Such 'sensitive policing' meant arresting fewer criminals, but more motorists.

Following the Macpherson Report, street crime immediately rose from 2,672 incidents in February 1999 to 3,300 in March – an increase of thirty per cent on the previous year's figures. In Kent it was sixty per cent. This predictably followed a drop of thirty per cent in the number of searches by cowed officers. The police were surrendering the streets.

The British constabulary consoles itself with the knowledge

that policing against serious crime is even less effective in France, where twenty-five Britons have been murdered since 1977. Of these much-publicized crimes their police have solved . . . just two.

We may also take some comfort from the fact that for all this it is still easier to survive in London. A study of murder and manslaughter in twenty-nine cities around the world has London in twenty-fourth place, with just over two homicides per 100,000 population. Washington DC has more than sixty-nine, Philadelphia twenty-seven, Dallas twenty-five, Los Angeles twenty-three and New York seventeen – despite zero-tolerance and rediscovered security.

There were 681 homicides in England and Wales during 1996 – though only eight per cent of those victims were shot. For perspective, 3,421 were killed on our roads in 1998 and 5,000 died from hospital-acquired diseases. Despite amnesties and new laws, armed British police were called to 12,000 gun incidents in 1997. Police calculate that hundreds of thousands of handguns are still circulating, most in the hands of criminals, or as cherished war souvenirs.

Since 1979 our crime rate has doubled and is going up far faster than in the US – a vindication of tough American zero-tolerance policing and an indication that we need to re-examine whatever cosy assumptions we have left about law and order. During 1995 more than six per cent of us were burgled – in the US, fewer than five per cent. Some three per cent of British car owners had their vehicles stolen; in the US – two per cent.

One explanation: American police forces have been reorganized and stimulated, their computerized intelligence sharpened. In the last ten years, in a massive effort to take criminals off the streets, their prison population has more than doubled, to 1,800,000 – or one in every 150 citizens. At that rate of increase, an American born this year has a one in twenty chance of going to jail; if black, one in three.

For the first time in many years New Yorkers now tell visitors it is safe to go shopping in Manhattan after dark. In 1990 there were 2,262 murders in their city; in 1998 'only' 629. So homicides are back to 1946 figures and celebrations are called for – though not, sadly, in 629 homes.

Success against crime has brought a predictable rise in complaints about the police, mainly because 'stop-and-frisk' – the US version of our old 'sus' law – is extremely unpopular with minorities. The NYPD admits that they may be disproportionately inspected in the streets, mainly because minorities are disproportionately involved in crime, and stop-and-frisk is a vital part of the Street Crimes Unit's successful anti-guns campaign.

An exasperated Police Commissioner Howard Safir asked those complaining of police severity at a public inquiry: 'How many murders will you find acceptable?' He admitted that his 40,000 men often failed to treat the public with sufficient respect. 'The NYPD's problem is not brutality, it is civility,' he said. They have a hard lesson to learn. Like most New Yorkers, policemen are rarely civil – even to each other.

American homicide rates remain far ahead of ours – for which the ever-present gun can take the discredit. This obsession provides the most blunt form of self-expression for those who would feel undressed without a sidearm – which is used in seven out of every ten murders. Always glorified as part of American mythology, the gun still stands for pioneering independence, rugged masculinity and the Sundance Kid. Not too long ago it was vital for survival. Sometimes it still is.

In the American race-memory of personal justice, notions of patriotism, self-image and guns interlock. Over an apocalyptic TV commercial for a pistol a resonant voice intones, 'Wrap your hand around history! There's only one Declaration of Independence, one Constitution, one Bill of Rights – and there's only one Colt . . .' Sadly that is not true; there are millions.

Yet in many public places in America it is now more acceptable to carry a concealed weapon than to smoke a cigarette. Smokers have become social pariahs, while no one seems upset if you are strapped (armed) and they catch a glimpse of your holster.

A popular item I was offered in one obliging LA gunshop was the Kalashnikov, which can fire 600 rounds a minute, effective up to 300 metres. Some seventy-five million AK-47s have been sold worldwide since 1947 for they are cheap, sturdy and simple to use – drug dealers, crime rings and the Mafia speak highly of them. It is hard to think of a legitimate civilian use for this malignant Weapon of Choice.

There was then a five-day waiting period at that gun shop to ensure that no buyer had a criminal record. A stern measure of control suggested by a governor of Virginia – afterwards adopted by a tiny majority in California – was that people should be allowed to buy only one handgun a month . . .

President Clinton had that idea, too. His modest attempt to restrict Americans' access to weapons of personal destruction was scorned by Charlton Heston, whose policies were less confused: 'When bartenders are responsible for drunk drivers' acts and gunmakers are responsible for criminals' acts . . . yet nobody is responsible for O.J. Simpson's acts – then something is wrong.' The old actor awakened longings for a better, simpler nation – that durable dream of America's idyllic Wild West past and Big Country present, with a leavening of Dirty Harry crusading through mean streets.

At the end of 1998 a new FBI data processing centre in West Virginia came on-stream, which permitted weapons to be purchased instantly, provided the buyer had no history of violence or mental illness. Anyone with a grudge could pause in the middle of a quarrel, pop into his local gunshop, pick up the week's Best Buy – and settle the argument there and then.

The Denver high school rampage stunned Americans, for the gunmen were not the usual suspects – black teenage junkies from broken ghetto homes – but white middle-class youths from comfortable two-parent mansions. Who to blame?

I had first become aware of the American attitude to lethal weapons back in the innocent 1960s while filming a *Whicker's World* in Texas. For a vox pop I stopped passers-by at random in downtown Houston to ask whether by any chance they had a gun? Every person I spoke to had one – even a couple of nuns, who told me they always carried a revolver in the Convent car. A newspaper-seller had a dozen.

I was appalled, and bemused. I then believed that guns were for soldiers, yet in the middle of rich, urban, sophisticated Houston found myself back on the Wild Frontier trying to cope with the Texan belief that to take away a man's pistol was to emasculate him.

A few days later, up in Dallas, President Kennedy was assassinated.

*

While in Houston I had become friendly with the city coroner, who was also an outsider: he had arrived from New England, where they had a less enthusiastic attitude towards guns – a more British attitude, you might say. Fresh from the cold sedate towns of New Hampshire, this new arrival told his Texan colleagues that he neither liked nor understood guns, and would not carry one. The people in City Hall thought he was *very* odd.

On his first holiday he set out to explore the vast emptiness of southern Texas with his wife and young daughter. They stopped to picnic in the middle of a wide prairie miles from anywhere and sat quietly relishing the space, the silence. As they ate they saw in the distance the dust of a lone car coming towards them through the haze – the first car they had seen all day.

It approached and passed, trailing its cloud of dust – a couple of young roughnecks in an old utility. They waved, and carried on with their lunch as the silence descended again, but when my friend glanced down the road after the dust cloud he saw that in the distance ... the car had slowed. Then it began to turn around. As he watched, it started back towards them.

With sudden instinctive fear he leapt up, pushed his wife and daughter into their car – and they hit the road, flat out, just as the utility reached them. They accelerated away and he saw in his mirror that one of the punks was angrily waving a gun. They outran the utility across that empty prairie – and kept going.

Back in Houston he went straight to a gunshop, and from then on always carried his revolver. He was never defenceless again. 'In that isolation we'd have been at their mercy,' he told me, shaking his head. 'They could have done whatever they wanted. How could I have protected my daughter or my wife against that armed trash?'

Today Texas has 470 gun shows each year; an estimated seventy million guns are in circulation – four for every man, woman and child.

In the National Guard Armoury at Glendale, one of LA's endless suburbs, I watched a chattering group of actresses and house-wives, nurses, law students and stewardesses uneasily handling revolvers for the first time in their lives. They were starting on a twelve-week course learning, not just to shoot, but to *kill.* That was the operative word the instructor kept impressing upon these frightened people.

Most of them had been robbed, or raped. A matter-of-fact stewardess told me, 'I don't appreciate having myself, my home, violated. I don't appreciate it one little bit. This guy with a gun busted in at three in the morning – and he wasn't there to say hello.'

The class filed into the armoury's shooting range, timidly holding newly acquired smallarms. They seemed like reasonable people, in an unreasonable world. Their instructor, a large aggressive man with an incipient paunch easing over his gunbelt, was a hospital carpenter and expert shot: Alex Goodrich was President of the Californian Marksmen. His wife Jackie was also instructing; she had once been raped. 'Quite viciously, as a matter of fact,' he said. 'That helps me when I teach women who've also been raped – there's a kind of empathy. Not that I can comprehend rape – no man can – but I think I have a better insight.'

With his uncertain students, he laid it on the line: 'You have all kinds of ideas I have to overcome – in the first place, you're not killers. I'm going to teach you vicious dirty shooting. That could involve killing a human being, OK? Unfortunately we have to prepare you for that. If you have to use a handgun, you use it to the maximum. You're going to blow this guy's head off.

'Do you have any idea what that's like? You've got a man coming toward you . . . *boom* . . . he's got a big hole in him and blood spurting out three feet in front of him all over you, and he's got pure hate in his eyes and he knows he's dying and he's still coming at you. *Boom* – you've got to shoot him again. OK, he's still coming. If you miss you're gonna die, it's that simple.'

Ammunition was issued, and they prepared to shoot at menacing black silhouette-targets. 'Ready . . . point, fire! Point, fire! Point, fire! Point, fire! Point, fire! OK people, fingers off the trigger. We have a kill, good, we have a wound but that's not going to kill him, it's going to rearrange his stomach but that's all. Very poor technique – I taught you to concentrate on the chest.

'Remember, people, you are *not* target shooting, you're combat shooting. All you've got to do is get a bullet into the man's chest. You've got to kill him. Ready, *go!* Take your time. OK, you jerked your trigger a little bit. Squeeze it. OK people, you've got to blow some sucker's chest out. Ready, *go!* . . .'

One of his class, a clergyman's son in his twenties, was about to be ordained into the United Community Church. He was thin and pale and earnest and, after he had put on his safety catch, I asked whether as a putative minister he could envisage blowing some sucker's chest out? He was quite certain that he could – if the man was trying to kill *him.*

'In the Book of Luke, Jesus Christ told his disciples "Go and get your swords", so there *is* a point where you don't turn your cheek. You just have to find the right balance. The crime rate is going up and up. Murder, rape, robbery – there's coming a time when it's going to get out of hand. People do not respect police officers any more, and they don't rely on the courts. They feel they have to take the law into their own hands. There's coming a time when we will resort back to the way of every man doing that which is right in his own eyes.

'In a situation where death could occur I would rather hurt than maim, maim rather than kill, and kill rather than be killed. When I read that some young lady's been raped it just turns my stomach. The courts are too lenient with these people. I feel they should be taken out and killed. A rapist if he's caught, take him to trial immediately and get it over with.'

'You're certainly the Church militant,' I said. 'Are you not a rather bloodthirsty Christian?'

'I have no desire to kill, I love people, that's why I'm going into the ministry. I love someone who does me wrong. I can forgive – but there comes a point when I can't see my own life being sacrificed. I'm not going out to walk the streets hoping for an encounter, not at all, but if the need arises I want to be prepared.'

Alex Goodrich also referred to the Almighty. 'With a gun in your hand, you're God. It's an awesome responsibility. I employ a little drama when I'm teaching, but afterwards everyone out there with a handgun is God, because you can take anyone's life if you choose to.' He constantly reminded his students that it was not wrong to fight back. 'You don't need to apologize for protecting your own life.'

The anaesthetist and his wife in the class were both middle-aged and mild. 'I was putting some things in the trunk of my car after making rounds at the hospital when a fellow – about nineteen years and dressed in dark clothes – this young guy came up to me without saying a word, put a gun in my chest and shot me, right before my wife and a friend.

'The bullet went in the downward direction through my chest and right diaphragm, liver, duodenal, right kidney, right renal artery and the vena cava. I had such low blood pressure they could only do the surgery under very light anaesthesia, so I was awake for about an hour of this four-hour operation. I could feel the incision being made. I lost my kidney and required twenty units of blood, and another ten later that night. It took months of recovery. This type of injury reduces one to an animal. You exist from bed to chair to sofa.'

On that awful night his wife had no means of defence against the young thug – evidently a junkie looking for drugs. She jumped into their car and frantically sounded the horn while her husband lay dying. Had they not been outside his hospital, she was sure he would have bled to death.

'If I'd had a gun at that time, even without any experience I probably could have killed the guy, or at least shot him. Now we just want to be able to protect ourselves and our family. We don't wish to be caught again. I was avidly against guns – I've never allowed one in the house. I feel differently now, though it's taking me a lot of guts to come here.'

Another doctor in the class offered a new and disturbing thought: 'Police forces are set-up for a civilized civilization. They can't protect you in one that's coming apart. It's not realistic to expect them to be able to do so.

'The criminal never has trouble getting weapons if he needs them, so it doesn't bother me that people who want to protect themselves can also get them readily. I'd rather have someone who knows how to use a gun than just have it at home in their dresser drawer, so kids pick it up. It's like starting to drive – you need lessons.

'As doctors we're called out at odd hours in the dark and we're obvious targets, with the drugs we carry. They're looking for us – they know where we park. I've never talked about this with other doctors but I believe that more and more they will quietly do things to protect themselves. It is either that, or refuse calls – which is unthinkable.'

His wife said: 'I'm starting to believe *any* human being could kill another, given enough persuasion. Even if I were threatened I don't know that I could do it, but if my children were threatened, by God I could do it *now*.'

A nurse recalled the night she and a friend had just left a laundrette to drive home. A man followed and exposed himself against the car window. She pulled out her loaded gun and pointed it at the flasher's closest point. He lost his ardour quite quickly. When arrested later he complained, reproachfully, that it was the first time he had ever had a gun pointed at him. 'He was married, he had two children,' she said. 'He had priors – he'd been arrested before, for this.' The prospect of an instant vasectomy had acted as instant therapy.

'By learning to shoot we're taking responsibility for our own lives, and you feel more confident having this class behind you. If you take aim, you're not just going to stop them or maim them – you kill them. That sounds vicious, but they're going to do it to you, if they get the chance. You're not going to ask them, "Are you going to kill me, or just hurt me, or tie me up, or just rape me and then let me go?" So if you have the drop on them, you kill them. Shooting somebody – it's called survival.'

While all these earnest doctors and nurses, students, secretaries, stewardesses and airport staff were being urged to kill, if necessary, I asked Jackie Goodrich whether there was anyone she and her husband would not teach? 'When we started this class I thought we were going to attract a weird sort, you know, and perhaps some waitresses who work until three in the morning, and mothers living alone with kids, but actually we're getting more professional girls. We really haven't had to ask many people to leave.

'OK, we had one woman who was a schoolteacher and she'd been attacked three times by the same guy in the same parking lot. Now she was going to get him, she just wanted to know how to do it, you know. There was no talking her out of it. I wasn't going to be responsible for that. Then we had another girl who was definitely on drugs. I wouldn't even put a gun in her hand. Another couple were heavy drinkers, and Alex and I just don't think shooting and drinking mix. It's too serious a sport. People lose sight of that. It's fun.'

Alex saw no future armistice in the national street war. 'If you're going to be robbed or raped, it'll probably be by some guy between sixteen and twenty-three, and it's a sixty-five per cent chance he'll be black or Latino. You have a million illegals coming across the border into California every year – they see all the goodies, they want some, they try to take them.

'We have 260 million people, we have about 200 million guns. We're not getting rid of them. Congress can pass any law they want. Prohibition, we didn't stop drinking. Confiscate handguns, we won't give them up. We're fed up, we've had it, we're not going to take crime any more, we're going to protect ourselves.'

Out in the mean streets again I went to see Carol and Russell O'Rea who ran that most popular target for armed hoodlums and junkies hunting for cash: a liquor store. Theirs was distinctive because of all the bullet holes around its walls.

They were in their sixties, he heavy and lugubrious, she a smiling bespectacled little old lady – but it seems that, in California, little old ladies can take care of themselves: 'This fellow, a white fellow, came in one night. Nobody around, just me and him. I was kind of jittery. He says, "I want a pack of Camels," and when I went to pick them up he had a 9mm German Luger automatic . . . I tell you, I just froze.

'He says, "Get down on the floor." He was such a mean-looking thing. I got down, and under the counter we had a 38/40, you know, one of those large old-fashioned guns, and I thought, Gee, this has to be, I've got to do something, it's him or me . . . So I put my finger in the trigger and – *bang*, I shot him right between the eyes.

'Still there's nobody around, nobody heard me, so I thought, Oh heck, I'll take another chance and shoot him – so I shot him in the neck, and down he went. I went around, I wanted to get a towel to wipe his face because he was bleeding so bad. He'd only taken $39, so I went to search his pockets to get the $39 back.

'I couldn't find it, but I saw his neck moving, so I ran outside and shot in the air, thinking maybe someone might say, "Look at that crazy person," and come over. Nothing. So I dial the operator. I says, You'd better call the police, I says, because I think I killed somebody. "Hold on," she says, and before I knew it I had seven cop cars and television and everything here. He was on the floor, but he was already dead.

'So I says, Listen, I says, take that money out of his pocket, he's got my $39 . . . and it was bloody. I put it in the cash register, and they took him away. I had dum-dum bullets, you know, they enter the skull and fly into hundreds of pieces, just pulverize the brain.'

So you didn't really need that second shot?

'No I didn't, I just wanted to see how it feels . . .'

Was it the first time you'd killed anybody?

'There's been a few more – about four – but I shoot twice, that's all I shoot. Third time I don't shoot. If I can't get them in those two, I quit . . .'

I went up in Hollywood's social world to see Juliet Mills, most English of stars. This daughter of Sir John was living in typical Beverly Hills style in a fine mansion high in the Hills guarded by a couple of Alsatians and – most emphatically – by her then husband Michael Miklenda, from Czechoslovakia. A keen gun enthusiast and collector, he always carried a handgun in his shoulder holster – even, he told me, under his dinner jacket. He opened a display case of guns: it was like Tiffany's. When he went away, he said, he stored the best in his bank vault, and booby-trapped the rest.

'All our close friends – I'd say about seventy-five per cent of them – have a gun and know how to use it,' said Juliet. 'Especially any woman who lives alone – she'd be crazy not to protect herself. I certainly would.'

Yet today such law-abiding householders not only face the danger of being robbed, raped or murdered by intruders, but of being sued. Juliet recalled a mutual friend who one night found an armed man inside her home. She had been taught to use her bedside gun, so before he could shoot, she beat him to the draw in real High Noon style and, as he ran away, shot him. He was wounded, but still escaped.

As he was then in her garden, not inside her home, this armed punk with a long police record was taking her to court, and she will surely be punished for defending herself against whatever it was he wanted to do. The police reminded her that three-quarters of an intruder's body had to be within her house when he was shot, to make it legal.

In his slight middle-European accent Michael recalled another way of handling the problem. 'Here in Beverly Hills, just nearby, there was a man who was burgled. He caught the burglar and had him with his hands up against the wall. He got a telephone and held his gun over the burglar while he dialled the police. The burglar said, "What are you doing?" He said, "I'm calling the cops, and they'll come and get you." The guy was laughing. He said, "You do that, you just do that. I'll get about six months. Then I'll come back – and I'll *kill* you."

'That made him think twice. He could see that every night when he came home to his wife and kids he was going to worry whether this guy was out there behind some bush in the garden. This year, next year – there'd always be that threat hanging over his family . . .

'Then as the phone was ringing for the police, he put it down, clicked the gun – and shot the guy, shot him dead. The police came and took him away. That was that. End of story.'

So as Britons surrender their guns, Americans buy more and are taught to fire first and stay alive afterwards – even if it means appearing in court. 'Better be judged by twelve,' says another bumper sticker, 'than carried out by six.'

Never thought of an airliner
as home before . . .

Moving around the world is so easy these days that some professional travellers find the need to create hardships, just to make their expeditions interesting: all those daredevil explorers and writers telling us what a tough time they're having – even a few gallant television men pushing on through White Men's Graves protected only by a production team with air-conditioned 4x4s.

You know how it goes: Around the World in 80 Days and total panic – but no flying, no reservations, no reason. Across the Sahara – walking backwards. Up Everest – by bicycle. North Pole to South Pole – blindfolded, of course. Every fearless adventurer struggling up the Amazon without a paddle – but with a camera crew – is boldly overcoming insurmountable obstacles he has painstakingly created for himself.

Once upon a time I also set off to go around the world in thirty-four days, but the object of that exercise – as any right-minded traveller will appreciate – was not to do it anxiously, the hard way, but to enjoy its Wonders as comfortably as possible. No silly self-imposed suffering, just nice 'n' easy – and let's face it, so it should have been with fares of £37,000 per couple, or more than £1,000 a day. That's £1 a mile to you, guv – right round.

It was the first time such a project had been attempted, and I was a natural for the expedition. I've been set in my airways ever since my first flight from Italy to Sicily during the war, travelling flat on my back in a DC3 air ambulance. When I began wandering *Whicker's World* out of uniform it took three days to reach

Tokyo in an Argonaut at a steady 250 mph, and another couple of days to get your hearing back. Travel has grown rather more agreeable since then – at least for the fortunates up front.

My first and Ultimate Package tour resulted in four programmes under that subtitle, and was a remarkable expedition. One television critic wrote: 'Watch this – you'll never see anything like it again.'

We flew around the world's Wonders in one mighty bound without pausing, hesitating or repeating ourselves. In a way we were blazing a trail through the skies, for in the future other great air tours may be attempted as each exotic destination in turn becomes familiar, and travel companies search for new stylish holidays.

Future international travellers will probably descend upon Easter Island as we did on this tour, for travel must always extend, always go beyond the next horizon. Spurred by the world's largest industry which employs 130m, we holidaymakers have through the years worked our way from Benidorm to Mykonos to Hong Kong and on to Bali. Because of the space programme, Easter Island – a grim and isolated South Pacific speck with 2,300 lonely inhabitants – already has a runway that can take Concordes. Not for much longer will islanders escape the soft seduction of descending travellers' cheques.

All travel fascinates: each serious lottery win, every sudden windfall is celebrated by a new car, a new home – then off around the world! With an eye to this rich market Thomas Cook celebrated its 150th anniversary by selling thirty-four days in a private airliner – after which you would not need to travel again, ever. Sated, you would have seen everything the world has to offer. Been there. Done that. You could then get on with your life, while staying comfortably ahead of the neighbours.

After a lifetime as a solitary traveller I found it a beguiling project: to experience edited highlights of the world without pain. No struggling with ticket desks and taxis, with Customs and hotel receptions, no anxiety about connections or reservations, no wondering which restaurant to use or which sight to see. There would be people to do the worrying as I settled back, while they moved the scenery and proffered frosty champagne flutes.

Set against that was the fact that I would be travelling round the world for thirty-four days, caged in with eighty-seven inescapable strangers.

Our itinerary – a fat Filofax full of the future – contained 170 pages of leather-bound instruction and guidance. It told us exactly what we would be doing for the next five weeks: when to get up, where to eat, what to look at, when to go to bed. It reminded me of the Army, and being told the day and time to change my boots and get my hair cut. This schedule was equally regimented but more softly spoken, full of kindly guidance and encouragement. It avoided my favourite package tour instruction, known to every hotel lobby noticeboard: 'Bags out of rooms at 6.30 am'.

We've heard of the Ship of Fools – ours could have been the TriStar of Fools; eighty-seven ill-assorted people paid £21,500 each to catch that magic carpet through five continents to Venice, the Pyramids and the tombs of the Pharaohs, to see the Taj Mahal and China's terracotta warriors, to walk the Great Wall, climb Ayers Rock, attend Sydney Opera, take a chopper over Tahiti, gaze at Easter Island's massive heads and the Falls of Iguazu, at Copacabana beach and the lights of Broadway . . . Think of a Wonder – and there it would be.

We travel in a *belle-époque* wagon-lit, a gondola, a felucca, a junk, a helicopter, a cable car – all linked by our armchair in the skies. Along the way we'll be entertained by Egyptian belly dancers, Indian musicians, Chinese acrobats, Australian didgeridoos, Polynesian hula girls, Brazilian strippers – and, for starters, the Band of the Grenadier Guards.

You might think an expedition costing each couple around £40,000, basic, would attract only run-of-the-millionaires. In fact some of us needed a bank loan to cover the fare. We had a harbour mistress, a retired mortician, a surgeon celebrating forty years in the operating theatre, a dealer in old watches and a breeder of shire horses. There were some successful and a few less successful property men, various widows and divorcees at a loose end. One or two of us were over eighty, another was nineteen; the average age was fifty-seven. A few were on their first and others on probably their last great adventure.

Most of us were British, of course, hoping to blend in with Catalans and Venezuelans, Swiss and Irish, Americans, Danes and

Dutch, a Monegasque, South African, Viennese – eighty-seven international strangers all paying highly to be carried through the skies in a new travel pattern.

All holidays are about fantasy – travel agents are selling dreams; but if you have just spent a fortune on a once-in-a-lifetime airborne experience, will you get what you think you've paid for? Can you be sure you'll enjoy yourself? That £40,000 could of course buy you a small apartment in Florida or Spain. You could drive off in one of the cheaper Jaguars, splurge the lot on three days' fishing for one rod on Scotland's River Beauly, or bid for a couple of bottles of Château Lafite – 1806, of course. We spend our pocket money in our own ways, and our reasons for travel range from self-improvement to sexual adventure.

The man who started the conquering craze for organized travel was a printer in Market Harborough. On his first excursion in 1841 he took 570 people eleven miles by train from Leicester to Loughborough and charged them a shilling each. For their bob they also got tea, speeches and a brass band – so at least the entertainment hasn't changed much.

His tours were intended for the workers – and teetotallers at that – but over the years Thomas Cook's passenger list grew into a sort of Victorian *Who's Who*: Queen Victoria herself, Gladstone, the Archbishop of Canterbury, Rudyard Kipling, Mahatma Gandhi, Winston Churchill, the Kaiser . . . It became smart to be packaged.

Just over a century ago he conducted ten passengers on his first round-the-world expedition, which cost 210 guineas. During those 220 days they faced prairie fires, wolves and Red Indians, but were far more afraid of social contamination: why, a chap might even meet his *tailor*.

Having taken that risk, one passenger – the Chief Justice of Hong Kong – set the romantic holiday tone by falling in love and marrying another traveller. Such behaviour, I'm told, still goes on.

Then Jules Verne picked up the idea, and going round the world became the Done Thing. A distinguished American who moved around in his own railway carriage, the late Lucius Beebe, once said, 'How you travel is who you *are*.'

We were seriously stylish, surely, with a great 320-seater airliner waiting at every airport, engines running and champagne chilled. It was like whistling up one's Bentley: when you were good and ready you strolled aboard and sank back into your favourite armchair in a friendly and familiar setting where you knew the staff by name, ordered whatever you wanted, and no money changed hands. It was home.

Even the smallest room became enticing, and sometimes visited eagerly when eating more meals than usual – and more unusual meals. I had hitherto never found tiny angular aircraft loos at all inviting, but in some places around the world ours became a luxurious target, a clean and fragrant haven quite unlike everything available – ugh – on the ground.

Day One of our extraordinary marathon began as we gathered rather apprehensively in a Piccadilly hotel for what they called the Gala Ball. It was really our First Date. We were getting to know each other.

We had already met the staff. They had just flown our TriStar over from California. There were eighteen in all – which seemed adequate for eighty-seven passengers. The Captain was a tall, lean Texan who had been flying with Braniff, and in the Gulf. In addition to the normal complement we had the unusual luxury of a sort of chef and a baggage master – neither of whom earned his keep.

Since we had to reach out-of-the-way airports like Abu Simbel and Xian, Easter Island and Iguazu, the navigator needed to know his charts. They came up to our London hotel from Gatwick, but got lost on the way. This did not inspire confidence.

That first night was the honeymoon stage, while Grenadiers played. Passengers were charged an additional £95 a head for the guests they had invited to see them off – and still had to buy their own drinks. This was something of a shock, after signing those £37,000 cheques. The Meridien charged only £29 a head, so Thomas Cook was already winning.

Next day was for real. Like all proper journeys our air cruise started at Victoria Station, where the Orient Express waited to sweep us down to Venice in carriages with mosaic floors in their loos. While one solitary disgruntled Sunday-morning porter struggled to handle 400 pieces of colour-coded luggage, I did my first piece to camera, walking the platform alongside the Pullmans and setting the scene for the four *Whicker's World*s to come. Took me five minutes just to give viewers the headlines. There was so much to say I almost ran out of train.

Waiting to board, sables and golden shoes stood on the platform amid worn tweeds and trainers. It felt like the first day at school. I studied the faces anxiously, wondering which would be the friends, the bores, the bullies, the ones who activate and the ones who're always late. It was hard to spot the life and soul of our coming party, the whingers or the wallflowers. We now had thirty-four days to find out more than we wished to know about each other.

Once in the Pullmans and rolling I set about meeting them all, for filming had started and there were four documentaries to make. A thirty-two-year-old Austrian stockbroker was about to cancel the whole holiday because he had discovered there was no satellite phone in the plane – and probably no phone at *all* on Easter Island; without twenty-four-hour communication he would be losing money. Josephine, a bubbly blonde widow from Highgate, was quite ready to meet her third husband but had so far failed to locate any promising talent; a heavy investment was in jeopardy. A retired couple with a combined record of seventy-nine years' work for the Isle of Wight Electricity Board were spending their savings on the journey of a lifetime. Two American women who, never having met, had agreed through their travel agent to save the £2,500 single supplement by sharing accommodation, discovered instantly how much they disliked each other – and faced five weeks of intimacy.

The expedition had taken two years to plan, while the project manager had been trying to sell Cook's most expensive holiday ever during the months following the Gulf War and a recession. Her international clients were predictably proving hard to handle: Josephine had called endlessly to discover in which countries her Carmen rollers might work and those in which, shock horror, they might not. To get her off the phone they sent to America and bought her a multi-voltage set. Others, elaborately casual, called in wondering how many single men would be travelling? If the number of available men proved fewer than first reported, I wondered, might they get their fares back? No.

Having served its usual excellent lunch, our Pullman train

came to an abrupt halt near Tonbridge. We waited, for hours. Everybody of course discussed the possibility of a Murder on the Orient Express, and the usual suspects were offering themselves for questioning. Then we heard this was not murder – but suicide. Someone had thrown himself from a bridge on to the line.

Some poor fellow, wretched within private agonies, had halted the ecstatic expectations of a trainful of fortunate people intent upon pleasure. His unromantic death sent a chill through veneered corridors that had been full of laughter and excitement.

We arrived at Folkestone four hours late. Our Boulogne ferry had left, and lowering grey skies brought a considerable gale. We finally lurched off towards France through a raging sea, eyes closed and clinging on. Most people became violently sick. Of a hundred or so in our jolly party, only a dozen remained standing. One passenger had a bad fall. An elderly woman was so distressed she could not remember who or where she was, and called for her mother. Waitresses became nurses and stripped off their jackets to keep passengers warm. The Harley Street doctor travelling around the world with us earned his ticket before he had found a seat.

The lounge looked like a battlefield. The pictures would have provided a most unusual opening for my series – except that the whitest and sickest of all the passengers was my cameraman. This was not in the script. He was unequal to standing up, let alone recording the event. The sound man was all right, just, but there seemed little point in recording groans, or worse.

We had boarded with two wheelchairs but at Boulogne needed eight to get everyone into the gleaming blue carriages which waited to waft us down to Venice.

The joy of the Orient Express is mainly in anticipation: it is not a journey, but an event. In the right company it stimulates a superb atmosphere, an exotic clamour in the piano bar, a deliciously decorative dinner, a buzz of expectation along mysterious corridors.

This time *mal de mer* removed sensual anticipation as shaky world travellers were shoehorned into their tiny compartments, each with two berths and no lavatory. I have travelled aboard the

Orient Express many times, always with enormous pleasure; but not even James Bond or Liza Minelli could make a discreet rendezvous in one of those berths seem exciting. For me the only mystery is how the train won its reputation for illicit passion; easier to make love in the back of a Mini. This time, no muffled laughter came from the next compartment.

Sometimes it was not heavy breathing you heard, but short sharp screams: travelling with us on a previous journey to Venice was George Barrie, then head of Fabergé, with his latest wife. During the night, making a move towards the loo at the end of the corridor, he forgot he was in a top berth and crashed to the floor, breaking his nose. Such a violent landing can have an unsettling effect upon any enchanted evening.

Our train rocked and rolled us to sleep; we awoke alongside Lake Constance. The only drama of the night had been gales, which meant trees instead of bodies on the line, and more delay; but we had not finished dinner until 2 am and from then on were securely horizontal.

Our itinerary expected us to arrive in Venice as the sun was setting across the lagoon. In fact it was midnight as the train crawled into Santa Lucia. A large boat took us aboard and set off, not down the Grand Canal which is such a glorious introduction to Venice, but along the Canale Guideca and past ocean-going steamers and derricks and the paraphernalia of the port.

At the Hotel Danieli we awaited our luggage, hoping to unpack and avoid tears before bedtime. It did not arrive. Venetian station porters, furious when a train bringing 400 suitcases arrived five hours late, had walked out on strike. This was tiresome, and our impatient eighty-seven exploded into the lobby: was this the way life was going to be for five weeks? There was some shouting; one eighty-year-old in a dressing-gown leapt from his wheelchair to remonstrate with the tour managers; still no suitcases. And so to bed.

That Venetian scene gave Simon Laxton, General Manager of Thomas Cook Holidays, the first of his many Bad Luggage Days. Because he was chartering an enormous Jumbo which was carrying only a third of its normal load and no freight, the Thomas Cook brochures had rashly hinted that this air cruise was a return to the good old days of wardrobe trunks: passengers could carry as much as they needed to cope with temperatures around the world, with shooting rapids and the Maharaja's Ball. It was like an ocean liner: bring what you want, and stack it in the hold. One woman brought ten cases – even some stewardesses had five.

Simon Laxton grew to regret this deeply: 'They just can't handle us,' he said wearily. 'Nobody even knows what 400 cases *look* like – and when they see, they give up. Can't wait to get to the Third World.'

When we came down next morning the luggage had arrived, somehow. We hired a gondola and went into the canals to film the to-camera diary which I was to do every day during the tour. This was a new style for me. Viewers normally see my best side: the back of my head. Now, rather to my surprise, I found myself lounging back among cushions as the glory that is Venice drifted by and confidentially recalling my happiest days – the sort of ruminative personal revelation with which I had never presumed to burden viewers.

It was not difficult to talk about a city where I lived for a year when editing the 8th Army newspaper, *Union Jack.* Anyone who resides in Venice instantly becomes bonded, to feel forever proprietorial: 'Who are these people littering my piazza?' In 1946 the soldiers had gone, the tourists had not yet returned; it was like living in an elegant medieval club and socializing over a negroni at the Florian or the Quadri, nodding to other members as Venetian life drifted through the Piazza San Marco.

I recalled being measured for my first post-war suit, my first silk shirts. More significant, opening my first account at Harry's Bar, then little known, with the late Harry Cipriani watchful behind the cash desk. Ernest Hemingway would arrive later, and make it famous. Having an account meant you suffered only one stunning blow rather than a series of unsettling shocks, and I felt most worldly strolling out through the swing doors without the vulgar necessity of handling money.

Even in those days, as I took contessas in my launch to Torcello for lunch or to the opera at La Fenice, I was aware that life was about as good as it was ever going to be. So it proved. I doubt whether Venice has ever been as lovely or as happy as it was in that post-war summer when it was an enchantment just to be alive.

So there I was in a gondola again, remembering when every day was springtime. Now, of course, every day is autumn – and not even nostalgia is as good as it used to be.

I was also breaking the disciplines of a television lifetime by offering viewers my memories and thoughts, rather than those of other people. Normally in *Whicker's World* the people I talk to are the stars – which must be the reason why our programmes have been on television for more than forty years, so far. However this effacing style also led me into an unwise career move: I turned down *Around the World in 80 Days*.

When offered this series, the unoriginal idea seemed too much of an ego trip: the camera always upon me as presenter, listening to whatever I had to say all round the world. During its traditional Jules Verne race there would be no time to talk to anyone in the exotic cities we passed, and too much time with no one to talk to while crossing the Indian Ocean in a felucca. Also, I had just returned from filming in Hong Kong and had eight programmes to edit and write.

So at an agreeable lunch with the BBC's Chief Executive Will Wyatt and his producer, I turned down their series. They finally recruited Michael Palin . . . who went on to become rich and famous beyond the dreams of *Wanda* – while I went on carrying my humble spear around *Whicker's World*.

Having rejected their demands for endless talking to camera, I then found myself locked in a TriStar for thirty-four days with eighty-six other passengers who had paid a good deal of money for their holiday and, just possibly, might not wish to spend much of it being interviewed by me every day. What to do? Do the talk myself, that's what. So I might as well have done it in *80 Days*, and got rich.

In addition to my reluctance to burden viewers with personal ramblings, I was now anxious about filming within our TriStar's closed community – though people are always so agreeable that in a lifetime of television I can recall no actual problems. We once spent six weeks on a *QE2* world cruise; a captive group of passengers is always liable to grow restless from cabin fever, and we were shooting four hours of television around them, sailing from Tahiti down through the South Pacific to New Zealand and Australia, then up to Papua New Guinea and Bali, into China and on to Japan.

The Cruise Director and I prepared a note to passengers, explaining that while filming a profile of the vast ship we would be careful to shoot around anyone not wishing to be photographed. Of some 1,200 on board, fewer than half-a-dozen passengers asked to be ignored – and most of them changed their minds when they found they were being excluded from the action. There is always a ripple of interest when a television camera appears on any periphery and turns some quiet party up a notch. In outgoing places like Palm Beach it validates residents' very existence, but even in more peaceful areas the sight of a professional camera can elevate everyday events into occasions at which people brighten up, present their best sides and smile a lot.

Rarely have I met anyone who has objected to joining me in *Whicker's World*. I was much gratified when Roderick Mann, the author, told someone why he was giving up his time to appear: 'Because it's fun.'

Thomas Cook's Ultimate Package Filofax explained, 'Alan Whicker's small film crew should add an interesting dimension to this great journey – to say nothing of producing a fascinating documentary.' I was encouraged by their confidence. They also wrote to everyone assuring them that any request for privacy would be scrupulously observed. Three couples said they did not wish to be filmed. One was Sir John and Lady Hall, who created Gateshead's enormous Metrocentre and rescued Newcastle United. They afterwards became friends – and so much on-side that he was an articulate and thoughtful star in each of my programmes.

After a few days a second couple also decided they no longer wanted to be left out; indeed most people are flattered to be interviewed on television, and affronted if excluded. Only one Englishwoman with a quiet Danish husband remained implacably hostile. Fortunately she was easily identifiable for her hairstyle had an odd topknot. She became known as The Hottentot. Should that menacing hair ever edge into frame, my cameraman would hurriedly look away.

As our air cruise was about to remind us, this is a small world: a year afterwards Valerie's aunt and uncle were dining at Tetou in Golfe-Juan when to their surprise they overheard my name bandied about at the next table. The cross woman with the curious hairstyle with whom I had hardly exchanged a word was still badmouthing me, after 37,000 miles – and a year off to recover. I am still saddened by our one failure among the gallant eighty-seven, however boring or bad-tempered she might have proved.

So although all the happier passengers seemed to find a television interlude could make a day more interesting, I tried to remain in the background; constant conversations might become tiresome for them – and perhaps for viewers. Instead I continued the daily sitrep recounting the tour's triumphs and tragedies, and grew to enjoy my chats with viewers. Such audio diaries have since become commonplace, but it was some time before I realized it was the very format I had told Will Wyatt I would never use.

Before we left Venice to fly to Cairo that Monday afternoon, I strolled back for a last wistful bellini in Harry's Bar, wondering whether after almost half a century my credit would still be good, and brimming with sentimental nostalgia for the happy days of long-lost youth at the start of a wandering life.

It was closed.

I turned away from my past, gulping and blinking, and headed towards the airport and the future. Venice never relaxes her spell. It was November, when you can hear every footfall, and the most blasé heart must miss a beat at the revelation of each misty Canaletto vista. However long your stay in that queen of cities, it is never long enough – and we had relished the merest taste, the perfect hors-d'œuvre before leaving to feast upon the world. That, we were to learn, would become the pattern of the next thirty-two days; we always moved on too soon.

A procession of launches took us to the airport to meet our TriStar, at last. Looking up from the tarmac, overawed, wide-bodies always seem enormous, each one a flying Waldorf Astoria. This Lockheed L1011–500 was twenty-five years old at least, well built and thirsty, but in lovely condition. It could carry 320 passengers, though for our tour was configured for 118. The seats were called first class, though by modern standards were sub-Club: little recline, no footrests. However cabin space was wide and uncluttered and, best of all, offered the luxury of a mingling area at the rear around a stand-up bar.

A crew out of Central Casting was lined up, Texan Captain lean and rangy, younger officers dashing. They were to give us superbly professional flights without a moment's consternation. The flight attendants were something else, and ranged from over-the-top blonde voluptuous to earnest anorexic college girl. Some had brought more luggage than the passengers – it was a once-in-a-lifetime holiday for them, too.

American TransAir handled chartered gamblers' flights from LA to Las Vegas, which seemed to be what they knew about: smile, offer dry-Martini-in-a-bag and Have a Nice Day. They were friendly and appealing and would suggest a sweet liqueur to start the meal, or maybe a sherry-and-soda with your steak? The meals were commonplace – McDonald's with wine – but the champagne was reliable and, as we flew towards Cairo, the whole atmosphere was secure and happy.

Whicker's Third Law states that the countries you least want to visit are always the hardest to enter. Every corrupt East European Mafia-state, any scorched diseased African dictatorship, each oppressed East Asian tyranny will insist you fill in endless forms, hand over photographs, suffer injections, wait for hours, buy expensive visas and piles of worthless currency. Upon arrival at some primitive and hazardous airport your forms will be incorrect, unpleasant officials will demand additional payment for anything they can think of, and you will be delayed for hours while luggage is mislaid or stolen. You then become aware of an unpleasant tummy upset, kidnapping and the strong possibility of being shot. Leaving the country will be *far* more difficult.

It would be unkind to categorize friendly Egypt so cruelly; it is after all the oldest tourist destination on earth – and come to that, my birthplace; but with its heat and those 16 million Caireans who are always standing next to you, with the poverty, questionable cooking, inefficiency and terrorism . . . it does not feature in too many Must-Go lists.

We arrived at 9.30 pm, well documented and well wishing. The vast echoing airport was empty; no other flight movements. It seemed a wise time to enter a notoriously bureaucratic country. Furthermore Thomas Cook had created Egyptian tourism and organized tours for more than a century, cementing the English love affair with the Nile. They owned cruise ships and fleets of coaches, and in a land of baksheesh always oiled the wheels of bureaucracy with gifts of breakfast tea – a disarmingly British way of doing business.

On this occasion, needless to say, the entente cordiale went wrong. Our documents, while correct and in order, duly stamped, completed and paid for, were unfortunately the wrong *shape*.

Our affluent party, small but significant, was exactly the sort of tourism poor Egypt desperately needed, but far from being welcomed we were caged for two and a half stifling hours in a deserted airport, waiting for a Customs check; in the end, nobody bothered. Presumably money changed hands, for we were finally permitted to leave the airport – though grudgingly, without passports and without luggage. Some welcome.

The magic of Egypt had evaporated and the shambles helped explain the decline in tourism. It also taught us that hand luggage should always contain a toothbrush.

Next morning, Day Five, and with no officials in sight, Egypt's fluctuating charm swung back into action. Cairo is a super-capital, seemingly bigger than its country. Within its heaving immensity there is a constant state of ferocious energy amid din, dust and disorder, smells, shouts and sunshine. This fevered state of irritable excitement quite overcomes Egyptians during the khamsin.

Coaches took our eighty-seven to the Cairo Museum, to park where terrorists later machine-gunned busloads of tourists. I followed by taxi, and discovered where battered Ladas go to die. We bounced along without hitting a soul, driver smiling, crowds amiable. No menacing sense of hassle haunted those teeming streets, no big-city insecurity. Women walked freely and, unlike Spain, Italy or Mexico, did not suffer unwanted attention. Even traffic discipline was surprisingly effective: cars were not treble-parked in French or Italian style, and the compressed millions of good-natured Caireans contrived to live without road rage.

Cairo always looks as though it's *almost* complete and should be ready in a year or two, just as soon as they've fixed the roads, removed the scaffolding, cleaned out the alleys and dusted the palm trees. In fact the city has been looking much like that since around 5000 BC, so we might as well accept it the way it is.

Only minutes from the centre, its strange desert-on-the-doorstep was revealed as we rounded a corner: the Pyramids. The most photographed image in the world, and our first Wonder. Splendid of course, though to me always faintly disappointing; perhaps they have been overexposed.

Later we drove out through the short twilight to Mena House, the historic hotel where Churchill and Roosevelt met during the war. Girls showered us with rose petals as we entered a magnificent party to sit on pouffes at low tables and dine from an enormous buffet spread around the moonlit garden. There were dancing horses to entertain us, but mainly and inevitably – belly-dancers. Writhing Egyptian girls with candelabra on their heads were modestly covered, relatively, but foreign performers wobbled bare bellies and large breasts at us. We were soon urged to submit to the traditional humiliation of dancing with them. First up, like a shot, was Sandy Pettit, the seventy-year-old funeral director from Chester. He proved himself very alive.

Next morning we flew ninety minutes south to Abu Simbel, the first wide-body to attempt to land on an airstrip which was long enough but might not hold our enormous weight. It did. However its steps were too small to reach the TriStar's exit, so we lowered ours and met halfway. The Captain had to leave the third engine running all the time we were being guided around temples so we would not return to a flat battery.

In the scorching midday, curling slightly at the edges, we trailed around the finest and largest monument in Nubia, and went inside the James Bond-style hollow hill they had created in solid gritstone when the Aswan dam forced them to move vast statues up the hillside.

Among our sweat-sodden tropical shirts and scruff order, the undertaker who had belly-danced the night away wore a blue serge suit and stiff white collar as he cast a professional eye over the tombs. It was plain that Sandy was going to enjoy his retirement. He told me he always did the packing for his wife because he was so experienced at tucking well-dressed bodies neatly into coffins. This was an aspect of undertaking to which I had not given much thought.

Our waiting airliner was purring away with its meter ticking, ready to fly us forty-five minutes down the road to Luxor. There

we boarded an elderly and slightly grotty steamer for a three-day
Nile cruise. The idea of three days without needing to pack and
unpack while sleeping in the same bed already seemed like
luxury – that is, until we saw the bed: narrow berths in a cramped
cabin. It was the Orient Express without the good food. We took
sleeping pills to blot it out.

Group travellers always find a level among their fellows that
pleases them. On the *QE2*, a one-class ship for world cruises,
some wanted to play bingo, others to study the Tang Dynasty or
Victorian watercolours. They instinctively sorted out friends, bars
and activities. On this Ultimate Package we did not enjoy that
dispersal area, so after a few late nights and dawn starts had
already begun to fragment restlessly.

Some of our high-flyers regarded the tour as a once-in-a-lifetime dream come true and were determined to relish every experience; delays and fatigue merely stimulated their blitz spirit and
dawning sense of shared adventure. However, the more experienced were growing less easy to please: they had expected ultra-
de luxe treatment but were merely getting standard upmarket
packages, strung together.

'I thought someone would thrust chilled white wine into my
hand every time we paused,' said Sir John Hall, grumpily. We
were concerned at these first signs of disarray, for it was only Day
Eight and they were our cast for the duration.

For convenience and identification we had by now created
nicknames for the more dominant among our passing parade: a
couple of elderly widowers, Reggie from Wales and Dennis from
Yorkshire, now drifting amiably from bar to bar, were The Last of
the Summer Wine. Josephine, the peppy blonde widow from
Highgate, had to be the Sex Bomb. The elegant Spanish, who
wore different outfits every day and alarmed the sensibly shod
English, were the Catalans. A pair of disapproving mature ladies
who complained about everything, The Ugly Sisters. The Duchess
and the Princess drifted around, aloof – and the furious
Hottentot would not even speak to her husband.

Younger single women, sizing up the paucity of manly talent,
began to look a little strained and tight around the lips. For one
or two the tour had been a serious investment, and each day they
watched the market go down.

The few passengers with physical disabilities were the most accommodating and easiest to please: one chairbound eighty-year-old who had originally appeared unlikely to get past Victoria, now refused to miss an excursion and found every day the best yet.

The happiest travellers were the older widows. Jolly and giggly, they had humour, energy and a certain wisdom which I assumed came from not bothering too much about men any more. I was wrong. When I sat behind a couple of seventy-five-year-olds in an airport coach, one was discussing her forthcoming remarriage. She recalled how she had slipped her elderly husband-to-be a tactful warning about their future love life: 'I told him, you mustn't expect too much – I'm not very keen on all that business *upstairs*.'

He was unruffled. 'Don't you worry about that,' he said. 'We'll get a bungalow.' It was not, I suspected, *quite* the answer she had been expecting, but she was undaunted and evidently prepared to face a new and fuller life at ground level.

The biblical landscapes along the Nile were tranquil and extraordinarily beautiful, but as we cruised along I sensed a certain restlessness among our world travellers. Most were sunbathing blissfully, but a few had gathered below decks – to plot a mutiny! Word reached us that at a revolutionary meeting they were psyching themselves up to roast the tour managers, so we hurried down to the ship's lounge. They were not yet chanting, but did look most resolute. I could see Simon Laxton was about to be set adrift in a felucca.

Their complaints ranged from legitimate to ludicrous. A few disliked the accommodation, not unreasonably. Others complained that male passengers did not always wear ties at dinner, when coffee was served incorrectly. One couple were bitter because a waiter had spilled their ferociously expensive champagne, and demanded reimbursement. Warned its exorbitant price would cost the wretched man two months' wages, they were not sympathetic. Some complained that the air crew took the best seats in the hotel lounges – and then expected to be bought drinks. Others pointed out that the three toilets at the back of the TriStar were marked Women, Men, Crew – and while two were usually empty, women queued.

One or two – and I know this is hard to believe – even complained about *Whicker's World*. Our taut Hottentot led for the prosecution: she had never seen our programmes, she explained with quiet pride, and knew nothing about them – but her servant in Denmark had thought the project was not a good idea. A hyphenated lady from Surrey had not much cared for my *QE2* series. It was hard to get a grip on those two charges against us, but in the end the verdict seemed to be Not Proven. After a long and inconclusive meeting no one had to walk the plank, though the mutineers doubtless felt better. The air was now clear, and they could carry on cruising.

It was my first glimpse of the simmering volatility among those who, having paid a lot of money for a holiday, were not absolutely convinced they were receiving their just dues – but found it hard to decide exactly what was wrong, apart from everything.

If our cameraman was not going to walk the plank, at least we could put him over the side to provide a distraction and to film the boat moving through scenery unchanged for fifty centuries; a glorious picture. For such mid-river shots the ship could find only a rowing boat with one pair of oars, so after we had sailed past them they could not row fast enough to catch up. The camera boat receded sadly into the distance, its weary crew drifting back towards Cairo. I was half inclined to join them.

There were then 180 such floating hotels cruising a Nile which, because of silt, weeds and irrigation, was running out of water, its level falling several inches a year. On deck I chatted with Dr Nigel Southward, the Queen's apothecary, who had come expecting a month's holiday but was instead working extremely hard. He of course was not as concerned about the level of the Nile . . . as what was *in* it. His cruisers were succumbing, day after day, to gippy tummy; after all, this was where it was born. He reminded me that the water offered on board the ship was in fact purified Nile water. It did not sound inviting but tests had proved, he said, that it was often purer than the bottled water in which we put our faith and cleaned our teeth.

Doctor Nigel was particularly worried about one passenger who, dashing along the gangplank towards a tour bus, had fallen into the thick yellow water with a despairing splash. This was not medically recommended. We both hoped she had kept her mouth shut.

We went on to the Valley of the Kings where the authorities, having charged visitors for a licence to take pictures, then confiscated their cameras. From the elegant Old Cataract Hotel, a sanctuary of cool cucumber sandwiches and China tea, we moved to a *son et lumière* in the Palace of Philae, and finally to Aswan. Then another 3,500 miles in our flying limo, to India.

At New Delhi, as though to reproach Egyptian incompetence, we were waved through Customs and Immigration, straight into rickety buses. The Maurya Sheraton public relations manager left me an effusive note explaining she had gone to Australia. More important, we had a large bed again, with lots of light – and a telly.

On Day Ten, during the traditional tour of the old town and the Red Fort, a local market sounded a promising film location – but turned out to be a dreary clipjoint selling carpets. Still, India is the last home of the craftsmen and you can go broke saving money. My diary piece was done while being tossed around amid the usual seething Indian crowd in the Street of Moonlight, which was not as magical as it sounded.

That evening we experienced one of the set pieces of the tour: the Maharaja's Ball to which we were driven in horse-drawn carriages – and grand vintage cars, as found in all Royal Indian garages. This evening's Maharaja turned out to be my old friend Babji Jodhpur and his enchanting Maharani, Hemlata. I had last filmed them thirteen years earlier, discussing their arranged marriage – which was still proving wonderfully happy, thank goodness.

After dinner I was called upon to draw the raffle tickets for the first Grand Prize of the tour: first-class returns to Delhi and a week's holiday, to which His Highness added another week of hospitality in his palace. I stood on the stage groping in a champagne bucket for the winning tickets, conscious I was about to make two friends – and eighty-five enemies who would hate me for the rest of the tour.

The first winner was seventy-four-year-old Mrs Babs Elvins, dauntless harbour mistress of Wareham, Dorset. She was one of

171

nature's permanent travellers who was first on the bus every morning with her stick and what I called her yellow underwater camera. Next, Mrs Charlotte Hepworth, a delightful old Doncaster lady of seventy-six whom we had filmed screeching with delight upon a camel at the Pyramids. Recently widowed, she had told me she feared this would be her last holiday.

They both wept, of course, at which the head of Indian Airlines jumped up from our table and offered them flights to anywhere in India. Then the Sheraton topped up the prizes with more free accommodation. They embraced, and it was all very touching – even though I happened to know they did not much care for each other.

I was happy not to have handed those prizes to some rich couple who could well pay their own fares – indeed they were so well deserving some passengers hinted darkly that it must have been a fix . . .

The four and a half-hour drive to Agra next day was an instant reminder of India's flavour: children beating on the windows for money, overflowing villages with markets full of fruit and vegetables and dirt, suicidal truck drivers overtaking on blind bends. Two trucks had crashed head on and were contorted on their sides and covered with scavenging monkeys. We had a hundred near misses, but only one hit: we knocked down a cyclist. Nobody was much concerned; bicycles, it seemed, did not count – they were expendable. Certainly all cyclists seemed to show a blithe indifference to approaching death.

This was one of India's busiest and most modern roads through a relatively affluent area at the upper end of their poverty scale, yet some of our global travellers were appalled by what they glimpsed in passing. They later complained to the tour manager that they should have been protected from such sights. On television the editing is done for you, but when driving along you need to censor your own pictures by turning the head or closing the eyes. They had not worked that out. It seemed they wanted to see the world – but not to *look* at it, even at 40 mph.

Outside Agra their brush with real life was wiped away by one of the world's dream destinations and its greatest memorial to love, the Taj Mahal. After 350 years the Taj is now often shrouded in industrial smog and dust from a refinery thirty miles away, so suffers marble cancer and begins to yellow; but it remains one of the sights of the world, and our second Wonder.

Our hotel employed a well-patronized astrologer in the true mould: small, skinny, emphatic and sharp. He sat cross-legged upon his bed in a white room off the lobby advising his first client – predictably, Josephine. She was looking for information about her next husband. 'I do not know if you will have a holiday romance,' he told her, 'but a near romance.' That must be better than no romance at all? 'Exactly,' said Josephine, 'I'm very pleased.'

Astrology, he said, was a guideline for mankind. We filmed him telling her she could expect 'a lot of success for your personal life and success in your business and career, as well as enjoying good health. I think your life is long, in my knowledge. You are going to live to eighty-five.'

Sadly, his crystal ball was clouded.

Our tour manager was a worldly Milanese, Dante Barbareschi. He had been guiding for more than twenty years, though this tour was much longer and much richer than usual. He took care of day-to-day transportation and sightseeing and, because he was always there, got all the full-frontal complaints.

I watched how he coped with irate and often unreasonable gripes. His method was to get his own moans in first. Since he usually had the mike in his hand, his complaints were the more emphatic. By the time he had told his captive coachload how tired he was after another long day, how hungry and weary after traipsing round temples and beauty spots, how fed up with waiting for buses and boats . . . he quite took the punch out of their protests. Since he was amusing and outrageous they felt protective, and started consoling instead of complaining.

As we flew for six hours from India to China on Day Thirteen we sat in the back bar, recalling the shock caused to our world travellers by the poverty, by a dead body we had passed on the road. It had illustrated the urgencies of India: its easy laughter and casual death.

'Yes, a dead body in India . . . I always say to my groups, particularly to the ladies, that India is the best place to murder your husband. You can commit a murder and nobody would find out that you have done anything. Shall I tell you why?

'I was with one of my tours at Agra and one couple came downstairs in the morning, but the husband was a bit tired and told her, "I'm going to have breakfast, you go on the excursion – I'll see you afterwards." It was a whole-day excursion, and the wife left quite happily. He went into the coffee shop, and there and then, he kicked the bucket!

'Some hours went by and the ladies were still on their excursion. In the afternoon Reception phoned me and said, "Mr Barbareschi, there's a plastic bag at the desk for you." I went down and of course in the plastic bag was the husband of this poor lady. He had already been cremated.

'I thought, "My God, what shall I do with him?" Then I said, "When she comes in give it to her, and tell her to call me." The tour came back, she picked up her key and they told her, "There is a plastic bag here for you." She said, "That's funny, I didn't buy anything." '

'Anyhow, she takes it and they warn me and I say, "Oh God, now I'll have to tell her." Then Doris, I think her name was, called me from her room and said, "I have a plastic bag here, what shall I do with it?" '

' "Take a stiff drink," I said, "and I'll come and tell you what's inside." So I went over and told her, "That's your husband, in there." '

'Her reaction at the beginning was very bad, but then the following day she had a long fax from London. Apparently there was a huge amount of money waiting for her, so she revived . . .

'Sometimes,' said Dante, 'life on tour is a bit of a problem for unescorted ladies, because unescorted men are very rare animals.' I recalled that on the *QE2* retired grey-haired ex-officers were employed to dance with some of the solitary ladies and do a little light escort duty.

'Yes, when I was on the *France* this was part of *my* duties. We had a lot of husbands who kicked the bucket. Husbands always kick the bucket and wives never do, do you notice that, Mr Whicker? Women are always the survivors. We had a long cruise of three months and quite a few husbands died. I remember we used to go up on the top deck and kick the bodies into the water. You could not put them in the refrigerator with the caviare and the lobsters, could you? Not in First Class, anyway . . . The wives were left as widows – but most of them got a lot of money, which made things easier.'

'Yes,' I said. 'They often go quite blonde from grief, don't they?'

'They change their hairstyle . . . We are a bit cynical, aren't we?'

'A bit.'

On its eventual transmission the subtitle of our first *Whicker's World* was: 'The Best Place to Murder Your Husband . . .'

At Beijing we swept through Customs once again, though Immigration dealt with us in alphabetical order – unhelpful if you happen to be a Whicker. Eventually we unpacked in a vast suite on the top floor of the Great Wall Sheraton, with kitchen, dining room and enormous bedrooms. I had risked an Indian lunch on the TriStar, inspired by the assurance that it was prepared in the Swissair airport kitchens. This proved too trusting.

Travelling around the world all my life I have been blessed with wonderful health and a cast-iron stomach, which happily survived Nigeria and Mexico; unfortunately it has one weak spot: India. I once filmed there for three months and when I left my suits were wonderfully loose; not a single straining button.

This time I had been too busy to eat much, but India got in a sucker punch as we left – just in time for China's horrifyingly medieval public lavatories. In addition, that night I suffered some curious allergy: my nose ran so fast it was dripping on to the carpet; not a pretty sight. Feeling sorry for myself I sat amid total grandeur, leaking from both ends. I was soon to learn how trivial my passing afflictions were.

At dawn next morning the phone was ringing; I assumed it was a wake-up call, and ignored it. It rang continuously, and eventually our PA got through; she told me that Jane, wife of our director David Green, had just given birth in Los Angeles to a baby suffering from Turner's Syndrome and unlikely to live.

Struggling to get David on to any flight out of Beijing was a nightmare, for we had entered on a group visa and Chinese bureaucracy could not cope with emergencies or individuals out of step. Simon Laxton was admirable and finally contrived to substitute him for a Thomas Cook staffer returning to Hong Kong. He reached LA in time for his baby's funeral.

We then left to carry on filming without him in Tiananmen Square, distressed by a real drama which at least put trivial complaints out of mind and allowed our cameraman – who had been grumbling rather a lot – to come up trumps and do an excellent job, while I directed from in front of the camera.

The Chinese permitted us to go into Tiananmen Square, those two square miles of dreadful memory, for just fifteen minutes. The vast and desolate square was empty of everything but bad vibrations. I was slightly ashamed to be there at all; it felt like condoning the tanks. On stones recently stained by the blood of their students I filmed a few conversations. Only one among our eighty-seven had the courage of her political convictions: Felicity Horwood, forthright wife of a retired Gurkha, refused to set foot in the Square. She rejoined us later in the Forbidden City, where Ming emperors were once served by 9,000 maids and 100,000 eunuchs. Time makes everything acceptable.

Then we drove some fifty miles to reach a Wonder upon which work started in the seventh century BC: the 4,200 miles of the Great Wall. After the searing heat of India, our stretch was bright, sunny – and just above freezing; it felt like climbing the side of a building to be brushed by winds from Russia.

Along the Wall one of our worldly group posed for a giggling tourist photographer operating a Polaroid. His prop was the carnival uniform of a Ming emperor, with toy sword. David Bellis, from Manchester, changed and stood posing with his sword and trying to look fierce, watched by a group of solemn Chinese on a factory outing. Then the Polaroid was passed around and we all studied it intently; West met East, in Toytown.

Eileen Brownsword, our jolly pensioner from Avon, was disappointed by the Wall: 'I thought it would be much older.' I suggested that it must have been worn smooth by the footsteps of twenty-eight centuries, but she was not satisfied.

Nor were the local bureaucrats, who for some enigmatic reason cancelled our side trip to Xian: capital of China for eleven centuries. This last-minute change of heart threw Thomas Cook into confusion, since along with Easter Island it was a crucial destination. Fortunately some friends of mine in Hong Kong were old China hands with powerful contacts in Beijing, so after a few phone calls the Terracotta Warriors did an about-turn and came back into the schedule. We had earned our seats on the tour.

Even so they would not permit internal flights by foreign aircraft, so the next day we flew the 600 miles to Xian in a 737 chartered from China Airlines. The aircraft was clean, and excellently flown. An anxious but eager cabin crew served a boxed lunch which quite reconciled us to TriStar catering.

The vast airfield at Xian was almost deserted. It had been built, presumably, to handle the oncoming tourist millions expected to beat a path to the excavated army. We, early in that queue, drove for ninety minutes along empty roads to their museum where photography was forbidden, though for a mere $800 we had received permission to film – for two minutes.

In a sort of half-excavated aircraft hangar as big as a football field, thousands of lifesize soldiers stood side by side – no two alike – a massive army risen from the soil. Its uncounted numbers grew and grew as the earth slowly surrendered the Emperor's buried warriors. Another 6,000, some of them mounted, wait to be resurrected.

I considered filming some interviews in this remarkable setting – a farmworker's discovery in the 1970s – but one of our local Chinese handlers muttered to a policeman; he shambled over and told us to come in, our time was up. The camera was banished. Soon after that two of our travellers, who had evidently not contributed $800, were arrested for taking pictures. This easygoing couple from the Isle of Wight were marched away to the police station, the wife in tears. Their camcorder had taped less than a minute of the statues, but this incriminating evidence was replayed again and again. After a long and raucous scolding, they were fined $20.

I was sure it was the first time either had seen inside a police station or been shouted at by uniforms. They found the experience shattering, so we filmed a reassuring and light-hearted conversation, mainly to make them realize it was not a capital offence, and that they were not on their way to the Chinese saltmines.

After lunch in a modern glass-sided hotel the handlers insisted that we visit the town Friendship Store, to buy. The authorities then adopted quite another attitude, and our coaches were led through main streets by police cars with lights flashing and sirens screaming. All traffic stopped. Pedestrians ran to watch. One of the lead cars had loudspeakers on its roof, screaming 'Move over! Move over!' at hordes of cyclists. The city came to a halt. It was like some breathless presidential motorcade, with a finger on every trigger – yet we were merely a bunch of tired tourists.

That kind of royal progress can be quite exhilarating, and we reached the Friendship Store in no time at all. Later our escort shouted and flashed and sirened our path through silent crowds, back to Xian airport. We returned to Beijing with China Airways and crossed the apron to our waiting TriStar without further conflict.

All this had happened during China's 'Year of Tourism', yet officialdom seemed confused about the promotion of a unique army soon to be one of the world's great destinations. They had built airports, roads, hotels to encourage hard-currency visitors – then banned photographs. Decided to allow two minutes' filming upon payment – then brusquely confiscated cameras. Made confused, but friendly, tourists feel like criminals. It was hard for visitors to know how to do right. The Pyramids and the Taj had a surer touch.

It was reassuring to be back in our aerial home as we flew in a state of euphoria out through the Bamboo Curtain, and down to Hong Kong. We had just lived through the bureaucracy of Egypt, the poverty of India, the authoritarianism of China . . . and now at last faced a half-term break in our great Far Eastern bazaar. The handover was still five years ahead, so the place had British standards and no one was going to be arrested for taking a happy snap.

What's more, we should be in one hotel room for two full days without having to pack or unpack, on what promised to be a relatively light schedule. We had just experienced a number of five o'clock calls, twenty-hour days and a bombardment of sights; half-way round the world we were getting a bit bushed. We had also lost our first passenger – not through exhaustion, but because the siren-song of the Vienna Stock Exchange was calling him home. That stockbroker would have had a better holiday had he left his mobile phone in Austria.

However the object of Hong Kong was simply to spend, spend, spend, and that always stimulates. Everybody prepared for an eagerly anticipated shopping spree, especially the Catalans who were intent and deeply businesslike about purchasing jewellery. I was told they carried $2m petty cash to buy their Christmas goodies. Certainly they were going to make some jeweller's day. The rich have a passion for bargains as lively as it is pointless.

I sent my cameraman along on one of their excursions, which was slit-eyed, intense and full of chattering calculators. Any salesmen other than Chinese would have been steamrollered by the determined and knowledgeable group from Barcelona. As it was I think they forced a draw, which is the most anyone can expect. Watching the eyes of the wives as they handled string after string of pearls was a revelation to me, a simple country boy unused to seeing souls exposed.

Chinese salesmen may be short on charm but they are unusually persistent, and still profit from the memory of the old days when everything the Colony sold seemed to be a bargain. In Hong Kong, even if you're not shopping – you're shopping. We shopped. Our eighty-seven were busy buying things they didn't want to impress people they didn't know.

In the vast lobby of the Marriot I did my half-term report to camera on the tour so far, and that evening went to a pretty party at Repulse Bay, attended by John Brooke, Chairman of Thomas Cook, and his Board. They were holding their biannual meeting to coincide with our arrival. Most of the massed blue suits came up to me during the evening to ask how the tour was being received; I had the feeling they were also auditioning for interviews, and so it proved; their PR man later wondered whether it might not be a good idea . . . ?

I would have been happy to have questioned them in that lovely setting but unfortunately my crew had already packed all the gear, which they said was required early by Customs. In actual fact what they really wanted was to get the cameras safely out of the way so they could concentrate on their own shopping; and why not? Film crews can be human, after all.

Our itinerary had been carefully arranged to spare us night flights, but for the 3,500 miles down to Alice Springs we had to pass our first night in the spacious but not too comfortable TriStar. We took off at midnight and flew for more than five hours to Darwin, where in the early heat of an equatorial dawn Australian Customs required all luggage removed from the aircraft, and checked. That took about two hours. Then another 800 miles on to Alice, where we transferred to a smaller aircraft for the final 230 miles across to Ayers Rock.

Before leaving Hong Kong we had enjoyed that lavish buffet dinner at Repulse Bay: then, filling in the night, a second dinner on the TriStar, with a snack on the leg to Alice. The Ansett 737 served a light meal into Ayers Rock, where our bedrooms were not ready so we were appeased with our fifth meal. Having nothing else to do, we ate them all. We were overfed, overtired and unamused. And that, son, is how digestions go wrong.

Halfway round the world, on Day Eighteen, we had finally run into what an Hawaiian hotelier told me was called The Warm Bed Routine – when arrivals overlap delayed departures. Last night's tourists were still in our rooms.

Ayers Rock, however, swept away all irritations. I had been to Alice Springs several times during various filming tours but had never found time for the 450-mile detour to Yulara and that sandstone monolith. When we finally reached Uluru, as the Aborigines call their desert cathedral, it was one of the most majestic sights I had ever seen. I could sense its mystical aura and well understood why that great God of the Dreamtime was a holy place, for it said something to everyone. Australians, less romantic, call it the Biggest Pebble in the World; six miles around at its base, and sunk four miles into the earth. With all its might and mass and mystery it was discovered only in 1872 – illustrating the vast size and youth of Australia.

We filmed it from a chopper and a coach with a chatty driver who introduced himself: 'I am your bus captain.' I wondered whether they had any bus admirals. He cautioned us severely against stealing souvenirs, like foliage – or even sand, which seemed plentiful enough. I was taken aback by the prospect of being frisked at the gates of that desert park, for *sand* . . . 'Sorry, Officer – just borrowing it for my birdcage.'

That evening the Captain drove us out to toast the desert sun as it set behind the vast red rock. White-clothed tables were covered with little Moussec glasses of sparkling wine, and we found they had circled the wagons: great six-wheeled coaches had come from all sides and unloaded hundreds of tourists eager to watch the rock change from red to purple to black, and the sun go down. Grey mist also arrived, so we saw only the sparkling wine go down.

Back at the hotel a themed dinner was staged in its courtyard. Amid flaming torches and Arabian music, strapping young Aussies wearing galabiehs served hummus and barramundi in tahini. There was a choice of grilled crocodile, antelope, buffalo, kangaroo . . . I had always wanted to say 'Chuck another croc on the barbie', but settled for the lamb.

Next day we relished two tiny triumphs: while filming a conversation with Basil Bushell, an ENT surgeon from Cheam, he noticed a passer-by and became distracted: 'Isn't that Geoffrey? *Geoffrey*!' It was a doctor friend from the Middlesex Hospital. He joined us, but instead of greeting Basil said, 'My God, that's Alan Whicker. My wife is sitting in our coach right now reading your book!' Serious readers are much valued, particularly in the Outback.

Even better: a group of eight from our gallant eighty-six decided to try and climb to the 1,200-foot summit of that bald rock – a considerable and, often, a dangerous feat. Temperatures can reach 47°C in the non-existent shade, which could melt roads and the resolution of the sturdiest world traveller. Notices warned: 'Don't climb – you'll die. Twenty-six people have been killed . . .' There were also plaques commemorating climbers who had failed on the way up, terminally. The prize for such a death-wish was a ninety-mile view across the red desert, and total exhaustion.

Upon their triumphant return to ground our eight rushed up to my camera crew, anxious to be congratulated and have their achievement properly recorded. One of them, however, was husband of the dreaded Hottentot who had protested so vehemently about our camera. We of course still had to respect her desire for privacy, so made our excuses and left.

Our flights back to Alice Springs and on to Sydney concluded with one of those moments when you appreciate how stylish travel can be: on the Qantas Executive side of the airport our TriStar taxied right up to waiting transport. We stepped from one to the other and drove unhindered to the InterContinental. Painless. Then we discovered how *irritating* travel can be. They lost our case.

It was the first piece of baggage to go astray out of the tour's 400 and growing – apart from the disappearance of a bag of Josephine's shoes which had caused hysteria but did not really count. This was a major piece, well identified by one of Thomas Cook's elegant brass (weight no object) labels. I heard Simon Laxton's exasperated, 'And of all people, it had to be *his*.'

He guessed I might be discussing that loss on camera, and assumed the large case containing everything that made life work had probably been misplaced within the hotel. All guests' suitcases were then checked; most were owned by Japanese about to leave for Tokyo. It was a surprising loss, since our tour even had a Baggage Master. After a day without my necessities and with growing irritation I called his hotel room to check progress. He was asleep.

Filming had to continue, so I sorted my wardrobe – most of which was evidently on its way to Japan. The Outback safari suit I was wearing and one remaining tropical suit would have to see me through the South Pacific, on to bleak Easter Island, to the beach at Copacabana and along the windswept avenues of New York at Christmastime. It was a chilly prospect, but did at least illustrate the world's most common travel headache, which always has surprising power to distract and destabilize.

Overdressed but undaunted, I drove to Bondi Beach by way of Double Bay and Mrs MacQuarie's Chair, and took tea with the underdressed Life-Savers. Then aboard a cruiser to look around Sydney's incomparable harbour. There another drama awaited: after much mutinous muttering a couple of big spenders had finally decided to leave our tour. They could stand it no longer.

This wealthy pair from a village near Newport Pagnall were travelling lavishly, having requested suites in every hotel – some costing an additional £1,000 a night. They were remembered for ordering that ill-fated bottle of Dom Perignon on the Nile steamer. Ray was a plump 47, probably in property, and known to my crew as Essex Man; Sandra was 29. They seemed quiet and agreeable, though even when lunching with them on the Orient Express at the start of the tour I had found they were already vaguely dissatisfied about most things – mainly because nothing was luxurious enough.

He told me he had tried to organize a truly de luxe round-the-world tour with a few friends in a private jet. When it was costed at £400,000, most of them backed out. So abandoning half this holiday and paying an additional £7,000 for first-class singles back to London must have seemed financially insignificant.

As we steamed under the Harbour Bridge in brilliant Australian sunshine I reminded him, 'You'll be missing Tahiti and Rio and all those good places if you leave, and when you get back to Chicheley it'll be raining. You'll be very sad.'

'Yes,' he said, thoughtfully. 'I probably will be.' They left, anyway, carrying their dissatisfactions with them; the first couple to follow the Viennese stockbroker and jump ship. We watched them walk down the gangplank and disappear for ever.

On such an elaborate holiday everyone's expectations are different; even among the remainder I could detect a certain fraying round the edges – though I suspected the metropolitan comforts of that great southern city would restore enthusiasm. Josephine and the two bachelors, Brian and Terry, who ran an hotel in Torquay, were also thinking of leaving: lack of time to lounge on beaches, journey not glamorous enough – and what's more they should not have been subjected to the sight of poverty in India, which was not in the brochure. However, surrounded by the new promise of Sydney's bright lights they perked up and decided to soldier on.

During the harbour cruise I filmed Reggie, six foot seven, and Dennis, rather small but with big white moustachios, the *Summer Wine* pair who were enjoying the tour. Reggie explained: 'It's an adventure – a bit like a week with the Territorial Army.' Said Dennis: 'We're having difficulty *not* getting up at half-past five . . .'

The loyal eighty-four returned to the hotel – and there, like some reward for being staunch, was my case. It had been in the back of the TriStar hold all the time. That night I was finally able to discard the blue tropical for a dinner jacket, and go to the Ball.

We had a five o'clock call, so I left before midnight struck and I turned into a whingeing Pom.

On the way to Tahiti on Day Twenty-two we flew through the alps in the South Island of New Zealand and landed at Christchurch, just for tea; didn't have the time to stay any longer, you understand. Maori warriors made the usual song-and-dance about our arrival, and we got our noses rubbed. My cameraman filmed the New Zealand Broadcasting Corporation filming me. At one point the two cameramen were shooting each other, purposefully. It was Arriflexes at Teatime.

After chocolate strawberries and Christmas cake on a hilltop overlooking that most English of Down Under cities, we took off for a night flight. For the first time in twenty-two days I managed to get to sleep on the aircraft – to be woken almost immediately by the captain announcing that we were crossing the International Dateline.

So we had Saturday twice, the second time in the South Sea island which entranced everyone from the *Bounty* crew and Gaugin to Robert Louis Stevenson. We all began to agree with Fletcher Christian that perhaps this might be the best place to jump ship. We had arrived in paradise and what's more did not have to pack again for three days – so it *had* to be paradise.

That night there was a small drama among my crew which I used for a diary piece, with much relish. They planned a midnight swim with Nigel the doctor and Russell the Thomas Cook PR. Camera assistant Paola, a sophisticated Carioca, knew the best beach so led them to a dark little cove nearby for a skinny-dip in the moonlight. They all ran joyously into the sea.

The first sign of chaos to come was when Mike, the cameraman, stepped on a sea-urchin. This was spiky and very painful. He leapt about – and trod on others. More noise and anguish. Led back to the beach in agony with spines sticking into him, he sat down – on another sea-urchin. The man was fated.

Catherine, our PA, grabbed a chair to allow him to sit safely, but as she wrenched it up in the dark it hit Russell in the face and knocked out one of his front teeth.

So there was Mike with the spines still in him and Russell bleeding all over the place and everyone else leaping about and not knowing what to do. Dr Nigel rushed for his black bag, but found his medications not much help. It was a scene out of Hieronymus Bosch – if only we could have been filming it.

Finally the injured pair were led back to the hotel, but at 3am there was no vinegar available to bathe the savage sea-urchin rash. The night porter told them there was only one reliable emergency treatment: 'Somebody has to pee on it.'

They looked around for a volunteer . . .

It was a telling moment, like being bitten on the backside by a venomous snake; you instantly discover your *real* friends.

Later when I discussed the emergency with our Flying Doctor, he praised the natural first aid some kindly person had provided. 'Usually, after we take all the spines out, the next day will be very painful. I was really surprised how well he was. I'm quite convinced there *is* something in that urination theory.'

As Doctor in Charge of the drama, how much had he contributed to the first aid? 'No, it wasn't provided by me – it's not part of my kit.' I was rather relieved that our programme budget was not going to be hit, because Harley Street pee can be extremely expensive – especially if delivered personally on a call out.

Next day we flew around the jagged peaks and gorges of Tahiti in a helicopter that almost lopped the treetops, then soared up alongside the highest mountain – over 7,500 feet – amid racing clouds and driving rain. As we swooped about over the dramatic emerald island I attempted to film a conversation with the enormous Reggie, on his first chopper flight, and Dennis. It transpired that Reggie was quite frightened and Dennis was quite deaf; finding the helicopter noise painful, he had disconnected his hearing aid. One way and another, it was an unusual interview.

When we landed a subdued Josephine told us it had been the most terrifying forty minutes of her life. She had kept her eyes shut during the entire flight, so much of Tahiti's beauty had escaped her.

That night there was an eye-opening traditional tamaara, a moonlight feast on a beach lit by flaming torches, with wonderful lobsters, oysters and mahi-mahi. The hula girls were enchanting. It was the classic dreamy South Seas set piece, as seen in the best brochures: grass skirts, soft melodies, moonlit waves, seductive hands . . . and the reason why people travel, in one shot. We were delighted with the experience and with our pictures. Later we discovered the whole roll had been lost in the developer's laboratory.

Another dawn, another Wonder: it was a six-hour flight on Day Twenty-five to the loneliest island in the world, lost in a million square miles of South Pacific: Easter Island, only five miles by fifteen, with a population of 2,300. The ultimate trophy destination – and one of only two places on our thirty-four-day itinerary that the harbour mistress and I had never visited.

It was first sighted by a Dutch admiral on Easter Sunday 1722; then some fifty years later, by Captain Cook. We had reached a true conversation-stopper, the place people brag about to neighbours who are merely going to Australia. Easter Island, a very long way from anywhere, can trump any other destination.

It used to be visited by only one ship a year, but now a couple of flights arrive each week from Chile, 2,500 miles away, bound for Tahiti, another 2,650 miles. It was not a route on which to run out of fuel. The nearest land is Pitcairn, eleven hundred miles away – a large rock with a population of forty-five, a dozen homes, a shop that opens one hour a week, and no airstrip.

Our arrival on Easter, the other remote volcanic dot, was a big event. Chilean Customs celebrated the rare visitation by insisting on inspecting *every* piece of luggage, including those in the hold. We had dealt without too much trouble with such notoriously finicky Customs officers as the Egyptians, Indians and Chinese, so were unprepared for the Islanders' rigorous assault.

After the Hong Kong and Sydney shopping sprees our luggage was edging towards five hundred pieces. The tiny Customs hall, about the size of a cricket pavilion, was not geared to international big spenders, and overflowed. There were few officials around to cope with the upheaval they had created, and no porters. For the first time on the tour we experienced total chaos: everyone shouting and struggling and trying to manhandle their round-the-world luggage; even Josephine began to suspect she should not have brought ten cases.

'What are they looking for?' someone snarled at my camera. 'A bomb?'

The Customs men were bemused by what they had done, but implacable in their determination to run their hands through every case. Amid the turmoil one of the Ugly Sisters declared it was all being done for the benefit of the film crew. Laugh or cry, there was no answer to that – except possibly a swift karate chop. It was a long night and, as our Torquay bachelors probably said, not in the brochure.

Eventually we arrived at our hotel – another collection of army huts. Each basic room in the prefab lit by a forty-watt bulb had a few hooks, a shower and a couple of narrow nursery beds. The walls were so thin we could hear someone complaining three rooms away. If we had anything indiscreet to say we learned to turn on the shower, the way we once fooled the KGB.

But after all those miles around the world, all our experiences, we were no longer tourists – we had become *travellers*. Nobody had promised us Easter Island was a rose garden. We world travellers had spirit, experience, and could cope. Without a murmur sex-bomb Josephine set about crushing her bedroom cockroaches with a golden sandal. A fortnight earlier she would have had hysteria, and fainted.

The hotel breakfast room, distributing greasy bacon on Day Twenty-six, was like the mess hall of a bleak army camp. We were already calling it Dartmoor-on-Sea. The efficient Thomas Cook had sent a girl out in advance to teach them how to cook eggs and bacon, at least; her lessons had not survived translation.

We left in rickety minibuses to cross the damp treeless island, like Rannoch Moor on a wild day, eager for our first close-up of the great heads. These moais were carved around AD 300 out of basalt rock and transported to the coast by worshippers, nobody knows how. They have stared disdainfully through the centuries, and remain the ultimate target for travellers who have seen everything. The smallest is ten feet tall, the largest seventy-three feet. My guide book said there were 394 of them, our tour guide 'more than a thousand'. There were a *lot*, all magnificent. Many more lie buried. Those not covered by moss, say the locals, are still alive. To stand before them was a humbling experience.

Endless theories surround the original Easter Islanders. Polynesian, or ancient Egyptians; maybe survivors of a sunken continent – a Pacific Atlantis. Some believe the statues were moved by the magic powers of an extinct race of priests, others credit extraterrestrials.

Wherever they came from, I thought it a great privilege to have seen their formidable home and, walking those misty acres in driving wind and chill rain, realized that the best part of a visit to such a trophy destination would be in talking about it *afterwards* . . .

We had been given a taste of what could happen when this last remaining travel target comes on the package route. Tourists already dominate much of the world, as I said before we started our journey. First, Spain, then flights from Luton Airport moved on to the Greek Islands, to Florida, to India and the Far East, to Australia. What destinations remain? Which land has not yet surrendered to travellers' cheques? Already the growth of tourism across the world is limited only by runway capacity. Because of the space race Easter could now cope with almost anything – though the Customs Department might need some rethinking.

The only souvenir I have ever brought back from anywhere in the last forty years is a copy of one of the Easter Island speaking tablets, the *kohau rongo-rongo*. It lies on my desk now – a slim elegant piece of woodcarving covered in hieroglyphics which no expert has ever been able to decipher. These baffling ideograms still exude a powerful message, adding to all the other unsolved mysteries of their inscrutable homeland.

And now for something completely different. I know you won't believe this, but once upon a time in the early 1970s the vibrant reality of *Whicker's World* was actually mocked by a very odd group calling itself Monty Python. A succession of awful imitation Whickers strutted with stick mikes across a beach under the waving palms of Felixstowe. It was supposed to be an island populated only by Whickers in grey suits and old school ties, talking to camera in Whickeric and desperation. In their pay-off line a Python complained that the problem was that there were now not enough millionaires left for Whicker to interview . . .

The skit was funny, repeated endlessly, and has bugged me ever since. I wrote my congratulations to John Cleese, etc., with a PS saying he would of course be hearing from my solicitors. By return they sent a number of signed photographs of the five

Python Whickers under their property palms, and a note saying, 'Here's some evidence for them.'

On Easter Island with my planeload of big-spenders I filmed an accurate and cathartic retaliation by doing the Pythons doing me, striding to and fro before those great statues and complaining that the *real* trouble with Whicker Island was that there were far too many millionaires, and not enough Whickers to interview them . . .

We were at the bottom of the world, our most southerly landfall. We had covered 28,000 miles and on Day Twenty-seven started on the last 9,000, uphill all the way home. After the vast distances to which we had grown accustomed, this seemed a shortish leg – though it was still 3,500 miles, or an Atlantic crossing.

We took off from the deserted airfield on a flight that seemed reassuring, for we were leaving the endless empty South Pacific, where you can feel very lonely, and flying towards land. When we finally saw it after five hours it was the towering Chilean Andes: magnificent, though still not totally comforting.

We flew high over Santiago and in the evening landed at Iguazu Falls, on the Argentinian side looking at Brazil and Paraguay. On a previous visit I had stayed at the old Brazilian hotel, which was stately but growing decrepit. Our Argentinian hotel was compact and modern and, after the best Easter Island could provide, felt like Claridge's.

Its seven-acre garden stood on the brink of the Falls, where thirty rivers thundered over a 200-foot precipice in hundreds of cataracts covered by a permanent cloud of spray. The Falls are so vast that when Eleanor Roosevelt saw them she said, 'Poor Niagara.' Iguazu is higher, twice as wide and seemed somehow . . . wetter. We were in an emerald jungle brilliant with orchids. Butterflies the size of soup plates landed on my shoulders, and spiders, big as a fist, happily did not.

Attempting 37,000 miles in five weeks may have taken some of the holiday out of travel but it provided almost every day a sight-of-your-life, and turned everyone into Action Man. To reinforce our new Indiana Jones image we went for the scenic helicopter flight over the Falls, which was even more hair-raising than the flight through the gorges of Tahiti. We swooped and dived over cataracts, clinging on for an exhilarating experience that would have stunned and petrified Mrs Roosevelt, let alone Josephine.

I flew upfront in one chopper while in another the intrepid Mike Fox – totally unconcerned by heights and aircraft – sat dangling his legs over the side and filming. With my vertigo, I couldn't even look at him.

I was deeply relieved to land safely, but was then instantly asked to do it again; the director wanted pictures of our chopper taking off and landing. Another spectacular flight. Returning to blessed earth, I feared my knuckles would remain permanently white.

Then some of us put on lifebelts and went to shoot the rapids. I got a few tour verdicts while crashing and bouncing upriver beneath the Falls. Someone said, 'We shall bore our families for years, talking about this holiday.' Clinging on anxiously, I listened and believed.

On Day Twenty-eight we went flying down to Rio in a heaven of blue. On the final 750 miles to the Atlantic, I got a faint presentiment of what was to come. Dante had something to tell everyone, and it was about the dangers of Rio – a city where muggings and even killings were frequent. As we drove through the jungle in the airport bus, he spread the warning word.

Our well-heeled eighty-four were cautioned never to walk anywhere after dark in that throbbing city, and in daylight to take the greatest care, even in main streets. We should use hotel hire cars rather than risk cruising taxis. Under no circumstances should we wear watches or even costume jewellery. Wallets and handbags, credit cards and cash must be left in the hotel safe. Cameras must be carried in plastic bags.

His warnings, reinforced by others, unnerved everyone. We prepared warily for an assault landing in the world's fantasyland, among eleven million Cariocas, the girl from Ipanema, and those bank and train robbers who could not get into the Costa del Sol.

It did not seem quite the right moment for me to add that when I was filming a *Whicker's World* around the cataclysmic Rio carnival a Swissair steward had been murdered outside the hotel where we were now about to stay. A gang had come down from their *favela* to plunder, and he was brave and foolish enough to fight back.

Simon Laxton tried to reassure everyone by explaining that

Thomas Cook had hired three armed security men to help protect us; they would always be there. Even *Whicker's World* would be guarded by an armed heavy. When we started filming, our solemn standover man with a revolver stuck into his belt kept walking sullenly into shot.

The depression was lightened when Dante recalled 'a personal experience I had with my last party here. There was this couple walking along Copacabana beach when two voluptuous ladies approached and started fondling the gentleman – or groping, is that correct? Anyway they started groping this fellow, sort of teasingly, and the wife laughed a little bit. Then the two girls disappeared – and when he felt in his back pocket, his wallet had gone.

'So I suggest to all my gentlemen that they leave their wallets behind and put just one dollar in their back pocket, so you get frisked by these girls, a nice little feeling, for one dollar. It's very cheap – the best value in South America.'

We had not filmed these warnings nor the cheerful postscript, for once again our cameras were packed and in the hold. We also did not get a single picture as we came flying across the most beautiful harbour in the world. There's always a hollow feeling of defeat when you are thoughtless or silly enough to miss superb sound or pictures; they can never be recaptured. You always console yourself for such defeats by saying, 'We'll pick it up later.' It never happens again. The moment has gone.

As though to counteract those ominous warnings, Rio Customs and Immigration waved us through, and we arrived at the Sheraton just after lunch. This hotel has a beautiful position on the sea between the beaches of Ipanema and Leblon, beneath a picturesque but menacing hillside *favela*. On my previous visits it had always proved perfectly adequate. This time it went into Fawlty Towers mode; most rooms unprepared, some still occupied, many unclean. It had only six lifts to serve 617 rooms and twenty-seven floors, and several were not working. From my twenty-fifth floor I often waited twenty minutes to get down to the lobby – it was as bad as hanging about for a No 9 bus. Schedules went to pieces. Moving between rooms was a major exercise.

This shambles placed our now-not-quite-so-gallant eighty-four in a quandary: they hated the hotel, but were afraid to go out. In addition the November weather was stiflingly humid. We retreated to our beds, muttering.

Next day some of us set off dutifully to tour the lovely city, scene of an endless battle between Haves and Have-nots. We were most certainly Haves, but were dressing down and stripped for tourism: every bag in sight was plastic, wedding rings in hotel safe, running shoes laced, cheapest sunglasses . . . We really were not worth a detour.

We climbed 2,000 feet up the Corcovado mountainside in the cogwheel railway to reach Christ the Redeemer, arms outstretched in benediction. I have always thought this the most wonderful statue, and in a diary piece at the summit recalled that one of our group had agreed with me it was magnificent – but added that she thought the one in Lisbon was a better likeness . . .

A Brazilian Tourist Board woman travelling with us heard my wry comment – and reported to her superiors that I had been attacking Rio. Another official later hoped we weren't going to talk about muggings and dangers. I told him my fellow travellers talked about little else.

A German courier with a Brazilian wife thought it the world's most dangerous city; every day there were pages of newspaper obituaries of unfortunates who had been murdered. Such conversations made everyone more aware of the heavy iron grilles over shop windows, the armed security, the predatory gangs of children living on the streets, the city's watchful tension. Our high-flyers, already timid, were now petrified. Amid their insecurity, they hardly noticed the beauty and excitement of the place and found it hard to appreciate grandeur when constantly looking over their shoulders. The inefficient hotel completed the high misery count.

That afternoon we went up the Sugar Loaf Mountain in one of those dramatic cable cars where I always expect James Bond and Jaws to be fighting across the roof. All was peaceful as we looked down towards the city and its wide beaches. That night our survivors went to a samba show, a sad touristy event and a pale shadow of Rio's throbbing samba schools that could make a robot dance.

Next day, with great relief, we left Rio – which still contrived to provide a last-minute drama: moving through the airport Brian, the bachelor from Torquay, was asked to open a case he was carrying for Josephine. After some language confusion he shouted in exasperation at the policewoman – and was promptly arrested and pushed against a wall. He was very frightened by this: 'I'd heard stories of people being taken off and shot.' The only help came from my crew, since the camera assistant spoke Portuguese. They attempted to get him released. This was admirably public-spirited, but not very professional. I would have preferred them to have taken pictures of that telling farewell.

So all in all *Whicker's World* did rather poorly in Rio – and the city did even worse. 'The most awful place I've ever been to,' said the thoughtful Sir John Hall as we prepared to fly away. 'A disaster from beginning to end.' Eileen Brownsword, who had loved the whole tour and never complained, wailed, '*Why* did they send us to Rio?'

It was all most unfortunate. Rio is one of the most dramatic and exciting of cities in a glorious setting and its endemic mugging and robbery can usually be avoided with reasonable care. Though some of our number became paranoid and were too frightened even to step outside the disorganized hotel, no ill befell those who did brave the city. Yet as our TriStar took off on the long flight to New York, relief burst out in cheers and applause. Ahead of us, the notorious streets of Manhattan would surely seem as safe and secure as Frinton.

Some time after my series had been shown, officials from the Brazilian Tourist Board came to invite me to return to Rio where everything, they said, was now peaceful and much safer. I made an excuse and didn't leave.

Released from Rio, we happily faced the longest airborne day of the tour: almost 3,000 miles north to a refuelling stop in the Caribbean, then another 2,200 miles on to New York. We were carefree as we crossed the Amazon basin and Devil's Island and landed in Barbados – to another curious reception.

On our flightpath much earlier we had refuelled on New Zealand's South Island, when the hospitable people of Christchurch organized a Maori reception, drove us round their cathedral city, gave us a delicious tea and allowed us to spend £3,000 in a quick dash through a gift shop full of sheepskin things.

To my surprise Barbados was indifferent to the big-spenders from the sky. Not only did they neglect to offer the passing heavy hitters as much as a rum punch, but they would not even let anyone off the aircraft. We had been sitting for six hours and had expected to stretch our legs in the airport shops before facing another five hours on to New York, yet were not permitted to set foot on the hot tarmac.

Despite that non-existent welcome we were so relieved to have left Brazil behind that we cheerfully took it in turns to stand at the top of the steps in the last of the sunshine that had followed us from Egypt. We each took a few illicit breaths of fresh air – for which the Bajan authorities made no charge at all.

That Sunday evening, Day Thirty-one, we landed in New York convinced that after our Brazilian demoralization, the last few days of the tour would be roses all the way. Wrong.

The much-criticized US Immigration and Customs nodded us through politely – but then our very own Thomas Cook, who had handled us so well around the Third World, fell flat on his face. When group travel works, it smooths your way; when it does not, you are better off on your own. I have never been a groupie, and at JFK I knew why. It was cold and wet and the wind cut through our tropicals, but worse – after a month of tender loving care according to Filofax, suddenly nobody cared. It was the end of an affair.

We were left to pick up our 500-pieces-and-counting of accompanied luggage and hunt for unmarked buses somewhere in the dark damp New York night. We never found the baggage trucks. It took a long long time to get ourselves and our suitcases together in that charmless airport, and head for the Waldorf Astoria.

There the buses dropped us at the back door, to avoid the Sunday evening traffic. This seemed sensible to me, but to our weary eighty-four it was the final insult: to be left at the trades-men's entrance to wander undirected through a strange 1,410-room hotel as cosy as the Albert Hall . . . The Ultimate Package, which had started in such high spirits, was disintegrating dismally.

On Day Thirty-two some of us dutifully went on the mandatory city tour and the harbour cruise, but most just wanted to hit the Fifth Avenue stores. We were beginning to look like our passport photos, so it was time to go home – and time for me to wind up the experience, to-camera, on Park at 50th.

We had circled the world in one aircraft on one journey, checked out the Wonders of the World, and caught occasional glimpses of the Himalayas, Andes, Amazon . . . an international kaleidoscope sliding by at 500 mph, six miles below. We had spent more than seventy hours in the air on a circuit made even more rigorous by the fact that we were going round the *wrong* way, travelling east against the sun – so discombobulating sleep patterns as well as digestions.

Most of us had now got all the trophy destinations we could handle but, surprisingly, the romance of travel never quite got through, though it had every opportunity: those moonlit nights on the Nile, the spell of the Taj Mahal, the stark beauty of the Outback, the seductive rhythms of the South Seas . . . nothing seemed to work. Maybe we were all too tired. I detected only one budding romance, between a couple of shy middle-aged loners. We were all happy about this most suitable affair and pretended not to notice.

I need not have worried about being caged up for five weeks with eighty-seven strangers, for almost all of them were pleasant – though the occasional boarding house paranoia did develop: he has a better seat, she has *two* eggs. We suffered a few perpetual whingers, as would any group of that size. One woman who had happily paid her £21,000 fare registered an official complaint because she had not been given the $3 T-shirt promised in some brochure. One protested because there were too many Indians at the Maharaja's Ball; another said the guides talked too much. The tour proved once again that pleasant people never complain – and nobody pays much attention to the unpleasant, because they complain all the time.

As for missing luggage . . . we decided that Josephine's shoes should be written off as a contribution to the Chinese. Or was it the Indians?

When we shot the rapids at Iguazu, Eileen Brownsword had told me, 'A lot of people watching your programmes are going to say: "I wish I'd been there".' After five weeks' hard travelling, the summing-up was: 'It's been pure magic – but not when you're tired.'

Emerson said no man would find anything in travel he did not bring with him on the journey. On this major expedition I don't think any of us got *quite* what we expected. We were divided between experienced travellers prepared to pay higher fares for a slower tour with more luxury and spare time; the majority who found schedule and price about right – and those who could only just afford it and were taking their first wide-eyed wondering and appreciative look at the world beyond their horizon.

In travel as in life, you get what you pay for, and everyone crammed a lifetime of experience into those five weeks, though they turned out to be not quite as easy and luxurious, not as privileged and stylish as promised.

I took this up with Christopher Rodriguez, then Thomas Cook's Managing Director. 'I think we've all learned,' he said. 'We have learned how to write to this target market – who are *not* brochure readers. They clearly have money, because this isn't a free trip. Other people buy a new Mercedes, new sound equipment; these people have said that travel's important to them.

'In future I would prefer a forty-day tour rather than thirty-four – but having said that, I would lay a bet that they'd then cram forty-five days of travel into forty, just as this time we've crammed forty into thirty-four. People are committed to getting every experience they can out of a tour, so if you send them to a beach for a couple of days they'll say "Why are we here, doing nothing?" It's Catch 22. Some of the fifty-year-olds haven't kept up with the seventy-five-year-olds, but that's life. No one has offered one of these tours before: it's a bit like the moonshot.'

To declare an interest, I must say I enjoyed my first package, though I was often too tired for logical thought; but then, I *do* like to watch people and see the world go by. I might even do it again – but not next week . . . I had never come to think of an airliner as home before – but there are far worse places.

Most of our high-flyers were distracted on Day Thirty-three by serious last-minute shopping around Manhattan, while Thomas Cook went into a frenzy backstage. Towards the end things had not gone well, and they faced disgruntled clients and doubtless, from the Americans, lawsuits. Determined to neutralize dissatisfactions in one mighty bound they worked desperately to make sure their first World Tour ended in a blaze of spectacle and happiness.

They had planned a 150th anniversary celebration on the Waldorf's Starlight Roof, flying in various VIPs from overseas. Peter Middleton, travel grandee and then Chief Executive of the Group who once spent three years in a cell, as a monk, told me he had authorized an additional £60,000 expenditure on that one party – topping up what had already been spent. This was just to end on a high note and wipe away any bad memories. It also wiped away any tour profit.

Party planners, decorators, lighting experts had been flown in, showgirls lined up, floor show organized. The charge for us to bring extra guests to that party was £195 a head. It proved a most elegant evening for the weary yet triumphant travellers; superb meal in a jolly end-of-term atmosphere which left most of them laughing – though a few grumbled, 'Why couldn't they have done it like this, all the way round?'

The main raffle prize for one fortunate passenger was to be the return of the ticket price: £21,000. I refused to draw the winner, having made enough enemies from the last raffle, but did agree to present the prize. The suspense was electric. Another guest dug down and handed me the winning name. I was aghast – and thankful I had not picked it myself.

Out of the eighty-four remaining travellers the winner, once again, was that Dorset Boadicea, the harbour mistress of Wareham. In our other raffle Mrs Babs Elvins had won a first class return fare and lots of free holidays in India. She loved travel, was always on parade on time and showed whingers no mercy, but even so most of us thought her remarkable luck was becoming too much of a good thing. She still sends me postcards from around her world – indeed once even ventured as far as my home. This tour must have been her first holiday to show a profit.

On our final shining night the Peter Duchin orchestra played 'Auld Lang Syne' and, as artificial snowflakes fell, I did a final diary piece to-camera, wondering whether our nest-eggs and our dreams had got together. Then it was midnight – and all the dashing world travellers turned back into workaday tourists.

Valerie Kleeman's postscript for another world traveller:

We got to know Josephine during five intense and frantic weeks. She had bounced into our lives the day we met our eighty-seven at the inaugural lunch, sweeping into a room full of quiet greying couples, a blend of *Funny Girl* and *femme fatale*. Blonde and in her early fifties, wearing a navy suit with Chanel handbag, carefully made-up and straight from the hairdresser, she stood alone at the door for a moment and cast a practised eye around the room.

In the seconds it took to scan the guests she knew her money was wasted: there was no husband potential. 'If I hadn't paid my deposit, I wouldn't be going,' she said later. 'There's not a single person in this room I want to have sex with.' Then she took a glass of champagne and braced herself to make the best of it.

Six weeks later, settling back in the Orient Express as we left Victoria, Josephine told us her story. She had married young, then fallen in love with her au pair's boyfriend. Taking her baby daughter, she eloped with him to Spain, where she discovered his patrician Catholic family was not thrilled with the idea of a married Jewish daughter-in-law. Isolated but in love, she stayed, feeling increasingly uneasy. One day on a balcony watching the traditional Easter procession as the Virgin was carried shoulder high through the crowded town by masked penitents, she panicked and fled back to London.

The next man who walked into her life was a married Belgian, 'the wedding-ring king of Europe'. Wealthy and gregarious, he gave her the high life she had always craved. For years they lived as man and wife, with her daughter believing them married.

On her birthday he took her out to celebrate. They deliberately avoided Mayfair, for Scott's had just been bombed by the IRA. Halfway through their meal in Knightsbridge the IRA struck again. Josephine and their two friends slid under the table, the Belgian stood up to see what was happening – and took the full force of the bomb.

Hours later in St Stephen's Hospital she was approached by two policemen. 'Can you identify this? We've taken it off a body.' She looked up to see her photograph had been found in her lover's wallet. His legal wife appeared, made the decisions, and drove Josephine home in a taxi. Since they had never married she had no rights; grieving and shocked, she was not legally a widow.

Next she married someone big in the bridalwear business and lived contentedly until he died, leaving her comfortably off but lonely and desperate to find another man. 'It was a lot easier last time,' she said.

'People always ask, "How are you?" I always say, "Fine." Who wants a miserable woman?' Now, she said, sex had to be either for love or for a *lot* of money. By the time the train reached Folkestone we knew her longings, hopes and fears. She, full of champagne, was asleep.

Throughout the next five weeks it was impossible not to be aware of her. She ate, drank, flirted, complained, giggled. She added a welcome frisson to any event. She was a restless presence drifting from group to group, looking for someone to make life worth living. Some single ladies referred to her grimly as The Maneater. Eyeing one happily married sunbather she told him, 'You look great naked.' His wife's lips turned white.

Josephine was a man's woman, a rare creature in today's world and, politically, totally incorrect. She lived her life to be pampered and adored, and returned the compliment. She was by turns maddening in her self-absorption and disarming in her generosity and warmth. She was also disaster-prone: if baggage got lost, it was hers; if there was a caterpillar in the salad, it would land on her plate. Several times she decided to leave and go home, but always changed her mind at the last moment when all arrangements had been made.

She was petrified on her helicopter flight around Tahiti, certain that she would be mugged in Rio – yet always survived to reach the next destination wearing a new outfit and a bright hopeful smile.

On our TriStar she was either asleep, or gossiping up a storm. Once, flying from Australia to New Zealand, she sat beside Alan for a couple of hours while he took a rare break. Two days later she complained that he had been ignoring her. 'It's *her*, isn't it?' she said, looking meaningfully across the plane at me.

'I don't think you quite understand our relationship,' he replied, amused.

'You don't understand women,' she said.

When I showed her a new brooch she was appalled that I had

bought it myself. 'You don't know how to talk to him,' she said, reproachfully. I felt I had failed the entire female sex.

My last glimpse of her was after we had landed at Stansted late at night, tired at the end of our five-week endurance test of a holiday. In an oversized T-shirt and leggings, she was waiting to go through Customs and, beaming from ear to ear, was chatting up a handsome young policeman. She was back on her home ground where there was fresh talent – and she was ready to start running again.

One night soon after our return we had a call from her Torquay bachelors. Josephine had been spending the weekend with friends before setting off on her travels again, this time to a Marbella clinic to have the facelift she longed for but dreaded. Full of joy and trepidation she took her old face for one last evening out. Driving home after dinner there was a head-on collision. She was killed instantly.

The baritone put a bomb
on board . . .

Mexico seemed like a blow in the face; we were stunned by its beauty, squalor and excitement, and from the first day of filming were nervous and stimulated. No one could be indifferent to so dramatic and passionate a land – tormented and violent, lovely and hateful.

The courteous Mexican, proud and vulnerable, has held on to an Indian heritage and, just as his land is both Garden of Eden and garbage dump, some Mexicans are chic worldlings while others move in the dark of superstition.

The red of blood and the black of death have always stained their nation, where many face a future that does not exist and a past they dare not remember. Today they lead the world's population explosion. In 1963 when we filmed there were 38m Mexicans. In 1998, after thirty-five years, 98m.

The *peon* who works all day for the price of a few *tortillas* and beans has but one compensation: his wife. Both now live a little longer and more of their children survive, so the benefits of progress are spread discouragingly thin; Mexico City stands ringed by its 'belts of misery'. Within sight of opulent high-rises, millions of homeless have parachuted, as they say, on to any vacant land.

The penniless and usually illiterate peasant, driven from the land by a government policy pandering to strong industrial unions by keeping agricultural prices artificially low, comes to Mexico City with his family to hunt for work, which he rarely finds. Such is the human spirit that sometimes, amid despondency, pride and amiability remain. At least the benevolent Mexican sun softens the harsh outline of existence.

Once the doorways of the capital were jammed every night with frozen bundles of newspapers that were homeless boys. Much of the population had no shoes, and for men the only protection against summer rains and winter nights was *pulque* – a spirit made from cactus – while for women it was cotton shawls, and prayer.

Girls of twelve with listless faces hung around the night streets. Prostitution has not disappeared from Mexico, but it is better fed and clothed, not quite as hungry and diffident, not quite as young.

It could be that in some ways these people are more free than at any time since the days of their magnificent ancestors, the Maya, who knew the zero fifteen-hundred years before Europe discovered decimals. In their savage and beautiful land we found the explosive mixture of peoples speaking fifty different languages was ruled by a race of amiable but moody trigger-men who ran the government while attempting to feed and house the ever-growing tide that washed against the borders of their capital.

We reached Mexico City at Eastertime, and were flung into the deep end of a country fervently religious – though officially atheist. We went to film the Crucifixion at Ixtapalapa, joining the solemn smouldering mass of a quarter of a million watching this fierce Passion Play. It could have been just such a crowd upon a dusty hillside at that other Calvary.

Tourists were warned to keep away. Pickpockets ferreted through the crush. We had organized a truck, and filmed from its open back amid the tumult. As we struggled to repel boarders, we received unexpected support from our escorting Man from the Ministry – a burly hovering figure. He took a gun from a hidden holster and waved it about. Occasionally he hit intruders with its butt, quite sorrowfully. I think he came from Public Relations.

Our day of awe and violence had begun before dawn, in peace – but already the promise of turbulence hung upon shimmering air. The morning sun fell upon a raggle-taggle brass band as it spread its unique *mariachi* sound across the growing mass of worshippers – and helmeted police standing ready with tear gas.

In the hot dust, amid realism heightened by a harsh and arid landscape, and by emotion, we waited to see the trial of Christ, the procession to Calvary, the Crucifixion.

Easter at Ixtapalapa was no simple demonstration of faith and religious conviction, for beneath the elemental medieval Christianity of a complex people, an ancient pagan tradition survives. They have a straightforward habit of taking mysteries literally: a congregation will send their Virgin Mary up to Heaven rather fast – with the help of a rocket.

The Mexicans are proud and courteous, poetic, cruel and violent. They regard the Cross as a potent symbol of the old Magic Calendar. It is not an abstraction, but is itself a wonder-working God. All the ancients of central America worshipped that Cross – which as a Christian symbol may still quite safely be invoked by pagans.

So, before us, an agonized Christ in his crown of thorns. He was an employee of the local office of the Ministry of Justice, and took the role of Jesus each year. With the two barefooted thieves, he was scourged through the streets. This was no gentle Oberammergau; there was little play-acting in the intolerable burden of this Cross.

Led through dust clouds by penitents, the three slowly climbed the arid rocky hill which once had been the site of the most significant Aztec ceremonies: every fifty-two years they awaited the end of the world, and priests sacrificed an honoured victim here, building a fire in the cavity from which they had just ripped out his heart.

The Aztecs – distant ancestors of the men we were filming – were a colourful and lusty race. The violent pageantry of their religious ceremonies could be matched, perhaps, only by the solemn ferocity of Inquisitional Christianity.

When the Church turned to kindness and paternal benevolence, to conversion by Christian example, the Indians, the would-be converts, missed the violence and orgiastic release of their old religion. Sometimes they would slip away for a surreptitious rain dance to their old God, Tlaloc.

So the good Friars, tempering their Christianity with practicality, decided to put a little more zing into their piety. They allowed Mexicans to adapt the Catholic hagiography to their own tastes and colours, their own sense of drama, their memory of the terror a deity *ought* to inspire.

Religion elsewhere in the world can become a weekly investment in peace of mind which need not intrude upon the practicalities of everyday life. In Mexico it is a central tragedy – the very core of pain and humility, the altar of guilt and self-effacement. Moaning peasants approach shrines upon their knees, their heads, necks, waists and ankles strung with spiky cactus leaves that tear the skin. At Ixtapalapa they were venerating the God who destroyed their own Gods – banished the Smoking Mirror, the Hummingbird Wizard, the Feathered Serpent. They had come to worship the greatest God of all, whose soldiers broke the old images. A God who for the first time did not exact human sacrifice – but instead, sacrificed himself.

It is impossible for most Mexican Indians to regard Catholic deities as distant, inscrutable beings. In some areas they are still on probation, still aliens who may just possibly turn out to possess unusual power. After almost five centuries of Christianity, they still treat their saints as idols.

As we filmed from our truck amid the awestruck mass, we wondered whether the dusty figure before us, struggling up the hill beneath the weight of the Cross, was seen by the worshipping, moaning, ecstatic crowd as man, or idol, or god.

All those taking part in that holy procession were living roles that had been handed down from generation to generation. Each dusky Indian centurion, haughty in his red velvet cloak, retained his family's role.

The intensity of their fervour created a disquieting air of reality. I was uncomfortably aware that all through southern Mexico there remain traces of a cult, a thin stream of memory or fanaticism which centres upon the Indian Christ – a dark Christ who was crucified *for* the Indians. Among both Maya and Zatopec, Indians have offered themselves for actual crucifixion on such days – a rite carried out in deepest secrecy and reverence.

They reason: 'The Christ who died far away across the seas, rejected by his own people, did not know the Indians; but if one of us should die upon the Cross of his own will, then we can be sure this sacrifice was truly made for us.' So token crucifixions have become fatally real and peasants have been nailed to the

Cross they carried, to die upon a hill before a hushed and reverent mass.

Dazed and drained by the heat and emotion of that day, we went on to Cholula, near Puebla in central Mexico, to film what must be the greatest concentration of churches in the world, yet serving only a few thousand people. There are said to be 365 in that gilded cluster, offering the very faithful a different church to attend each day of the year.

Cholula was once the holy city of the great Aztec Confederation – the Aztec Rome. Hernando Cortés, the Spaniard who conquered that warlike race with 500 men, sixteen horses and ten brass guns, passed through in 1520 on his triumphant march to the capital of the Aztec empire, Tenochtitlán – now Mexico City.

He ordered every temple razed and a church built upon its site. So inside those new Christian churches, anonymous Indian artists mixed their ancient complex imagery, drug inspired, with the heady inspiration of the ardent Spanish friars. They painted an army of angels with knowing faces, and robust cherubs inspired by village babies. Their dark-skinned saints with slanting eyes were stocky as the Cholulans, their totem-pole faces looking down from a profusion of ornamented arabesques. Not one inch of wall or ceiling remains uncarved, unpainted or ungilded. The figure of Christ is not the bland, antiseptic symbol we know in our churches. The Mexican adores his doleful, flayed Christ.

Over the centuries, it seems, anonymous Indian artisans have applied themselves to a catechism in reverse: the angels are Indian, the saints are Indian – even God is Indian. The ghosts of those slaughtered Aztecs must rejoice to see how victorious Catholicism has been Indianized.

After such tortuous and intense days, we escaped with relief into a fiesta – and there is no better place to forget the terrors of the Hereafter and the frustrations of the Now than at the San Marcos Fair in Aguascalientes, most famous of all Mexico's festivals. From the capital it was a long day's drive, and of course when we arrived there was No Room At The Inn. We bedded down, gratefully, in a hotel's cheerful and crowded lobby.

As we began to film the fiesta we were constantly told by escorts and officials that some French photographer wanted to meet us. Amid the noise and confusion such an invitation was low on my priority list, until a white-haired man forced his way through the crowd – and turned out to be the great Henri Cartier-Bresson, taking pictures for a book. We fell about, and of course from then on he travelled with us, and shamed my cameraman by being twice his age but more than twice as active.

The fiesta, Mexico's highest expression of social life, proved the most shapeless, most ragged of combustions – a happy explosion of the communal soul. Festivals are constantly breaking out somewhere in Mexico, because every day belongs to some saint. For run-of-the-mill saints, fiestas last a day or two. Very miraculous saints are saluted for a week. St Mark was acknowledged by two weeks of carnival. The texture of his nights was thick – a heady tropical mixture of heat, sweat and religion, and the endless assault of the deafening noise all Mexicans love.

This was a brilliant reversal of the reticence and silence of their ordinary lives and one of the rare occasions when the Mexican opened out to the world – shouting, dancing and firing his pistol in the air. Men who had exchanged only formal courtesies during the year traded confidences, got deeply drunk, discovered they were brothers – and, on occasion, killed each other.

In such an outpouring, the flashpoint of the average Mexican is as low as can be. As a rare foreigner exposed to such dangerous amiability, I faced the nice judgement of how chummy to get with a group of befuddled characters who wanted to be friendly and welcome a stranger – and carried knives in case such friendship was spurned.

There was the further anxiety of just how much one could drink and remain safe socially, as well as internally. Add to that the unforeseen but deadly insult of looking too long at some young woman – or, in some cases, of not looking long enough.

The risk of a sudden outflow of personal blood was increased by the presence of our camera; this delighted some, but confused and infuriated others. Along this delicate tightrope we were forced to take some adroit side-steps to resist thought control by ministers and officials, with the ever-present risk that if those steps were too obvious we could be flung into some dank Mexican slammer, for ever.

There have been many attempts around the world to impose views and attitudes upon me. Revolutionaries, police, politicians, dictators, bureaucrats, pressure groups and public relations men have all, in their various ways, tried to influence my reports, but so far I have never submitted the content of any programme to censorship. Such determined independence can demand fast footwork – and so it proved in Aguascalientes.

We had been casually introduced to a teacher of English, a rather seedy little man out of Graham Greene who leeched on to us and offered his help as interpreter and contact man, in return for meals and drinks. We tolerated him as a grey and shadowy sponger and he followed us around, amiably. Then, filming one night amid the noisy excitement and running into a little local difficulty with some police, our unctuous interpreter forgot himself. He flashed a badge which broke up the argument and caused the officers and everyone else to step back a pace. It revealed him as a powerful officer of the State secret police. We all went rather quiet and thoughtful.

First we had to try to remember what he had seen and over-heard – which was plenty. Then we had to take evasive action and make sure he was decoyed whenever we filmed or recorded anything that might upset him and his superiors – and, afterwards, us.

Though no doubt he could have called for thumbscrews and clanging cell doors, he was not very frightening. When we left town he presented us with some ashtrays he had stolen from a restaurant, and suggested a token tip. May all our secret policemen be as mild.

It was not easy to film in Mexico, but the programmes we sent back must have conveyed some of the flavour of that cataclysmic land, for the commentaries of the *Whicker Down Mexico Way* compilations won the Screenwriters' Guild Award. For any reporter, awards for writing are always the most appreciated.

One of the twenty caused more uproar than the rest put together. It was not the squalor and distress of the *peons* or their bloodthirsty religions that upset viewers but, predictably, some birds doing what came naturally. Within seconds of the end of

Alan Whicker
our programme on cockfighting, the BBC began to receive furious complaints.

Though outlawed in most countries in the world, this activity
was regarded in Aguascalientes as family entertainment. Cocks
with long steel spurs fitted to their claws fought to the death in
the cockpit every night before more than 2,000 people, before
women who seemed bored but watched every fight and men who
came only to bet. All of them I am sure believed that we
Europeans, with our harsh voices and cold indifference to others,
were cruel to our children.

The high point of the carnival was another traditional and
tragic ceremony of savagery and ridiculous courage well suited to
the Mexican character, which made cockfighting look positively
bucolic. It was, furthermore, on the BBC banned list: a bullfight.

We joined the 9,000 who had paid scalpers' prices to be pulled
back several centuries, spectacularly. The heavily edited version
of our film was the first *corrida* ever seen on British television. The
subsequent uproar was a small sample of what was to befall us two
years later when, in *Matador*, we devoted a whole *Whicker's World*
to the famous *torero* El Cordobés.

If you have been brought up in the pure RSPCA spirit, I told
viewers, you'll be horrified at the sight of a magnificent animal,
ribboned barb of the breeding-ranch stuck in its neck, tearing
into the ring pained and infuriated, to be tricked, turned,
speared and killed in a conflict not between bull and man – but
between bull and a great mob of armed men. This bloody and
sickening spectacle can stimulate every unpleasant instinct.

If, on the other hand, you have an investment in the controlled
insane courage of men – even the odd narcissistic ones who
become *toreros* – it is quite an experience to see a slight man
dressed like an expensive doll in his silken suit-of-lights standing
effeminate and alone in the arena holding high two frilled
banderillas to place together, and exactly, in the bull's hump as he
meets and eludes its fearful charge.

At its best, a bullfight dispels the conflict: it is not man against
bull as much as man *with* bull in a magnificent duet, stately and
magical as in some ancient rite.

Such courage is the epitome of the *machismo* which seemed to
me the scourge of Mexico: the need for every man to prove

208

himself very male – preferably by some outrageous and pointless show of courage. If he could not fight a bull, he could demonstrate this by driving through red lights, by knifing someone for an imagined affront, by exerting some brief authority, by establishing a *casa chica* he could not afford, by siring a great number of children. There were endless ways, large and small, but always and above all things every *hombre* had to be *macho*.

How does one explain this national trait? Deep ingrained Indian pride and fatalism, perhaps. The adoration of blood and death common to Aztecs and Spaniards. The years of conquest and cruel class distinction. Such displays of excessive strength grew painfully out of debilities and guilts, out of mixed blood, hunger and unemployment and the knowledge that, through the centuries, he had always been tricked and cheated – first by foreigners, then by his own countrymen.

The outcome, caught in the defiance and narcissism of the bullfight, is a fragile ego, a violent pride, a low flashpoint, and one of the highest murder rates in the world. It also shows itself in great charm and gallantry. It is inescapable.

So unfortunately is *la mordida*, the Bite, which over centuries has become an established national practice. Certainly money talks everywhere in the world, but in Mexico rather more simply and openly. From the traffic policeman who leans on motorists, through underpaid bureaucrats who must be bribed before anything happens and count such bribes part of their salaries, up to ministers who may demand a twenty per cent kickback on the cost of building a dam.

It is expected, and accepted, that most politicians will emerge from office very rich indeed. Resigned and envious Mexicans-in-the-street merely hope that, while enriching themselves, they will help the country too. Sometimes, very rarely, they do.

The few who overplay their hands and cannot buy their way out can end up in Mexico's Black Prison of Lecumberri, where we went one Sunday afternoon to watch convicts enjoying conjugal visits. Wives and girlfriends arrived in a high old state of Latin excitement to spend a few hours in the cells, helping relieve tension.

It was a primitive prison, and the convicts I talked to were inside for crimes of extreme violence – though they seemed an unusually jolly group. This could have been due to the regular and softening influence of their womenfolk, which certainly was the intention of the practical and understanding authorities.

The prison choir sang for us, most beautifully, and just loved being filmed. It was led by a stout and jovial baritone who had once insured all the passengers on an airliner – and sent a bomb along with them, air freight.

Indeed the Mexican attitude to death is very different from ours, as was shown by the gruesome mummies we filmed in the catacombs of old and battered Guanajuato. They are still regularly visited in a friendly fashion by their relatives – like popping round the corner to make sure Gran's all right.

Mexicans have an awareness that Life is the preparation for Death – just the other half of Death. Life may be short and sick and dismal, but death is long; that at least is certain. It is life that is uncertain, so the Mexican displays his coming death as an adornment, a jewel.

To us, death is no joking matter; in Mexico the idea of dying can have something luminous about it – something almost light-hearted. At first sight, the attitude seems playful. To prepare for All Souls' Day, the Day of the Dead, Mexican women bake the Bread of the Dead, fashioning shrouded, appetizing and sweetly smiling corpses, all crisply cinnamoned and glazed. Children walk around munching skulls made of sugar and marked with their own names, or gobbling up chocolate skeletons.

This national holiday became a macabre carnival, for there are few Mexican families who do not make a pilgrimage to the cemeteries to picnic around the graves of dead relatives made merry with candles and flowers. Marigolds are most popular, for they are the traditional Aztec Flowers of the Dead.

Happily mourning families light their candles and begin the night's vigil, eating and exchanging recollections of the person whose grave they are using as a picnic table, and cemeteries seem covered by a dancing legion of will-o'-the-wisps, and enchantment. In Mexico the grave may be fine, but it is *not* a private place . . .

They celebrate in their cemeteries until dawn. Though not all the living may feel fully at ease on such eerie occasions, the dead are supposed to enjoy them very much indeed.

Since this is the day when the Dead are expected to return to visit the Living, improvised altars stand ready in Mexican homes and upon each one are offerings for the departed, usually some enticing titbits – the kind that person once most enjoyed. To the Indians, all dead – particularly family dead – are the subject of real and continuous concern.

In southern Mexico, where people still regard death as the beginning of an actual three-year journey to the next world, they believe that though their souls are 'in glory' they still have human feelings, so upon their annual return visit they are treated with great consideration. Their favourite food and drink is offered, the songs they liked best are sung. Women wear their Sunday clothes and gaudiest necklaces, and children are kept on their best behaviour, exactly as though an honoured guest were in the home.

Next day, after the visiting Dead have enjoyed the essence of the proffered food by inhaling its odour and extracting the flavour, it may then – wisely and economically – be eaten by the household.

In Oaxaca there is a further charming tradition of hospitality to poor old souls who have no families to come back to, no one to entertain them upon their return visit. Separate candles are lit and thoughtful offerings spread, so that no solitary soul need feel lonely or neglected during the general happy reunion.

For days before and after this Day of the Dead, death is everywhere present. In sweet shops, candy skulls have bright tinsel eyes. At toyshops children beg for little coffins out of which jump, at the tug of a string, tiny skeletons. Death-bread leers invitingly from bakery windows. Great papier mâché death's heads are on sale as decoration alongside tissue paper garlands which are the Flowers of Death. Señoritas present their boyfriends with skeleton tie-pins.

Throughout Mexican art, death joins in daily life – macabre, but familiar and not fearful. 'If I must die tomorrow,' they sing with yearning, 'why not at once – today?'

Until quite recently in this violent land, human life had little value. There are many reasons: the insignificance of man amid nature's savage grandeur, the unimportance of the individual in pagan dictatorships, the indelible background of a primitive religion which demanded human sacrifice on a scale unequalled in any other culture.

For centuries Central Americans were convinced that every fifty-two years they faced the end of the world: so they awaited universal death. In our nuclear age we begin to get an inkling of this terror.

They believed that by intense prayer and sacrifice throughout the whole cycle they might be able to keep their gods kindly disposed. At the crucial moment of decision, all mankind had to pray together so that its clock might keep ticking.

Individual death, the Aztecs believed, was not destruction but transformation – so handsome young warriors went happily to the sacrificial slab. It was reasoned that for man to survive, the gods who permitted his existence must also wax strong, so they received the best nutriments, the most precious offerings from the very hearts of men, wrenched by priests from living bodies. At the dedication of one Aztec temple, 20,000 people were sacrificed. Some were skinned, and sometimes their arms and legs were eaten.

Since then in Mexico, where peasants still bury their dead as though planting seeds, death has been domesticated, the skull turned into a popular decoration, the corpses of friends and relations carefully preserved. This familiarity, this intimacy with death that we avoid, does not necessarily mean fearlessness; it could mean a dread that demands elaborate propitiation.

To find Death at the door is no less awesome for Mexicans than it is for us; but in Mexico it knocks more often, and must more frequently be admitted.

Luciano, you *have* to sing tonight . . .

An invitation to an island-warming is hard to resist, should you be inclined to islanditis. I live on one, and have paid my dues on Bali, Easter Island, Western Samoa, Norfolk Island. This party was to be held on a steamy speck of green in the Straits of Malacca, off the west coast of Malaysia. Quite far-flung, for a weekend.

Pangkor Laut – 300 acres of rainforest and smaller than Hyde Park – suddenly became as elegant as it was isolated. The owner of this fantasy island was Francis Yeoh, a third-generation Chinese-Malaysian and strong player on Asia's Bamboo Network. He was planning to jazz up natural perfection and offer guests two major attractions, each well worth the 14,000-mile jaunt. In the end, both of them came together in a ninety-minute *Whicker's World* Special.

Guest of Honour was to be Malaysia's prickly Prime Minister, Dr Mahathir Mohamad, with whom I had passed an agreeable dinner while filming the inaugural run of the Oriental Express from Singapore up to Bangkok. Soon afterwards, the volatile PM declared a trade war against Britain under the slogan 'Buy British Last'. During seven months it cost British companies thousands of jobs and millions of pounds.

He was then refusing to meet Her Majesty's ministers of any rank but – such is the penetrative power of television – he did agree to consider the whole dispute with me, before the cameras. On Pangkor Laut we shared another meal – breakfast, this time – and a long discussion which was later transmitted in ITV's 'serious' spot at Sunday lunchtime.

The other attraction was just as unsettling – and even bigger. Francis Yeoh was offering his few guests an unusual floor show: the world's greatest tenor, Luciano Pavarotti, accompanied by sixty-four members of the Manila Symphony Orchestra. This equatorial event was small but exquisitely formed: a private concert on a private island by the voice of a lifetime – with almost as many people on the stage as in the audience; not an invitation for the Perhaps file.

So, a week later, a couple of hundred of us sat in tropical moonlight perspiring quietly into our evening dress while lightning flashed along the horizon behind the palm trees, experiencing a sort of perfection. We tried to react as ardently as the 850,000 who cheered 'Fat Lucy' in Central Park, or the quarter-of-a-million sodden enthusiasts standing behind Princess Diana's umbrella in Hyde Park, but I suspect he noticed the difference.

With two such powerful reasons to cross eight time zones, we had set off for Kuala Lumpur in a hurry; eleven hours with a good tailwind in an impeccable Malaysian Airlines 747–400. The first 7,000 miles were easy; then it grew more complicated – but paradise islands *should* be hard to reach, right? Otherwise everyone would go, and there's paradise lost.

At Kuala Lumpur airport, still woozy, we considered a variety of tortuous routes towards the end of the rainbow – but then gave in and went the expensive way. Taxi to the helicopter base for a 200-mile flight which swept us away from the world's tallest buildings, over endless neat housing estates and symmetrical palm-oil plantations towards a dark-green island in a shallow azure sea with a coastal fringe of palm trees and silver sand.

The final leg was a short buggy ride from Pangkor Laut's chopper pad to our villa in the sea. I had been thirty-three hours without sleep; a testy Prime Minister and petulant tenor were bearing down upon me and ninety minutes of television waited to be filled . . . but the silver silhouette of that tropical magic isle was calming. Conrad, Somerset Maugham, Gaugin, Noël Coward and all the other South Seas enthusiasts would have been equally transfixed.

During the two days of preparation before the PM and the Voice descended upon us, I strolled a perfect beach with Patrick, Earl of Lichfield, as we filmed the setting sun at Emerald Bay.

'The reason people come to places like this, or Mustique,' said the international photographer, 'is because famous though they may be in Paris or Bonn or wherever, they are *not* famous on tiny islands. They also find privacy, which is something you can't buy. One's not trying to keep out the Great Unwashed, but to be able to relax without a lens being pointed at one.'

After I had told my crew to cut and Patrick had taken a few shots, we wandered off into the sunset, shaking our heads over the frightful intrusion of cameras, which today seem to get *everywhere*.

Pangkor Laut was once a leper colony, but things improved. The unhappy lepers departed and it remained uninhabited until 1943, when a British officer running from the Japanese Army escaped from the mainland. After hiding in its jungle for many months, Colonel Spencer Chapman DSO swam out to be rescued by a Royal Navy submarine. This mode of transport is now hard to organize.

Twenty years later the Sultan of Perak discovered the appeal of his own island, and stationed a guardian there. Ah Pei lived alone for twenty-two years, until his death in 1986.

Then Francis Yeoh hit the place with Malaysian dollars. He ran YTL, a construction conglomerate then capitalized at £100m, so seemed the ideal man to transform a remote equatorial dot into an exclusive hideaway with a couple of hundred wood and rattan villas.

This was not as bad as it sounded. Most paradise isles can be gentled and improved by a little civilized tweaking, and this one had been occupied surreptitiously. The green jungle unchanged for two million years was not scarred by a concrete jungle; instead a sea village as picturesque as those at Bora Bora was built along a patch of coastline, with villas and walkways on stilts, as in a traditional Malay fishing village.

The ethnic look of the brand new *kampong* was deceptive; each of twenty-three stilted pavilions had air-conditioning, bar and jacuzzi opening on to a wide wooden terrace and an equatorial vista, plus other amenities the local anchovy fishermen did not enjoy. Also a massive fruit bowl on which Col. Chapman could have survived for a week.

The natural décor was as prolific and elegantly intrusive as ever: great seabirds soared overhead, yellow pied hornbills made house calls along with crab-eating macaque monkeys about which the resort warned: 'They are primarily good-natured but it is not wise to interact with them'.

Interaction once grew so intense and troublesome that hundreds of monkeys were rounded up and transported to the mainland. The remainder then bred themselves back into mischievous dominance again. Francis Yeoh – the owner, no less – found them scrounging for breakfast remnants on his terrace, and chased them away. They returned later, huffed, and threw his shoes into the sea.

Having reached a paradise isle and come to terms with the monkeys, you then find there is absolutely nothing to do. That's how it is, in paradise. The beaches may be silver and well mani-cured, but the sea is usually grey and uninviting – and there be sea urchins. Extreme heat and humidity limit energy for the everyday windsurfing, scuba-diving, waterskiing, sea cruising – but then, you can get all that at home. No one could lie for long around the elegant dark blue mosaic swimming pool under so fierce an equatorial sun. It was as breathtaking as India, where I once sunbathed before an electric fan; felt *very* odd.

In search of local colour and a life-saving straw hat, I took the staff ferry to the larger island of Pangkor, passing one of the resort's six security men on the jetty – a tubby little figure with large stomach, terrible teeth and a lovely smile.

As we waited I chatted in careful basic English until it tran-spired he had spent years in London working for the Sultan of Brunei, had watched and remembered my programmes and spoke better English than I did. He gave me a thoughtful critique which was welcome but unexpected from a relaxed guard on a remote isle in the Straits of Malacca.

We reached the real Malaysia across a mile of calm sea, and it turned out to be Graham Greene country: a dusty village pervaded by the stench of its speciality – dried fish. Open drains, a few shacks and shops, but no non-plastic hats; I checked every stall, decided to settle for slight sunstroke, and caught the next ferry back to comfortable unreality.

Passing time on Pangkor Laut by gin-slinging yourself into the traditional tropical stupor could also stun your bank manager. Malaysia, fervently Islamic, does not ban alcohol as do other

Muslim lands, but seeks to tax it out of popularity. In the two restaurants the cheapest bottles of Californian Cabernet Sauvignon were £45, the better £52; since the same tax went on Château Latour as on plonk, it paid to go for the good years.

There was no television, so this was the ideal honeymoon resort; indeed I ran into one happy couple from Barons Court who had gone there to be alone for ten days. They were then hit by the Pavarotti circus, along with a few score presidents, princes, potentates – and *Whicker's World*. It was a different way to start a marriage.

They watched ruefully as a theatre was built on three tennis courts and a constant clatter of helicopters ferried in glitterati and heavy-hitters. They were finally reconciled to enforced-Pavarotti after calculating how much people paid to hear the Voice at close range.

Converging upon their hideaway honeymoon came the former President of Chile, the Prime Minister of Peru, Asian noblemen, English aristocracy, various magnates and politicians – a motley mass of international movers and shakers, not all of them with their own wives. To protect such a guest list in a kidnap zone, a Malaysian warship hung around offshore, and three commandos were unleashed to prowl the surrounding jungle. Our two stars brought their own personal defence; as befits a contentious Prime Minister, Dr Mahathir had eighteen security men.

Pavarotti's party of twelve, led by an unusually charmless manager, included three hyperactive German bodyguards with whispering earpieces who circled the Maestro like sharks. By force of Pav-power they came to dominate the Prime Ministerial security and the guests as though controlling paparazzi outside a Fifth Avenue party, putting their hands over camera lenses in the traditional way. They showed the charm and technique of doormen at some Manhattan disco, treating visiting ministers as though they wanted autographs.

The heaven-sent Voice is now controlled by American management who in a cloud of fine print extracts astronomical fees from every impresario along the operatic flightpath. Pavarotti will not get out of his reinforced bed without contracts covered in zeros, as the Italian taxmen well know.

We prepared for his arrival by filming everything that moved

217

around the island – even a brief conversation with Pavarotti's school friend from Modena, Leone Magiera, who was conducting the Manila Symphony, and with the young flautist Andrea Griminelli. To be brutally honest, I recorded that break in rehearsals mainly to be polite, as we whiled away the afternoon. Their massive star totally overshadowed everyone else and although ITV had allocated our documentary an unusual ninety minutes, the scintillating guest list meant that a flautist was fairly low on my billing.

I was therefore taken aback when the Rudas Theatrical Organization of Nevada Inc. heard of our chat and hurriedly presented a demand for $6,500 for those five aimless but dutiful minutes. When transmitted after editing I found we had used only four of Maestro Magiera's words – all of them charming, but hardly worth £700 a syllable.

After petulant Pav and his stroppy manager, Magiera and Griminelli were so relaxed and agreeable it was a relief to talk to pleasant people, who were also gifted. While we were filming that expensive conversation, Magiera suddenly announced in mid-sentence that he had to go to the loo. He got up and walked out. He had gone to spend £100! I *like* decisive Maestros.

We kept the camera turning while Griminelli showed me the Japanese 14-carat gold flute he had bought from his teacher, James Galway: 'Pavarotti's very demanding about music. He doesn't allow mistakes, so you have to be really perfect.' Finally, Magiera returned, relieved after his natural break, and we eased him back into the conversation. As I always say, in Whicker's World we look at real life as it happens.

In the curious hot-house atmosphere of a concert tour Pavarotti's every whim had to be instantly gratified – preferably before he noticed that he'd had one. When his circus hit town, opera houses and impresarios trembled, for he had a Little List; well, fifty pages, actually. It always preceded his arrival and detailed the Maestro's demands, plus a few extra from his manager.

Among the requirements: nine extra pillows, one-piece mattress, humidifiers, medical scales in kilograms, films in English and Italian, no strong-smelling flowers. 'Lilies cannot be tolerated. No fresh paint or cleaner used in the previous five days.

Eight extra policemen who must be dressed well, and not rude or crude.'

Nothing may be left to chance, from the make and colour of the limousines (Mercedes, white, two – plus three for management) to the number of shower caps in the great man's bathroom (six extra). Also, the stage must have a firm floor; that at any rate seemed reasonable.

Food requirements in his residence were exact, though varied with each current diet. He also required a snack in his dressing room, to include 'large plate of assorted cheese; plate of grilled chicken – sliced; two club sandwiches, toasted; minimum of ten fresh lemons, not sliced, and refreshed every day' and so on, and on, for fifty pages.

In the hope of pre-empting dramas, Pangkor Laut had imported an Italian chef from Singapore who spent his days making pasta and hanging it on a washing line, just like Mamma used to do.

The carpet to the stage had to be three feet wide, and red, the backdrop curtain sufficient to hide unsold seats. Surprisingly, such a veil *could* be required. On an earlier British tour sixty-five per cent of the tickets at Wembley were unsold. At Sheffield eighty per cent remained; not even a backdrop curtain could cover that shame, so the concert was cancelled. 'Time to throw-in the hankie?' wondered the British press, unkindly.

Pavarotti, known backstage as Fat Lucy, was adored for his voice and smile, disliked for his insincerity and autocratic manner. 'A grotesque carnival king for the masses,' sniffed his own local paper, Milan's *Corriere della Sera.*

Certainly his public relations could hardly be worse, though once beyond the barrier of managers and agents, handlers and minders who were protecting their meal tickets, one sometimes caught a glimpse of a genial and simple Italian who was lonely and liked ladies, horses, food and football.

Yet he had for so long been guided and controlled by slit-eyed agents that he seemed to have joined them and become moody, self-obsessed and spoiled. After a lifetime singing his way up the scales, with that sort of history and that sort of management – how could he be otherwise?

In addition to the unpleasant manager, his caravan included a dietician, masseurs, co-ordinators, assistants and secretaries – for one of whom he soon afterwards left Adua, his wife of thirty-five years.

This tenor may be a great spoiled baby beset by self-doubt, cosseted, protected and isolated, but as soon as he lumbers on stage on his new artificial knees, breathes in and opens his mouth you can forgive him for anything.

Orchestra and technicians, their working lives totally dependent upon this voice, travel like a repertory company from one engagement to the next on a concert treadmill that is intense but rewarding. Climates and time zones change weekly. After breathing cold recirculated air in their aircraft for hours, they emerge into sodden equatorial humidity, then into air-conditioned cars and hotels.

This affects the larynx of every longhaul traveller, who just takes a throat tablet and a hot drink; but for the man who sings for his and a hundred other people's suppers, the hot/cold damp/dry air can be a ruinous cocktail. The Maestro and his fixers can control everything but his fragile throat – the delicate instrument which is his life and future. His multimillion income and the careers of his entourage depend upon that larynx. It *has* to be in great shape – supported as it is by lungs of such power that when he inhales, curtains are drawn towards him horizontally.

On his way to sing at this party before two hundred of Asia's élite, Pavarotti broke off for a holiday in Bali. When he arrived in Manila for his first-ever concert in the Philippines, the worst thing in the world that could happen was happening: he was losing his voice. Faces were also about to be lost all round.

On the island we waited for him to arrive – with or without voice – in the owner's yacht. He is frightened of all aircraft, and positively bans helicopters. Our agitated host Francis feared his approaching trophy-tenor might arrive as a whispering baritone, even sulkier and surlier. Sleepless nights, anxious conferences, desperate fail-safe substitutes considered. Anyone know Barbra Streisand's phone number? How about Liza Minelli? Is Placido available?

I considered the drama with the ever-smiling roly-poly Dr Roberto Tan, who held the Maestro's hand in Manila while tending his fragile throat. From this jolly Chinese-Filipino I heard the backstage will-he-won't-he saga of the world's most valuable vocal chords.

A specialist with an ENT clinic in Binando, Dr Tan had been called in to put this enormous Humpty-Dumpty together again. He had to restore Pavarotti's voice and bolster his confidence to fulfil million-dollar contracts in Manila and Kuala Lumpur – and finally at Pangkor Laut. To this daunting task Dr Tan brought faith, psychology, an ICI beta blocker, humanity and considerable charm.

It had all started in Manila, when he was summoned to examine the famous throat, then feeling several degrees under. He waited for an hour outside the Maestro's hotel suite, while handlers treated him like an autograph hunter. Then the curt message: 'The Doctor can go away. I'm feeling better.'

Next evening, still an enthusiastic fan, Dr Tan arrived at the Opera House clutching his prized and expensive ticket, and found – disaster. The voice had gone, the audience of 4,000 was going. Outside the cancelled concert, the 50,000 camped before a giant public screen were dispersing.

Next day Dr Tan received a frantic but suddenly polite call. 'The Maestro needs you, Doctor. He's *begging* you to come and see him.'

Dr Tan was not about to be caught twice. 'First I want to hear from his own lips that he really wants me, this time – and that he will see me as soon as I arrive. Secondly, whatever instructions and medication I give him, he must follow to the letter. And thirdly, if he gets better, he must sing for all the Filipino people who were turned away last night.'

There was a long pause. Then on an extension he heard a very famous but very faint voice whisper four words: 'Yes. Yes. I will.'

At the hotel Dr Tan was met by the German minders and an anxious entourage. This time he was not just local labour; the red carpet – at least three feet wide – was out.

'When I walk into the Imperial Suite I see a huge man lying totally exhausted on a sofa, his hand trailing on the floor, cold clammy perspiration pouring down his face. I took his temperature and tested his lungs. The thing that struck me most was that in my thirty-four years as a doctor I have never seen lungs with such a volume. When he inhales it's almost like a wind tunnel!

'I could see he was suffering from bronchitis and that he might be starting pneumonia, so I gave him an injection of a special antibiotic I'd brought back from the States, and I told him to rest. I stayed with him for three hours. Then he slept.'

On Sunday morning there was another urgent call: 'Please come instantly!'

Dr Tan, who is his own man and splendidly unawed by the massive Maestro, gave them his priorities: ' "It's Sunday morning and the first thing I have to do is go to church. Next, I have to visit my patients in hospital. Then – and this is the *most* important thing – I have to be with my family for lunch, because that's the Chinese tradition. I have prescribed the medicine and all he has to do is follow my instructions. I will come at three o'clock." '

'When I arrive at the hotel, the Maestro is a different man – jolly, laughing, full of life, so I sat down and told him how years ago I had first heard his glorious voice, and how it inspired me.

' "One night," I said, "I was at home after a long day in the operating theatre – routine operations, nothing complicated – when suddenly I was called back to the hospital. One of my patients, a banker, was in post-operative shock. I rushed to his bedside and saw an enormous haematoma on his neck. I performed a tracheotomy so he could breathe, and applied ice compresses. I did all I could and prayed for him – but I was deeply troubled that night and couldn't sleep. When I touched a button on my bedside radio, out flooded the voice of Pavarotti singing 'Nessun Dorma'.

' "I didn't understand the words but I said to myself, 'If such a person can perfect his voice in such a manner, there is no reason why I as a doctor cannot solve my problems.' At dawn I returned to the hospital feeling very calm. I examined my patient again, diagnosed the problem – and operated. He recovered."

'Luciano listened to my story, then he translated the words of the aria. I'd never realized that the song all the football fans sing is about a sleepless night.'

But next morning Pavarotti's mood and voice had changed. 'I returned to find he was still insisting that the concert could not take place. He said, "Roberto, send me the bill for your services and the medicine." I said, "Luciano, my services cannot be measured in terms of money. I am offering them as a gift from the Filipino people." '

Pavarotti always practises for ninety minutes before a concert to loosen his voice, and at six o'clock Dr Tan listened to his rehearsal. After two arias the Maestro turned to the conductor: 'Cut! Forget it – I don't have the voice and my diaphragm isn't moving. The song that's coming out of me is not mine.'

'That was at 6.20, ninety minutes before curtain call. In his dressing room he said, "Roberto, I am very very sorry. I know you tried your best, but it just isn't there."

'I said, "Luciano, you *have* to sing tonight. If you don't sing I won't have a job any more! Everybody knows I am looking after you. I am a professional man from the best medical school in Asia – I cannot let down my college or my university." Then I opened my purse and gave him a gift. I said, "Luciano, this is something I always carry with me. This rosary was made by a nun who'd been blind for seven years. I operated on her and restored her sight. She made this rosary for me, and another for my wife. Keep it with you and I'm sure the good Lord will see to it that you can complete the concert tonight." '

(When this *Whicker's World* was transmitted on Malaysian Television his reference to the nun's gift of crucifixes was removed to protect Muslim sensibilities.)

'Then I said, "Don't just believe in God's power alone because, as the Bible says, God helps those who help themselves. So you have to take this medication too."

' "Is that another piece of poison you're giving me?" he asks. I said, "No, it is Inderal, a medication I take every day before I operate. It gives strength to my heart, makes me calm and able to work more effectively." But I tell him, "We doctors can only help. It is God who cures."

'At 7.45 he still refused to put on his tuxedo. He said, "I don't think I'll be able to make it." I said, "To be a successful man you must follow the 'R' principle – I use 'R' because my name is Roberto. R is for Respect. You must respect the laws of nature, you must respect the expectations of people, and at the same time you must respect the Supreme Being and ask for help. And R is for Resourcefulness – if you're in a predicament you must find ways and means to correct whatever mistakes you're bound to commit. So if you're on stage and suddenly mucus comes into your mouth, hold your handkerchief, pretend to bow – and wipe it out. If mucus comes out when you're singing, make a gesture with your hand and wipe it away as if you're trying to express the meaning of a word." Then I gave him a spray to hold in his hand and use between songs, if his throat felt dry.

'I was in the audience when Pavarotti went on stage, and sang. He was coughing a lot, wiping his mouth and taking my medicine. When the first half ended the intermission seemed rather long. Suddenly I was called backstage. "Roberto," he said, "the spirit is willing – but the voice is not there."

'So I told him, "Luciano, don't let your body control your mind, let your mind control your body. If you say you will, you *can* do it. Unless you go out there you will not understand the meaning of courage. He thought about it. "Let's *go!*" he said.

'For three days I had been saying special prayers, and as soon as I heard Luciano's first song after the interval, and the volume in his voice, I knew he had been given divine inspiration and that my prayers had been answered. At the end of the concert the audience gave him a standing ovation, but by the second encore even I was cold with perspiration. I didn't think his voice could hold out much longer.

'When he came on stage for the third encore, he said: "I want to dedicate my next song to Dr Tan. Without him this concert would not have been possible." I sank down in my chair. He said, "I know you're in the audience, Roberto – come up and shake my hand. If you don't come up, I'm not singing." So I went up on stage, and he sang "Granada" for me! As I watched him I thought, "This is a miracle, a gift of God to the Filipino people." '

So, triumph in Manila, for both of them. Then, despite it all, the voice went again. The next concert in Kuala Lumpur was cancelled, to conserve any remaining top notes for us in Pangkor Laut.

Back on the island we awaited the operatic circus. All was ready: stage completed, competitive peacocks expelled to avoid discordant notes, security for politicians in place – commandos creeping through jungle, warship circling warily. Could it be that, after all, we were about to hear the voice of God – assisted, in a small but enthusiastic way, by Dr Tan?

He had told me, with one of his conspiratorial giggles, that in Manila he watched *Whicker's World*: 'When you are on, I turn off the football.' That put me in excellent voice and sent me back to face the mute Maestro's management with the reassuring feeling that, however unfortunate some attitudes, people are basically good.

The sixty-seven musicians of the Manila Symphony had arrived, and at rehearsal competed with helicopters bringing guests from everywhere. The ethnic welcome on the island's jetty was provided by local musicians: drummers worked up to a frenzied crescendo as exotic dancers in pink silk greeted the massive tenor. He walked uncertainly along the Pangkor Laut jetty on his new artificial knees, leaning heavily on minders. His mutinous throat was muffled in what looked like an old tablecloth. Despite the rosary, the medicine and all those Filipino pep talks, he did not seem happy.

'I said *no* steps!' he growled, as he lurched towards the Pavmobile – a specially imported electric golf cart. He might have been grumpy, but at least there was still *some* voice in there. He was driven up to a hillside villa overstocked with shower caps, pillows, Häagen Dazs and enough favourite food to hold him until the concert tomorrow.

His entourage seemed divided between the Unspeakable and the Delightful. His amiable English sound engineer Jim Lock has been travelling with him since 1963 – which said something for both of them. He controlled the formidable sound system at concerts, and was a quiet rock in a rolling sea. 'After all this time, he calls me his brother,' Jim told me. 'At the end of the day, he's 100 per cent professional – but if we see he's in a mood, we all keep out of his way.'

Next morning nobody kept out of his way; Pavarotti emerged cheerful and almost friendly, for his voice was returning. The large black eyes sparkled, the smile was engaging, the hesitant English improved. He was most satisfied with his surroundings: 'This place is a paradise! When I wake up I go out on the terrace and I was really moved, almost crying, to see what beautiful things God has done, huh?

'The tenor voice is something very very difficult to put together – exciting when it is good, and very problematic when it is bad,' he explained. 'You recognize immediately when a tenor is not well, but it is not inconsistent, otherwise I could not have done this work for thirty-two, thirty-three years. My father is eighty-one and he's still singing and expressing something new.'

He discussed his repertoire: 'I would consider any pop song that is coming to me, if I like it. I have already done a record with Sting. There is a song called "Caruso", which is not classic at all, but it's the best song written lately, at least for me. Even a religious song, if it suits me, because I began singing with my father in church. My début, like a solo, was when I sung "Ave Maria". I sang the part of the tenor and the priest sang the part of the baritone, Don Riccio. "Ave Maria" is always "Ave Maria" – it is so beautiful, even from pop singers. An incredible piece of music.'

Pavarotti explained his trademark handkerchief: 'It began when I made my first recital, I practise in front of the mirror and I saw myself making incredible gestures – too much or too little or too nothing, and the face loses the real expressions. So I took a handkerchief and put my hand stiff. That was the reason – to stop my hand. Since that moment, because it brought me good luck, it is always with me.'

The insecurity of the world's most magnificent voice was obvious: 'If you make me think about my concert tomorrow night, I begin *now* to be afraid.'

But next night Pavarotti walked carefully along the three-foot-wide red carpet on to the temporary stage, seemingly unafraid and ready to break the sound barrier. He was not discombobulated by the tiny audience that could not fill the rows of chairs, the ceaseless chorus of cicadas, the threatening tropical storms and distant lightning . . .

The Manila Symphony was inspired, the setting sublime. The voice, once again, was Semtex in syrup. Everyone surrendered.

Later he drove his Pavmobile to the after-show party and strode into dinner ahead of the Guest of Honour, the Prime Minister. The other guests, the great and the good and the fortunate, submitted obediently as his handlers corralled and directed. It was Pavarotti's last night on Fantasy Island.

Malaysians, endlessly courteous and smiling, had dressed

magnificently for the occasion, as had other guests. Amid the bejewelled and scintillating gathering Pavarotti's manager lounged at the top table wearing a sports coat and slacks, bringing a stale breath of Broadway. Guests pretended not to notice.

The banquet was served in sixty-five minutes because the Prime Minister's wife did not like going to bed late. Waiters moved at the double, and not even Pav's bouncers could slow them down.

Next day, before my camera, I discussed with Dr Mahathir the rather more significant business of Anglo–Malaysian relations, which were in total disarray; but even with the serious theme of that international crisis we could not avoid talking about our operatic experience the night before. 'It's almost unbelievable to see him performing in these surroundings, knowing the place as I do,' said Dr Mahathir. 'We didn't expect Pavarotti to come here, much less to perform.'

He had noticed another thing: 'He's not as fussy about his food as people make him out to be. He had second helpings!'

I had first met Dr Mahathir while taking a second helping of the *opulentissimo* Orient Express – a stylish expedition across the frivolous frontiers of the new Age of the Train. On its inaugural run the Eastern and Orient*al* Express set about creating international rail travel through South-East Asia. It crossed jungles and kampongs along the length of Malaysia, instead of foggy Balkan borders.

We departed from sedate and tidy Singapore and, after forty-two hours, 1,200 miles and three countries, were scheduled to arrive in chaotic and raffish Bangkok. Despite a remarkable cast list, the train was the star of this event, though it had inherited no history, no exotic legends grown stronger than reality. No beautiful spies seduced Kings' Messengers in its elegant wagons-lits; no murders, yet, on this Oriental Express – where James Bond did not battle and ladies did not vanish. It was more rubber planter than Archduke, more Singapore Sling than French champagne, and not at all like that line of resurrected Pullmans that slid gleaming into *Whicker's World* on platform 8 at Victoria in 1982, along with various dukes, duchesses, film stars and glitz. That

Express on its very first run swept us in great style down to Venice – delightful of course, though hardly the Orient.

This expedition began in the Republic of Singapore, so the waiting train had to be the *real* Oriental Express facing a future with absolutely no memory of Grand Dukes or Mata Hari, fun-loving princes, courtesans or randy Balkan priests. This international Pullman had no past, not even a reputation, as it set off from Keppel Road Station – good grief, even the *name* was unromantic.

The train had come from staid New Zealand and now had to learn to cope with South-East Asia, with jungles and tigers and opium arriving through the Golden Triangle, with bandits, maybe, or anyone ill disposed towards such bravado, to such opulent progress through our drab days.

Its route did not cut through the legendary Alps nor foggy middle-European frontiers. Instead, the single track wound sedately across bright green rice paddies, through tropical rainforest, past mosques and temples. It might not have the urgency of an Express – well, no train is perfect – but its route was indisputably Oriental.

We had an eclectic passenger list; royals, near royals, wannabe royals, royals' groupies . . . down through a star-studded spectrum. At our first stop, Kuala Lumpur, the Prime Minister of Malaysia, Dr Mahathir, would board and so unsettle the nicely balanced protocol of rank established by the enforced pecking order of royalty/nobility/film star/politician/tycoon/celebrity through which the Train Manager was already picking his way, anxiously.

First to arrive at Singapore's dull but immaculate station were Lord and Lady Norwich, straight from a thirteen-hour London night flight – a brave way to start a long journey in an unknown train. Next, tiny pert Jane Powell and camellia-complexioned Arlene Dahl – sweet of face and elegant of leg but, in between, great of body. This ill-matched pair of Hollywood survivors of the 1950s had both been Fred Astaire's partners and still smiled with starry confidence – though they looked like Little and Large.

Then the Earl of Snowdon with a pocket camera that actually went into his pocket and would doubtless shame all predatory zooms. Prince and Princess Michael, royal standbys ever ready for any international host. Adrian Zecha, Balinese hotel mandarin with impeccable taste and dainty feet. James and Shirley Sherwood, who conceived and nurtured the train as they did the Venice–Simplon Orient Express. When the Singapore launch ceremony began I noted that he was recycling much of his 1982 Victoria Station speech.

At a Monte Carlo auction in 1977 he had bought two wagons-lits built in the 1920s. These inspired him to locate old rolling-stock in those sad grey yards around the world where famous trains go to die. He collected another thirty-one Pullmans and sleeping cars with exotic histories – some famous for transporting kings and presidents, others infamous for accommodating German officers' brothels. In restoring those historic carriages, re-creating their art deco, marquetry, lacquerwork and Lalique panels, this anglicized American was restoring the waning Art of Travel.

In South-East Asia he planned to re-create the legendary era of tea planters in rattan chairs taking tiffin and tea-dancing with other men's wives – the days of Mad Dogs and Englishmen in those Malay swamps where the python romps, while in Bangkok at twelve o'clock they foam at the mouth and run . . .

He found no history of dramatic trains. The railway was how you travelled when there was no other way to go. A few sluggish local services carried pith-helmeted planters home on leave along a single line that ran through village streets – and much of that needed to be restored, as the Japanese had taken tracks away to build their Death Railway across the River Kwai and into Burma.

Before the Oriental Express appeared no one wanted to face the 1,200-mile journey from Singapore to Bangkok by rail; every-one took a two-hour flight. Adventurous ground-level travellers were offered three classes of train: Express, Rapid or Ordinary. Locals translated these as Slow, Very Slow – and *just* moving.

Since there were no vintage carriages in the Orient to restore to splendour, Sherwood had to find modern rolling-stock – and distress it. He bought twenty-four restaurant- and sleeping-cars that ran between Auckland and Wellington in the 1970s – a worthy, if not a very sexy provenance. As they lacked instant nostalgia, he set about making them more interesting.

In Singapore the Japanese-built carriages were stripped to their shells and rebuilt with triple-glazing, anti-vibration paint and air-conditioning that could cope with tropical humidity. They were painted cream and – quite suitably – jungle green. Unhindered by frowning Nanny States, he was able to create a unique observation car at the rear by using some giant tin-opener which peeled back the steel and left an open platform to be surrounded by brass rails.

Carriages were numbered in accordance with Chinese superstition: no 4s – which signify death – no negative numbers like 5 and 7. Instead, combinations of lucky numbers 2, 3, 6, 8 and 9. Mata Hari and the Grand Duke, slipping stealthily along those midnight corridors, would have been baffled and frustrated.

At Grand Central Station someone may have sat down and cried, but she could not have felt sad that morning at Keppel Road, a 1932 art-deco station where we were encouraged upon our way by lion dancers, big-headed dolls, men on stilts and children in violent make-up. Princess Michael, trailing her inevitable *Hello!* photographer, made animated one-way conversation at all the children, who found her totally incomprehensible. At least they were undisturbed by the regally wooden Prince Michael, who stood around gazing silently into the middle distance.

Inaudible speeches, old and new, ricocheted around the echo chamber of the concourse, the band struck up 'Murder on the Orient Express' in an encouraging way and, in a surge of champagne, we got the show on the railroad. Within minutes we had left Singapore's Manhattan skyline, crossed the first border and were heading into the little-known.

The E&O is not a dramatic train; I doubt whether it will appear in many movies. Its two sad diesel locomotives could not compete with the extravagant décor behind them – nor could most of the passengers. But it was comfortable; our air-conditioned cabin had two full-length beds, a luxury after the restrictive upper and lower berths of the European express; we could have travelled for a week without pain. Best of all, the tiny shower room had a loo, so there was no longer any reason to go creeping along corridors at night. The Grand Duke would have been dismayed.

The train had a crew of fifty-two who worked six twenty-hour days, then took a week off – rather like being at sea. Excellent meals were prepared under an English master chef, and the Thai service was of course superb. In the Piano Bar, the resident entertainer flexed his Noël Coward repertoire, as though on a loop.

Like all good rail journeys, the Express was slow enough to maintain contact with the passing scene, and we meandered comfortably through Malaysia. In the observation car at the back passengers could lean against shining brass rails as though part of some presidential whistle-stop tour, graciously acknowledging any passer-by who looked as though he might appreciate a well-intentioned wave.

The lounge car at night resembled one of those publicity pictures where stylish but stiff models sit around showing their best profiles, holding champagne flutes and smiling brightly into space. In fact few of us in that striking setting had met before. Lord Snowdon joined us, and wondered who I could identify among the brilliance. 'Who's that?' he asked, nodding towards one good-looking woman sitting alone and studying Malaysia through the window. I recognized her as the Editor of Australian *Vogue.* After a while he murmured, 'What do you think her reaction would be if I went over and introduced myself?'

She was obviously in need of someone to talk to, preferably a man, hopefully a famous man – possibly even someone once married to the Queen's sister. 'It would be delight,' I told him, firmly, 'to the point of orgasm.'

So it proved. I was less enterprising – and then Tony's empty chair was occupied by Princess Michael who put me at my ease with small talk about the train and, of course, Noël Coward.

We arrived at the Malaysian capital's beautiful British-built railway station in the humid heat of the sultry night; the Moorish minarets, keyhole arches and scalloped eaves of this Islamic wedding cake were lit by fairy lights. The improbable building had been designed in 1911 by an English architect, its completion delayed because British Railway specifications insisted that its equatorial roof had to be able to support a three-foot covering of the right type of snow.

We drew in to find the platform had been turned into the hubbub of a village bazaar: food stalls, musicians, exotic masks, dancers, fortune-telling birds, snake charmers – and two poor skinny tigers, symbols of the Eastern and Oriental Express, one called 'E', the other 'O'. In their cage they are prodded into reaction by a German trainer whom we filmed, and hated.

The Prime Minister arrived, surrounded by a wedge of heavies pushing people aside, including the Earl of Snowdon – who was not too steady on his pins, anyway. They also removed – with greater difficulty – the statuesque Princess Michael. She almost ended up under the train, and was not amused.

There was no doubt who was the star on that colourful platform: Dr Mahathir was at the heart of the opening ceremony, while foreign royalty and nobility watched from the back of the crowd along with the rest of us. Speeches and excitement over, we reboarded in an atmosphere so harmonious and reassuring that it was decided the Prime Minister would be safe with only six bodyguards.

As the train rumbled north we prepared to enjoy a stylish night, but an extended Malaysian family with wives and children took over the Bar Car and sang 'My Way' lots of times. The din was not evocative. It transpired that the musical family had put up one-third of the financing for the Express – so they could sing whenever they wanted. The other two-thirds of the train belonged to Francis Yeoh – who also owned Pangkor Laut – so he could sing twice as often, or twice as badly.

In fact he was stage-managing the important dinner that night, where I found myself at his table opposite the formidable Prime Minister, with whom I was anxious to film a conversation. He was a peppery and erratic leader, the last of the Asian old guard. He had become *very* indignant when the 14,000 Malaysians studying in Britain were asked to contribute towards their college fees. When he did not attend an Asia Pacific summit and the serpentine Australian Prime Minister Paul Keating said he was 'recalcitrant', he practically declared war on Australia. He later blamed the economic instability of South-East Asia on 'a Jewish conspiracy' and imposed capital controls.

Dr Mahathir was then sixty-eight and had undergone a triple bypass, but despite a noticeable lack of political balance, had a good smile and looked about forty-five. He was Asia's longest-serving ruler.

As we began dinner he asked which of my interviewees, during a lifetime in television, had been the most interesting? I always find this a tough one, but mentioned the merciless Papa Doc, Dr François Duvalier, President of Haiti, who had been a strong leader, a caring country doctor – yet, paradoxically, a murderous dictator.

This was perhaps not the best example to venture, for the Prime Minister then pointed out that he too was the leader of a nation and had been a country doctor. He offered no further comparison.

I had the feeling I had not given him the most encouraging role model, so cast around for someone more suitable, and recalled a previous visit to Penang when I had interviewed that major Malaysian statesman and admirer of Churchill, the late Tunku Abdul Rahman. I enthused about this amiable Father of the Nation who had taken me to see his racehorses exercising on Penang's beaches. Dr Mahathir, smiling a steely smile, pointed out that the Tunku was an enemy who had frequently attacked him in Parliament, a hostile political opponent he much disliked. I changed the subject before I inadvertently insulted his mother.

Despite that uphill opening the dinner went on for hours as we rode through the night, and was most jolly. The Prime Minister decided he would be happy to be interviewed – despite his belief that Westerners looked down upon all coloured races. He had never forgiven Britain for his failure, while studying in London, to become a lawyer. Medicine was his second choice, and he still held that enforced change of career against us though, like the menacing Papa Doc, he had not done too badly with only a medical background.

When I filmed a conversation with Dr Mahathir next day, his security men were scattered casually around the carriage. I wondered why they were needed in such a secure place? He shrugged them off: 'It's become the custom,' he said; he used them for errands. As we started our conversation one of his staff stuck a cautionary tape recorder on the table between us. I had the feeling someone was going to read me my rights.

I had noticed that he responded well if I teased him; his laugh was infectious. With great good nature we discussed the sensitive subject of his various trade wars with Britain, from the impending visit of John Major to his original battles with Margaret Thatcher, with whom he had since come to terms: 'When you get to blows with somebody, after that you understand each other better.'

That night we were rocked to sleep by Malaysia's interesting railway track and awoke in Butterworth. While our workaday diesel was being reversed on a turntable, we prepared for a lightning assault on the isle of Penang. Drummers and 115 trishaws took us from the train to a jetty which had been prettily decorated and furnished with long tables covered with bottles of champagne and caviare canapés. It was just 8.45am. There were also Chinese fortune tellers, much patronized despite the hour.

While trying to do justice to the spread I wondered when the boat would arrive to take us across the Straits to the island – when suddenly the whole jetty slowly set sail. This lurching progress was not caused by early-morning champagne but because the function was being held on the working deck of a vehicle transporter, massive but frivolously dressed.

At Penang 200 classic cars gathered from all over Malaysia waited to drive us to the Governor's residence. The Prime Minister stepped with a gracious smile into the first and most stylish model. The Michaels, noticeably lower on the running order, stood around disconsolately, the Princess plaintively demanding a different car: 'No, *no*, Minister, we'd like an open one. Perhaps you'll go and find one – I think I'll die, otherwise . . .' Such royal precedence as they could muster did not count for much at the court of Dr Mahathir.

The rest of us boarded old Bentleys, Jaguar XK120s and cherished MGs in a disorganized but stylish cavalcade. A Malaysian lawyer with a tweed deerstalker and a flat at Swiss Cottage carried me off in his burnished 1950 Morris Minor convertible, which proved an ideal camera car.

At Government House we watched unsettling displays in which enormous bamboo poles were balanced on dancers' heads, then tossed around and caught on other interesting and doubtless sensitive parts of the body. Such stoical dexterity may be slow to reach Europe.

By lunchtime we were back on the mainland and safely inside our fantasy island on wheels as it ran through mile after mile of lush green jungle and plantation in a stately rock-and-roll which made some American passengers queasy.

Rex Reed, the acerbic film critic and *Myra Breckinridge* actor, protested that each time he looked out of the window he expected to see Jennifer Jones and assorted colonial memsahibs being marched off to Burma. On the Kuala Lumpur platform he had survived a close encounter with a cobra: 'It came at me, hood and all. The Princess told me I had not learned the secret of travelling through the Orient: I should have been carrying a piece of turquoise to ward off snakes and the Evil Eye. I wanted to say, "Does it work with the English Press?" '

He found the E&O experience enervating: 'After all, how many rubber plantations can you *look* at.' Heading for bed, he offered me a final weary confidence in genuine 18-carat Beverly Hills blasé: 'Who do you have to screw to get *off* this train?'

Arlene Dahl, on the other hand, expressed a fascination for the East and wondered why 'so many of our boys didn't come back from Vietnam'. It took a while to work out that she was not worried about America's thousands of casualties, but rather the fate of those young soldiers who decided to marry Asian girls. She saw that as a different sort of defeat. 'American women were curious.'

The supposedly reserved British contingent also had its surprises: John Julius Norwich kept the bar car jumping into the night, not by debating the style and qualities of Venetian churches but by singing 'Mad Dogs and Englishmen' with far more conviction than the jealous resident entertainer.

His companion around the piano, Princess Michael, had by now adopted the Asiatic mode and turned tittering roguishly behind her fan into an art form – quite an accomplishment for a six-foot blonde Valkyrie. She laid down her fan to join in a Noël Coward singalong. We glided and clattered through the jungle night, begging Mrs Worthington again and again to keep her daughter off the stage.

'We sounded quite wonderful,' said the Princess afterwards, 'or so we thought. The joy of it is that very little talent is needed.' Prince Michael did not join in the upmarket singing; indeed I did not hear him utter during the entire journey. His main sign of life was an occasional cross gesture at photographers.

Across the Thai border next morning the train stopped at the royal resort of Hua Hin, where the King has a country house. A group of us were sent to the temple to present parcels of food to a line of nine Buddhist monks in saffron robes. They in turn blessed us and sprinkled holy water on the train. Baby elephants danced for us and rouged children offered gifts of painted sweetmeats. These turned out to be inedible, but much appreciated by the elephants.

I was doubly blessed – first by a holy water sprinkle from a monk, then by a baby elephant who peed on my foot. It had to be an auspicious day.

As we neared Bangkok, villages and temples grew closer together. Finally we were among urban back-street humanity in its teeming millions. From insulated air-conditioned luxury we saw a side of Thai life hidden from the road-bound. At railway crossings massed lines of vehicles stretched away out of sight. Bangkok is so clogged that most road journeys require refreshments, reading matter and sometimes chauffeurs' aids to support motionless hours in a fume-filled gridlock. Guards under bridges reported our progress to someone as we trundled slowly into the middle of the city.

Leaving the train at Hualamphong Station was like being pushed out of the nest. Friendships had been forged, animosities revealed. Did the Michaels *really* not speak to the Snowdons during the whole fifty hours of jollity they shared, cheek to cheek? Could it be they were still upset that when asked to name the worst Christmas present for an enemy, Snowdon's son Viscount Linley had suggested, 'Dinner with Princess Michael'? *Surely* not?

Yet Snowdon confessed to me that he had been pointedly ignored. So, were the social sins of the Son visited upon the Father? Even on such a happy travel-orgy among such frivolous people, it seemed that tropical nights could stimulate long-dead feuds. Somerset Maugham would have loved every venomous twist and glance – not to mention the inescapable Noël Coward.

During a night in Bangkok we and the train were refreshed, and next evening set off to film the return journey, with a completely new cast. This one was rather more jazzy and uninhibited, and included Serena Scott Thomas, who had just played Princess Diana in an American television series, and the actress Susannah York.

Koo Stark was there with a diamond stud in her nose which I found hard to take my eyes off while we talked. She was accompanied by Bertie Way, formerly of the Brigade of Guards but now working with Sir Tim Bell and handling Brunei's public relations, which must have kept him busy. They were both so affected by the romance of a train journey through the jungle that they got engaged. This arrangement lasted several months, before the Oriental spell wore off.

Even on such a splendid train passengers were visited by one of the torments of air travel: missing luggage. One couple, baggage still in Bangkok, sat with composure in the bar car, he wearing a borrowed dressing gown and she a large Thai tablecloth bought at a passing station. I said I hoped she had bought two, since I would not wish to lunch with the kind of girl who'd wear the same tablecloth twice.

Keith Schellenberg and his new wife then owned the Hebridean island of Eigg; he was a sportsman of action who had once taken me powerboating off Whitby, the kind of thudding crashing marine madness in which you just hope to return with most of your teeth. This time he organized a Scottish reel at Hua Hin. The welcoming orchestra was playing some Thai air in which Keith detected a Highland echo. His dancers on the station platform included the British Ambassador to Thailand, Christian Adams. They were watched by silent and bemused children and local farmworkers, all adjusting their ideas of the stuffy British.

After a convivial dinner that night the train pulled in to Kuala Lumpur at 2am, and Keith arranged a cricket match on the deserted platform, supported and inspired by salmanazars of champagne. The station echoed to jolly cries of *Howzat!* until a late drive past silly mid-on broke a waiting room window. Sadly the Malaysian station master was not up to speed on English eccentricity and failed to see the traditional humour in it all.

We headed south, on the last leg, while struggling to get exterior pictures of the unusually long train. We filmed forward from the observation car, hoping to catch sight of the serpentine progress of our two locomotives, away in the distance. This proved difficult for the train was so long they were always a quarter of a mile ahead and out of sight around the next bend.

That afternoon, we embarked upon another fifteen-minute corridor trudge from our cabin, up to the observation car. The train slowed to a halt, and we sat chatting over passionfruit tea and admiring the equatorial greenery around us.

After a while it began to dawn that the front of the train could well already be in Singapore station, having arrived at the end of its journey. We, at least twenty-two coaches behind, were still sitting out in the countryside – possibly even across the border . . . Our graceful expedition had ended imperceptibly. Singapore is a very small place.

'Land on that island,' said my boatman, 'and they'll shoot you. We cannot even get too close.'

I considered this unexpected warning. I'm not Dick Daring, but sudden death out of the blue on a tranquil sunlit afternoon in the Gulf of Thailand seemed improbable. 'Let's go in and take a look, anyway,' I said, encouragingly.

We were sailing off the Isthmus of Kra, away from the coast of Koh Samui and my seaside hotel, Baan Taling Ngam (pronounced with some difficulty) faced small islands of volcanic rock. They rose deep green from the smooth warm sea – some eighty in this archipelago, a spectacular scattering across one of the world's loveliest settings.

The boatman, muttering, changed course reluctantly towards a cluster of five green rocky outcrops: the Birds' Nest Islands. 'You go in front,' he told me urgently. 'You get better look.'

I went forward obediently and stood in the bow as we chugged towards the towering isolated rocks. I knew his concern was not for my point of view, but because he believed that lookouts watching through binoculars from the bamboo huts perched high above us would observe that I was not an adventurous fisherman invading their territory but merely a nosy foreigner and not worth the cost of a warning shot.

All reports of guards and guns and fierce dogs on these placid green dots have solid financial support. It is not a drug-run they are defending but, as the name implies, the supply of birds' nests. The walls of every cave on the islands' precipitous sides are decorated by the edible nests of *aerodramus fuciphagus*, the white-nest swiftlet, and *aerodramus maximus*, the black-nest swiftlet. These tiny birds build their nests by regurgitating sticky saliva in long thin strings against the rockface.

Throughout the Chinese world huge sums are paid for this delicacy. In Thailand one nest alone is worth an average month's salary – and thousands wait to be collected. The swifts arrive in dark evening clouds to exude their white gold – which Chinese medicine regards as the very finest tonic.

The birds' nests are not aphrodisiacs in the traditional rhino-horn category which we know and disbelieve, but the equivalent of a shot of B12. Each nest is concentrated predigested protein.

The cathedral-sized caves are lined with bamboo poles and ropes thick as your wrist. With such basic climbing equipment, the gatherers scale the slippery sides of sea caves and the dry razor-sharp walls of higher caves, sometimes climbing sixty or seventy feet up swaying bamboo to reach the nests. The casualty rate is considerable, and the nearest stretcher several islands away from these goldmines in the sky.

One Mr Big controls the sale of nests and has a jealously guarded unwritten contract with the authorities, whoever they may be. His twenty collectors live on the islands for three months at a time. He discourages them from leaving as he does not want talk of their profitable activities spread around home villages. When a small bowl of birds' nest soup can cost £35 in a Hong Kong restaurant, and dried birds' nest sells at up to £2,000 a kilo, you can appreciate his desire for discretion – and why shots occasionally ring out.

We sailed around the pirate islands at full chug. I took a few hurried pictures while listening for that warning shot across the bows; but all was peaceful – indeed I got a wave from one armed lookout. Somehow he had detected I was not a tiny Thai fisherman.

My boatman became almost cheerful as we left the five little islands and their valuable droppings and headed back to carefree beaches where a bird's nest was just a pretty photograph. Next day I flew on to face another threat, in Bangkok: suffocation, by traffic.

Any motorist complaining about the M25 would be silenced by such a poisonous Asiatic gridlock. Thais looking for work pour into the sprawling airless capital, cars are relatively cheap, bus services spasmodic, the water table too high for an underground. Every journey seems to take ninety minutes. One hour is your good luck.

Citizens organize their lives around necessary movement. Their live-in cars have telephones, entertainment, food, portable loos, sometimes beds. The wife of a friend drives her children to school each day – a short journey of a few miles and, usually, a couple of hours. Then another two hours to get home – and soon afterwards she must think about collecting them. Eight hours a day through blue carbon monoxide, going almost nowhere.

I had first stayed at the Oriental Hotel on my way to the Korean War, when Randolph Churchill and I raced our trishaws undisturbed through Bangkok's quiet country lanes. Today it is sensible to avoid the solid sultry streets and approach by riverboat, before sinking into the deep deep peace of the Somerset Maugham Suite in the Authors' Wing. This has two four-posters amid fuchsia-silk day beds, and butlers trained to unfrazzle nerves. Even faster unfrazzling is available in the spa just across the river.

It is hard to get a decent massage in Bangkok, if you take my meaning Squire, but there amid marble, orchids and lilyponds, the hands-on technique is correct and therapeutic; for the jet-lagged, the massage is the message.

Outside amid fuming streets and the occasional oasis of exquisite tranquillity, Bangkok blends the best and worst of city life; as the twenty-first century arrives, an example to relish – and dread.

Amid that urban nightmare I passed a woman crouching on the pavement before her tray of birds' nests in plastic bags. If the massage doesn't work, those swifts can fly to the rescue . . .

Last assignment . . .

An elderly Rolls-Royce collected us from Edinburgh's North British Hotel. In stately comfort we drove out to Port Edgar, and down on to the quayside. On the deck of the waiting destroyer sailors were busy with last-minute buffing-up before the arrival of the First Sea Lord. They paused, impressed, as we stepped down from our lofty limousine. 'Good start to the voyage, anyway,' murmured Richard Sharp. 'Lot of face, in a Rolls.'

We were covering the three-week cruise in northern waters of Admiral of the Fleet Lord Fraser, who was to visit Atlantic Pact capitals and meet Ministers of Defence and Service chiefs, flying his flag in HMS *Nepal*. The old destroyer's teeth had been drawn, allowing plenty of space on deck for cocktail parties and marching Marines.

It was soon after the war, in 1949, and I was covering the story for the combined press, Richard for radio. It was an early assignment for the news agency Exchange Telegraph, which was later to send me to wars and excitements around the world. Richard planned to record the ceremonies when King Haakon of Norway and King Frederik of Denmark came aboard.

The First Lieutenant showed us to the sickbay, the only sleeping space left after the Admiral's party and all that gold braid had been accommodated aft. The cabin was small and dark, without cupboards or drawers, and cluttered with equipment. There was one bed, and a hard narrow couch. Resigned, we tossed: I lost, of course.

With all the old Rolls-Royce knocked out of us, we went on deck to await the Admiral and consider the cruise from a news angle. The handsome Sharp, former BBC war correspondent in the Far East, had silver hair but still looked younger than his forty-seven years. He agreed there would probably not be one good story in our whole itinerary, despite Royalty and Ministers. The full A-list range of ceremonies, parades, parties, pomp and circumstance in five different countries – but no story.

As we smoked in the pale sunlight he grimaced and clutched the deck rail. 'Shocking pain,' he said at last. I followed him back to the sickbay and watched helplessly as perspiration soaked his face. After a while he muttered: 'Morphine. Need some morphine.'

That was not something I knew much about. Worried, I ran off to look for the ship's doctor – who turned out to be a twenty-year-old sickbay attendant, a National Serviceman on his first sea voyage. Lone destroyers do not carry doctors for their 200 men, not even when the senior officer of the Royal Navy is aboard. 'Doc', as he was known, hurried away to ask the coxswain for the key to the painkiller cupboard. He did not inspire much confidence.

Through the scuttle I watched Admiral Fraser, small and ruddy, striding along the quay with his Naval Assistant, Captain Jellicoe; his First Lieutenant and Secretary followed. They passed out of sight. Shrill whistles as the Admiral was piped aboard announced the destroyer was ready to sail.

Richard was on the edge of the bunk, face glistening. The little tube of morphine arrived. After an injection, he sat back and lit a cigarette. By now the buzz that one of the correspondents was ill had run round the ship. An officer looked in to say that a doctor was coming from the naval shore hospital.

'I'm all right,' Richard said, frowning. I knew what he was thinking: if he gave in and went ashore and the pain was just indigestion and gone in an hour, he could never catch up. We should be out in the North Sea and, story or no story, he would have fallen down on the assignment.

'If he's sick we'd better put him ashore,' said the agitated Captain as we waited outside the sickbay during the doctor's examination. He already had a First Sea Lord to worry about, and did not need a sick correspondent. 'We've got a tight programme planned to the minute, with all these Royals. Can't risk anything going wrong.'

I said nothing. I knew how bitterly disappointed Richard would be if he were left behind.

The doctor, a Lieut.-Commander, came out. 'He can go if he wants to,' he said briskly, and went ashore. It must have been a traditional service medical inspection. Five minutes later we cast off. A quarter of an hour behind schedule, on a fine Sunday morning at the end of April, the *Nepal* sailed for Oslo.

Richard, pale but relieved, came on deck as we passed under the Forth Bridge with the fourteen-man Royal Marine band playing cheerfully. Then he went back to our sickbay to lie down. Three hours later the effect of the morphine had worn off.

Kindly but misguided hands, seeking to help – 'This'll fix you up, mate' – gave him a large tot of Navy rum. It set his stomach afire in a blaze of pain. The day went slowly for him as the destroyer rolled along in the swell. He did not eat or leave his bed, but took more morphine and lay back, silently awake.

That night we got little sleep, but talked. He was deeply in love with Elizabeth, a Chinese girl he had met while working out of Singapore. She had returned to England with him so they could stay together, and he had just made the decision to leave his wife. They'd had a terrible scene that morning, he said, before he left for Edinburgh. He had told her he was not going back.

I lay on the hard couch alongside his bed and we discussed their future, quietly, until he fell into a shallow restless sleep. During the night contractions of pain forced soft groans. Once he murmured, 'Sorry about all this noise.' Before dawn I was racing round the ship, trying to find more morphine. The pain was worse.

During the afternoon he dictated a message to Radio Newsreel at the BBC reporting his condition and adding 'Some improvement today but impossible tell if will continue'. He advised his newsroom to watch for my stories on the ExTel tape – which within six hours was to report a drama.

I looked in to the sickbay again before dinner. The young SBA was sponging Richard's face and combing his hair as he lay stiff, trying not to move. 'Getting ready for the bright Norwegian lights?' I asked. He grinned, a wan boyish smile from the pillows. 'Anything I can do?'

'No, Alan, thanks very much,' he said. 'I'm not too bad now.'

I went out and along the deck. The destroyer was pushing gently through the North Sea at an unhurried twelve knots. The wardroom was cheerful. After the statutory pink gins we sat down to dinner. The meal was almost over when the ship's engines suddenly throbbed louder . . . and still louder. We looked round in surprise. Vibration shivered the table, and cutlery chattered. Nobody spoke. I went to a scuttle and looked out: a few feet below the waves were slipping by in a turmoil of white foam.

A knock on the wardroom door; a sailor, pale and wide-eyed, saluted the First Lieutenant: 'Sir, it's Mr Sharp . . .'

Up on the quarterdeck the night was cold and clear. Brilliant stars sprinkled the sky down to the unseen horizon. *Nepal* was slashing through luminous seas like a speedboat, leaping and bounding into the darkness. Something dreadful was happening: the furious hum of the engines, the endless threatening ocean racing past and away into the night, the white face of the young seaman, the quick deliberate dispersal of the officers . . . and all the time, like ghostly background music to some drama of the high seas, the muffled thunder of the waves.

I raced up to the sickbay. Richard Sharp was unconscious. Under the hard white light his face was ashen. Two Petty Officers had begun artificial respiration. His lips moved gently as air was forced into his lungs. I waited in the tense silent cabin, took my turn at the bedside, then stumbled down to the signal office.

Within minutes the Morse operator was tapping out my first message to Portishead receiving station and ExTel:

DIOCLES LONDON
DESTROYER NEPAL CARRYING FIRST SEA LORD
FRASER ON CRUISE ATLANTIC PACT COUNTRIES
NORTHERN WATERS TONIGHT RACING TWENTY
KNOTS THROUGH SKAGERRAK TOWARDS OSLO TO
SAVE LIFE BBB BBB CCC CORRESPONDENT . . .

I cabled 200 words, and went up to the bridge. The Captain had decided to put in to Larvik, a coastal town some seventy-five miles south of Oslo. A radio message went out calling for a doctor and ambulance. Suddenly, as though brushing through a curtain into a room full of smoke, the speeding destroyer ran into fog.

Without slackening her urgent pace *Nepal* raced on. Now the siren was howling in the night.

Back in the warm sickbay unscreened lights threw great shadows on to the clinical green cabin walls as sweating men leaned over the unconscious figure. Above the bed hung a grotesque Davis submarine escape apparatus; every few minutes Richard was given a whiff of its pure oxygen.

In the background, watching the silent intent men, a small silver-haired figure with eight bright rows of medal ribbons: the First Sea Lord, his cheery red face grim, the light glinting on his golden sleeves.

Twice Richard's heart stopped beating. Twice it was coaxed back to life.

... FRASER WATCHING ARTIFICIAL RESPIRATION IN SMALL SICKBAY TOLD URGENT MEN WORKING STRIPPED TO WAIST QUOTE YOURE DOING FINE JOB STOP KEEP AT IT AND YOULL PULL HIM THROUGH UNQUOTE AFTER HALF HOUR RESUSCITATION SLIGHT COLOUR RETURNED SHARPS ASHEN FACE BUT HE STILL UNCONSCIOUS STOP AS NEPAL RUSHED THROUGH THICK FOG SIREN BLARING PETTY OFFICER LEANING SHARPS CHEST FORCING AIR INTO LUNGS SAID QUOTE HES JUST TICKING OVER THATS ALL UNQUOTE SINCE NO DOCTOR ABOARD CAUSE COLLAPSE UNKNOWN ...

I sat in the radio office staring angrily at my typewriter, while behind me morse keys stuttered the copy away. The awful thing, the unforgivable thing, was that this was what we called a *good* story; it had action, drama, names, suspense ... Richard and I had agreed that this diplomatic cruise would provide no story – but now he was dying, and leaving me to write it.

Up in the sickbay again the unconscious form seemed somehow heavier, greyer, different. We kept up the respiration but all of us – Admiral of the Fleet, young National Serviceman, burly coxswain, newspaperman – all of us knew that it was no use any more.

... AT ELEVEN OCLOCK SHARP THOUGHT TO BE
DEAD BUT FOUR MEN WORKED ON SWINGING ARMS
PRESSING CHEST IN CASE SPARK LIFE LINGERED
WHICH COULD BE AWAKENED BY NORWEGIAN
DOCTOR EXPECTED IN BOAT BRINGING PILOT TO
GUIDE DESTROYER INTO QUAYSIDE LARVIK ...

The warship cut through the night, its banshee siren wailing
dismally until, as suddenly as the race had begun, the urgent
speed dropped away and the bow came round to starboard. The
siren fell silent. *Nepal* cruised on at half-speed.

... AFTER TWO HOUR STRUGGLE FOR LIFE RICHARD
SHARP ABOARD DOCTORLESS DESTROYER THE FOUR
PERSPIRING MEN FOLDED HIS ARMS ACROSS CHEST
AND RELUCTANTLY STOOD BACK FROM NARROW
BUNK STOP HE WAS DEAD PARA HOPELESS EFFORT
SAVE HIS LIFE BEEN ONCARRIED DESPERATE INTEN-
SITY FOR THIRTY MINUTES AFTER ALL IN TINY CABIN
KNEW HED GONE PARA ADMIRAL FRASER INFORMED
AND AGAIN VISITED SICKBAY WHERE SHARPS BODY
LAY COVERED BLANKET QUOTE YOU DID ALL YOU
COULD FOR HIM POOR FELLOW UNQUOTE HE TOLD
SILENT MEN STOP DESTROYER ALTERED COURSE
CONTINUED OSLOWARDS ...

My first takes to ExTel had gone out in time for the early editions;
news of his death caught the finals. In a round-up for the
evenings I included Admiral Fraser's signal to the widow: 'He was
a man well-known to the services and greatly respected by all.'

My last piece got away at 4.30 am and I chainsmoked the night
away in a wardroom chair. We learned later that death had been
caused by a perforated stomach ulcer and subsequent peritonitis.

Early next morning the warship steamed up Oslo fjord. On
deck the band stood silent, its cheery martial music unread. The
Marines played only the National Anthems. High above the flag
at half-mast, grey skies threatened and as the *Nepal* tied up in
Oslo town and the stretcher was carried out across the decks, a
violent storm broke and lightning flashed through unnatural

Dawn Champagne with Lord Snowdon while crossing to the isle of Penang …

On another island – the privately owned Pangkor Laut – a lonely tenor searches for seashells, just like any other beach-comber …

At Hua Hin station I was doubly blessed: first by holy water from nine Thai monks, then by a friendly local – who peed on my foot …

Prime Minister of Malaysia, Dr Mahathir, arrives in Pangkor Laut – and in the welcoming group my sound recordist is the best dressed. Anyone who knows camera crews will appreciate a unique picture …

Aboard the Oriental Express, Princess Michael cues Lord Norwich for yet another chorus of 'Mad Dogs and Englishmen'. Prince Michael actually smiles: another unique picture …

Romance on the Oriental Express: Koo Stark and Bertie Way became engaged. The effect soon wore off ...

On Pangkor Laut, the Pavmobile takes the strain from the new Pavarotti kneecaps ...

Princess Michael, adopting the Asian mode, titters shyly behind her fan ...

The *QE2* became the first big ship to visit the port of Qingdao while the bamboo curtain was still in place. Welcoming musicians, rather to their surprise, found themselves being conducted by the ship's bandleader, Joe Loss …

At a celebratory football match a scratch team of *QE2* stewards and stokers played the regional Chinese. The *QE2*'s hundred supporters made far more noise than the 20,000 local fans …

As our film crew arrived on the pitch, the *QE2* stand chanted: 'Whicker's here, Whicker's there, Whicker's fuckin' everywhere…' for quite a long time. It was hard to tell what the docile and inscrutable Chinese made of this incantation …

In the Asaro Valley of Papua New Guinea, the lithe skinny figures of clay-caked Mudmen in grotesque helmets emerged silently from the forest. The spectacle was disturbing …

A more conventional welcome at Goroka airstrip from the isolated people who have somehow jumped a century or two: the first wheel some Mudmen saw was on an aircraft …

The peace of Symi, in the Dodecanese, was disturbed only by Mr Bob the Spongeman, who gave that little harbour his Whickeric version of me – which was quite good, if you like that sort of thing …

At home in Jersey, with local luxuries …

I'm convinced my Bentley Continental is older than I am – though in rather better shape, I'll grant you that. One reason why: a complete facelift and make-over, right down to the metal …

The way most viewers believe I live my life …

… though this is more like it: going to work by tram – but in Rio …

… or taking the train – but in Alaska. It did pull up for me – and it wasn't even a Request stop …

darkness. Norwegian newspapermen came aboard and placed a hurriedly gathered bunch of tulips and irises upon the Union Jack covering the body.

An elderly Rolls-Royce ambulance waited on the quayside and, as ship's officers saluted, Richard Sharp was piped ashore at the end of his last assignment – from which there had been only one story.

Postscript

I wrote to Elizabeth in Singapore to tell her what had happened, and of his love for her about which he had spoken during those last hours. Later she told me she had adopted a child born at the exact moment he died, so that Richard's spirit might live on with her.

That whole sad dramatic story would have been even stronger had I chosen to reveal what Richard Sharp told me during his last agonizing hours.

'I think my wife has killed me,' he whispered during the night. 'She put something in my drink before I left home. She knew about my ulcer – and that when I got back I was going to leave her.'

I did not know Mrs Sharp, but protested that such a monstrous action was surely inconceivable. 'No no,' he said, 'she'd do it. I know what happened.' He died without telling his dreadful thoughts and fears to anyone else.

I continued with the First Sea Lord's tour, as planned. When we reached Copenhagen the BBC sent out my friend Doug Willis to replace Richard. Later, back in London, I went to Broadcasting House to leave some of his effects with Pat Smithers, who was running Radio Newsreel and had sent him on his last assignment.

He was the only person I ever told what Richard believed about his death. When I did, there was a long silence. Then he said quietly: 'When I rang to tell Mrs Sharp the first thing she said – the *only* thing she said – was that she wanted him cremated in Oslo, right away. She did not want his body returned to England.'

The other side of the one-way mirror . . .

Leading a camera through the minefield of money and expensive pleasure is going in at television's deep end and risking resentment, for everyone's reaction to the invisible barrier of wealth in others can be intense and self-revealing. Few of us would be what we are today if we could afford to be different, so depending upon the attitude of the viewer, any of my attitudes and questions on camera could seem naïve or censorious, deferential or aggressive.

To film a series of four *Whicker's World*s on the *Queen Elizabeth 2* we travelled around the Pacific from Tahiti to Japan with 1,400 cruisers of a dozen nationalities, all able and willing to spend much time and money on a hedonistic holiday of up to three months. Observing such a fortunate group at play it would have been easy to sink into the familiar television hatchet job: intercut parties and diamonds aboard with distress and poverty ashore, add lofty commentary and retire complacently – having settled *that* problem.

We all know television reporters who base their careers upon injustice, seeking out unfortunates anywhere in the world, dealing with refugees and poverty in terms of easy professional pity or wholly useless anger. Rail against an uncaring unfair world, demand that *they* do something about it – then into the Jag and off home to Wiltshire or Islington, smugly on the side of the angels.

Dismissing envy and occasional venom, the rich remain a secret society which can be experienced as a pageant, a glittering entertainment we read about constantly and, occasionally, see. Like the poor, they are everywhere, and usually harmless. Through application or luck or intelligence they have accumulated more of everything than the rest of us, so we struggle to join them by hard work – or by a short-cut through the Lottery.

On television the enjoyment of any group intent upon its particular pleasure can be a problem to convey to viewers sitting at home before their spyhole in the corner. We are familiar with our reaction of distaste or irritation as we watch celebrating football fans, a druggy rave or a tipsy hunt ball.

Whicker's World filmed the inaugural run of the Orient Express down to Venice – a jolly house party on wheels attended by a *mélange* of duchesses and railwaymen's widows, film stars and earnest train buffs. It was certainly not a solemn occasion – though the commercial enterprise and investment behind it were serious enough. Its excitement and style produced much fun for viewers, and a few disapproving letters for me.

The viewer of such a celebration may react like a drinker who has gone on the wagon but then attends a convivial party: everyone seems noisy and silly and not half as funny or clever as they think they are.

Looking soberly and often disapprovingly through the one-way mirror of television it is easy to be impatient with revellers when you have not been invited to share their fun, which is rarely contagious. Nothing makes a woman prettier, wittier or more desirable than a couple of drinks in a man – and surely vice versa – but viewers at home come cold and sober to their screens.

A gentleman from a Norfolk village wrote critically about our Orient Express expedition. In reply I wondered whether a film of one of his calm Sunday morning gatherings at home, viewed the next day when a few dry sherries behind those on camera, might not leave most of us a little impatient with his jolly guests as they joshed the vicar and teased the doctor's wife? After reflection, he withdrew his courteous censure.

On a cruise all the other guests are chosen for you, and their enthusiasms can seem baffling to straightforward normal viewers like you and me. Some are resolutely exhilarated by aerobics or trapshooting, art appreciation or golf, astrology, boozing, jogging, disco dancing, gambling, bridge or graphology – you name it, they're at it, while we sit quietly at home getting mildly irritated because they are having more fun than we are, even though some of it may be regulated jollity.

Once it seemed that Sea had lost its battle with Air, for few travellers were boarding luxury liners to sail away into nostalgia. Today the seafarers are returning en masse in search of a comfortable adventure. *Whicker's World* had looked at early cruisers within their spaceship back in 1965 aboard the Royal Mail Line's *Andes*. In 1978 we went round Indonesia on the 9,000-ton *Prinsendam*, a splendid little Dutch ship which then sailed off to Alaska – and sank. A fire on board had started, unsportingly, in the Fire Control Centre.

All those adventures made revealing viewing, but following our six-week consideration of *QE2* passengers it took television another fifteen years to wake up to the fascination of such captive groups; then we had *Airport*, *Hotel* and a deluge of less-successful series.

The *QE2*, up close, was overwhelming; long as a street, tall as a skyscraper, far too big to see. This leviathan had stopped being a liner in the classic transatlantic tradition back in the 1970s and become a resort hotel that followed the sun. As soon as the anchor was raised and the human chemistry within started to react, an unreal shipboard life with new and different perspectives took over.

Separated from the familiar artefacts of their identity, like homes and friends and jobs, cruisers thrown into this international mishmash sometimes found it a problem to identify the social and financial status of the people from the next cabin, the next table. They would gather tentatively in territories where they felt most at ease: at dainty Devonshire teas or bingo or in the casino, on bar stools or at business seminars or the nightly round of parties. From their selected bases they sounded out their companions, and began to gell.

In mid-Pacific, floating free, we became remote from all things usual, as that vast place, thirteen storeys high and a fifth of a mile long, pushed through the South Seas at 30mph, with 1,400 strangers milling around and getting to know each other.

Going among them I filmed Floyd 'Ike' Ingram, a retired engineer from Utah on his tenth *QE2* cruise. He spent five hours every day doing a giant jigsaw, with several loyal helpers. I wondered why he didn't just buy a jigsaw, do it at home and save the fare? He explained that when not on holiday he would never have time to mess with it.

Mrs Betty Sinclair was only on her ninth cruise, but still a knowledgeable passenger for she had run the Gleneagles Hotel in Torquay where John Cleese and a group of Monty Pythons once stayed. Her late husband, a retired Naval officer, had evidently not been much in tune with the attitudes and demands of that television team, and out of Mr Sinclair's irascibility grew the distinctive Basil, and *Fawlty Towers.*

Mrs Sinclair told me there had indeed been a Manuel – called Pepe – but when I enthused about the series she gave me a thoughtful look. 'You mean,' she said finally, 'you mean you thought it was funny?'

Well, er, actually, yes. 'Oh,' she said, coldly. We moved to less controversial matters, like how she put up with those awful people at the next table.

Another noticeable passenger was John Meek, a New Zealand optometrist with multiple sclerosis who told me that with luck he had ten more years to live. He was on his way to Germany to have his blood changed. He darted around the ship on a tiny scooter designed by Lord Snowdon and found the wide decks, smooth corridors and twenty-four lifts an ideal holiday setting, though admitted gleefully that he had 'ridden over a few toes'.

Some women passengers dressed well; some followed Danny La Rue. At one casual penthouse party our hostess was wearing double emerald earrings, a number of hefty rings surrounding another egg-sized emerald, and a sort of emerald breastplate. I wondered what she wore on important occasions when dressing to impress.

A more elegant Lauren Bacall-type matron never appeared twice in the same outfit. She changed three or four times a day. Warned that I was not only watching but counting, she admitted with a worried frown that one day soon she might have to wear something twice – though after only thirty days aboard still had a couple of wardrobes to go. Most cruisers with nostalgic memories of cabin trunks do tend to travel heavy.

A rich Mexican bachelor who enjoyed dancing was much in

demand. He told me that fearing boredom he had brought a lot to read, but first planned to fill the hours redoing his address book. He had already been aboard for forty days but was only halfway through the As.

In the restaurant Valerie and I sat next to the patrician Brookes-Walkers, great-grandparents from San Francisco's Nob Hill. Invited to their stateroom we found it stacked with an enormous cache of champagne. This was deceptive; they had planned a large party for their extended family before sailing, but an IRA dockside demonstration kept visitors behind the police line. The abstemious Brookes-Walkers, on board for eighty-two days, were trying to drink their way through their aborted send-off hospitality, and finding it something of a chore. We did what we could.

The *QE2* then accounted for one-third of the world's consumption of caviare – some 20 lbs a day. Also on board: 3,000 tins of *pâté de fois gras*. Chefs boasted they could prepare any order, however exotic – and also add a pound a day to every waistline, for most cruisers did their best to masticate their money's-worth. Since the galleys prepared 4,000 meals a day, they were offering mass catering to their caviare clientele with recipes starting: 'Take 2,000 eggs . . .'

Such meals were the events of the day, social occasions requiring dressing up. The *maître d'* always inquired what dish we would like for dinner. Bluff oysters? Saddle of lamb? Beef Wellington? After a while I ran out of favourite dishes and it became a chore to offer the galley a daily challenge. Most passengers soon fell back upon anything that cost a lot. One conspicuous consumption standby was *saumon à la Russe*: smoked salmon wrapped around caviare. Presumably had they worked in *foie gras* it would have been even more desirable.

On an average sailing the *QE2* carried 1,600 different items of food – three times as many as a hotel of comparable quality. Provisioning can be a problem, for should stock run out no supplier waits at the end of a telephone. On an inaugural voyage American Family Cruises ran out of bananas. The line is no longer in business.

During television's bad old days when its trade union, the ACTT, was at its most destructive, Granada's splendid *Brideshead* series was interrupted because union technicians demanded £10 a day hardship money to film aboard the *QE2*, and another £10 for disruption of domestic life.

In the Pig and Whistle, one of the crew's four bars, a steward told me he had been looking after my old friend Ben Lyon when he died on a *QE2* cruise in 1979. 'We got back to Los Angeles and there was a posh hearse, a Cadillac, waiting to collect him – but his body was just carried ashore stitched-up in canvas. Seemed strange.'

The man who sewed that canvas around a corpse at sea, he said, was traditionally rewarded with a bottle of rum. The last stitch always went through the nose. If the body did not notice, it was safe to carry on with the burial.

The *QE2*'s hospital, with surgeon, doctor, dentist and four nurses, could cope with any emergency up to minor brain surgery. It took an average of four minutes to get any stricken passenger into hospital, so it was the ideal place in which to have a heart attack.

As we steamed out of New Zealand's capital, Wellington, on a soft summer evening, there was a 'Starlight' call on the speakers: three cardiac arrests among the passengers – and a fight in the galley. Someone had stabbed a cook, who fought back with a cleaver: a conventional scene. Casualty list: one eye, nearly, and thirty-four stitches. All the heart cases survived. It may have been peaceful Upstairs, but Downstairs it was all go.

The *QE2* was greeted at every dockside by impressive music – martial or traditional. A massed pipe band played us out of Wellington. At Raratonga it had been a hula group. Bandsmen of the Royal Australian Navy welcomed us to Sydney. At Bali a gamelin orchestra, with temple dancers. Chinese girl pipers marched alongside at Singapore, and at Yokohama Japanese Police belted out the *River Kwai* theme. For our welcome at Brisbane, a group called the Ran Ran Bush Band came booming from disco speakers across the sunlit water: 'First I'm gonna sing yer a little song about a pub . . .'

The more adventurous went ashore in Port Moresby and flew into the Eastern Highlands of Papua New Guinea to meet the Mudmen. Landing at Goroka, cruisers travelled another thirty miles into the Asaro Valley and there, during their first hesitant minutes in a clearing among some huts, became aware to their alarm that Mudmen were advancing upon them silently, like gesticulating apparitions from the forest. They were caked in clay that had dried almost white, and wearing grotesque helmet masks.

In silence broken only by the whirring of tree insects, the lithe skinny figures advanced slowly, eerily, until their little grey hands reached out to touch the tourists, who flinched and backed away. The spectacle was most disturbing.

It seemed that once upon a time the Mudmen's village was attacked by a hostile tribe, and survivors took refuge in a river. When they crept back to their homes, still muddy, the enemy thought they were ghosts come to avenge their dead, and panicked. Since it had worked so well the ploy was adopted, and the village was never attacked again.

It was easy to understand such fear. They seemed from another planet and, in a way, they were; they had jumped a few centuries. The first wheel some Mudmen ever saw was on an aircraft.

After this ghoulish arrival they took off their helmets and posed impassively for photographs. Some brash cruisers put on the heavy masks, and regretted it afterwards.

Poor but dignified, the Mudmen's village had little for sale except a few knitted 'bilum' bags and pig's-tusk ornaments, some fragile spears and clay effigies – yet in its dramatic simplicity theirs was a memorable expedition into the past.

Another much discussed expedition from our four programmes was the crew's ecstatic run ashore at Pattaya, where they were instantly immersed in Thai boxing and, even more deeply, in topless bar girls. They had such a good time and provided such good pictures that several crew divorces followed.

During editing I showed Sir Nigel Broackes, then Chairman of Trafalgar House which owned the *QE2*, that memorable sequence and the telling confrontations with tiny Thai temptations: 'You may not win us many new passengers,' he said thoughtfully, 'but you'll certainly get us a lot more crew.'

From Hong Kong some cruisers ventured into China, through Macao, driving to Shiqi by way of Sun Yat Sen's birthplace. Returning to the frontier again after a few hours we were faced by stern questionnaires: 'List jewellery you carry, including male jewellery and the name of the watch.' I admitted mine was usually called George. We were also asked the names of antiques we had bought. All that was on sale even in that relatively affluent Pearl River delta farmland was a little fruit and a few basic Mao jackets; nevertheless the Chinese seemed to fear cruisers might trade their Patek Philippes for oranges and pink plastic sandals.

We sailed towards Qingdao, on the Yellow Sea north of Shanghai. None of us had ever heard of the place, though it was eight times the size of Manchester. Passengers assembled to learn what awaited them in a hitherto hidden land; in 1989 ours was the first foreign liner to put into that port. The Chinese had to dredge the approaches and build a new wharf since the *QE2* was seven times bigger than any ship that had docked there before.

Officials from the China Travel Service attended a briefing to warn us that 16mm filming was forbidden – though 8mm was all right – and offered to answer questions. Cruisers en masse can be surprising; more than a thousand of them, mainly Americans preparing for their first descent upon an unknown nation of well over a billion, had little to ask except, 'Can we get western food?' Stuffed to the gunwales with weeks of the richest meals, the first tourists to go into China were wondering how to avoid its food. 'Are there taxis?' 'Will my electric curlers work?' Intrepid they were not.

Our indulgent and enviable lifestyle in which the only problem each day brought was what to wear for dinner . . . may have had something to do with that lack of alert concern about the world outside our space capsule.

Buses had been brought to Qingdao from hundreds of miles around to cope with the influx of 1,400 plus crew, and city streets were emptied of traffic for the swift drive through town. Speeding down centre lanes past saluting policemen and a million solemn fascinated faces, we felt like Party leaders.

Passengers had all dressed down and were led, bored and bemused, around carpet factories, mills, hospitals, Friendship stores . . . and everywhere greeted by chanting schoolchildren in stage make-up. Women, all in trousers, wore none. Advertising was then restricted to a few billboards offering maxims like 'Keep Your Saucepans Clean'. At this first meeting of two cultures, both sides were serious, uncertain and watchful.

Next day things lightened up; in the city's football stadium

Qingdao faced a team hastily put together from the *QE2* crew. The 20,000 spectators were all in regulation dark blue, with a few greens, and had been queueing since 5.30am to watch the foreign devils at play. As many again had been turned away to line rooftops or climb trees in the hope of catching a glimpse of the game. Around the stadium stood untold thousands of spindly interlocked bicycles, a chaotic Chinese puzzle. I could not imagine how anyone would get their own bike back.

Amid the quiet and respectful sea of blue filling the stands, one small section had been reserved for *QE2* crew. Their hundred supporters made far more noise than the Chinese thousands. Spotting my camera team, they unleashed a familiar capitalist chant: 'You have lost your lea-der . . .' When I arrived for filming on the touchline they switched to the even more familiar 'Whicker's here, Whicker's there, Whicker's fuckin' everywhere . . .' They were not at all inscrutable. Hard to imagine what the Chinese made of it.

Their team were regional champions, fit and professional. The *QE2* lads, press-ganged at the last minute, included a singer from the Joe Loss band, a few cheery stewards who had just served lunch, and a couple of stokers. 'We should be playing a scratch team from one of their ships,' said Cunard Director Terry Conroy, ruefully. So it proved.

Qingdao soon scored and seemed ready to go on, and on – until down from the directors' box came an order that could not be ignored: 'Win – but not by too much. Smile a little more and run a little less.' Their players eased up, noticeably, and allowed *QE2* to equalize. The game was much enjoyed and the final score a diplomatic 5–2. No faces were lost. *QE2* spectators joined their team in a lap honouring their defeat – and were resoundingly cheered. It was indeed a friendly game; far more was done for international goodwill than by any World Cup match.

The *QE2* was a fast old lady and could move between landfalls at a businesslike twenty-eight knots, or a good 10mph faster than today's much bigger and more economic megaships. She had much character as a cocoon and provider of fantasies. Also, if you will, a cabaret, country club, health farm, gambling den, school and endless house party.

Her disasters were always front-page news. My favourite was a small and secret upset: the wheel on the bridge was not at all like Captain Ahab's, but tiny and discreetly elegant. It was once detached and carried off as a souvenir by a visiting schoolboy. Aghast, they had to steer their 70,000 tons with a screwdriver.

Another untold story of the *QE2* is for me the most cunning scam of the High Seas. It brought comfort, though no financial gain, to its perpetrators, but an enormous loss to their shipping line.

Through the years the crew of this great liner contrived to trick its owners out of millions of pounds, without detection; had the swindle run for the life of the ship it would have cost them more than £100m. The mastermind has never been discovered. Maybe there wasn't one. Maybe it just evolved . . . a floating con trick that shanghaied profits and will become a legend. Hard to believe it was so successful, for so long.

This intriguing trickery before everyone's eyes finally came to light when the ship passed to its fourth owner, Micky Arison, hard-nosed Chairman of Carnival Cruise Lines of Florida. An amiable and soft-spoken Israeli, Micky followed his formidable father Ted to head their fleet of enormous cruise ships. As part of his maritime training he had worked below decks for nine years, during which he learned the tricks crews pulled – and how to stop them. The *QE2* needed him, for he had seen it all – yet of course there's always the next scam waiting just below the horizon . . .

Cunard's magnificent flagship had sailed through a turbulent sea of dispute, deceit and dishonesty from the day the keel was laid at Clydebank in 1965. Until she was launched in 1967, pillaged furniture, carpets and every type of fitting surreptitiously left the yard to furnish the homes of the eager DIY Clydeside shipworkers, their friends and clients. This was called 'squirrelling', and the supporting jobs-for-the-boys thought was: the more you stole from a ship, the longer it took to complete it.

Resigned to such traditional daylight robbery – dismissed as 'perks' – the venerable Cunard line drifted along in its comfortable way, pretending not to notice. In that grand era it was not only the shipyard mateys who were skimming: some directors had permanent accommodations on board and when they were not crossing the Atlantic the ship sailed with empty staterooms. This did not strengthen the profit-and-loss account.

Nor did the dominant unions; they had grown so strong that, in effect, they controlled the ship. When Cunard, mismanaged and financially drained, sunk into memory after takeover by what was originally a property company, the Chairman of Trafalgar House, Sir Nigel Broackes, told me that the unions still decided which crewmen they could employ, and in what capacity. The ship had to accept those sent for employment and could do little to control, punish or dismiss. Some seamen imposed upon the owners were petty criminals, some Neanderthals, some good decent men struggling to survive in a floating thieves' kitchen.

I write from some experience: I had many happy times sailing aboard the *QE2* – but in 1972 suffered a crippling theft, which an unsurprised ship Security philosophically shrugged off as par for the voyage.

After endless disputes Trafalgar managed to curtail some of their excesses, but the *QE2* was still partially crew-controlled when the company was taken over by Kvaerner, a Norwegian conglomerate which wanted most of Trafalgar's assets but was not too enthusiastic about the *QE2*.

After some unprofitable years Kvaerner sold the *QE2* to Carnival Cruise Lines of Florida, a sharp company which knew all about running superliners vivid with casinos on a seven-day Caribbean holiday circuit. Their forty-six ships had a fast turnover and usually almost 100 per cent occupancy, their crews were well paid and honest, or else, and their passengers lined up to pay moderate fares – because the casino took the strain.

Going through the books upon purchase, the one fact that always eluded Arison was his initial basic demand: how many passenger cabins *were* there on his new liner? This reasonable query always produced vague and uncertain answers.

Persisting, he buried himself in plans, charts and records, and eventually discovered that over the years, each time the 2,000-passenger liner had gone into dry dock for a refit – she had emerged with fewer cabins! Somehow over the years seven per cent had disappeared behind the bulkhead, to become crew accommodation.

This stealthy manoeuvre had been initiated, it seemed, by the ship's non-maritime complement – the entertainers, hairdressers, shopkeepers, croupiers, PE instructors and other members of the cast who saw themselves as a shipboard élite and were always anxious to travel in the more comfortable passenger cabins. So each time the ship was in dry dock someone – who? – arranged that the bulkheads be moved back a bit . . .

When Carnival finally uncovered this mysterious movement, it emerged that thus far about fifty cabins had gone behind the crew curtain. No previous owner had noticed this creeping encroachment, this stealthy deflection of money-making capacity.

The income the crafty scam cost the owners was phenomenal. The missing fifty double cabins would have earned, say, £100 per passenger per night, so if the ship sailed 350 days a year – allowing two weeks out of service for maintenance – there was a loss of £3.5m a year. In addition, the on-board passenger spend in bars, shops and so on would have averaged £10 per person per day. Another £350,000 shanghaied. In all, a missing £3,850,000 a year, minimum.

After a normal liner's life of thirty years, that scam would have manoeuvred the owners out of more than £115m – quite enough to sink a shipping company. You could buy the *QE2* for that, with enough change left over for a couple of jets and a hotel.

Today cruise liners have polarized into big-and-flash, and small-and-chic – the buses and the Bentleys. The *QE2* is an elderly but comfortable bus, which held the Biggest Ship in the World title unchallenged for more than a quarter of a century. Now every liner launched is bigger and flashier than the last. Among competitive shipowners, adding the odd thousand tons above the 100,000 level does not much affect the economics but does satisfy that rampantly macho breed who long to crow: mine's bigger than yours!

We flew out to Miami for the inaugural jaunt of what was then the biggest ship in the world. At 101,000 tons *Carnival Destiny* was 31,000 tons larger than the *QE2* and built to carry more than 3,400 passengers and 1,000 crew on Caribbean cruises timed to the minute: 'It's Friday, so it must be Ocho Rios.'

With fourteen decks and a nine-storey atrium, *Destiny* was a floating Caesar's Palace full of apple green and pink neon, fruit-machines, dazzling flesh-and-feathers cabaret shows in an enormous theatre, and twenty-four-hour action. Such 'fun ships' promised at least five meals a day with plenty of umbrella drinks in between, plus the easy availability of slots and close companionship. On holiday their passengers believed in Life, Liberty and the Happiness of Pursuit – so inhibitions went overboard early, along with style.

Several thousand fun-lovers swung from the rigging for a few days while the liner moved imperceptibly from one sunny Caribbean freeport to another – though ports of call were incidental. The holiday offered a new horizon every day, but to passengers eagerly chasing fun it mattered little what had come over that horizon or where their piña-colada palace sailed. The ship was the destination; indeed not too many seaside towns would wish to cope with a floating Waldorf Astoria that suddenly disgorged 4,000 cheery foreigners and then, as the clock struck, removed them all and sailed away.

The intention of the shipping line was to make sure that a surfeit of holiday fun was provided on board, in and out of the casino. Should the shopping and partying ever slow down, *Destiny* offered fifty-six different organized activities on every cruise, from hairy-chest contests to nautical knot-tying seminars. The ship was so vast that most passengers were still learning their way around when they landed back in Miami, holiday over.

Such cruising has joined the mass market and is the fastest-growing segment of American holiday business. The fact that it enjoys higher customer satisfaction levels than any land vacation does suggest that shipowners know what their customers want, and how they should be treated. Larger ships are more economic to run, so the world's shipyards now concentrate on super-cruisers. Four thousand passengers can be handled for little more than your average leviathan spends on a thousand.

Voyager of the Seas, 142,000 tons, is already cruising its ice rink, golf course, rock-climbing wall, basketball court, five-deck-deep theatre and feeble food around the Caribbean, and will soon be joined by two sister ships. The coming *Queen Mary 2* will be at least 8,000 tons larger than that massive trio.

By 2001 there will be a dozen liners larger than the poor little *QE2*. Passengers hitting those decks will be able to forget they are

on a ship. Should they ever get a salty whiff of the ocean, someone will come in and fix the air conditioning.

The oldest and cheapest liners, the so-called 'bottom feeders' of
the industry, today charge cruisers around £50 a day. *Destiny,*
catering for the 'contemporary' class, charges £150–75, the refur-
bished *QE2* around £225–50.

At the top end of the floating scale, an international flotilla of
some thirty little ships with shallow drafts sails imperturbably into
secret harbours, charging their few pampered passengers
£550–75 a day but providing opulence and service five-star hotels
envy. They attract the cruiser who could probably afford a decent
yacht, if prepared to face all those seafaring decisions and a lazy
overpaid crew who, on his rare visits, would resent him as an
intruder.

I joined one of those boutique cruises in Bordeaux. The
Seabourn Pride had come seventy-five miles up the Gironde to
anchor at the bottom of the main street, and was waiting quite
alone in the city centre, the only vessel in that empty yellow river.
When we sailed her 10,000 tons cut through the Bay of Biscay at
eighteen knots without sound, vibration or sense of movement. It
was uncanny – so I went up to see who was driving.

The bridge was a white film set out of *Batman*, with the
Captain's blue armchair the most visible piece of equipment.
There were small levers for manoeuvring the ship backwards,
sideways – and upwards, for all I know. Bridges used to be full of
stern windswept men in oilskins shouting urgently at each other;
that carpeted observatory was as hushed as a laboratory.

The passengers were mainly silver-haired soft-spoken
Americans from the covers of *Fortune*. Sitting next to us in the
restaurant was a distinctive trio: he carefully groomed and well
into his seventies, she a doll-like wife of similar age. Facing them,
a solemn thickset young man. During long and exotic meals, they
seldom spoke. I later discovered the sombre figure was their
guide. It seemed curious that such an apparently worldly couple
should come on a carefully guided well-guarded cruise to be
cosseted and watched over by many minions, yet still pay to bring
their own guide – especially one who was plainly not a bundle of
fun.

At Vigo, almost at the end of their holiday, they gave their burly young escort an afternoon off and went ashore to sightsee. It then transpired that they did need him, rather badly. They missed the ship.

Seabourn Pride, most upset, finally had to sail without them, leaving that elderly couple still shopping. Their chastened guide was put ashore to locate them. They then had to fly 300 miles back to Madrid to get passports stamped and fly another 400 miles north to Bordeaux to re-embark. For that bemused couple, a permanent escort must have been an economy measure.

Before we landed the American travel manager had some expert advice for us all about British Customs: 'Go to the oldest officer you can see – he may have a better-developed sixth sense but he's not trying to make a name for himself, he's seeing his time out. Never never go to a woman Customs officer.'

The *Seabourn Pride* could carry 200 passengers, but had only 100 on board. She claimed to be a ship 'with yacht-like qualities', so did not need to dock amid the bleak wastes of Tilbury or Southampton but could sail right up the Thames, through the Barrier and under Tower Bridge. I felt that, given encouragement, she would have veered to port a bit and dropped me at my home jetty in Bouley Bay, Jersey. As it was, we stepped ashore in the Pool of London opposite the Tower, unhassled by Customs officers of any age or sex, and hailed a cruising taxi in Tooley Street, SE1.

Sea Goddess II was even smaller: 4,250 tons and fifty-eight staterooms. Built in Norway, she was taken over by Cunard and, as the demand for luxury grew, was soon supported by a sister ship: Mediterranean and Caribbean in summer, then East Africa, Seychelles, Indian Ocean and on through the Orient – with Alaska and a quick dash up the Amazon fitted in somewhere.

The upfront fare could stun, but did include flights, excursions, those worrisome gratuities and as much rich food and expensive drink as you could absorb, day and night. We were greeted by roses at the airport and Dom Perignon in the stateroom. Such a cruise, if you can afford it, offers exclusivity and the indulgent calm of a yacht run like a private club.

When we boarded in Piraeus there were only sixty-five other passengers, looked after by a polyglot crew of eighty-seven.

Before we left port our neighbour, a Norwegian, came in to dinner without his wife. 'She's being sick, already,' he said, resigned. It seemed probable she at least would not get her money's-worth.

*Whicker's World*s on previous cruises have been enlivened by a variety of flamboyant passengers, but the *Sea Goddess* did not attract extremes. Cruisers were calm and went their solitary ways. Peace was what they were paying for, not activity; the only thing they had in common was the ability to pay the fare. I never heard a tannoy announcement and became convinced that if the ship were sinking they would send round an engraved card: 'The Captain requests the pleasure of your company in the lifeboats . . .'

Unlike the bigger ships, boutique cruising is not a happy hunting ground for romance. These are not Love Boats; the passenger list is too small for productive chance encounters. With only thirty couples on board you need to get along with your partner – or pack some good books.

The ship had no organized entertainment – not one balloon-bursting competition; merely a discreet pianist supported at night by a small band. In the dining room, no sittings or table allocations. It was said a splendid buffet breakfast awaited up on deck somewhere, but I never quite made it. An urbane *Great Gatsby* quartet from Long Island agreed: 'I don't do breakfasts,' said one, declining public involvement before the first Bloody Mary around noon.

That was one of the appealing facets of *Sea Goddess* passengers: you did not notice them. Better still, they did not notice you. They rarely mingled, never carried handycams or plastic bags full of local kitsch.

At around 7.30 pm they would gather quietly in the Main Salon for a salvo of corks and small eats, usually supported by a giant tin of help-yourself caviare. *Sea Goddess* got through £2,000-worth a day – spending more on caviare than fuel. I *like* that in a ship.

We dined with a pleasant and substantial American who had been in control of all the Spam factories in America. His product was not available on board. The romance of that name awakened memories of wartime rationing and Monty Python – but the poor innocent knew nothing of either; he did not realize he was presiding over Britain's bravest hours.

There was no Captain's cocktail party, so we were spared the regulation lining up and being greeted and having photographs taken shaking hands with a golden-sleeved old sea dog. What's more, because of civilized dining arrangements, the Captain did not even have a table. You had to invite him to yours, should you feel like salty reminiscence.

Experienced cruisers say that when you've seen one Captain, you've seen 'em all. However, few of my skippers have been in the burly Jack Hawkins mould. The Commodore of the Cunard fleet invited us for drinks in his quarters on the *QE2*. He and his wife were both young and attractive, and unusual in every way. She was an actress, and they met while she was performing on board. Forthright, stylish and funny, she had ME very badly – a valid excuse for not doing any Captain's-wife chores that did not appeal. Their quarters were crammed with teddy bears, all of which had names and were spoken to very seriously.

The Captain of this mighty liner talked with them, walked them about, and tucked them into bed at night. It took a while to appreciate this was not a leg-pull, but a charming eccentricity. I had a lot of photographs taken with the more socially active bears, to be sold later for charity.

On *Sea Goddess II* our Norwegian skipper had been with the ship since she was commissioned, and lived in Lavenham, Suffolk – you could not ask for better judgement. His ship moved discreetly at night, so each morning we awoke to find he had steered us to some new sunlit island.

Affluent guests do not buy staterooms or berths or seats; they buy experiences. At Santorini we anchored in an extinct volcanic crater upon a still sea a quarter of a mile deep. The anchor-chain going down with a scream next to our for'ard cabin took a long time to hit rock bottom, and was an adequate wake-up call.

There were three ways to reach the tiny town perched upon the crater's brink, as on a balcony a thousand feet above: by donkey, by cable car or, for those concerned with waistlines, by climbing 587 steps. Those steps were regularly used by the plodding regiment of donkeys, so we were advised not to wear shoes we planned ever to use again. Donkeys were fed when they returned to the port – so a mounted downhill journey could be rather faster than expected.

Mykonos, where I filmed that jolly plate-smashing Barclaycard commercial, was delightfully empty. Best of all, enchanting Symi, where the sponges come from, looking like some Dodecanese Portofino. In the evening when the tourist ferries from Rhodes had gone, it stood sleepy and almost deserted.

As we wandered past a waterside café I was accosted by a T-shirt which said 'Mr Bob the Sponge Man'. I had seen him working the crowd outside his store that morning. Bob had left Fleet Street after some heart trouble, came to the Greek Islands to de-stress and sell sponges, and apparently specialized in imitating me. His café friends had dared him to practise his Whickeric at source, so as the sun set on the translucent water of that tranquil little harbour, I stood listening to his version of me. It was weird – though quite good, if you like that sort of thing.

The indelible memory of our cruise up the Turkish coast came from Ephesus, built in the twelfth century BC and once ruled – I recalled as I observed my affluent shipmates – by Croesus. It grew to become Rome's greatest Middle-Eastern city. We strolled the Arcadian Way on stones trodden by Alexander the Great, Antony and Cleopatra, St Paul, St John . . . and were suitably awed.

Its grandeur and magic were enhanced when we returned after dark. The ruins had been taken over for the night and lit by blazing torches, just for us. We were greeted by Vestal Virgins holding baskets of fruit and flowers, and solemn Centurions looking more like Woody Allen than Charlton Heston. Before the façade of the Celsus Library, we took champagne and supper in the moonlight. A string quartet offered a classical concert concluding, unexpectedly, with the *Godfather* theme.

Hire of ruins, plus togas, cost the *Sea Goddess* around $10,000, but the experience of that party in the moonlight was unforgettable. We sailed away during the night towards the Dardanelles and said our goodbyes in the heart of Istanbul.

Cruising has long been scorned as the pastime of the geriatric rich. Hearing I was about to sail before the mast a haughty Jersey matron well into the autumn of her years told me disdainfully, 'I'm too young for cruising – I'll go when I'm older.' It seemed unkind to recall that cruisers' average age is now usually around forty; indeed each day the jet skis using our water platform were rather too noisy, the disco thumped away and the gymnasium torture machines rumbled ominously.

Having spent a lifetime flying around the world I am aware that the slower you travel, the faster you unwind. Also that every place looks lovelier from the sea – so those few hours of closer examination in that quaint port are often quite enough thank you, where's the tender?

Cruising can become addictive: some passenger lists show eighty per cent repeat business. On our voyage an American of a certain age was presented with a brooch commemorating the 500 days, and counting, she had spent on that ship – which meant that cumulatively she had been on board for almost two years. So how dare she be so *thin?*

As *Sea Goddess II* sailed on towards East Africa, a British-born American boarded in Alexandria, with two friends. A constant cruiser, he had bought tickets for six months' travel for around £350,000. I dread to think what will happen – not to his bank balance, but to his *weight*.

If you must be personal, I put on 14lbs in eleven days, without visible effort. One solid stone. No pigging-out, merely living comfortably as did other fortunate and equally abstemious folk: light breakfast, buffet lunch, few glasses of champagne with the evening caviare, pleasant three-course dinner. Nothing unreasonable there, surely, when on holiday?

I avoided those cheerful pre-lunch sessions, fattening cream teas, treacherous midnight buffets, punishing the Perignon and all excessive celebration. I was reasonably active. How then did a stone settle so stealthily about my person? I think we should be told.

Forty new cruise ships – most of them giants – will be launched by 2005, eleven within the next few months. The world market for this ascendant holiday is climbing from seven million passengers in 1999 to nine million in 2000 – so will they *all* put on a stone?

Probably. There's a price to pay.

A land of wild and preposterous death . . .

The small blonde chatting with me politely in a husky monotone across the teacups was fourteen times a Grandee of Spain – which meant that if she were a man she could have worn her hat in the presence of the King. She often received letters addressed to Her Majesty – a confusion easy to understand for Cayetana, 18th Duchess of Alba, was head of a family so impossibly aristocratic that since 1063 it had collected sixty-eight significant titles. The most titled British family, the Dukes of Athol, makes do with ten.

Her family tree read like a roll-call of history, from the twelfth-century Chief Constable of Toledo by way of the third Great Duke, who conquered Portugal. One of her ancestors was an English King, James II. She lived surrounded by more wealth and splendour than most royal families, in four palaces and various modern homes around Spain, in many farms and several castles. The Duke could not remember exactly how many, so gave us our programme title: 'I wouldn't say we have many castles – we have a *few* castles . . .'

Such a loose grip upon possessions was not, I suppose, unusual in a nation where a Duke could once ride across Spain from the Atlantic to the Mediterranean without leaving his own land, where the Albas still maintained the right to name the priests of at least 300 parishes.

I was taking tea at No 20 Princess Street, Madrid, better known as the Liria Palace – a sort of Buckingham Palace set in six sunlit acres in the heart of the capital. My visit was television's first move towards the consideration of hitherto inaccessible royalty and nobility. Thirty years later this social climb reached its zenith in the unhappy interview Prince Charles gave to the BBC, when he was invited publicly to shatter, once and for ever, the public's memory of what was left of the sanctity of his marriage to Princess Diana. His misguided reply to a heartless question set under way the decline of British royalty.

Back in 1965 I had approached the Duchess with some trepidation, for those who displeased the Albas seldom fared well. In the family tradition the Great Duke took care of anyone who neglected to take care of him. Asked on his deathbed if he had forgiven his enemies he was able to reply, with quiet finality, 'I *have* no enemies – I've hanged them all.'

During our tentative tea the Duchess agreed to invite me into her life and, with the Great Duke in mind, I grew to understand during filming why the artist who had once painted her in her youth swore never again to paint a child, and never did. She had a challenging blend of imperious timidity, of autocratic reticence. She was also unpunctual, unreliable and moody – and of course had the perfect right to be all those things; but on the other hand . . .

Having arranged to her satisfaction a complicated shooting schedule, we flew a crew out from London and had them standing to attention, ready to film. It was thus a considerable headache to receive every few days a casual ducal decree: 'Don't feel much like filming today, so I'm going to the country. We'll leave it for a couple of weeks.'

I wrote about the tribulations and triumphs of filming the Duchess of Alba and her Few Castles in Spain in *Within Whicker's World* when, in her land of brown and magnificent monotony, this aristocrat with the grandeur of royalty but none of its obligations confronted the new disciplines of television.

In order to keep my camera crew usefully occupied during the Duchess's moody off-days I cast around for a second programme to shoot, and finally decided to tackle a documentary on bullfighting.

This project had been in my mind since the success of our *Death in the Morning* on fox hunting and the Quorn, which the BBC put in for the Italia Prize. We had a brief but telling experience in Mexico, so appreciated the problems we could face in considering their Death in the Afternoon.

When I told the Duchess we were planning to look at her national spectacle she recalled she had once fought bulls herself, on horseback: 'I don't really like to kill animals, but bullfighting is different. The bull is fierce, and it's fair play. We all have it in the blood – we love it. I think shooting deer and fox hunting is *much* more cruel.' Everyone has an opinion about bullfighting.

Our programme on this fierce drama – *Matador* – became a time bomb for BBC Television, which was hypnotized and horrified when we first displayed the lurid and tawdry ritual of the bull-ring. Though bullfighting was regarded throughout the Spanish-speaking world as the noblest national pastime, it had been the policy of the BBC not to allow it to be seen in Britain. It was believed impossible to show it truthfully, for the moments of inevitable cruelty would be unacceptable to many viewers – yet if the cruelty were omitted the whole spectacle might seem white-washed, or even glamorized. Many people were distressed by the thought of the pain involved to bull and horses and sometimes, to man – though that of course was his own fault. So should the Corporation protect, or shock – or continue to look the other way?

It had long seemed to me time for television to extend its para-meters, to attempt a positive and thoughtful view of a significant international activity; mature consideration need not imply acceptance or approval. We took a deep breath – and a deep look.

In Spain all senses are heightened as though by some elevating drug – the air is clearer, the sun brighter, the people more gracious, more cruel, more grand. To me the whole land just felt *more* – which may be why it has always stood apart. Nothing expresses that lonely quality as well as the ritual of the *corrida*, which can reveal all kinds of unexpected instincts: it repels the stranger, yet makes his blood race. As with drinking wine or watching ballet or making love, the degree of enjoyment must, I felt, be in direct ratio to knowledge of the subject.

In the bullring, when the trumpet sounds and the gate swings open, the spectator is overwhelmed by the glare, the colour, the mass emotion – and even more by the pageantry. The plaza feels like some giant dissecting room where all that is worst in man is exposed by a merciless sun.

Its beautiful sadism is not always a pleasant spectacle – critics see it as barbaric and primitive. It must be closer than anything else in the world to the Roman Circus, to that moment in the Colosseum when the lions sprang out upon Christian gladiators.

And all around, the crowd waits – eager to jeer or applaud, reeking of eau de cologne, little cigars clenched between its teeth, eyes protected by cardboard sun-visors, bottoms by hired cushions. It is animated only by a brutish lust for blood, while down before it in the sand . . . one man longs for glory.

An unsettling experience; yet such is the contagion of Spain that anyone who watches long enough may succumb to the savage magic as the bloody parade continues and the young gods are cheered around the arena or whistled out of sight. The evening shadow creeps across the ring and the spectator feels himself half united with the fierce multitude, sensing in spite of the bloodlust and intolerance, something of grandeur emerging among the circus tinsel and high tragedy, as brave and skilful men dominate and kill brave and powerful bulls. That was the emotive scene we set out to capture.

As I feared, the problems of creating a programme within such an intense world of blood and money seemed at once insurmountable – even getting the camera into a bullring required days of fixing and leaning and bribing. We ran into much wary hostility: anyone who wanted to film in such depth must surely be hostile, they reasoned, for it was well known that the less people knew about bullfighting, the more they hated it. Why facilitate lofty Anglo-Saxon sneers?

After much conflict, we filmed in Seville and Cordoba, in primitive portable bullrings put up in country villages, in the magnificent Madrid Plaza. We concentrated upon the controversial Beatle of bullfighting who in five years had turned from peasant-boy to multimillionaire international hero: El Cordobés.

The setting up had been difficult enough, but it was when we got home and many hours of film were being edited that our problems really began. At the first whisper of the project, a tremendous row had blown up at Westminster. A group of MPs headed by Marcus Lipton (Lab, Brixton) and Sir Cyril Black

(Con, Wimbledon) tabled a motion asking the Postmaster-General, Anthony Benn, to ban the programme. After consideration he refused, declaring, 'I really can't become a censor of bull-fights.' The RSPCA and the Animals Defence League were predictably outraged. Newspapers published editorials, for and against. I received a mass of mail, damning in advance.

Richard Cawston, Head of BBC Documentaries, saw the film with some consternation and passed it to Michael Peacock, Controller of BBC1, who passed it to Huw Wheldon, Controller of Programmes, who passed it to Kenneth Adam, Director of Television, who passed it to Sir Hugh Greene, Director-General, who passed it to Lord Normanbrook and his fellow Governors. Even at that altitude there were upheavals: after several viewings, three of the eight Governors were reported as threatening to resign if the programme were shown.

The row continued in public and in private for weeks – at a moment when I had little time to spare for public scenes; I had embarked upon a demanding monthly series of *Whicker's World*s for BBC2 and its Controller David Attenborough. At that rate of strike I had no time to get my retaliation in first.

It had proved an exacting commentary to write, but as in the earlier fox-hunting programme, our many judges seemed to agree the approach was balanced, the camerawork and direction excellent. That was all upon which they did agree.

Yet to my surprise when the film came down again through all those censorious echelons, we were merely asked to cut some shots of a dying bull – which meant a certain loss of balance – and some scenes in an abattoir, which I was delighted to see on the cutting-room floor. During editing I had always closed my eyes at that commonplace butchery.

In the end, after all that delay and dispute, we had to make do with only half a victory. My look at that savage theme had been a little before its time. The BBC finally tiptoed the film out on the air in a shamefaced sort of way, as though hoping no one would notice.

Matador was surreptitiously transmitted as the second half of two programmes marking the thirtieth anniversary of the Spanish Civil War. The Corporation heavily publicized the first – a compilation of library footage with commentary by my old friend James

Morris – and slipped ours out on the next night with hardly a mention. 'Those who feel unable to face this aspect of Spanish life should not watch,' warned the *Radio Times* and the continuity announcers – who were supposed to be on our side. Unlike the Alba film, it was never repeated.

In fact the programme won an enormous audience and awards, and most viewers got out of it exactly what they took in; it is no easy task to open a closed mind. Two heavy headlines illustrated the spectrum: 'Sickening BBC Bullfight film' (*Daily Telegraph*); 'Artistry of Bullfight film' (*The Times*). Everybody took sides, of course, but few were as clear-eyed as the American showbiz bible *Variety*: 'Honest and pitiless truth'.

We had wanted to film that blood-in-the-sand in colour, but in 1965 the available stock was not quite good enough and it was feared the bullring's famous creeping light-and-shade would cause the cameraman too many headaches. Cordobés could speak no English, so we had the classic commentary-and-picture programme: we went and watched, and then I tried to explain what it was all about.

During our filming he was injured again and again – which was I suppose what the crowds were paying scalpers' prices to see. He also lolled in his hacienda with girlfriends and admirers, and lived it up at parties – which was I suppose why he was risking his life, week after week.

Across the world boys dream heroic dreams, see themselves as cowboys, racing drivers or spacemen. Spanish boys see themselves only as bullfighters, a dream that speaks of glory, conquest and impossible wealth. For Manuel Benitez it all came true: orphan, chicken-thief, bricklayer, he grew into El Cordobés, matador – an illiterate millionaire who was to millions the most famous face in the world. In this *Whicker's World* he was our hero – or villain.

Even in 1964 this tousled phenomenon, unknown outside the Iberian peninsula, Latin America and Mexico, could earn £36,000 in three afternoons. After making several million pounds in a few years, he was just learning to read and write – so he could sign his cheques. We filmed him bleeding in the ring – and then with equal determination, struggling with his alphabet. He had come late but resolute upon education, and was guided through his lessons from a child's picture Bible by his friend and confessor, Father Arroyo. He received a thousand begging letters each week from those who had more faith in his reading ability than he had himself.

Only a few years before he had carried his wooden sword and Dick Whittington bundle towards Seville and its bullring, one of the band of *maletillas* – the young hopefuls who sleep rough and hang around impresarios, yearning for a chance to face a bull. Each youngster dreamt of the day he would be like the man our cameraman Brian Tuffano was filming on the afternoon of the *corrida*, lying languid upon a hotel bed alongside an adoring girl, attended respectfully by admirers and spongers and staff.

Most matadors come in the sleek sad Rudolph Valentino mould, but this new millionaire version had carefully dishevelled hair, an engaging smile and mouthful of white teeth. Disentangling from the girl, he dressed slowly in one of his *trajes de luces*, his suits-of-lights – the most spectacular male attire in the world. He needed six suits each season for although, after a goring, the blood washed out easily, the embroidery was hard to repair.

He had killed a thousand bulls so far, and that afternoon was facing two more. For any matador, four o'clock on the day of a bullfight is a thoughtful time. None, however brave, could ever bring himself to smile. Asked why he was so serious, Manolete, greatest of them all, had replied, 'The bull is serious.'

A couple of hundred bullfighters have been killed in the ring during the last hundred years, and many more crippled. Every bullfighter is eventually gored, more or less seriously, and sheds his brave blood first. One Mexican *torero*, Carnicerito, suffered more than fifty gorings, each pronounced 'fatal'. The last one took.

Juan Belmonte fought 109 *corridas* in 180 days, back in 1919. He was that most unusual type – a matador with a sense of humour. 'The most difficult thing to do in the bullring,' he once confessed, 'is to spit. I have been wounded fifty-eight times – three times in the place where a man least appreciates it . . .'

So, I wondered, what makes a man fight a bull? The idea of anyone toying with death for fun, rather than for Country-Home-and-Mother, is alien to Anglo-Saxon minds. Many theories have been offered to support reasons as diverse as religion,

homosexuality and thwarted matricide. The main thrust is probably something as simple as power or recognition or money, for
in Spain a bullfighter's glory eclipses all others – film stars, footballers, pop singers – and such adulation cuts across class and
age barriers.

During the season of daily bullfights *toreros* live within a small
preoccupied world of managers, handlers, assistants and hangers
on, a closed world which we had penetrated; but Cordobés was
not just another bullfighter – he was a public fetish and an industry. He had changed bullfighting from a classic stately minuet to
a heart-stopping and terrifying brawl, and cheerfully broken
through the melancholy mystique surrounding all matadors, in
and out of the ring.

Bullfighting is indefensible, but irresistible – a ceremony rich
in the Spanish love of ritual and preoccupation with emotion and
courage and death. The great crowd which awaited his cortège in
the Seville Plaza – most beautiful of Spain's 350 bullrings – would
have been unaware of any need to defend it. They had come for
delight, and took no pleasure in cruelty to animals – they just did
not see it. Stoical and indifferent to suffering themselves,
Spaniards are astonished at the foreigners' suggestion that bullfighting is cruel. There is nothing sadistic in the crowd – they are
strong-stomached and unimaginative and not at all upset at the
sight of the bull coughing up its lifeblood. It is only foreigners,
bored or thrilled or nauseated, who have their susceptibilities
gored.

No Spaniard can accept the idea that animals should be shown
as much concern as humans: *corridas* are for bulls, just as nests are
for birds and kennels for dogs. Unfortunately, *corridas* are also for
horses – the victims of the fiesta.

In Spain, only bullfights start on time. The bull hurtles into the
ring like an express train, black and gleaming, meeting a
dismounted man for the first time in its life. The morality of the
spectacle that follows the trumpet fanfare is always in doubt, but
unquestionably it is a tragedy in three acts; we filmed each one
several times, always with fascination and horror.

The first act is perhaps the most exciting as the bull, fresh and
uninjured, makes its preliminary passes at the great cape – crim-
son raw silk one side, yellow poplin the other – and the matador

feels the ground around him tremble beneath its terrible hoof-beats.

Then the picadors use their lances to weaken neck muscles, so its head will be low enough for him to reach over the horns and kill by a sword thrust. The picador, a semi-comic figure loaded with protective armour, is the most hated of men: tourists hate him because he is hurting the bull; Spaniards because he is *spoiling* the bull and making things easy for the matador – who pays him.

The moment when he sticks his ten-foot pic into the bull's shoulder muscle and leans upon it, screwing it in deeper, is the moment when most of the women, a few of the men and all of the tourists look away . . .

Once, six thousand horses were gored to death each year in the bullrings of Spain, for the horse is there to give the angry bull some encouragement after so often charging the cape and hitting nothing. Since 1929 the pitiful nags have been covered by the *peto*, a thin quilt weighing 34 lbs. This was adopted when tourism became important to Spain in an attempt to disarm the main criticism of bullfighting. The padding does not protect the horse from anguish, pain or internal injury, but it does protect the sensibilities of the spectators.

The horse's slow patient agony is found preferable to sudden and ugly death in front of the public. Ernest Hemingway rationalized that, like drains in a fine house, the horses were necessary but regrettable; no way had been found to do without them.

Then, in the second act, the *banderilleros* go dancing across the ring with their pretty barbed sticks which anger and torment, and stop the bull striking in a favoured direction. Unlike everything else in a bullfight, the planting of these three pairs of spikes is not quite as dangerous as it looks.

Having watched all this from the *callejon*, the service corridor around the ring, a tight-lipped Cordobés exchanged his working cape for a small piece of red serge, the *muleta*. He had now, on pain of death, to convince the bull that this cloth was its real enemy.

The *muleta* is red by tradition – the shortsighted bull is colour-blind and enraged only by movement. Hurt and cautious, the bull is now far more dangerous. Its former confidence in a terrible ability to kill anything that moved has been replaced by a wary foreboding, and the deadly algebraic formula has started to work: the bull learns at the rate at which it tires.

Cordobés was no traditionalist, with none of the classic matador's respect for the noble beast or the ancient structure of bull-fighting. He was more reckless than other matadors, braver than most and less skilled than many; but like all of them he was swept along by the deep swell of the crowd's *Olé!* The sound of a bull-fight is so full of feeling it makes any Cup Final uproar seem empty.

In a short and violent career Cordobés had often suffered for his fame – face down in the sand, beneath the horns; and so it happened as we filmed. He was thrown again, and the anger that drove him back towards the furious animal brought the crowd to its feet. While other *toreros* play the bull, lead it through a prescribed ritual, Cordobés fought it all the way.

Despite his tossing, he then faced the final and most dangerous act in the drama: the lightweight sword he had used to save his wrist was replaced by a businesslike 33 inches of steel. This was the moment of truth when, unprotected even by that piece of cloth, the matador must offer his body to the horns.

To kill well, the sword must enter the bull's neck at an angle of forty-five degrees. Sometimes it does and the bull dies immediately. Far more often the sword catches bone, jars the matador's body and wrist, and he must then attempt the kill again – and again.

In such a tragedy, the death of the bull is inevitable. That fact alone removes it from the uncertainty of sport. There is no suggestion that it is an equal contest – the outcome is known. Each year five thousand bulls are killed in the plazas of Spain and in each fight all that is in doubt is the amount of damage they can do to those who torment them, before dying.

Nobody is distracted or amused at a bullfight; something else goes on there. The majority of those who detest the very idea know little or nothing about it. Their reaction is natural and kind, for certainly there is cruelty – as there is, say, in some circuses, in stag hunting and factory farming and fur trapping, in the abattoirs that provide our daily dinners.

Much depends upon whether you are most a friend of bull, or

of man. Britons always identify with the bull; Spaniards have grown up with the spectacle and naturally see themselves in the place of the man. Some foreigners succumb to the savage magic even after watching third-rate *toreros* on the Costa Brava, but few attend the important *corridas* in Madrid or Seville; bullfighting does not depend on tourist money, for it offers little if the spectator is untaught and does not know what to look for.

Certainly there are many ugly moments in the *corrida,* but it is conducted in hot blood amid a swell of emotion. The killing of a bull is not a cold sadistic performance – though it may suffer from a monotony of sacrifice. Spain has always been a land of wild and preposterous death.

Today bullfighting is still far more representative of the Spanish soul than soccer. In the seven-month season a top matador eager for wealth is either fighting or travelling. He will appear at more than a hundred bullrings in Spain, Portugal and southern France – and afterwards fly to Mexico for the winter season in Latin America. In one month Cordobés faced sixty-two bulls in twenty-one cities linked by 10,000 air miles.

We flew in the aircraft he had just bought to carry him between bullrings. In recruiting a pilot, he told me he had searched for a careful man 'with at least fourteen children'. We went to Palma del Rio, the little town outside Cordoba where he was born in 1935, where four years later his mother died. His father, a waiter, died when he was seven and their five children went into an orphanage. After ten years young Manolo, unemployed, was thrown out of town under the unwritten 'law of layabouts'. He found a job on a Madrid building site, and as office boy in a macaroni factory. He also hung around bullfight managers and at the age of eighteen appeared at a country bullfight in a rickety ring of old dried wood and rusted iron supports. He was useless.

The sons of wealthy men rarely become *toreros,* for they escape the initial stimulus of an empty stomach. Spaniards say, 'The horns hurt – but so does hunger'. When Cordobés first left his village to face the bulls, he told his eldest sister, 'I shall buy you a house – or dress you in mourning.' She got the house.

If Seville and Madrid are bullfighting's Wembley, portable bullrings are its village greens. They trundle around like travelling circuses and create everywhere a local fiesta. From such rings his fame spread across Spain, for his style was sensational. He was also the end product of clever publicity: the stunts, cash and cunning of his manager made his name long before he earned it. He was called a Beatnik *torero,* a graceless travesty, an idol without an art. Writers said he handled his cape the way a woman shook a rug out of a window: the matador who does not bribe the critics often gets the reviews he deserves.

Earnest aficionados also detested his dramatic break with cold, classic tradition. Sometimes even the crowd found it easy to jeer, for when he fought he doubled and quadrupled the prices they had to pay – and when they had paid, did not always fight well. His manager sometimes had to bribe people to carry him through the streets.

When not fighting, Cordobés filled his new rich life with the animals he loved – breeding them, enjoying them, killing them. We went with him to his splendid hacienda where, like any autocratic Spanish nobleman, he was master of land, man and beast. He employed 300 labourers and also owned a hotel, houses, an apartment block, a farm and an enormous ranch with 600 fighting bulls. Unlike dignified landed gentry, this Young Master drove around taunting them with a car horn which sounded like the mooing of a cow.

In Spain the bull is admired because he is great and capable of fury, and the Spaniard requires such ferocious force against which to display his most precious possession – his courage. So the bull is bred to kill, to die in hot blood at the crest of his rage. He will die anyway, and Spaniards consider he dies more heroically by the sword in an arena than by the mallet in some stockyard. He spends the first years of life living peacefully off the fat of the land, the last fifteen minutes in mortal combat. There are worse ways to live, and to die.

Cordobés was one of some 300 bull breeders in Spain, but only bulls from one ranch would fill a plaza, whoever fought them: the Miuras. One of these Bulls of Death killed Manolete. As we filmed them I was transfixed by the rage and hatred in the vicious eyes of the monster which thundered towards me – even though it was, I believed, secure within its stockade.

I had only once before seen such malevolence, and that was in the evil eyes of a taipan, most deadly and ferocious of all

Australian snakes, as it was milked of venom at a snake farm in Queensland. A stare of such hatred can never be forgotten.

I then understood why no leading matador would face a Miura, not even Cordobés; they were left to ambitious second-rank *toreros* who would take any fight offered on their climb to make their names in the Madrid Plaza.

Miuras, end product of four centuries of breeding, are cunning, beautiful, lethal wild beasts, whereas a matador's ideal bull is a fearless fool of vicious and unswerving stupidity. An intelligent bull, a bull that can reason, is dismissed scornfully and fearfully – and very quickly – as 'a bad bull'.

In his own home, we watched Cordobés preparing to fight again; he was serious and preoccupied as he dressed. The strain of the season, of fighting every day for his life and the bull's death, had begun to show. The needs that first stimulated him had long been satisfied; the money was no longer needed. Now he was staking his life twice a day merely for fame and applause.

The *corrida* is always held late in the afternoon, but no matador will eat before fighting so if he is gored the surgeon may operate at once. Cordobés had already been gored fourteen times, and as we filmed that evening in Cordoba the bull's horn ripped open his upper arm, leaving a deep wound several inches long. This was the right arm which had to drive a sword into half a ton of thundering muscle and bone. The wound would have kept any normal man out of action for weeks.

He was taken to the infirmary to be patched up while one of the *cuadrilla* circled the ring with the ear he had been awarded. The ear, now an accolade, was once the receipt with which a hard-up matador could claim the carcass.

The local governor, that afternoon's president, joined doctors and officials urging him not to return to fight his second bull. He could retire without disgrace. Bandaged and bloody, Cordobés brushed them aside and went back into the ring to face a fresh bull: sometimes he could be even more courageous than the crowd demanded.

He killed again, and honourably. Banks of waving handkerchiefs told the president he should cut two ears this time. Cordobés had won another gamble, added to the legend, survived.

He had arrived at the plaza in a *torero*'s full glory, but left in a decrepit ambulance for hospital and eight more stitches. In a few days he had to fight again at the most important *corrida* of the year, the Feast of San Isidro in Madrid, where for three afternoons' work he would earn more money more quickly than anyone, anywhere.

Our camera was turning as he faced his first Madrid bull, the stitches from Cordoba still in his sword arm. The tiny glittering figure down in the sand of the vast arena fifty yards wide was gored again, in that same arm. Yet he went on to kill and, after another visit to the infirmary, returned to the ring to cape his second bull.

Only in bullfighting must an artist put up his life as forfeit against his ability – pitting experience and courage against the bull's strength in a primitive and savage ritual. Certainly there is cruelty in that ring – though not all the time. There is bravery – but not every afternoon. The one constant is danger – danger is always there.

We watched the injured matador return to his second bull before the fierce crowd which was, perhaps, the worst beast in the Plaza. It was just such a crowd that killed his boyhood hero, Manolete, for they demanded more and more until all that melancholy matador had left to give was his life. So he gave them that, too.

People who do *that* can finish up dead . . .

It was like some bizarre Ealing comedy, where a cast of digni-
fied and most important characters pretends not to notice
what's going on around them – a sort of *Carry On Up the Rock*.
   I was talking with the amiable Governor of Gibraltar, Field
Marshal Sir John Chapple, at a small dinner party in a quayside
restaurant on the marina. Our host that sunlit evening was
Gibraltar's peppy Attorney-General, Katie Dawson; among her
guests, the Lord Chief Justice and the Chief Minister's Legal
Adviser. Hard to find a more significant judicial group.
   As we chatted at our waterside table there passed before us a
rakish speedboat, its 200 hp outboard burbling. It was setting off
on a cigarette run. Sitting on the saddles inboard were three men
in black wetsuits, like Ninja warriors: a trio of the notorious
Winston Boys at work.
   They didn't exactly wave to our elegant gathering as they slid
past, purposefully, but you felt that had they not been so tensed
up, so intent upon a hard night's smuggling, they would at least
have acknowledged us in a friendly way.
   Some of our side – the great and the good – glanced at the
boat without much interest as it cut through the marina, but its
businesslike departure interrupted no conversation. It was totally
commonplace.
   At least a hundred of these 50-knot £30,000 rubber and fibreglass semi-rigid boats were berthed before us. Some earned their
keep running hashish and hard drugs from Morocco into Spain;
others, manned by Winston Boys, just carried cigarettes around
the Rock to La Linea, in Spain. Their departures were always

peaceful and legal, their cargoes paid and weighed and exported legitimately: 'Look, Guv – the manifest!'

However, when the craft reach Spanish waters a few miles away they are no longer always ignored, or smiled upon their way. Reception could be hostile. They might be fired at by the Guardia Civil or buzzed by helicopters, their crews tear-gassed, arrested, flung into gaol. Spanish reaction is quixotic: sometimes fury, sometimes total disinterest. Such mood changes may depend upon many things – but mainly, I suspect, upon whether pesetas have changed hands.

At the end of their short run, boats usually unload on a known beach outside La Linea, though still within sight of the immense 1,400-foot Rock. As each boat runs up into the sand, every man in a waiting gang grabs one box of 200 cartons of cigarettes, races across the coast road – where their womenfolk will be holding up the traffic – and disappears into a kasbah of anonymous one-storey buildings. On that short international journey, every one of the millions of cigarettes has increased in value three times.

The empty craft then returns in quiet dignity to Gibraltar, re-entering the harbour as a respectable legally registered boat owned by a local resident in good standing. On the longer and more serious drug deliveries, pilots – as they like to call themselves – can earn the price of their boats in two runs.

Such activity of course infuriates the Spanish, and their protests to London put us on the verge of a constitutional collision. Smuggling and the resultant money laundering by Gibraltar's booming offshore bankers – which is a problem, anyway – could lead Britain to suspend the Crown Colony's Constitution and bring back direct rule for the first time since the Second World War.

So, after fending off Spanish claims of ownership for almost three hundred years, Gibraltarians brace themselves to face an equally unwelcome threat, but this time from our side. The Rock has always lived in the eye of the storm. Few places in the world have as turbulent a history as this arrogant symbol of British imperialism which has always tormented fragile Spanish pride.

Money-laundering is perhaps more easily controlled than the smugglers, so many are they, so rich and cunning and well orga- nized – indeed, in some quarters, so popular. Occasionally, they are caught. While I was there a sixty-year-old Frenchman had a ton of hashish in his elegant white powerboat as he headed for Spain, alone. What he obviously did not have were the right connections. He went straight to gaol, to start the long slow legal process.

One of Gibraltar's immediate judicial problems in handling the Winston Boys is that, with its isolated population of some 30,000 on a peninsula not much bigger than Hyde Park, it is not always easy to find twelve good men and true who are not related to the accused – or at least on very friendly terms. The pool is further reduced by the fact that women may not sit on juries.

So Gibraltar lives with its Jekyll-and-Hyde personality: a tranquil self-governing dependent territory in a dramatic setting which yearns to stay British – but also a flourishing centre for powerful mega-rich drug-runners.

Smuggling and tourism meet occasionally, and not always happily. A holidaymaker snapping away in the marina near our jolly dinner party was confronted by a young tough who jumped off his boat, snatched her camera, tore out the film and snarled, 'People who do *that* can finish up dead.'

Normally Winston Boys are careful not to make such hostile waves; too much easy money is at stake. They do not need to be violent because they're not usually caught – or even noticed. Indeed the smuggling is so open and everyday it is said that if a tourist finds himself short of holiday money he can go down to the quay, help them load the cigarettes – and pick up a packet of pesetas.

However, the Spanish and Gibraltarian authorities do still co-operate in a more hazardous field: the endless struggle against the hashish and heroin boats. They collect their cargoes in Morocco – together with an armed stand-over man who is on board to keep the crew honest, in their particular way – and then hurtle back across the Straits to some Spanish beach.

Police guarding their coastline fire only rubber bullets. 'They can't puncture a boat but they can put an eye out,' a Gibraltarian Customs man told me as we cruised the Marina, past the long line of tied-up smuggling boats. To cope with that enemy fleet, he had six men and one 55-knot twenty-one-footer. His boat, with two 150 hp outboards, was a shade faster than the smugglers'. With it, his Fast Team was expected to control several hundred drug-runners who suffered only one legal restriction: their motors had to be less than 200hp. 'But they can be tuned-up,' said the two-ringer, ruefully. 'Please ask the Governor to get me another boat . . .'

The Winston Boys boosted local economy. They supported the casino, entertained señoritas, bought powerful cars and expensive apartments in the new blocks around the marina – so they could live over the job. It was all easy come – even the lookout man posted high on the Rock with a radio to warn boats of approaching police was paid £5,000 for every run he oversaw.

Yet in other ways Gibraltar remained peaceful and pleasantly old-fashioned. The Attorney-General told me that she would happily walk alone at night anywhere on the Rock – mugging was unknown, and you did not really need to lock your home. However, she and the authorities feared that if new laws were introduced and smuggling finally controlled, the five hundred lawless hard cases with unexpected time on their hands might go looking to make up their wages, and upsetting a peaceful equilibrium that had lasted for ever.

So it proved. Goaded by London and Madrid, in July 1995 Gibraltar finally confiscated sixty of the smugglers' speed launches. These seizures provoked two days of unprecedented riots and looting, disturbances followed by counterbalancing mass demonstrations by businesses and trade unions in support of the anti-smuggling measures. The Spanish also approved, and border controls were eased.

Then the death of a civil guard while chasing smugglers in April 1996 led to their reimposition. Madrid threatened another total closure of the frontier, and in the meantime made border life as difficult as possible for everyone.

My first experience of the sun and shade of Gibraltar life came in 1949 when I flew out to board HMS *Amethyst* on the last stage of her triumphant voyage home from the Yangtze. In that twilight of gunboat diplomacy, the warship had been caught in bitter fighting between Chinese Communists and Nationalists during their civil war. Sailing 180 miles up the river from Shanghai on her way to Nanking, seat of Chiang Kai-Shek's government, she was ambushed and heavily shelled by four Communist shore batteries. Out of a complement of 192 officers and men, seventeen crew were killed and many wounded. The Captain later died of his injuries.

The 1,490-ton frigate was pinned down for 101 days, and shelled if she moved. As rations ran out and a plague of rats arrived, the Assistant Naval Attaché at the embassy in Nanking, Commander J.S. Kerans, smuggled himself on board the crippled warship and, one silent Saturday night, commanded a gallant dash for freedom under the guns.

Despite heavy artillery and machine-gun fire *Amethyst* reached the East China Sea, with only nine tons of fuel in her tanks. It was a traditional tragicomic victory for the British Empire. Amid the post-war gloom, the Royal Navy organized suitable coverage of the plucky little warship's return to her home port of Plymouth.

Representing the combined British press I went on board in Gib with Frank Gillard of the BBC and an enterprising Fleet Street photographer who titillated the Navy – and particularly Simon, the ship's champion rat-killing cat – by arriving with a crate of carrier pigeons. These were to fly his negatives off the ship just before we reached Plymouth, thus giving his pictures a useful lead over shore-based competition. Not yet space-age technology, but journalistic enterprise of the Old School.

The Navy quickly recovered from its surprise at such unexpected cargo and as we sailed the wardroom stewards set before us all a most tasty dish; the poor chap only noticed the menu was offering 'Pigeon Pie' as he was masticating his scoop.

When we sailed into Plymouth several days later the Hoe was ecstatic with cheering crowds. As at Dunkirk, the whole nation had turned this daring retreat under gunfire into a victory, and was deep in Amethysteria – fuelled no doubt by my daily reports from on board. The Admiral signalled: 'Well done, Tiddy Oggy,' and before going ashore the Captain mustered all ranks and warned, 'Put on your drinking caps.'

It was a rapturous Devon welcome – and those pigeons were all right after all. The Captain was awarded the DSO and Simon the Dickin Medal, the animals' VC; he was also Mentioned in Despatches – but only for killing rats.

Gibraltar hove into my sights again in 1954: Prince Charles and

Princess Anne had sailed out aboard the *Britannia* on their first foreign jaunt to meet their parents, who were on the last leg of their Commonwealth Tour.

I remember going up the Rock with the royal children to take a look at the famous but scrofulous apes on whose continued existence British occupation is believed to depend. They had the unnerving habit of leaping down upon visitors and grabbing anything that seemed interesting, or could be eaten.

Prince Charles was five and a half. In his sailor suit he hid behind his nanny, plainly terrified. He hated them, and so did I. Princess Anne, not quite four and smaller than many of the pugnacious monkeys, was totally unperturbed and scampered happily among them. It was her first display of deep commitment to animals.

Arriving in Gibraltar by air is always a shock. You land on the runway built out into the harbour alongside that towering colossus of rock – one of the Pillars of Hercules. The other, Djbel Musa, can be seen across the Straits, looming over Morocco.

Customs Officers are cheery: 'I've got your intro written for you,' one told me, on my last visit. 'Gibraltar – banana republic of sun and sea . . .'

'Already used that,' I said. 'Years ago.'

The tiny duty-free fortress has been reassuringly British since 1704. Though the British garrison sailed home in 1991, telephone boxes and double-deckers remain red, policemen wear proper helmets and the Rock Hotel offers sedate afternoon tea and views across the bay to Algeciras. There are thirty-two miles of tunnels within the gigantic limestone rock – but outside, only twelve miles of roads.

Days are endlessly sunny, skies are blue and everything is as it should be – except when you try to leave that two and a half square-mile peninsula, and visit Spain. Then, perhaps understandably, you suffer the spin off of years of rancour, smuggling, laundering and jealousy.

Gibraltar has lived through fourteen sieges, so a rigorously controlled border is nothing new. Leaving the Rock is usually painless, but on return you can sit fuming in your car or coach for seven hours in a queue stretching miles along La Linea's seafront boulevard.

The Spanish have proved ingenious at devising legally correct ways of slowing traffic: inspecting officers first make sure the car has a fire extinguisher, warning triangle, first-aid kit and a blanket in the boot, in case of accidents. Then they go painstakingly through each piece of the luggage. Finally – this is a good one – should the driver wear glasses, he must be carrying a spare pair. Who would have thought of that? Brilliant.

Coaches need a complete tachometer record, not only for their current journey but for every journey the coach has ever made. One missing record can cost a £1,000 fine.

Locals cope with such truculent 'Spanish practices' with a system that speeds their frequent crossings; you need a motorscooter, and a friend. We had both. After spending a night in Sotogrande, half an hour along the coast towards Marbella, our host James Gaggero put the car into his garage in La Linea, and took out a scooter.

Strange how motorcycles everywhere seem above the law; at Gib they go straight to the head of the queue, rider and pillion passenger proffering passports and ingratiating grins. Guards on both sides go along with this ploy. Their only stipulation: skidlids. James took Valerie across, returned for me – and we had cracked the mile-long queue without aggro in ten minutes.

It is more complicated if you have luggage, as I discovered when we later returned from Jerez, but passage can be speeded by abandoning the hire car in Spain and turning to porter, trolley and folding money. Another solution for residents is to keep cars on both sides of the border. For the affluent the compensation for such outlay is that no resident who lives there for more than thirty days a year, not even a megamillionaire, can pay annual tax of more than £19,750.

Everyday commerce is also affected in large and small ways, all irritating. The anxious manager of the Rock Hotel: 'We have a bar mitzvah with six hundred guests at lunchtime, so at 5 am I sent to Spain for flowers. They still haven't arrived. Nor have the musicians – and they should have got across last night . . .'

These exasperations give any visit a frisson of the unusual – as did watching the sinister Ninjas heading out towards a tiny risk and a big reward.

So what exactly is it that Spain covets so desperately that it must stimulate decades of pointless hassle? A small infertile peninsula two and a half miles long, less than a mile at its widest, with no agriculture, no livestock, no fresh food, no mineral resources, no rivers or streams, no railway, no indigenous culture, no skills, no style . . . populated by 30,000 people who must import everything they sell and eat – even fish.

Yet the Rock has great visual appeal; back in 1965 *Whicker's World* filmed at least one sight that will surely never be seen again: the Home Fleet at anchor. In one shot, seventeen mighty warships. Today the entire United Nations would be hard put to assemble seventeen warships.

Then the frontier had just been closed again, and the Rock was suffering another economic siege. One evening in 1965 I sat in the garden of The Convent, the Governor's stylish residence, under the shade of trees planted by every royal visitor since Queen Victoria, and talked to Sir Gerald Lathbury. He told me Gibraltar's main worries were smuggling and the frontier – and gave me our programme title: 'It's an unpleasant business if you're not friendly with the chap next door.'

Exactly thirty years later I was sitting under the same trees with another Governor, Sir John Chapple, who said the main worries were smuggling and the frontier: 'Spain's being particularly beastly at the moment.'

Time, it seems, does *not* march on very rapidly in this southern tip of Europe – which explains much of its appeal . . .

Just forty miles west along the coast there is another haven for hard men: Marbella was the flashy follower – at a considerable distance – of Monte Carlo, once the acknowledged sunny place for shady people. In the 1960s Marbella grew sunnier, and shadier. My guest for lunch at the Don Carlos was one of the shadiest.

He was a compact middle-aged man, brown and rather crinkly, steel-grey hair carefully blow-dried. Laughter lines, good smile, clothes with that slightly flared 1970s look; a jovial Jack-the-lad villain out of *Bergerac*.

At that time he was known as 'Britain's most wanted man', and had evaded two deportation attempts over the £7m Security Express robbery at Shoreditch. There was also that other matter of Brinks-Mat bullion worth £25m.

His life was a B-movie script: crippled semi-literate East End tearaway becomes West End club owner and friend of Krays and Richardsons. Leaves wife to marry sexpot film star who saves him from years in gaol when accused of hiring a hit man to murder his brother's killer. Acquitted, he leaves her for a younger woman, and when suspected of two violent robberies involving £33m – for which two brothers and a nephew were gaoled – escapes to a villa on the Costa del Sol with police outside waiting to take him back to Britain in handcuffs . . . And those were just the opening chapters.

Ronnie Knight arrived for lunch with his wife Sue, whom the tabloids pictured as rough and tough. This was unfair: she was tall and attractive with a hard but rather pretty face and seemed to be the boss.

Before our meeting I had talked to the Boswell of the usual suspects living along the tabloids' Costa del Crime. Nigel Bowden was Fleet Street's resident eye on every crime story, supplying all the Heavies with a certain headline glamour, doorstepping their swimming pools and sometimes, when they decided tabloid money might be safer and easier money, ghosting their tell-almost-all stories.

I wondered whether these East End criminals – on the run or semi-retired – found being respectable in Puerto Banus easier than life up the Elephant, or down the Angel? 'They say it's Bethnal Green in the sun,' he said. 'Others who can't get back to England for various reasons call it an open prison.'

We were strolling along a row of drug-running boats in that picturesque port, most of them lean and battered – working craft, these, and a long way from the indolent white gin palaces tied up alongside.

'The Costa del Sol's always had a history of smuggling,' he said. 'Years before it became a millionaires' playground, Gibraltarians used to smuggle in coffee and nylons and things like that, and take back sausages. Then drugs came along, and British guys learned the art of smuggling. Most of them have not got criminal records for bank robbery or violence – they're just smugglers. That's their game, and they're proud of it.

'When the drugs boom became big in Britain, organized crime living down here decided it was a good way of not just laundering money but of *multiplying* money they'd made through bank raids or bullion robberies. The infrastructure's here, and the people know how to do it.

'We have a lot of hash gangs – a dozen or so kids in each gang. They've come down here to live the good life, and they get organized by a couple of guys who know the drug trade. Three or four kilos of hash are strapped to them, and they're sent back on tourist flights into provincial airports where Customs are more relaxed than Heathrow or Gatwick. They have a short life expectancy, but if it's working well a hash gang can get a hundred kilos back every month.

'Charlie Wilson was killed over some Afghan hash that was going into Britain. He had mentioned some names, so a couple of guys came down from Holland, shot him – and kicked his dog, which had to be put down. Two months later the guy who ordered the killing was also shot dead, in a bar in Amsterdam.

'Ronnie Knight and people of his ilk are a constant stone in the shoe of the Spanish police because people always talk about them. What *would* put the cat among their pigeons is if they thought there were British police officers actively working down here, because the Spanish police are good but they really have not got to the soul of the British villain. There's no one better at doing that than a British copper.'

I was preparing a *Whicker's World* series of eight programmes on Spain; in any tour of that horizon Marbella was unavoidable, but could not be considered without its resident villains – so I had invited the most high-profiled of them, Ronnie and Sue, for an exploratory get-together to see if I could get to his soul.

I had read his two autobiographies in which he wrote touchingly about the problems of running his carefully named Charing Cross Road club, the Artistes and Repertoire. Members included almost every villain, stand-over man and hard case in London, so he had to handle a turbulent thieves' kitchen every day. This he managed quite easily. The secret, he explained delicately, was that he had to 'contain their natural high spirits'.

It was hard to avoid the thought that his members' high spirits had probably left a few non-members in concrete waistcoats or motorway foundations.

Ronnie obviously enjoyed being a known character, though I

suspected that in the eyes of resident villains his hard-man image was softening. As a just-tolerated foreign resident he needed always to be on his best behaviour in Spain to avoid extradition. To be seen to be doing something honest and useful he and Sue bought an Indian restaurant, the Montaz in Fuengirola, and later a club they called Knights.

He had grown weary of these investments, he told me, because they meant he had to go and sit in the restaurant for five hours every night, making sure the cash flow was not being redirected into the pockets of his staff. Also, as he said quite reasonably, 'If you've got a name and you use it to front a place up, you've got to be on the scene – that's what pulls in a lot of punters.'

However, the fact that convinced me I had to include him in my programme was that . . . he played bowls! The idea of this professional East End villain, thieves' kitchen owner, former husband of titillating Barbara Windsor and all-round tearaway appearing in whites and panama on the local bowling green was most appealing.

However, it was a bucolic picture no criminal reputation could survive. As a hard man, he was becoming history, overtaken by local drug dealers and thickset hit men in shades who rarely if ever played bowls.

Also, like any innocent abroad he was always getting screwed, and not only by his restaurant staff. Well, there is a lot of dishonesty about.

While tiptoeing around being law-abiding in Spain he had co-operated on his first autobiography from which he expected to earn £100,000. Two of his friends 'borrowed' the manuscript and sold it to the *Sun*, in advance. He ended up with £19,000.

The man happily drinking Cava and orange with me by the pool now seemed more of a benign *Dixon of Dock Green* villain, protesting his total innocence while eulogizing his Malaga brief, Fernando Piernavieja, who had foiled the extraditions. He claimed he had made his suspiciously ready cash by selling that London club and by various property deals and press payments. Certainly he had bought his hillside in the La Capellania development at Benalmadena during the 1970s for 180 pesetas a square metre, and believed it then worth 4,000.

Sue had been with him for eleven years and longed for a baby, 'but he's got a low sperm count'. She played tennis, did charity work, presided over his club and lived with constant stress and tension: his ulcer perforated and he lost seven pints of blood; she returned from shopping to find he had been arrested. Then she was arrested, too. They ended up together in the sinister cells of Malaga police station, as illegal aliens. It just wasn't a peaceful life.

Though I sensed he rather enjoyed attention by press and public, she hated her long-running role as gangster's moll and longed to be treated as a normal person. He usually tolerated photographers with a weary smile, but she expressed her feelings more directly – thus allowing the *Sun* to splash a picture of her emphatic New Year's Eve two-finger gesture at the inescapable paparazzi under the memorable headline 'Auld Lag's Sign'.

They had married in Marbella four years earlier, with an escort of telephoto lenses. The bride arrived at the reception at the El Oceano beach club in Mijas Costa in a lemon-yellow vintage car, the groom in a Range-Rover. Their hundred guests included most of the coast's criminals. The Anglican chaplain, the Revd Ronald Matheson, conducted a short service; the hymn was 'Love Divine, All Loves Excelling', so the collected East End villains in their best suits carried on singing 'Pure and spotless let us be'.

At the lunch afterwards Ronnie sent a couple of bottles of champagne out to the hacks sweating in the afternoon sun. Two waiting Scotland Yard detectives and an armed Spanish officer taking pictures of wedding guests from a hillside overlooking the club were not included in the toast.

They had already photographed Frederick Foreman, known locally as the Mean Machine and soon to be extradited by a posse of seven Spanish policemen and sentenced at the Old Bailey to nine years for handling £363,000 stolen from Security Express, and for using a false passport. Their album also featured John Everett, John James Mason, Clifford Saxe and others. The police believed the event to be the biggest recorded gathering of British expatriate criminals.

The bride wore a ring said to have cost £20,000, and her present from the groom was a BMW convertible; it was almost as though he had come into money. Scotland Yard suspected he and his friends had actually come into £5,951,000 after eight armed and masked men raided the Security Express depot. A guard who was not co-operating was doused in petrol and a matchbox rattled in his ear. Then six months later there was that bullion robbery, when 17,000 gold bars and a few bags of diamonds went missing . . .

At 3 am, after many festive hours, an initialled purple heart on El Oceano's beach spluttered into flame, and the £10,000 party ended. Ronnie had finally made an honest woman of live-in lover Susan Haylock, then his third wife.

Sitting by the Don Carlos pool, we discussed the light and shade of their life in exile; they had often enjoyed *Whicker's World*s so were quite ready to join in my look at Marbella. Exposure in such a programme, they believed, might dispel some of the tabloid image Ronnie had accumulated.

A northern freelance journalist who acted as a sort of agent and go-between, arrived to join us; he was small but his sense of double-entry bookkeeping was perfectly formed. Certainly a few free lunches from me could not compare with the tabloid pay-out a much wanted villain might command, occasionally, if sufficient beans were being spilt.

I explained that it was going to be difficult enough for me to get Ronnie's appearance in my programme past the BBC hierarchy – let alone any idea of paying him a fee. That was a non-starter, for the Corporation was not into chequebook journalism. Ronnie and Sue seemed ready to go along with this, believing it would help him to be seen in the right company, so we went ahead and planned a couple of days' shooting.

The night before we were due to start filming I had an embarrassed call from Sue: their agent had convinced them not to take part, as they were hoping to sell the story elsewhere – maybe as a drama-documentary, or another book. The possibility of tabloid cash had conquered all; so I never got anywhere near his soul.

Soon afterwards Ronnie Knight, for a variety of reasons, left his Villa Limonar and flew back to England in a plane chartered by a tabloid, to put his hands up. 'I was drinking too much and the white powder I was taking to give me a lift was turning me into a zombie,' he wrote. 'Right or wrong, cocaine is enjoyed in Spain as a social pleasure. A little here and there to loosen everybody up, no harm in that, but I was overdoing it and it was beginning to frighten me.'

He had first been tempted to return in 1994 by an offer of £150,000 from the *News of the World*, which came to nothing. He had, he said, turned down £100,000 from *The Times* and £25,000 from the *Cook Report*, but then went for advice to the same agent/journalist who had intervened in our plans. He converted Ronnie to a £50,000 offer from the *Sun* and Sky; but once again at the end of the day he ended up out of most of the money.

Britain's Most Wanted Man was crossed off the list at Luton Airport. Back in the Scrubs little had changed. Bail was refused, and there was a warrant out for Sue's arrest too, for handling stolen money. She stayed in Spain. It all ended in recrimination – even with Barbara Windsor, who had defended him so valiantly when he was accused of murder.

He was charged with handling £314,813 Security Express money. The judge told him, 'I think you know more of this robbery than you are prepared to say,' and sent him down for seven years. He was released after four.

Considering such villainy in a glitzy setting was all part of Marbella's particular lifestyle, a blend of the traditional sun, sangria and sex which had grown up since Prince Alfonso Hohenlohe arrived in 1946 in what was then a fishing village. He noticed there was a microclimate behind the Sierra Blanca which protected beaches from the north winds, and bought 120,000 square metres of seaside property for £1,000. His farmhouse grew into a guesthouse, a hotel, and finally a smart club – the very first jet-set destination.

In the next forty years the surrounding Costa del Sol became the easy-going retirement home of Europe, with little tax, cheap wine, no planning – and no extradition.

I talked with the Prince and his Princess Marilys, a Gibraltarian, in their hilltop home, and then at a golden gala at the Don Carlos where I interviewed the guest of honour, Adnan Khashoggi. He was celebrating the sixty-sixth birthday of one of his employees: Jaime de Mora e Aragón, a local socialite, brother of the Queen of the Belgians and pianist in a local bar; *there's* the character of the Costa del Sol in one sentence. Among the 500 golden guests we sat next to the mysterious figure of Sheikh Ashmawi – who looked like a desert hawk but turned out to be the local Rolls-Royce dealer.

There was no mystery at all about Marbella's Mayor, Jesus Gil y Gil, at the next table. A property millionaire who had been sent to gaol when some of his buildings collapsed, he was also Chairman of Atletico Madrid and after election in 1991 placed a bust of General Franco in his Town Hall foyer.

That night Gil was acknowledging his fans, for he was immensely popular. To establish a climate which appealed to business and new residents, he had just shaken up local government and local criminals: surrounded by police and guards he descended upon Marbella's nightlife area around the port at three o'clock one morning, shouting insults at voters sitting around drinking and calling them, among other things, 'scum' and 'drug addicts'. This caused some Spanish discussion, during which thirty were injured and a police car was burnt down to the bumpers.

In 1999 the Mayor was, in turn, arrested – this time for channelling public money from Marbella to his Madrid football club. Thrown into gaol again, he was soon released on 'humanitarian grounds'.

Unlike Gibraltar, time *does* march on very rapidly in Marbella – which explains much of its appeal . . .

The public execution drew an appreciative crowd . . .

I left the war in Korea in the early 1950s, thankfully, and flew off to cover the Egyptian revolution – which turned out to be almost as noisy, though shorter.

In Cairo rioting mobs put a match to Shepheard's Hotel and went on to throw elderly English residents out of the Turf Club windows to disembowel them in the street below. Down in the Canal Zone snipers shot soldiers – and a few correspondents – across Ismailia's foul Sweet Water Canal. 'Death from the bougainvillea' we called it, of course.

When Nasser took over from Neguib, King Farouk and the British Army finally gave up and sailed away. I followed as fast as I could, grateful to be escaping fever-heat and hostility; why stay in your birthplace when the locals are shooting at you? With luck and baksheesh I found a seat in an elderly DC3 of Air Liban bound for Beirut, where I could pick up a London flight.

The rickety Dakota was full of nervous Arabs and crates of equally unhappy chickens. Our low-altitude flight through heat thermals above the Nile Delta was eventful, the upheavals within the smelly little aircraft basic and violent. They had not yet got around to sickbags. I kept reminding myself it was safer than sitting by the Sweet Water Canal.

At Beirut Airport, vastly relieved to be in tolerable shape, I jumped out of the fetid creaking Dak and climbed up into a cool calm BOAC Comet which had just whistled in from Singapore. The champagne was chilled, hostesses crisp, dark blue lounge seats soft and enveloping. It was so immaculate I became aware my desert boots were dusty. After that DC3 turmoil, the Comet was bliss, and the change of scene from chaotic Arab insecurity to smooth early jet-set was like transferring from a tumbril to a Rolls-Royce.

Strange to realize, now we know about metal fatigue, how much *safer* I was sitting miserably on those chicken crates . . . Soon afterwards Comet Yoke Peter crashed off the coast of Italy with thirty-five passengers and crew; that DC3 is doubtless still flying.

It was my first fraught glimpse of Beirut – then called the Paris of the Middle East and a place of correspondents' R&R. I returned to film that booming city for *Tonight* in 1959 in a MEA Viscount which needed to refuel at Rome. The Casino du Liban was opening and the city was *en fête* to welcome this new target for high-rolling Gulf Arabs.

The Lebanon seemed the luckiest of lands and Beirut the most cosmopolitan and elegant of Middle Eastern capitals: a European city yet still oriental, with something voluptuous and exciting in its air, at once frantic – and indolent. The operative word was *boukra*; tomorrow was always soon enough.

It was also an international financial and espionage centre at the crossroads of three continents – just as it had been for Phoenicians and Romans. With a climate as good as it gets, anywhere, with no rain from June till September and 300 days of sunshine, swimmers enjoying the good Lebanese life could leave the warm sea and within the hour be skiing amid 6,000-foot peaks.

This shallow speck on the Mediterranean coastline only 140 miles long stands bounded by Syria and Israel. It grew from a privileged blend of civilizations and rulers, from Ramses II to General Spears by way of Nebuchadnezzar, Alexander and Napoleon. Its towns bear resounding names – like Tyre and Sidon. Byblos, the oldest continually inhabited city in the world, has 7,000 years of history; even the Phoenicians found it quaint.

It was here that the handsome youth Adonis was turned into an anemone – his death lamented every year by Phoenician virgins in wild ceremonies which the Ministry of Tourism has yet to revive.

In his 1958 book *Lebanon*, Farjallah Haïk explains its history: 'Greco-Roman mythology, Phoenician subtlety, Egyptian technique and Arabian art. England, France, Italy, Germany all enjoyed a certain continuity but,' (he adds with unknowing perception), 'Lebanon was pushed into shape by jerks.'

Well, yes. That's not what he meant – but it is the way it turned out . . .

Poor Beirut was shattered by the racial and religious madness of a seventeen-year civil war that turned its centre into Passchendaele and, with the assistance of the Israeli army, blitzed much of the city down to a stark ruin. Its lucky lifestyle was destroyed by explosives and kidnappings and cruelty.

I had returned to a strangely peaceful Lebanon soon after that war, approaching high over the bay – and there's Beirut on its promontory in the lee of snow-capped mountains, serene as ever. As we lose height it becomes horribly evident that many of the buildings are skeletons and the open spaces are not parks, but bomb sites.

The airport is quiet, almost hushed, with little movement and few passengers. Amid some anonymous aircraft on the tarmac one small white jet is marked in black Gothic: 'Luftwaffe'. On its side, a giant Iron Cross. I looked around for a Spitfire, to restore the balance.

My return to 'the city that would not die' after its years of self-destruction recalled all the threat and fear of those days. I had arrived on a British Mediterranean Airbus 320, landing at dusk amid the sultry confusion of a wartime airfield where abandoned MEA Boeings had bullet holes. We had been delayed because venal Yugoslavian air traffic controllers demanded $1,000 for a flyover already arranged. Nobody was willing to offer them cash or Barclaycard, so we took the scenic detour and left them to it.

The young Englishwoman sent to meet me at the gloomy airport was waiting – but her Al Bustan Hotel limo wasn't. The driver, impatient, had disappeared about his business. My escort – an appealing blonde – ran impetuously into the road and stopped the first cruising car, assuming it must be an airport cab. This was unwise – but she was anxious to get me to a delayed meeting.

With any thought I would have refused to get into the car, but I was still disorientated by the confusion of a delayed arrival. I did not know what was happening, but *did* know that John McCarthy had been kidnapped by Hezbollah on his way to this airport and bundled into just such a cab to be held in squalor and darkness for years. In another, foolish Terry Waite went trustingly into captivity. Political kidnapping had become less popular though in a destitute land, kidnapping for cash had not. You entered a strange car at your peril.

The driver of our suspect vehicle heard where we wanted to go. It was quite a way up into the mountains. He sized up the ravishing girl and affluent foreigner who had dropped into his jalopy out of the night, and thought it was Christmas.

We lurched off erratically towards the dark city, pausing only to pick up another muffled man who looked even more villainous. As we bumped on through a Stalingrad of blitzed buildings standing gaunt and skeletal, I grew more unhappy. 'Sorry, I panicked,' she said. 'Can we get out?' It was going to be difficult.

The dark streets seemed ever more threatening. I have seen wars around the world, but am always unprepared for a city-centre blasted down to a shell. Sections of Beirut around the old Green Line that separated Muslim and Christian areas looked like the Somme or blitzed Berlin – some stricken city shattered by total war. I could see right through the framework of the few tall skeletons still standing. Sheets of reinforced concrete hung like curtains over pockmarked walls.

Yet there were people squatting in those ravaged blocks behind empty staring holes that had been windows. In front of some gaping shell-holes hung torn scraps of red curtain. A precious bicycle had been carried up five storeys. There were even a few plants. Some squatters sat high up, feet dangling, watching the dusty street scene below.

We went crashing through potholes, the driver trying to explain – I gathered – that he did not know the road through the mountains to the hotel. My inadequate Arabic certainly could not absorb what they were saying to each other in the darkness, but I was not happy about what they could have been considering. Like all other jobless youths, they surely had guns – and if rape and robbery were in the script, this was the perfect set-up: rich bemused foreigners.

They requested money – but only for petrol. We stopped at a garage next to a small bar – a pool of light in the darkness. While they were outside happily counting the first instalment, I kicked the car door open, grabbed her arm – and we ran out into the sanctuary of the bar. The lights and noise and people were reassuring. While she went to telephone for another car, I waited at the door to repel boarders.

They did not attempt to come in. Finally, after some shouting and confusion, the car lurched away into the night. They had not done too badly – and at least no blood had been shed. Once they had disappeared I tried to convince myself that in real life they loved their mothers and were both on The Knowledge.

War-torn Beirut certainly had a fearful impact – even without sinister chancers on the make. The city had been captured and destroyed many times by armies or earthquakes since its founding in the third century BC. In the convulsions after 1975, Muslims fought Christians to a standstill – and blew the US Marines out of town. In 1982 the Israeli army besieged and occupied part of the city, to eject the PLO. The Israelis withdrew in 1987. Then the Syrian army arrived to help the Lebanese take control.

On paper the government of this polyglot republic is so well apportioned that it is hard to understand how they fell into such bitter internecine strife. Under a national covenant in 1943, the President must be a Maronite Christian, the Prime Minister a Sunni Muslim, the Speaker of Parliament a Shiite Muslim and the armed forces Chief of Staff a Druze. Power and control would seem to be well enough balanced to keep everyone happy. It was not.

In this self-destruction the central district was shelled by everyone, and devastated – though the Riad Solh and the Stock Exchange were almost undamaged. This was the Wall Street of Beirut, and each warring faction seemed anxious to preserve its bank accounts. Even artillerymen bent on killing people at random were careful not to destroy their own financial records and balances.

Today the new airport terminal is a broad vista of shining grey marble. Almost all roads are being repaired or rebuilt, so gridlock stays in place; tunnels and underpasses and flyovers spread the traffic jams. It can take hours to edge a few miles through the centre. However they are reconstructing a city, so have some excuse for chaos. The ring road network opened for traffic nine months ahead of schedule. Where I come from, that sounds unfamiliar.

As soon as they started rebuilding downtown Beirut they faced problems Stalingrad never knew, for in this ancient heartland of civilization eight cities have been built on top of each other. Now they work to create the ninth.

Some Phoenician and Roman remains revealed by the devastation are being excavated under UNESCO grants, and must be preserved. The developers sought advice from the British Museum on how to incorporate archaeological treasures into modern buildings.

There is a shortage of skilled craftsmen; most fled Beirut during the war and are not interested in returning to the rubble. Heritage buildings still standing – some put up under the French mandate – are being restored, along with the remaining skeletal but economically important blocks like St George's Hotel, the massive Holiday Inn and the Hilton. The three souks are being rebuilt in traditional style.

The old carefree days saw an architectural free-for-all; anyone with the cash could build anywhere and anyhow. Beirutis will be happy to lose junk buildings which survived the shells but have no merit. From now on there will be controls.

Normandy, a magnificent site on the seashore, was used for twelve wartime years as the city garbage dump. This health hazard four storeys high covers acres alongside a polluted sea, producing poisons and lethal gas.

Another unique complication is that after centuries of inheritance, ownership is fragmented. Some buildings have 1,000 owners; those with seventy-five are common. In an Arab world such title deeds take a certain amount of unravelling; like, for ever.

A friend returned to the damaged hotel he once managed. It was occupied by 150 semi-permanent squatters. To eject them would have started another war. Around such chaos a million people – a third of the population – still live in post-war Beirut. Outside the stricken areas, life bustles. In my undamaged hotel, room service offered Dom Perignon at 500,000 Lebanese pounds. Half-a-million looks daunting in *any* currency; this was about £200.

On my last visit to Beirut I travelled in a small group that included Michael Knipe, a *Times* correspondent there during the Civil War. He was too close to an exploding shell which left him with damaged hearing for the rest of his life, yet he retained an affection for the place.

We were joined by the MP Gerald Kaufman, a mild man gripped by violent certainties on every subject. He seemed less sure about Arab sensitivities, and created a small upheaval at London Airport when it was discovered his passport, unsurprisingly, showed visits to Israel. You would have thought this former Shadow Foreign Secretary might have been aware of the Arab reaction to Ben Gurion Airport Immigration stamps . . . Indeed so sensitive are they that media promotion of Lebanese–Israeli relations is forbidden by law; seems a pity that peacemakers are not blessed, but punished.

Gerald's papers of identity were briskly organized in Terminal 4, and we set off on the four and a half hour flight across Europe. At dinner I was pleased to find on the menu an interesting omelette, a happy alternative to the inevitable plastic chicken or sinewy beef. The stewards later apologized for giving out breakfast menus.

'What do we have instead?'

'Chicken or beef.'

In the pleasing restaurants of Beirut, all meals start with the inevitable mezze: endless side-dishes of hors d'oeuvres, lots of little packages of something-or-other wrapped in leaves, great green piles of health-giving vegetables, *hummus* (chick peas blended with sesame oil) and *fool* (hot beans in olive oil). Chopped meat is scattered around – much of it uncooked. Only just in time did I stop myself swallowing some shiny appetizing segments – which turned out to be raw liver covered in a health-giving meat sauce.

Once you have eaten yourself to a standstill through all these small mystifying dishes, the real meal begins: waiters wield serious platters of giant prawns, swordfish and steak. The conviviality of the ubiquitous refectory tables is improved by the constant replacement of glasses of *arak*, which gets the conversation going, or pleasant red wine from the Bekaa Valley.

The Lebanese are traditionally hospitable. For dinner one

night we approached the home of the merchant banker George Asseily along the brightly-lit Corniche at Raouch. Restaurants were open and every hundred yards little white vans offered ice cream to the few strollers. This stylish scene could have been in some Jacques Tati film.

Asseily's home in an elegant traditional building in the Christian sector had a nightclub upstairs; he said it was quieter than the previous occupant, who let his hi-fi torture the Mediterranean night.

One of the guests was the British Ambassador. Her Excellency was followed around by two attendants: one controlled her white poodle, the other was watchful and *quite* a different speed – a massive SAS-type in a bulging hunter's waistcoat. In Beirut, a highly desirable walker.

My indelible memory of the pre-war city was that its drivers were the worst in the world. Crash for crash, they had it over Pakistanis, Nigerians – and Spanish, a charming race which brings its love of danger from the bullfight to the road. In a recent survey it was found that seventy-seven per cent of all Spanish drivers jump the lights on amber, twenty-one per cent on red; fifty-seven per cent never stop at pedestrian crossings, and forty-three per cent drink-drive. The Beirutis plan to reach those standards, in time.

They can still buy driving licences – which does simplify administration. This uncomplicated practice spares everyone those tiresome driving tests, and any aggressive or suicidal tendencies can be preserved unhindered. During the war, of course, nobody cared about such scraps of paper.

Taxis are the only public transport, so every vehicle must be kept running, somehow. Each battered sedan has the standard villainous driver – and we're back to John McCarthy.

Drive out of the city towards the Bekaa Valley and Damascus and road blocks proliferate. Given the easy availability of instant death, these are almost comforting in their way, and manned by three alternating armies. Each stands anxious to reinforce its presence, and offering a choice of captors with different coloured berets: the home team, the Lebanese army; the occupying Syrian army; and the fighters and kidnappers, Hezbollah.

Each block is manned by equally bored soldiers who merely

wave traffic on its way and occasionally shout at photographers. The road to Baalbek climbs through mountains snow-capped from December to May. Most of the summer villas had been picked-off by shellfire; over the summit and towards the Syrian frontier, they are undamaged.

Towering above the approach road the stupendous 'City of the Sun': Baalbek, an immensity of temples. Perfect harmony of proportion disguises massive scale, and the six gigantic standing columns have a strange power of decomposing light and changing colour.

All is overlooked by a Hezbollah command post on the hillcrest, which at least no longer sends out patrols. This is their town; every woman is covered, and westerners visit on sufferance. There is also a presence of Syrian soldiers amid ruins which at least they did not create.

Baalbek has known many such masters: a Phoenician sanctuary in the fourteenth century BC, and occupied by Assyrians and Greeks before the Romans. The Arabs arrived, closely followed by Crusaders. Through the ages it was besieged, pillaged, destroyed . . . yet today stands, pagan and humbling – but still patrolled by indolent soldiers with guns. There's progress for you.

Within the Bekaa, an immense fertile plain unlike any other rift valley in the world, there is a smiling and undamaged town where I have survived long lunches in vine-covered restaurants by the Bardani River. Zahle, capital of the national drink *arak*, also knows two sides of mysticism: religion – and hashish. At such a high altitude it grows well in deep damp chalky soil. I passed fields of hemp standing high, like sunflowers, next to the main road. Once sown, it needs little attention and is generally rotated with tobacco. It's illegal, of course – but during the war there were no laws to break. Now it's illegal again, though production seems unaffected.

Like much of the Middle East, the Lebanon gives the impression of considerable chaos – yet almost everything works. It may not yet be quite ready for a tourist invasion, but it is certainly open for businessmen. Soon the traffic lights will return. Maybe even driving licences – though I wouldn't bet on it.

So Beirut rises from its ruins and calls itself 'The Ancient City of the Future'. With the casino flourishing and fashionable shops opening, it hopes once again to become the Paris of the Middle East. However differences do remain, some of them quite emphatic. While I was there a public execution drew an appreciative crowd.

At Tabarja, a coastal resort fifteen miles north of Beirut, two twenty-four-year-olds were hanged at dawn for killing a man and his sister during a robbery. Gallows had been erected outside the police station in the main square, which was packed. Two executioners in white gowns and hoods placed nooses over the heads of the condemned men. As they dropped, at least 1,200 spectators lining balconies and rooftops applauded. Afterwards the executioners administered *coups de grâce* with savage tugs on their ankles, to more applause.

It seemed a long way from Paris – though perhaps not all that far from the Bastille.

My anxiety tube was a poor investment . . .

In Vienna, once upon a time, the very first psychoanalyst discovered Sex, and the Viennese felt so guilty about it they sent him, if not to Coventry, at least to exile in London. Viennese have never much cared for reality.

It is not hard to see why. Their mellow musical metropolis has suffered the discords of the ages: one moment they were ruling Europe, the next lining up at soup kitchens. So, not unreasonably, they found it more satisfactory to invent their own legends . . . and then believe them.

When producing my series on cities around the world I returned eagerly to film in their capital, which has always been part of my life – each visit full of pleasure or alarm. Some of these dramas I recalled in my first volume of autobiography *Within Whicker's World* – particularly the crowded day when armed men came belting out of the Russian Embassy and, with screaming tyres, chased my camera crew around the Ringstrasse.

We had been shooting the Russian Embassy – photographically, you understand – for a programme about spying, when suddenly they all rushed out, shouting and threatening and seemingly anxious to make the shooting more real. After the chase, when both sides had been captured and subdued, the furious Chief of Police pounded his desk: 'Vienna is not the Wild West!' He then dismissed the diplomatic Russians and, after a sympathetic chat, the undiplomatic *Whicker's World*.

Vienna has always been an unreal capital, frozen in Imperial memories of Congress Dancing in Blossom Time while up in the

Vienna Woods the Widow made Merry with Chocolate Soldiers. Surrounded by the baroquery of the last romantic city, my cameras turned from the sinister threat of spies and searched for reality: how about singing choirboys eating chocolate cake on white stallions?

Like Venice and Hong Kong, Vienna rates any detour, and is an enticing early break when flying East. On one visit I was taken formally to the dramatic monastery of Stift Klosterneuburg; beneath its green cupolas I was intronised as a Most Noble Officer of the Order of Wine Barons. During a ceremony in the noble wine cellars I was nobly gowned and duly received a scarlet and white sash with golden insignia. Being intronised had at first sounded a mite painful, but proved agreeable – though could be habit-forming.

Viennese still act out their lives in a rich and reassuring dream of Yesterday, when theirs was the home of the masters of Europe. For six centuries their city ruled millions of subjects, yet now controls only a tiny republic with a population smaller than London. Having lost an Empire, the bitter-sweet city in its prosperous European cul-de-sac has learned what London must face: how to be unimportant, and like it. Its brilliant sons have often faced that cruel reality. Mozart was buried in an unmarked mass grave; hard to find a less important genius.

Sigmund Freud, another spurned son, lived and worked in the Berggasse for forty-seven years, amid hostile indifference; Catholic Viennese saw in the sexual theories of that brilliant Jew a threat to their beliefs and prejudices. When Hitler's Nazis arrived to a delirious welcome in anti-Semitic Austria and banned his science, he fled to England and looked back sadly: 'I still love the prison from which I have been released.' He remained almost unacknowledged in his city until, forty years later, the Municipality turned his gloomy apartment into a rarely visited museum, where we went to film. The old anxieties he had dragged to the surface still seem to agitate the calm city which has, unexpectedly, the highest suicide rate in the western world. In these days of population explosion it must be the only capital to implode; in the past sixty years its population has decreased by a third, to 1,600,000.

Vienna remains a rare centre for the individual craftsman;

there are 150,000 small businesses producing things like green Tyrolean hats, *petit point* spectacle cases and rocking horses. At one of their famous bakeries they created for our cameras the largest *apfelstrudel* in the world, which filled a room. We strolled around it where it lay, looking more serpentine than flaky.

For the first time in my life I risked trying on a top hat – an emotional moment which made me feel like a debonair Fred Astaire but look a proper Charlie Chaplin. In the home town of *angst*, the Viennese call that harmless old silk hat an 'anxiety tube', for it was the standard headgear of the Emperor's secret police.

Habig was the last producer of toppers. When this famous hatters closed it had been selling 20,000 a year, for £40 to £80 each. Most were bought by sharp dressers in New York's Harlem, though they were still part of the uniform of the better class of gravedigger and chimney sweep, magician and diplomat. Whatever you might believe, top hats are not lifetime invest-ments, because people *will* sit on them. Such regular comic destruction should have supported Habig's turnover but evidently was not regular enough, or funny enough.

While yearning for Yesterday the Viennese, with their forlorn lack of hope, are also drawn towards a sombre Tomorrow. They appreciate cemeteries and see them, not as mournful places but as somewhere to sit and enjoy the scenery. They call a corpse 'a 71' – the number of the tram which goes to the Central, biggest of Vienna's fifty graveyards, where, beneath a staggering array of monumental masonry, two million lie buried. Every day a hundred stately and ceremonious funerals add to the display – so there is always plenty to watch. The Viennese say their vast suburb of death is 'half as big as Zurich – and twice as funny'.

On that elegant city-stage I met again a jaunty aristocrat whose wedding I had attended at Nancy in 1951; but for a slight acci-dent of history, Archduke Otto or, as he preferred to be called, Dr Habsburg, would have become one of the world's mightiest rulers. I filmed a conversation with this senior member of Europe's twenty monarchs-in-waiting among the loveliest exam-ple of Vienna's baroque, the Belvedere – which if things had worked out differently would have been just another of his palaces. That morning only tour guides recognized him, though legitimists still genuflect and address him as Your Majesty.

When the Great War ended, the Habsburgs were banished. They returned hopefully after the last war – only to be kicked out once again, this time by the Russians. In 1967 the Austrian government finally permitted the Archduke to return when he renounced all claims to the throne – despite the stern disapproval of his formidable Mother, the Empress Zita. He became President of the Pan European Movement – an earnest talking shop – before handing over to his son Karl, and lived with his seven children in a modest house in the village of Pocking outside Munich which local Bavarians called Pockingham Palace.

Though titles were banned in Austria in 1918, Princes and Palaces still go together, like Wiener and Schnitzel. Next door to the Belvedere another Austrian nobleman was less displaced: with much foresight the Schwarzenburgs activated the Swiss side of their family at the start of the war, and so preserved their palace from everything: Hitler, Russia, Allies – even the Municipality. In one wing, the Swiss Embassy and an expensive hotel; their main palace can be hired to throw a ball or launch a new car. Like British stately home owners, Prince 'Karli' Schwarzenburg came to terms with his city's Socialism. A businessman, he told me he hoped his noble line had the survival power of the hedgehog, not the dinosaur.

Allied occupation ended in 1955 and the Viennese watched the Red Army march away – the first time Soviet troops had given up territory. It was a turning point in the Central European drama. The Red Army's battle across Austria had been followed by ten years with half its land and much of its capital occupied by Russians. The repressions of Czechoslovakia and Hungary were just across its frontiers; so, not surprisingly, the Austrian Communist Party immediately almost disappeared. Unlike the French and the Italians, the Austrians knew only too well the reality of life under Communism and how it felt to be conquered – so Vienna had no hard left-wingers, Militant Tendencies or rebellious students, and fewer than two people in every hundred voted Communist.

After the poverty of the 1930s and the trauma of the war and its aftermath, the penniless Austrians decided to be rich and Swiss, to go after comfort instead of children. Theirs was the first

Catholic country to make abortion legal. Today Vienna is one of the few cities in the world where women can safely stroll the streets at night – so, paradoxically, it must be a reassuring place to raise a family.

For a city that has known such inflation and economic depression, it is comforting to see how Vienna has risen from ruins to riches. Its economy is flourishing, there is little unemployment or crime, and political parties get on so well that strikes are rare. They may be trapped in waltztime memories of Imperial grandeur, but the gross national product has increased many times in past decades – so they have not been dancing *all* the time.

Vienna has no rich and no poor, no slums or minorities. In this peaceful, reasonable place contented citizens fall back for stimulation upon extremely rich food. They tend to eat all day long: five or six meals, usually, with a restoring snack or two snuck in between – mostly *mit schlag*. A quarter of the population of this elderly city is over sixty; in 800 parks there are seats which allow 92,000 people to watch the world go by, all at once.

Amid such tranquillity the Viennese flung themselves into an unlikely paroxysm of chaos; in the 1970s they started building an Underground. Unlike London – where they find a quiet corner of Green Park, dig a hole and disappear down it for ever – the Viennese unzipped whole streets and left the evidence lying around. For fifteen years the heart of the city was opened up and rendered chaotic – to make living easier.

The reasonable quality of life rose above such upset: when any ten shopkeepers or residents found the noise, vibration and dust too much to take, they could get together and bring about a change in building methods. One engineer did nothing else but handle such public complaints; the fact that he was a burly six-foot-six no doubt helped keep work on schedule. As you might expect, the Viennese regard trees as untouchable totems; to spare one linden the line was re-routed at a cost of £54,000. It died, anyway.

The trains then introduced are so automated they need no crews, not even drivers – though to reassure nervous passengers unused to hurtling unguided through the dark, a man sits in the driver's cab, merely opening and closing the doors . . .

Apart from such progress, Vienna remains one of the gracious capitals. To enjoy the new wine on a sunny afternoon in a *Heuriger*, a wine house amid vineyards on the gentle slopes of the Vienna woods in Grinzing, Sievering or Nussdorf, is to experience the art of civilized drinking – closely followed by the traditional new-wine headache.

Sadly, Vienna's famous café society has fallen upon harder times. Many of the old red plush establishments on the Ringstrasse have been converted into car showrooms or airline offices. In the few well-worn survivors you may still sit for hours over your choice from among twenty varieties of coffee – anything from a *kleine Mokka* to a *Doppelschlag* – while reading all the papers and magazines or dealing with your mail. Herr Ober will not insist upon showing you the menu.

The only conflict in this determinedly neutral nation was the Sachertorte war which rumbled on for half a century. We reported from the war zone: a table at Sacher, the hotel where Emperors enjoyed their raffish nights out. On the other side, Demel, the pastry shop founded by an Imperial chef. In this bitter struggle over the original recipe for that chocolate cake with apricot jam filling and who could use the name (Sacher finally won) it seemed wise to remain neutral – and eat both their offerings, indiscriminately.

Filming around Vienna we tried to sidestep the obvious, to go easy on all its well-loved clichés. We did not consider the Spanish Riding School, the Third Man and those echoing sewers, the Opera House, Hitler's bunkers, Schönbrunn Palace, spies, St Stephen's Cathedral, *Gemütlichkeit*, the Boys' Choir, Mayerling, the Vienna Woods, Congress Dancing, Josef Haydn, Ludwig Beethoven, Franz Schubert, Johannes Brahms, Gustav Mahler, old Uncle Johann Strauss an' all . . . What you leave out of a programme is as significant as what you put in.

As we packed and flew on to our next city I ruminated once again upon the wisdom behind the Viennese lifestyle, enlightened by the phrase I long ago used about the place and still try to work into all commentaries from the Kärntner Strasse: an illusion that makes you happy is better than a reality which makes you sad . . .

A hot mother on the dark edge of magic . . .

We were off to see the Shepherd . . . Hunting for a certain Pocomaniac camp I went wandering, not along a yellow-brick road but through a maze of alleyways deep within Kingston's worst shanty town. There were said to be 150 hidden camps in Jamaica, for Pocomania – a little madness – was the most powerful and active of the unorthodox religious cults, and the most secretive.

While I was researching, the Member of the island Parliament representing that slum constituency had warned me that they did not welcome strangers; he had waited nine months, he said, before being permitted to join his Pocomaniac voters at their worship. However a political scientist at the University of the West Indies, Rex Nettleford, urged me to try and reach one particularly dynamic but elusive group, led by a formidable woodcarver called Kapo.

Such was my plan, that night. I had paid off the taxi which brought me down from my hotel in the hills above the city and was stumbling around among the fetid shanties as the Caribbean dusk dwindled into night. I knew I was being watched as I moved deeper into that blighted shanty town which even then was known to be dangerous; certainly no white visitors ventured into its menacing maze.

I was mildly uneasy in that strange dark place, but not fearful. In such situations I always feel invincible – which is very foolish indeed. This myth grew out of my days as a professional observer of war and revolution – as a neutral, not a protagonist: 'Don't shoot – I'm not fighting, just watching.' This sweet reason was unlikely to sway Chinese hordes, terrorists or muggers, and certainly offered no protection against shells, rockets or Saturday-night-specials. Can't think why I still believe it.

The heavy death toll of correspondents down the years should have disabused me of this silly notion – but fortunately that charmed-life belief is hard to lose. Up to now, it has worked.

I was alone in a Kingston shanty town at night – but this was 1964, which indicates how the world has changed. Today despite the invincibility myth, the percentages have changed and I should hesitate to go there in an armoured car escorted by SAS.

Those few years ago no harm or fear came to me as I wandered among the shacks, asking anyone I saw for Kapo the Shepherd. Finally I stumbled across his church, which was just another shanty but with a larger yard outside. Eventually Kapo arrived: a magnificent giant with a deep throaty theatrical voice and the presence of an illiterate Paul Robeson. He was a carver and sculptor of note and talent – I still have some of his work in my home. I explained my project while he observed me thoughtfully with steady staring pop-eyes. Plainly he was not a man to cross.

After much discussion he agreed we could film his group at worship, so next night we carried our camera gear and lights into that forbidding ghetto, watched by a thousand eyes, and began to set up in his church. A few listless lolling men muttered, and moved out into the night. Silent children watched, wondering. There seemed little dynamism around.

After a while, just as we were deciding he had changed his mind – in strode Kapo, already shouting and controlling the flock of women swarming around him, plus a few men with drums. His white turban and swirling robes were dramatic – copied, I was later told, from those seen in illustrated Bibles.

Instantly, the place took off! No one gathered breath until dawn. Hour after pounding hour, the beat of the drummers became so compelling it was impossible to stand still. Obsessed Pocomaniacs forgot our lights, our camera, our white faces, forgot everything except the Shepherd's booming voice and their fevered hypnotic rites.

We returned on several nights to film the whole disturbing frenzy. In Kapo's unusual domination, in the way he controlled the reactions and emotions and minds of his flock, was a distant echo of the hysteria of Father Divine's angels, the rapture of Beatles groupies, the fervour surrounding the Charismatics, the Jesus People, the Moonies, the Bhagwan – even Billy Graham. There was also, I suppose, an uneasy memory of that procession of demagogues leading down to Hitler and Nuremberg. Total dominance is always disturbing to the unaffected.

Pocomania seemed to be semi-Christian, with a strong Revivalist flavour; semi-pagan, with overtones an African witch-doctor would recognize. It satisfied the worshippers' need to be mystified and exhalted, and led them gradually towards the dark edge of magic.

As we filmed, the whirling Shepherd regulated his drummers' endless beat, orchestrating communicants towards the auto-hypnotic state they reached after hours of hand-clapping and chanting, dancing and groaning, drumming and stamping. All of these are hypnotic exercises. They were aiming to 'get the Spirit', and the most effective method of making such 'close connections with the angels', of achieving shallow self-hypnosis, was by 'trumping'. This regular and forced exhaling from deep within chest and belly caused overbreathing. So they stamped and clapped in an endless rhythmic circle, gasping to the ceaseless drumbeats – just as African nomadic tribes trumped for hours before lurching ecstatically into battle.

A determined Hot Mother can reach the reeling trance-like state that ushers in possession almost at once, when she begins to speak in tongues. Pocomaniacs stoutly claim this gibberish is some little-known language – perhaps Greek, they say, or Chinese or maybe Latin. At any rate, it is the voice of the Spirit which possesses them.

When a Pocomaniac receives a personal revelation and reels away for her own private gyrations and groanings, eyes rolling and insensible to pain, she is in what psychiatrists call 'an hyster-ical fugue state'. Yet however deep the trance I noticed that every now and then one of them would suddenly do something quite rational, like moving a bench, or looking for a handkerchief . . .

Despite its gentler moments, its communion around a home-made altar complete with bread and wine – bottles of English Ruby Red, and orangeade – before candles in shoe polish tins,

Pocomania is condemned by orthodox religion as a debasement of Christianity. For emergent middle and upper class Jamaicans it carries some of the self-conscious stigma a solid English Protestant might suffer if caught attending a Black Mass. As in any parish church, women are the mainstay of the congregation at meetings most groups hold three or four times a week and, conventionally, twice on Sundays.

Pocomania is sometimes regarded by its adepts as just another Protestant sect; in fact it is a complex phenomenon which includes all the emotional excitement of Revivalism with swinging Moody and Sankey hymns, plus the elemental thrust of pagan Africa and the Spiritualist practices of possession, laying-on of hands, healing.

We watched one solemn fearful girl brought in by her friends; she had been struck dumb by some illness, they said. In the midst of the frantic drumming and trumping as the service progressed, the hands of the Shepherd massaged the scalp of the silent, confused girl. She could not tolerate what she felt from his fingers, and tried to escape. Grinning, he pursued her, triumphant in his effect, his evident power. He knew she would speak. She did.

Despite its drama, Pocomania is based upon Fundamentalist teaching, and its form of communion ended with the breaking of bread. Kapo slowly lowered the temperature for a tranquil climax, a quiet return to reality, to sanity. His services lasted ten hours at least.

When the frenzy had drained away, worshippers ate bread and drank a mixture of honey, milk and wine. For others, for the frantic drummers, there was only exhaustion, deep and beyond words.

The girl who had recaptured the trick of speech sat and wept silently. In the dismal dawn, the church which throughout the convulsive passions of the night had been filled with some sort of powerful magic, became once again a small ramshackle shanty. It was another day.

To consider the frenzy of the night in perspective, I recalled to camera that during two centuries of slavery in Jamaica, all religious practices by black workers on the sugar plantations had been regarded as dangerous in themselves and likely to encourage rebellion. In a dual-society of masters and slaves, conversion was not encouraged: it might lead to an undesirable sense of equality in the slaves and disturb the basis of the slave-owners' carefully contrived morality. The official attitudes of Britain and France – the two leading nations in that trade – were directly opposed; it is hard to decide which was the more cynical.

The French were able to convince themselves that slavery was good for slaves, that bondage was their salvation: it was the only way lost black sheep could be gathered into the fold of the true church. The British, on the other hand, thought it improper for a Christian to hold his brothers-in-Christ in bondage, so slaves were allowed to remain heathen and without baptism. There was also the danger that missionaries might teach them that all men were equal before God. When Christian slaves were captured by one side or the other, such dogma had to be hastily rearranged. So the Negroes lived in a spiritual vacuum, forbidden to continue their African customs, yet not considered suitable for Christianity.

Emancipation came in 1838; suddenly 311,070 black slaves in Jamaica were free citizens and able to choose their own religion. Their white masters were primarily Protestant, so not surprisingly most Negroes joined the Catholic church, finding satisfaction in its elaborate ceremonies, its more obvious protection against Duppies – those troublesome night-wandering ghosts of ancestors – and against Zumbies, Bugubugumen and other malevolent spirits.

Despite the continued acceptance of black magic, few Jamaicans would today admit to going to an obeahman, a witch-doctor, for such practice is illegal – though they would certainly be most fearful to learn an obeah, or spell, had been placed upon them.

Outside our little Pocomaniac church stood its balmyard – lovely word – where the Shepherd performed his magic healing by a mixture of prayer and superstition, bush remedies and commonsense. Because of the persistent belief that illness is caused by spells, even the more educated will attend a balmyard if 'the doctor's medicine doesn't work'. To any Jamaican unsure of himself or his place, the balmyard and the cult remain important.

It is impossible to separate the religion, magic and folklore ingrained in the Jamaican soul. The most complicated theologies co-exist with primitive magical beliefs, for Christianity was grafted on to the surviving remains of the jungle religions of Africa. After the slaves were freed, missionaries busy at conversion and familiar with the staid British mode of worship became appalled – as they can be today – at the growth of native churches incorporating in their services all the Negroes' natural physical enthusiasm.

In the people of the West Indies there is, they say, a genuine inability to cooperate for long, to maintain interest in anything in which they cannot take an active part – so their Christian fervour soon burst free from the restricting orthodoxy of solemn, mumbled religion.

The Revivalist version of Christianity was absorbed into pagan rituals which, three centuries ago, the early Spanish masters of Jamaica had seen as 'a little madness'. In such abandoned hallelujahs, Negro hearts found just what they had been pining for: the comfort of Christianity without the need to sit and listen to some distant droning cleric. So these natural extroverts were allowed – even encouraged – to sing and to shout, to pray fervently at the tops of their voices, to dance in righteous glee to the throbbing tempo of the Revival choruses which replaced those sober hymns.

For generations, economic and social privations had forced blacks to rely more and more upon promised deliverance from above, since experience had taught them there was precious little to be expected here below; so Pocomania came to satisfy a deep need.

The emotional outlet is evident – the dressing-up and the singing, the dancing and feasting offer entertainment and social life in a poor community starved of group activity and pleasure. There is also the opportunity for leadership, acknowledgement and identification. Each group has its appointments and offices, its Governesses and Deacons, Captains and Mothers. A humble woman existing in poverty and squalor can be transformed each night into the Grand Sword-Bearer of the Mount Carmel Icelandic Church, complete with authority and yellow sash, and so experience the sort of elevation that Freemasons enjoy.

For a few hours Pocomaniacs are absorbed in some powerful spiritual world where their material state does not matter, where each has a sense of importance, where incantations produce exciting physical results and there is reassurance transcending the bonds of poverty and colour. The cult offers an outlet for oratory and music, for poetry and self-expression, and an elevated, almost lyrical experience certainly not present in daily life. Pocomania is escape.

There is another side. It can be a dark and frightening ritual. Its secret rites take place at night, usually away from prying eyes; strangers are liable to be stoned, or worse. When getting the Spirit, the flight of consciousness demonstrates man's power over man. Trances can be very deep indeed – Pocomaniacs may keel over and lie stiff as boards, without waking or sleeping, for three or four days.

The minds of communicants in a state of extreme suggestibility are blank and empty. Seeking comfort and salvation, they have placed themselves completely in the hands of their Shepherd. He conducts the tempo, plays upon the more susceptible, controls their emotions and perhaps, in the end, could destroy reason.

When minds are controlled, almost any message can be put across. Men of strong character have always used such methods, for good or ill; in Kingston we watched, stunned, while the whirling Kapo spread . . . a little madness.

Why should I travel when I'm already *here* . . . ?

A foreign landing can disorientate, but wintertime Boston seemed as though we had never left home: cold grey suburbs, narrow winding lanes and, amid elegant tree-lined Georgian and Victorian streets, an abrupt and reserved people; indeed elegant Beacon Hill believed itself 'more London than London'.

The United States may be a noisy nation of equality, but we were there to study some most unusual Americans in their tiny oasis of reserve and reticence, of blue blood and special privilege – a unique dynasty of American aristocrats for whom railways have changed their timetables, stores their shopping hours and courts their statutes. Together, Boston's First Families formed one of the most exclusive closed societies in the world, the gates to which shut tight a century ago – as explained by some elderly doggerel:

> and this is good old Boston
> the home of the bean and the cod
> where the Lowells talk to the Cabots . . .
> and the Cabots talk only to God.

In 1962 I found them no easy group to infiltrate – even though *Whicker's World* had often looked into closed societies, as in Broken Hill and Palm Beach, Haiti and Paraguay. Ready as ever for American first-name amiability, I found it unexpectedly refreshing to confront rare transatlantic snootiness. We filmed conversations with several splendidly unAmerican Brahmins, including a magnificent old matron who dismissed my query about holidays with the famous reply: 'Why should I travel when I'm already *here*?'

With classic grandiloquence another described their rather ordinary city as 'the hub of the solar system'. Boston is still known as 'The Hub', still takes itself most seriously, proud to be a chill on the feverish pulsating surface of the United States. Salesmen call it 'the graveyard circuit', and Mark Twain, appearing before a local audience for the first time, declared he was 'facing 4,000 critics'.

Presiding over their stern capital from Georgian homes upon Beacon Hill live the Adams and the Forbes, the Lawrences, Peabodies, Jacksons and Lees who for generations have married each other with the determination of European royalty. The historian John Goreham Palfrey believed that, as cousin wed cousin, a purer strain of English blood survived in Boston than in any English county.

Certainly they have always looked towards London – their Boston accent and set ways formed a bastion against the exuberant invasion of Irish, Germans and Jews. They still appreciate five o'clock tea, Gentlemen's Relish, fox-hunting, Dundee marmalade – and the separation of the sexes after dinner. Their clubs stand modelled upon St James's and Pall Mall, impregnably masculine within that matriarchal nation.

'I fear there will be no dessert this evening, sir,' murmurs the suitably imperturbable head waiter at the Brookline Country Club. 'The kitchen is on fire.'

Their man-to-man view of the Hereafter was expressed by one relatively dissolute First Family member from his death-bed. Urged to repent if he wished to go to Heaven he announced, after careful reflection: 'I'm about as good as Gus Thorndike, Jim Otis and Charlie Hammond, and *almost* as good as Frank Codman. I prefer to go where they go . . .'

Their womenfolk also go together to the regular rituals at the Boston Symphony. They exhibit customs but no manners, plus an Amazonian disregard for fripperies: 'I come from Boston,' one told a New York shop assistant, 'I'm a Unitarian and I wear drawers. *Now* you know the kind of hat I want . . .'

They remain superbly independent: one ignored for years some friends who had rented the house next door because, she explained, 'I *never* call on people in hired houses . . .' Sarah Palfrey toured Europe alone at the age of eighty-eight 'for a last look round' and came home to start learning Hebrew. She wanted to greet her Creator, she said, in his native tongue.

It would surely be considered tactless to recall that only one of them, Mary Chilton, had arrived on the *Mayflower*; the First Families missed the First Boat by several generations. Each made up for this lack of foresight during the 1700s, however, by producing at least one great merchant or shipowner. If not exactly running pirate ships, they were at least Viking in their seaborne activities, easing severe New England consciences by describing the profitable rum and opium trade as 'West Indies' goods' and launching new ships, not with champagne, but with bottles of pure water.

Colonel Thomas Perkins, offered the position of Secretary to the United States Navy by George Washington, had to refuse and explain apologetically that he already *had* more ships than the Navy, thank you, Mr President.

Money could not get you into their closed society, but lack of money would surely get you out, so some dabbled in real estate. One bought what he described with proper understatement as 'a farm mortgage in the west'. This turned out to be six square miles in the heart of Chicago.

Robert Bennet Forbes financed a Scots professor who was running a Boston school training teachers of the deaf, while in his spare time tinkering with some crackpot invention. The Scot was Alexander Graham Bell and he called his invention 'the telephone'.

Their investments were usually made with cautious and canny conservatism: 'I never invest in anything I can't see from my office window,' said Phillip Dexter. Those who had little brilliance, like the early Cabots – possibly through conversing only with God – had at least the ability to marry money. So Boston suffered 'grandfather on the brain', a cult dating from the days when the grandfather–merchant was the key figure in the whole society system and entitled to almost godlike respect.

We found the most durable custodian of the city's Old Guard

tradition was the Boston Athenaeum, founded almost two centuries ago as a private library for shareholders. It stood at 10½ Beacon Street, opposite the Old Granary Burial grounds – indeed it had the air of a shrine for the last rites of Brahminism. It held the personal library of George Washington, bristled with reaction, and had in its time banned the works of H.G. Wells, Sinclair Lewis, Sherwood Anderson and Ernest Hemingway. Even the expurgated edition of *Lady Chatterley* was kept under lock and key in 'the scruple room'.

It was said that if a Proper Bostonian sent her daughter to the wrong dancing school, the family would not recover its social position for three generations. There was no question, of course, as to where the sons would go: just across the Charles River, to Harvard, where nine generations of Saltonstalls had studied alongside eight generations of Wigglesworths, and so on. The attitude of the Brahmins towards their 350-year-old University was summed up by Henry Higginson who declared that, while Franklin Delano Roosevelt could be regarded as 'generally satisfactory' as a President of the United States, he unfortunately 'lacked the necessary judgement' to become President of Harvard.

The Irish controlled the city's government, and a model of graft and corruption it was too; but those powerful men were regarded by the Brahmins as the poor downtrodden majority. Some, like the Kennedys, had not done too badly, but were still the kind of people who when asked, 'How long have you been in Boston?' could not reply 'Since 1730'. Certainly they bought their own furniture.

The Brahmins' impregnably snooty attitude can still make the rest of America rather sour. When a Chicago bank asked a Boston investment company for references on a young Bostonian under consideration for employment, they were informed he could be highly recommended: his father was a Cabot, his mother a Lowell, his background a prestigious blend of Appletons and Peabodies.

'We were not,' the bank replied in bleak acknowledgement, 'considering him for breeding purposes . . .'

From that rarefied atmosphere we moved across the river to Cambridge, to consider Harvard at close quarters and, in particular, the Department of Social Relations and its Center for Research in Personality, where they were undertaking 'The Streetcorner Project'.

This seemed, at first glance, somewhat simplistic: various cornerboy layabouts would be recruited and put in a closed studio with a chair and microphone, which they called 'The Womb Room'. Thus isolated, they were encouraged to talk at random, rambling on about anything that came into their minds – while before them, a meter clicked away. At every click, they earned one cent. Should they stumble upon a subject which interested the psychologists – sex, I suppose, or violence or deprivation or mother fixation – the clicks came faster.

The streetwise kids soon learned how to increase their earnings; it was harder to fathom what the researchers learned.

While we were filming this ludicrous but earnest project I was approached by a young Englishman from Cambridge: Michael Hollingshead was working at the centre, and was a fan of our *Tonight* programme. He was anxious that I should meet one of his associates who was, he said, little known but remarkable.

We drove out to 64 Homer Street, Newton Center, to have supper with this doctor the world was soon to know, for he advised a whole generation to 'Turn on, tune in and drop out' – and many thousands of young people did just that. He was Dr Timothy Leary, then conducting a research programme at the centre into 'Consciousness-altering substances'.

His enthusiastic use of mind-expanding hallucinogenic drugs and his effect upon young America were soon to transform him into a world guru for millions. For even more millions he was the Pied Piper of lost souls.

When we arrived his house was in darkness. We discovered that he and his friends were at that moment coming down after a five-hour trip on psilocybin, and were zonked out in the bedrooms. This drug had the effect of LSD or mescaline and was then being supplied, legally, by its manufacturer so that Leary's 175 university volunteers might undergo ecstatic instant mysticality, and report upon it. The Establishment's attitude towards drugs has changed considerably since 1962.

There was always somebody standing by with a straitjacket, I was assured, in case one of the trippers became psychotic.

Despite tremendous enthusiasm from all the volunteers it did not sound to me a very appealing experiment, and I declined invitations to take part.

Soon afterwards Leary was asked to leave Harvard – and later found it wise also to leave the United States. He escaped to Mexico but returned and, after a jail sentence, went into a commune.

That night, as we sat with the rather vague but agreeable man in his kitchen eating takeaway junk food, I did not appreciate I was supping with the future Prophet of the Beat Generation. Drugs seemed already to have removed the edges of his character; I found him too bland and vague a man to impress anyone about anything. However, millions were soon to get his message.

We considered filming his experiments but, knowing the BBC's horror of drugs, decided against it – thus I suppose missing a scoop, of sorts. There were then three subjects the Corporation regarded as unspeakable: drugs, Fascism and bullfighting.

Four years later I filmed a *Whicker's World* on the Beat Generation and Leary's disciples among the hippies of Haight Ashbury, in San Francisco. The BBC was still acutely fearful of LSD, and Mick Jagger had just been busted by the Kent police – so for the first and last time transmission of one of our programmes was delayed until the story cooled. Can't think how those innocents would have reacted had we introduced Timothy Leary to the world just as he was tuning in . . .

To experience a different sort of doctor we drove north to the cleaner air of Vermont. This State enjoys a brilliant springtime, a lush summer, a famous and breathtaking fall and a scintillating crystal winter. In its whole splendid year there are only two weeks when the climate is, without fail, wet and abominable: Vermonters call it the Mud Season. We arrived right on cue. At Barre we talked to Dr DeForest Jarvis about Vermont folk medicine. His book commending apple cider vinegar, honey and kelp had been in the best seller lists for years, at the very start of America's back-to-nature kick, which since then has never waned.

He had proved to himself and to the satisfaction of millions that natural foods, conditioning the body so that disease would not attack, were preferable to the synthetic chemicals supplied to pill-poppers by the corner drugstore. Primitive man and animals used plants and herbs to maintain health, and Dr Jarvis collected home cures and old wives' tales in a compendium of horse sense that was good for whatever ailed you – right down to a hangover. He was an excellent advertisement for the natural life: eighty, yet still attending to his practice, his books and his hobbies.

He told me his old Vermont method for determining ideal weight: measure your height without shoes, multiply the number of inches over five feet by five and a half, then add 110lbs. The formula then seemed a mite overgenerous to me, but I have grown into it. Should this total be less than your weight in pounds, he recommended two tablespoonfuls of apple cider vinegar in a glass of water at each meal – and guaranteed any paunch would disappear within two years.

Vermont went in for simple remedies. Robert Morse, a young farmer, let me into the established tradition of hibernation: in poor mountain communities, he said, they could not afford to feed and keep elderly people who did no work during the winter, so these ancients were left out in the snow to freeze, and carefully stored away in the barn under piles of snow. There they slept until the spring, when they thawed out and awoke, rejuvenated.

It was my first experience of cryogenics, but I never saw a frozen body until I reached the San Fernando Valley in California, years later – and was still not convinced that those icy perfused remnants had a future.

We had eaten sensibly long enough, so headed south to the Catskills and the Concord Hotel at Lake Kiamesha, to overeat and film what was then an innovation: a Singles weekend. This was a savage and somehow saddening experience.

Hundreds of Singles had converged upon the hotel's marriage-go-round. Most of them were lonely New York Jewesses, desperate for company yet savage in their scorn of any approach by equally lonely males whom they found below the standard of their dreams. It seemed a cruel ritual.

The senior Social Hostess, Rose Ahrens, was known as the Catskill Cupid. Her job, she told me, was to 'meet 'em, greet 'em, mix 'em, match 'em, mate 'em – and run like hell!'

At the entrance to the vast dining room, tableplan flags showed the declared marital status of each guest, and a junior Cupid arranged the seating suitably. If the way to an unmarried Single's heart was through his stomach, the hotel set out to render him susceptible with massive determination, serving a lavish as-much-as-you-can-eat Kosher dinner to 3,000 guests in forty-five minutes.

Our camera tracked out from the noisy ordered chaos of the kitchens in the middle of a line of waitresses exiting at the trot through swing doors on which a sign ordered: 'Smile!' The fastest-moving matzo balls and cheese blintzes on the borscht belt were distributed in a room inspired, the management believed, by the Great Hall at Versailles – only much larger, of course. I found it as intimate and romantic as Victoria Station; but the food was better.

Despite a promising ratio of two or three women to every man, I got absolutely nowhere with the clientele, however desperate. This was hurtful and shaming, but the proffered and unshakable reason for such rejection was that I was GU – a condition unacceptable to any woman at the Concord. It was evidently lethal; end of story, goodnight and goodbye.

After being spurned quite often, I was relieved to discover it stood for Geographically Undesirable.

The wantability factor . . .

We are all entitled to one weakness, at least. Mine seems to be Bentleys. I have driven them for more than forty years, undeflected by any yearning for change and ignoring the crafty Wantability factor created by Madison Avenue which urges us to covet built-in obsolescence. In America, as we know, everything on and off wheels is anxiously exchanged for a later model to avoid social disgrace, and stylish matrons move home constantly so they can redecorate in this year's colours.

Relentless pursuit of the dissatisfied Joneses has never appealed; I have been cautious, not to say dogged, in my pensive selection of life's permanencies: companion, home, craft . . . having noted that, if prepared to be patient, there was no need to accept second-best.

Take, for example, the car – that regulation necessity always about to be traded upwards. I decided early in life that, for my modest tastes, a Bentley Continental was just about right. I was delayed in achieving this reasonable target by one minor inadequacy: ready cash.

There was also another major obstacle, this one nationwide: I had started towards my fantasy Bentley during the austerity days after the War. Assembly lines which had been producing bombers and tanks were returning tentatively to domestic transport – yet a new car was still an impossible dream. Those few leaving the Midlands went for export, while the home market grew ravenous and desperate. Treasured cars which had survived the War on blocks were sold for many times their original prices.

Much of this time I was abroad – a foreign correspondent admiring shining new British cars in countries fortunate enough to have been neutral, or defeated. I can remember the excitement when, driving a small 1937 Jaguar through Belgium, we spotted a shining streamlined 1949 Standard Vanguard: exotic, unattainable, priceless – the future, with a funny rounded rear.

In 1951, returning from an uncomfortable period covering the Korean war, I flew thankfully into Hong Kong with Randolph Churchill, another homeward-bound war correspondent. During our euphoric week of R&R I was briefly clear-headed enough to dash in and buy a British car: an export Humber Hawk.

To be still alive after the unpleasantness around the 39th Parallel was happiness indeed, but to top it all – just take a look at this brand-new gleaming blue four-cylinder Humber with bench front seat, sunshine roof and steering-wheel gear-change! Wow. The ultimate post-war trophy and warrior's reward.

Back home, greatly envied, I drove this practical car 72,000 miles along the relatively empty roads of happy memory – though knowing all the time I was meant for another. After a few years I moved towards my Continental target, exchanging that workaday Hawk for a mistletoe green Bentley Mark VI, just as old with just as many miles on the clock – but by Crewe's engineering standards, comfortably run-in.

At last I was involved in serious motoring, and learning new techniques. Because of some baffling pre-war design decision, Mark VI doors opened from the front. Reclosing a rattling door while in motion could prove challenging: the onrushing airstream would fling it wide, dragging you from your driving seat. Even in those days of light traffic, it was not a wise move.

The gear change was down on the right-hand side, by the door, a chromed lever that sliced smoothly, as through butter. However the clutch pedal required such pressure that after much city driving my left leg grew noticeably muscular. It also ached a lot.

Nevertheless, she wafted me around Britain in some style during my formative *Tonight* years. Filming in a rainswept Welsh valley in midwinter I would escape into the back seat, put my typewriter up on a picnic table and, as the heater murmured reassuringly, sit back thinking creative thoughts. Grateful interviewees would join me behind steamy windows in this warm and welcoming roadhouse.

However for the sake of left leg and right arm muscles, I moved on to a pain-relieving steel grey R-type, which was automatic. The chunky lines of this elegant model with its larger rounded boot still appeal; after almost half a century, it still looks like a real car – the way those Stirling Moss motors of the 1950s are the last real racing cars.

As the years passed I progressed to an S1, a dignified limousine with ambassadorial presence which made its replacement, the Bentley T, look like a German taxi. The classic always retains its looks. I would be driving LUG 2 today had I not faithlessly sold her for £2,500, with only 36,000 miles on the clock. Not, it would now appear, a smart financial move, but I had been seduced by my target – a two-door Continental S3 in dawn blue.

Only 110 'Chinese Eye' Mulliner Park Wards were made, and sixty went for export. After twelve years of redesigning, it seemed to me that Rolls had finally got it exactly right. Car-struck cognoscenti agreed: Patrick Lichfield, David Frost, Terence Donovan, David Hemmings in the cult film Blow-up . . . All icons seek style.

Knowing I was in this relationship for life, I fitted a deep Webasto sun-roof and deflector – and one of the first telephones, which in those days had to go through Aircall operators, who became twenty-four-hour secretaries: 'Topaz One: please tell my office I'll be late, and book a table at Burke's.'

This was the end of 1964 and I believed myself truly mad to hand over so much money for a mere car – even though it was the most beautiful machine on the road, and not all that mere. It cost me – wait for it – £8,250. Its value today says a lot for Bentleys, not much for sterling – and nothing at all for economic stability.

In the late 1960s I passed much of my life on the brand-new M1, for I lived in Regents Park while Whicker's Worlds were transmitted by Yorkshire Television from Leeds. I put 53,000 miles on the clock effortlessly, then took the Continental to live in Jersey. In the past twenty-seven years we have quietly added . . . 6,000 miles.

Around 200 miles a year seems an insult to any virile motor but, as I always explain defensively to R-R engineers, the island's only nine miles by five and has a 40 mph speed limit; so where do you go? Despite the occasional airport run (twenty minutes) she has not cleared her throat since 1973.

At the age of thirty-six my Continental retains all her looks – though the salty air of this pleasant island is corrosive and a slight scratch appeared (the shame of it) caused by a fast-moving granite wall. Finally I gave in, had her stripped down to the metal, resprayed and Connollized. After eight months' attention we might have driven straight from the Motor Show catwalk.

I have always regarded the 'Chinese Eye' as the last beautiful Bentley. The T was just another Silver Shadow, and nothing special. The projected P 90 with its ugly hatchback was soon seen to be a mistake. The ageing and now replaced Corniche could hardly be taken seriously at that price, except in deepest Beverly Hills or Cannes. The Camargue was altogether too lorrylike, the concept Java interesting but unlikely to survive German management.

I went up to Crewe for the presentation of the Silver Seraph, which Rolls-Royce handled brilliantly – a magical revelation of car and floodlit assembly lines stretching into the distance. After that inhalation of surprise the Seraph seemed to sink slowly out of sight, as did the excellent £145,000 Bentley Arnage. Superb engineering has less impact, these days.

The last Bentley built before the German takeover was a fitting monument to the marque: a Sedanca Coupé, on the short wheelbase of the Continental T. By cutting the roof to allow front seat passengers their sunshine, the huge crossbracing needed to restore structural rigidity bumped the weight up 350 lbs to well over 2.5 tons – a lot of tonnage for what is basically a two-seater, with 0-60 mph in 6.1 seconds and a top speed of 155 mph.

At £245,000 this Continental SL is the most expensive car ever produced by Crewe – and exactly thirty times the price of my earlier model, which shows the damage thirty-six years can do. Last to be designed and delivered before the company fell into foreign hands, she drew a line under a seventy-nine-year history and, as Volkswagen moved in, was a stylish and muscular parting shot to signal the end of Bentley's illustrious life as a British car.

Also slipping under the German gun was the last in a long line of legendary Open Tourers: the Azure, bred from the thunderous Blower Bentleys which dominated Brooklands and Le Mans in the 1920s. The marque has driven a long way since those days of wind and goggles. In this seductive car I drifted along the

Moyenne Corniche of – quite suitably – the Côte d'Azur on a glorious sunlit morning, experiencing the way everything instantly felt exactly *right*.

Though the radiator's winged-B is now in a blue surround, Rolls have not decreed: any colour you want, as long as it's Azure. My model was Ebony – a paler shade of black. Within, the usual hand-stitched hide and mirror-finished walnut veneer; an integrated console flowed between driver and front seat passenger, packed with dials monitoring the 6.75 litre turbocharged V8's performance, controlling split-level air conditioning and entertainment – all those in-house decisions.

To stow the hood, for example, no longer requires a prolonged finger-pinching blasphemous struggle with clips and studs and straps; at the touch of a button the hood rears up, leaps about – and tucks itself away in a fascinatingly complex 30-second motion that draws crowds and applause. It also transforms the Azure into a very sexy beast indeed.

From behind the wheel, the bonnet slopes away at such an angle I forgot the size of this two-ton titan and developed the urge to drive a very great distance, just to relish the comfort and seamless power. The Azure reaches 60 mph in 6.3 seconds; its governor kicks in just when you're getting going, at 150 mph – should you drive like that. We also pottered happily along boulevards, drawing appreciative reactions and a few Gallic cries of admiration. You don't usually get that from the French.

Seems vulgar to mention price, which is £31,000 more than the Sultan of Brunei's Continental. That £231,000 would provide six Jaguars – not all that humble a marque – and some change. Unlike the £634,500 McLaren F1, this is a street car – preferably the better type of street, of course.

Talking of street-smart, another two-seater is on the market for £1,112,000. Mercedes-Benz built twenty-five CLK GTRs, and sold twenty-one instantly. This 250 mph racing car equipped for the road reaches 60 mph in 3.6 seconds and 125 mph in under 10 seconds – so at the lights you usually find yourself in pole position. For that sticker-price you get power steering, air conditioning, compact disc player and electric wing mirrors; almost as lavish as our Honda Civic.

What hit me was the official urban fuel consumption for this monster: 8.9 mpg. In town my sedate Continental gets around 9 mpg. Puzzling . . . but there is rarely logic behind acquisition and common sense plays little part in emotional decisions. Bentleys just happen to be the perfect reason for wanting to be rich.

Crewe also happily invaded my television life. The Maharaja of Jodhpur provided a vintage scarlet Rolls convertible from his collection for filming across the desert of Rajasthan, which fortunately I did not have to drive. Down in Sydney my mate Len Evans OA ran a dawn blue Continental S3 only a few chassis numbers from mine. We would cross the Bridge in fine Pommie style, though she had been modified in various teeth-clenching ways by overconfident and insensitive Australian garages. Aussie mechanics handle Bentleys brusquely – the way they would a sheila.

A retired elevator operator I filmed in Laguna Beach had suffered similarly. He had been persuaded by a smooth Beverly Hills salesman that it would be a smart move to cash-in his insurance policies and buy a much-used Bentley Continental – as an investment, you understand. After a respray it gleamed proudly in his trailer park; whitewall tyres, of course. He was enraptured, and insisted I experience its poetry in motion.

As the loose steering took us wandering about the freeway and the brakes reacted hesitantly, I urged a quick authorized service: we were riding in his life insurance, which was about to be much missed.

We rented a more satisfactory Corniche for a programme about Sunset Boulevard – it had the right Hollywood touch. Best transport of all came while filming my *Living With Uncle Sam* series around America: in New York I had run into an old BBC friend, Reg Abbis, then looking after Rolls' transatlantic public affairs. He wondered whether I might care to borrow a Spirit for a few days?

After weeks in sordid cabs and bland airport rentals, this offer took several seconds to accept. Next day, leaving the Algonquin to film upstate, there waiting in 34th Street was a gleaming scarlet Spirit. Life improved instantly.

We set off, singing. Carefully avoiding Harlem, we headed north on the Henry Hudson Parkway and turned left over Washington Bridge into New Jersey. Only minutes away from New

York's intimidating downtown we were floating silently along the Palisades Interstate Parkway through incomparable fall foliage. Life could hardly get better.

For a few glorious days we filmed around the Catskills, then reluctantly headed back towards the city – which had been easy enough to leave but, amid swirling freeway traffic crossing dismal suburban flatland, was not easy to rediscover.

Being unable to locate downtown New York may seem like failing to find the Grand Canyon, but outside the city directional road signs are mainly for locals. They do not say Manhattan, but Mission Road and Delaware Drive and such, and are of no help to a fast-moving foreigner.

Wedged into the endless traffic speeding night and day through sad suburbs and spaghetti junctions, take one wrong lane, miss one turn-off, and you are deep in the Bronx – and there be dragons. This is not a happy experience, even if you have not read *Bonfire of the Vanities*.

I did not knock anyone down, but did get seriously lost. Where have all the skyscrapers gone? Our highly desirable scarlet Rolls, heading south, went floating in a sheen of splendour through derelict streets along which I would have hesitated to drive an old Chevvy. No Lord Mayor's coach could have so stunned the sidewalks. I began to feel sort of . . . unwelcome. Then I noticed other drivers were waving.

They were not waving.

We had been so happy in rural upstate New York that I had forgotten there were plenty of urban drivers who were quite ready to loose off a few irritable shots if they did not like the way a car was driven, or its colour scheme.

After a few fraught miles trying to ignore the battered wrecks rattling alongside full of gesticulating Puerto Ricans – all marksmen, no doubt – suddenly there on the distant skyline through a gap in the tenement blocks was that wonderful castellated silhouette. Follow that skyscraper!

A fast U-ie, scattering escorting bangers, and foot down towards the relatively secure avenues of New York, New York. Never have Manhattan's snarling avenues seemed so welcoming, so downright convivial.

Getting lost is bad enough, but breaking down can be a

nightmare – a moment of dread on any American freeway. On television motorists are constantly warned to barricade themselves into their cars and wait for a police black-and-white to come patrolling along. Sound advice it would seem from the daily reports of mayhem by the armed crazies or opportunist muggers who cruise the urban jungle and wide country turnpikes like sharks.

Returning one evening from California's Napa Valley my slick brand-new rental suddenly expired amid the traffic streaming back to San Francisco. As the light faded, we were stranded at the roadside – unarmed foreign innocents helpless amid a heedless helter-skelter racing for the Bridge.

Ignoring all sensible warnings, I was outside the car peering baffled under the bonnet when a sedan pulled out of the stream, and stopped. No gun was produced. Then, doing everything wrong, we jumped with relief into this stranger's car. Far from mugging or kidnapping, as in the regulation horror scenarios, this kindly real estate agent drove us to his office in a nearby suburb, gave us a telephone and a drink – and a salutary reminder that there are probably more good Samaritans in the US than anywhere else.

There is one place in the world where everyone is guaranteed to be a good neighbour: the Outback of Australia, that stark empty Northern Territory where homesteaders can be relied upon to help anyone in trouble. Like lifeboatmen, the people of the Never Never are selfless, reliable and instantly friendly. It's called survival. In that harsh land they well know they might need a hand themselves tomorrow, so they learn to depend on their mates. This is where mateship began.

Knowing this tradition I was not too worried when we ran out of petrol on the Stuart Highway somewhere between Tennant Creek and Katherine. In that vast empty territory road signs deal in daunting figures. One warning of distances outside Darwin reads: Tennant Creek 969 – Alice Springs 1,479.

It is a lonely place, with a shack every few hundred miles, yet I knew the first car or road-train to arrive across that barren scorching wasteland would rescue us, and doubtless offer a cold beer. It's like being at sea, or crash-landing in Alaska – everyone comes to help.

In that fearsome desert furnace without shade we waited by the road, which stretched away into a haze of infinity. Without its air conditioning, the car was suffocating, the steering wheel too hot to touch. Outside it was even hotter, and flies descended in clouds. There was no movement, no sound but their pestilential buzzing.

After a long despairing wait – a cloud of dust in the distance. Saved! The car approached – and hurtled by, trailing its sand-storm. I was stunned. Did he not see me? Was he asleep, on that endless dead-straight highway?

An hour later, a long road-train. At last, a knight of the road! Passed without even a wave. And so it went. Not one of those friendly mates and cobbers even slowed down – they all shot through without a backward glance as I clutched my throat. They made the Bronx seem positively friendly. I could not believe the way they were ruining their reputation.

After a couple of hours the water situation was getting desper-ate and I was beginning to imagine piles of bleached bones. Finally another car came towards us through the heat-shimmer. It was driving more slowly than the others: a good sign. I went into my despairing arm-waving routine.

It stopped. 'Alan Whicker!' said a voice from the cool interior. A couple of Poms, on holiday. They gave us a drink and a lift up to Katherine.

Viewers never let you down.

Acknowledgements

As always, my thanks go first to Valerie, who took the pictures while I pointed out that there was a far better position over *there*. I could not have managed without her advice, judgement, loyalty, over-reaction and, best of all, her company.

So, thirty-eight pictures by Valerie, five by Nigel Turner – a friend from Yorkshire Television days.

My gratitude also to colleagues behind and around the camera for skill, patience and friendship. To Laureen Fraser, who once again captured all these words from the air, shepherded them out into cyberspace, and back again on to paper.

Then there are the friends and those I ran into along my flight-path who enriched our kaleidoscope and made life interesting, and fun. As I always say: if you're not here, don't go away – there'll be another one along in a minute!

Index

Abu Simbel 167
Agra 172
Aguascalientes 205, 207–8
Ahrens, Rose 325–6
Air New Zealand 34
Al Fayed, Mohammed 6, 124
Alan Whicker Appreciation
    Society (AWAS) 13
Alba, Duke and Duchess of 267–8
All Soul's Day, Mexico 210–11
Amboseli National Park 43–4
Ames, Kenneth 123
Anderton, Chief Constable James
    101, 103–4
Antarctic toilets 132
archives, BBC 78–9
Argentina 189
Arison, Micky 257
Around the World in Eighty Days 162
Asprey, John 11
Asseily, George 303
Atlantis theme park 53–4
Attenborough, David 271
attention span 72, 92
audience ratings 75
Austria 306–11
Ayers Rock 180
Aztecs 204–5, 212
Azure, Bentley 330–31

Baalbek 304
Bandar Seri Begawan 4, 7
Bangkok 236, 239–40
Barbados 193
Barbareschi, Dante 173–5
Barber, Noël 131–2
Barber, Steve 123
Barrie, George 160

Barclaycard 37–48
Baverstock, Donald 81
BBC programming 73–5
Beatles, The 81
Beijing 175
Beirut 296–305
Bell, Mariam 16
Bell, Sir Tim 47
Bellamy, Dr David 35
Bellin, Dr Howard 99–101
Belmonte, Juan 273
Benitez, Manuel *see* El Cordobés
Bentleys 3, 12–13, 234, 327–32
Biggs, Ronald 99, 101
birds' nests 238–9
Birt, Lord 74
Boston 319–22
Bowden, Nigel 289
Braden, Bernard 35
Branson, Richard 64
Bremner, Rory 82
bribery, Mexico 209
British European Airways 32–4
Broackes, Sir Nigel 254, 258
bronchitis, Pavarotti 222–4
Brook, Kelly 83
Brooke, John 179
Brookes-Walker, Mr & Mrs 252
Brunei, Sultan of 1–31
bullfighting 208, 269–80
Bushell, Basil 181

Cairo 166, 296
Calman, Mel 116–17, 118
Cambridge (Mass) 322–4
campaigns, television 89–90
Captains, cruise liners 264
Carlton Television 87–8

Carnival Destiny 259–60
cars 12–13, 22, 234, 327–32
Cartier-Bresson, Henri 206
casinos 54–5
cemeteries, Vienna 308
censorship 122–3, 269, 271
Channel 5 50–51
Chapple, Sir John 281
Charing Cross Road club 290
Charles, Prince of Wales 285–6
China 175–8, 254–5
Cholula 205
Christ the Redeemer, Corcovado
   192
Christianity
   Mexico 203–5
   Pocomania 314–18
Churchill, Sir Winston 133–4
classroom massacres 136, 144
clones, Alan Whicker 70–71
Clutterbuck, Dr Richard 108–12
cockfighting 208
Coe, Dr Malcolm 106–7
Collett, Dickenson & Pearce 37
Collins, Joan 63, 66
commercials 32–48
Concorde 133
confessional television 90–91
Conroy, Terry 256
contestants, Miss World 61–3,
   65–6
Continental S3, Bentley 329
Cook, Arthur 123–5
Cook, Thomas 156
corridas 274
court etiquette, Brunei 7, 20, 29
crew, *QE2* 254, 256, 257–9
crime 136–52
   Britain 141–2
   Gibraltar 284
   QE2 257–8
   Rio de Janeiro 190–92
criticism, television presenting
   81–2
Cronkite, Walter 121
Crucifixion at Ixtapalapa 202
Cruise 85
cruising 248–66

customs inspections 165–6,
   186–7, 262
Cutforth, Rene 120

Dahl, Arlene 228, 235
Daily Mail 126–9, 133
Davies, Derek 130
death
   at sea 253
   bullfighting 273, 276
   firearms 138–9
   on holiday 174
   Mexico 210–12
   Richard Sharp 244–6
Deknatel, Jane 97–9
Dempster, Nigel 60
divorce 116–18
doctors, taking lives 148–9
documentary programmes 76–7,
   86–8
Dorchester Hotel, London 2, 31
driving 328–35
Dyke, Greg 75

Easter, Mexico 202
Easter Island 154, 186
Eastern and Oriental Express
   213, 227–38
Edinburgh 241
Edward, Prince 16, 17, 28
Edward VIII 135
Egypt 165–7, 296
El Cordobés 208, 270, 272–80
Elizabeth II, Queen 31
English, David 125–6
Englishness, Boston 320
Ephesus 265
Evans, Len 332
excavations, Beirut 301
ExTel 244–6

fashion 112–13
Feast of San Isidro 280
Ferdinando, John 13
firearms training 140, 146–51
folk medicine 324–5
Forbidden City 176
foreign correspondents 130–35

Fraser, Admiral Lord 241, 245
Freud, Sigmund 307
frontier, Gibraltar 284, 286
Full Circle 86

Gaggero, James 287
Gairy, Eric 67
Galbraith, John Kenneth 97–8
Getty, J. Paul 2
Gibraltar 281, 288–95
Gil, Jesus Gil y 295
Gill, A A 71
Gillard, Frank 285
Goldsmith, Harvey 60
gondolas 161
Goodrich, Alex 146
government
    Lebanon 300
    ministers 114–16
Great Wall of China 176
Greek islands 264–5
Green, David 19, 175
Griminelli, Andrea 218
gun ownership 136–8

Habsburg, Archduke Otto 308
Haïk, Farjallah 297
Hall, Jerry 68
Hall, Sir John & Lady 163
Hanbury, Bridget 21–2
Hanbury, Major Christopher 2, 11
Harrods 6, 27
Harry's Bar 161, 164
Hart, Derek 94
Hatmen, the 129
Haylock, Susan 292
Hayward, Doug ix, 38
Healey, Edna 114
healing 315
Hedren, Tippi 105–6
helicopters 185, 190
Heston, Charlton 136–7, 144
Hezbollah 304
Hill, Benny 51
Hillary, Sir Edmund 132–3
HMS *Amethyst* 284–5
HMS *Nepal* 241–7
Hohenlohe, Prince Alfonso 294

Holland, Jools 71
Hollingshead, Michael 323–4
Hong Kong 126, 178
Hopcraft, David 42
Hua Hin 235–6
Hudson, Hugh 105, 107
Hughes, Richard 129–30
hula girls 185
human sacrifices 212
Humber Hawk 328
hypnotic trance, Pocomania 314,
    318

Iban People, Brunei 25–6
Iguazu Falls 189
Independent Broadcasting
    Authority 33–4
India 171–4
Ingram, Floyd 250–51
interviewers 83–5, 94–6, 126–7
Inzarillo, Gerry 58–9
Islamic fundamentalism 23–4
Isthmus of Kra 238
Ixtapalapa 202–5

J. Walter Thompson 32–4
Jackson, Sir Geoffrey 107–12
Jamaica 312–18
Jarvis, Dr DeForest 324–5
Jay, Antony 113–14
Jefri, Prince 11, 22–4
Jersey, driving 329
jewels, Sultan of Brunei 20–21
Jodhpur, Maharaja of 171, 332
Johnson-Smith, Sir Geoffrey 94,
    113
Josephine 158, 198–9
judging Miss World 66, 69

Kampong Ayer, Brunei 7, 9–10
Kapo the Shepherd 313
Kaufman, Gerald 302
Kenya 40–47
Kerzner, Sol 52–60
kidnapping 107–10, 112, 299
Kilimanjaro 43, 45–6
Kingship 5–6
Kiwaiyu 40–41

Kleeman, Valerie 198–9
Knight, Ronnie 288–94
Knipe, Michael 302
Korean war 111, 120–21
Kretzmer, Herbert 98
Kuala Lumpur 214

La Linea 282
Lake Kiamesha 325–6
Lamarr, Hedy 36–7
Lathbury, Sir Gerald 288
Lawrence, Stephen 141
Laxton, Simon 160–61
Le Vien, Jack 130, 133–5
Leary, Dr Timothy 323–4
Lebanon 297–305
Lecumberri prison 209–10
Leslie, Ann 126
Lichfield, Patrick Earl of 214–15
Liria Palace 267
Lloyd, John 48
locations, interviews 94–5
Lock, Jim 225
Locsin, Leandro 8
Lost Palace resort 56–8
Lott, Professor John 137
luggage 160–61, 182, 237
luxury travel 169, 261–4

McCarthy, John 298–9
McDonald, Trevor 35–6
McLaren, Malcolm 112–13
Magiera, Leone 218
Major, John 30, 35–6
Mangope, President Lucas 55
Manhattan 333
Manila 220–24
Manila Symphony Orchestra 218, 225, 226
Mann, Roderick 163
Manolete 273, 278, 280
Marbella 288–95
Mark VI, Bentley 328
Marsh, Peter 97–8
Marvin, Lee 117
Masai warriors 45–7
Matador 269, 271–80
Medlicott, Francis & Simone 19

Meek John 251
Mexico 201–5, 206–12
Michael of Kent, Princess 230, 235
Michelmore, Cliff 34, 94
Middleton, Peter 197
Miklenda, Michael 151–2
Mills, Juliet 151–2
Milne, Alasdair 73, 78
Miss World 49–52, 60–69
Mitchelson, Marvin 116–18
Miura bulls 278–9
Mohamad, Dr Mahathir 213, 226–8, 232–3
Mohamed, Prince 23, 25
Moir, Jim 126
Mombasa 41, 42
money, Sultan of Brunei 3, 15
money laundering 282
Monty Python 188–9
Morley, Eric 66
Morley, Julia 51, 61, 67
Morocco, smuggling 282
Morris, Jan 125–6, 271
Morse, Robert 325
Mudmen, Papua New Guinea 253–4

National Rifle Association 136–7
natural history programmes 77–8
'Nessun Dorma' 222
New Delhi 171
New York 194
New Zealand 184
news reporting, war 120–22
Nile, the 168–9
Norwich, John Julius 228, 235
nuclear hijacks 108

Olivier, Laurence 32
Omar Ali Saifuddin Mosque 7
O'Rea, Carol and Russell 150–51
Orient Express 157–60, 249
Oriental Hotel, Bangkok 124–5, 240

pagan religion 316–18
Palfrey, Sarah 321
Palin, Michael 162

340

Pangkor Laut 213–27
Papua New Guinea 253–4
Paradise Island 53
Parkin, Molly 112–13
Pattaya 254
Pavarotti, Luciano 214, 217–27
Penang 234
Piazza, Ignatius 140
picadors 275
Pilanesberg National Game Park
    62
plastic surgery 99–101
plays 102–3
Pocomania 312–18
police
    Chinese 177
    Spanish 283
politics 14–15, 25, 113–16
polo 11–13
popularity polls 70
Potter, Denis 101–4
poverty, India 171–3
Powell, Jane 228
production-time 86
propaganda 122
Pyramids, the 167

QE2 162–3, 248–60
Qingdao 255

R-Type, Bentley 329
racism 141
radio interviews 84
Rae, Daphne 102, 104–5
Rank Xerox 35–6
Reed, Rex 235
religion, Brunei 9–10, 23–4
Rendlesham, Lady 112–13
restoration, Oriental Express 230
Rio de Janeiro 190–91
Rodriguez, Christopher 196
Rolls-Royce 330, 332–3
Rook, Jean 131, 133
Roumeguere, Carolyn, 47
Russell, William Howard 119

S1, Bentley 329
Saatchi & Saatchi 35

Sachertorte 311
safaris 62
Safir, Police Commissioner
    Howard 143
Saleha, Princess 16
Salmon, Peter 72–4
San Marcos Fair 205
Santorini 264
Schellenberg, Keith 237
Scott Thomas, Serena 236
Sea Goddess II 262
sea urchins 184–5
Seabourn Pride 261
security, Rio de Janeiro 191
self defence, guns 146–52
Sepiuddin, Pengiran Dato Setia
    Yusof 20
Servadio, Gaia 99
Seville Plaza 274
Sex Pistols 113
Sharp, Richard 241–7
Sheldon, Sidney 64–5
Sherwood, James 229
shipping, Boston 321
shopping
    Hong Kong 178–9
    Sultan of Brunei 21–2
Silver Jubilee, Sultan of Brunei
    28–30
Silver Seraph 330
Sinatra, Frank 58
Sinclair, Betty 251
Sindall, Adrian 16–17
Singapore 227–8
singles weekend 325–6
slavery 316
Sloan, Professor Stephen 108–12
Smithers, Pat 247
smuggling 281, 289–90
Snowdon, Lord 228, 231, 236
society, Boston 320
South Africa 52–3
South Pole, the 132–3
Southward, Dr Nigel 170, 184
souvenirs, holiday 188
Spain 267–95
Spencer, Ivor 124–5
squirrelling 257

Stark, Koo 237
statues, Easter Island 187
Stift Klosterneuberg monastery
   307
subway, Vienna 310–11
Sufri, Prince 17–18
Sugar Loaf Mountain 192
Sun City 55–8
Sydney 182–4

Tahiti 184
Taj Mahal 173
talk shows 91, 94–9
Tan, Dr Roberto 220–24
television programming 72–5
Terracotta Army 177
terrorism 107–12
Texas 144–5
Thatcher, Margaret 17
Thomas Cook's Tours 154–200
Thompson, Tommy 123
Thyssen, Fiona, Baroness 116–18
Tiananmen Square 176
Today programme 83–4
Tonight programme 79–81, 83,
   94–6
top hats 308
touring, Pavarotti 219
traffic
   Bangkok 239–40
   Beirut 303
   Spain 287
transport, Sultan of Brunei 9–14
Trump, Ivana 63–4, 66
Tswana tribe 58–9
Tuffano, Brian 39
Tupamaros 107, 109

Ultimate Package Tour 153–200

Valley of the Kings 171
Vanessa 73, 91
Venice 160–62
Vermont 324–5
Vienna 306–11
Vietnam war 121–2
violence on television 103–4
Voyager of the Seas 260

Wachtveitl, Kurt 124
Wagner, Kathy 99
Waldorf Astoria, New York 194,
   197
war correspondents 119–22
Way, Bertie 237
weight-gain, cruising 266
Westmoreland, General William
   122
Whicker! programme 96–118,
   130–35
Williams, Billy Dee 68
Willis, Doug 247
Wilson, Charlie 290
Windsor, Duke of 134–5
Winston Boys 281–3
Wonders of the World 155

Xian 176–8

Yates, Jess 91–2
Yentob, Alan 77
Yeoh, Francis 214–16
York, Susannah 236

Zecha, Adrian 229